THE MEDITERRA

THE
MEDITERRANEAN
PASSION

*Victorians and Edwardians in
the South*

JOHN PEMBLE

Oxford   New York
OXFORD UNIVERSITY PRESS
1988

Oxford University Press, Walton Street, Oxford OX2 6DP

Oxford New York Toronto
Delhi Bombay Calcutta Madras Karachi
Petaling Jaya Singapore Hong Kong Tokyo
Nairobi Dar es Salaam Cape Town
Melbourne Auckland

and associated companies in
Berlin Ibadan

Oxford is a trade mark of Oxford University Press

First published 1987 by Oxford University Press
First issued as an Oxford University Press paperback 1988

British Library Cataloguing in Publication Data
Pemble, John
The Mediterranean passion. Victorians and
Edwardians in the south.
1. Europe. Mediterranean region. Travel
by Britons, 1830—1914
I. Title
914'.0428'08921
ISBN 0—19—282207—1

Library of Congress Cataloging in Publication Data
Pemble, John.
The Mediterranean passion: Victorians and Edwardians in the South
John Pemble.
p. cm.
Includes bibliographical references and index.
1. Great Britain—Civilization—Mediterranean influences.
2. Mediterranean Region—Description and travel. 3. British—
Travel—Mediterranean Region—History. 4. Great Britain—
Civilization—19th century. 5. Great Britain—Civilization—20th
century. 6. Travelers—Mediterranean Region—Biography.
7. Travelers—Great Britain—Biography. I. Title.
[DA533.P455 1988] 941.08—dc19 88—12409
ISBN 0—19—282207—1

Printed in Great Britain by
The Guernsey Press Co. Ltd.
Guernsey, Channel Islands

Preface and Acknowledgements

BETWEEN 1830 and 1914 travel to the Mediterranean became a significant part of the British way of life and the British way of death. My aim has been to amplify our knowledge of the way Victorians and Edwardians lived and died by harvesting the small ocean of literary material that their journeys created. I abandoned Lytton Strachey's technique of sinking a bucket, in order to trawl a net; and the result is neither biography nor a monograph, but an essay. It deals less with what made people distinct, than with what they had in common. Specialists will find in it a lot that is familiar; but I hope that the unfamiliar faces it introduces, and the new setting it provides for old faces and old truths, will make it interesting even for them.

As a proportion of the total population, the number of Britons who travelled so far was very small. The Mediterranean was almost inaccessible to the lower middle class; and the only members of the working classes to whom it was accessible were servants, soldiers, and sailors. But if travellers were few, they were prolific; and in order to make the subject manageable some further limits had to be set. I therefore decided to deal with the leisured, the literary, and the artistic—those who went because they chose, rather than because they were obliged, to go. Consequently I do not write much about servicemen, diplomats, merchants, or missionaries. But beyond this principle of exclusion my aim has been comprehensive rather than selective and, resolved to risk being shot down, I have roamed without a passport across disciplinary frontiers. This means that I have forfeited all claim to be exhaustive, because even within the limits imposed the range of material is very wide and every expert will think of something or someone that I have omitted and might have included. I rely heavily on the inductive method, and I am, in Clough's words, rebuked by a sense of the incomplete. You cannot decipher the murmur of a crowd from the echoes of stray voices. What I have read is only a fraction of what has been published; what has been published is only a fraction of what was written; and what was written was only a fraction of what was thought and said. And as if that awful fact were not rebuke enough, there remains the possibility that what was written was not an accurate record of what was thought and said. In justification I can plead only that, since omniscience is impossible in human affairs, speculation is the alternative to silence; and the case for speculation has been argued by a far more powerful advocate than I. 'You must', wrote Matthew Arnold, 'begin with an Idea of the world in order not to be prevailed over by the world's multitudinousness.'

I wish to thank the staffs of the Public Record Office and the University of Bristol Library for their courteous and efficient assistance. I acknowledge a special debt to the Inter-Library Loans service. Without this precious facility my book would have taken much longer to write and might not have been written at all. Among colleagues in the Arts Faculty at Bristol I am particularly grateful to Michael Liversidge, of the Department of the History of Art, for his generous permission to consult and quote from the papers of William Boxall which are in his possession. Hugh Tulloch, David Large, John Vincent, and Peter Warren helped with advice, loans of books, and the stimulus of conversation; Gordon Kelsey and his staff in the Photographic Unit prepared the illustrations for publication; and from undergraduates studying Doubts and Beliefs of the Victorians I heard questions and answers which compelled me to rethink my own. I should like to thank Anita Hathway for typing the copy and John Steeds for help with the illustrations, and to record my gratitude to my old schoolfriend Laurence Measey, who somehow found time in his life as a busy Consultant to check my medical chapters to save me from some embarrassing gaffes—without, I must add, in any way making himself responsible for the errors that remain or the opinions I have expressed. Material from the book formed the basis of three talks for BBC Radio Three and the text has benefitted considerably from the critical comments and advice of Alison Richards, Senior Producer with the Radio Science Unit. The comments and suggestions of the readers and editorial staff of Oxford University Press were invaluable, and if the book has any merit, this is due in great measure to their painstaking efforts on its behalf. For the map I am indebted to Simon Godden, Cartographer in the Department of Geography, University of Bristol.

J. P.

Bristol, July 1986

Contents

List of Plates   ix

Principles of Annotation   x

Map of the Mediterranean   xi

INTRODUCTION   1

PART ONE: WAYS AND MEANS   15

1. Journeys   18

2. Destinations   39

PART TWO: MOTIVES   51

3. Pilgrimage   55

4. Culture   60

5. Health   84

6. Hidden Motives   96

PART THREE: EXPERIENCE AND ATTITUDE   111

7. The Light of Recognition   114

8. Civilisation   128

9. The Life of Life   149

PART FOUR: ATTITUDE AND EXPERIENCE   165

10. A Wreck of Paradise   168

11. The Gift of Prophecy   182

12. Sacred Art   196

13. Abominations of the Earth   210

14. Decline and Fall   228

15. Death and Resurrection   240

CONCLUSION   257

Biographical Notes   277

Index   299

List of Plates

1. (a) 'Ordered South'. *The Illustrated London News*, 1892.
   (b) Descending the Mont Cenis pass in winter. *The Illustrated London News*, 1864.
2. (a) The cholera epidemic, 1884: passengers from Marseilles being fumigated at Paris. *The Illustrated London News*.
   (b) Cholera quarantine at Marseilles, 1884. *The Illustrated London News*.
3. (a) The Caffè Greco in Rome. *The Illustrated London News*, 1850.
   (b) The Campo Santo at Pisa. *The Illustrated London News*, 1860.
4. Tourists in Venice. *The Illustrated London News*, 1881.
5. (a) The ascent of Mount Vesuvius. *The Illustrated London News*, 1872.
   (b) The Promenade des Anglais at Nice. *The Illustrated London News*, 1886.
6. (a) The Café de Paris at Monte Carlo, *c.* 1900. Photograph in the possession of the author.
   (b) The Terrace of the Casino at Monte Carlo, *c.* 1900. Photograph in the possession of the author.
7. (a) The Promenade at Menton, looking west, *c.* 1900. Photograph in the possession of the author.
   (b) The Promenade at Menton, looking east. *c.* 1900. Photograph in the possession of the author.
8. The Jardin Public at Menton, *c.* 1900. Photograph in the possession of the author.
9. The Victorian vision of the Dead Sea: Holman Hunt's 'The Scapegoat' (1856). National Museums and Galleries on Merseyside.
10. (a) 'Starting for the Pyramids'. *The Illustrated London News*, 1874.
    (b) 'The English in Cairo: Visiting the Howling Dervishes'. *The Illustrated London News*, 1893.
11. (a) The Protestant Cemetery at Rome, *c.* 1890. Photograph in the Symonds Archive, University of Bristol.
    (b) British graves in the Old Cemetery at Menton. Photograph by the author.
12. A glimpse of Arcadia. (An unattributed photograph, *c.* 1890, from the Italian albums of J. A. Symonds.) Symonds Archive, University of Bristol.

Principles of Annotation

Published sources identified by title in the text have as a general rule been omitted from the notes.

Full names and titles, and dates of publication, are given in initial references only. Thereafter abbreviated names and titles are used.

Linked references are included in a single note at the end of the relevant section.

Place of publication is omitted where this is London.

Supplementary information about British travellers and expatriates mentioned in the text is given in the BIOGRAPHICAL NOTES.

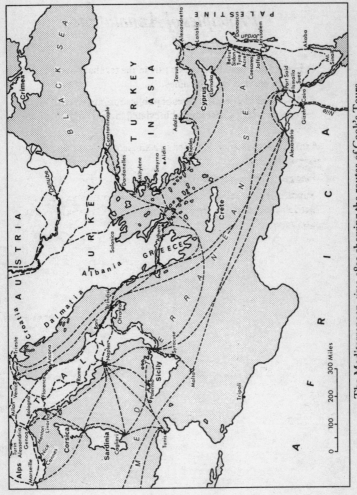

The Mediterranean *circa* 1890 showing the routes of Cook's Tours

INTRODUCTION

In VICTORIAN and Edwardian Britain the superior classes were travelling classes. They were always going abroad. Their lives were a constant bustle of arrival and departure, their portmanteaux and hatboxes were plastered with foreign labels, and many of the myriad letters that they wrote and received carried the postmarks of exotic places. 'The only remarkable thing people can tell of their doings these days is that they have stayed at home', declared George Eliot in 1869.[1] Absence was in fact so conspicuous that it became recognised as a national characteristic. 'The English', wrote Théophile Gautier in 1840, 'are everywhere except in London, where there are only Italians and Poles.'[2] It has been estimated that in the 1830s something like 50,000 passengers left the country every year by the Channel ports alone; and by 1913 the corresponding figure was in excess of 660,000.[3]

Most Britons who went abroad before the First World War travelled for professional or commercial purposes. They were colonial bureaucrats, service officers, traders, and missionaries, and their destinations were scattered over the two hemispheres of Britain's global empire. But a minority travelled at leisure—from choice rather than necessity; and this minority grew steadily larger as a rise in wealth and a decrease in the cost of travel made foreign holidays accessible to the lower reaches of the middle classes. 'Those who can be allowed to enjoy themselves quietly at home,' observed Anthony Trollope in 1866, 'or eat shrimps through their holiday quietly at Ramsgate, are becoming from year to year not fewer in number, but lower down the social scale: so that this imperative duty of travelling abroad—and doing so year after year—becomes much extended, and embraces all of us who are considered anybody by those around us.'[4] By Edwardian times even artisans and their families were being enticed across the Channel by organizations like the Toynbee Workmen's Travelling Club, which assured its members that 'foreign travel [was] as easy as home travel

[1] Gordon Haight, ed., *The Letters of George Eliot* (New Haven and London, 1954–6 and 1978), v. 67.

[2] Théophile Gautier, *Voyage en Espagne* (new edn., Paris, 1929), 349.

[3] John Pimlott, *The Englishman's Holiday* (1947), 189; Frederick Ogilvie, *The Tourist Movement* (1933), 92, 97. The first figure includes non-British travellers.

[4] Anthony Trollope, *Travelling Sketches* (1866), 101.

and ... the expense of a visit to the Continent ... probably less than
that of a week at Margate.'[5] The principal destinations of these
leisured travellers were the towns of northern Europe (chiefly Paris,
Brussels, and Boulogne), the Rhine, and Switzerland; but Switzerland was a parting of the ways, because the group identified by
Ruskin as 'the noblest born, the best taught, the richest in time and
money'[6] continued further south, to the shores and cities of the
Mediterranean.

It was here that the missing apex of the British social pyramid
was to be found. Victorian and Edwardian cabinet ministers, peers,
dowagers, heirs to landed fortunes, and members of the Royal
Family all travelled to the Mediterranean—not, like the Grand
Tourists of the eighteenth century, as strangers on a unique excursion; but rather as regular visitors coming to a home from home.
Coroneted carriages paraded the public squares and thoroughfares
in the principal Italian towns; titled hostesses received with Mayfair
magnificence in Roman palaces and Florentine villas; liveried
gondoliers ferried passengers with names in Debrett or Burke along
the canals of Venice; aristocratic yachts steamed between the Greek
islands, North Africa, and the Levant; *jeunesse dorée* from Oxford
and Cambridge poked about the galleries, churches, and ruins of
Italy and Greece; noble English residences multiplied along the
Riviera; crested dice were thrown in the Casino of Monte Carlo and
the gambling haunts of Cannes; and the Hotel Excelsior in Nice
added 'Regina' to its name to commemorate three visits by Queen
Victoria.

But Victorian and Edwardian visitors to the Mediterranean were
not exclusively or even predominantly aristocratic, because in the
second half of the nineteenth century rising incomes and facili-
tated travel combined to bring more and more members of the
middle classes to the South. 'Money increases quickly', wrote
Trollope in 1866, 'and distances decrease; wings that a few years
since were hardly strong enough for a flight over the Channel now
carry their owners safely to the Danube and the Nile; Jerusalem
and the Jordan are as common to us as were Paris and the Seine
to our grandfathers.'[7] The man who did most to mobilise the
British bourgeoisie was Thomas Cook, the Leicester Baptist and

[5] S. A. Barnett, *Canon Barnett, His Life and Friends* (1918), i. 365.
[6] John Ruskin, *The Stones of Venice* (Everyman edn., 1907), i, Appendix 25.
[7] A. Trollope, *Travelling Sketches*, 92.

temperance evangelist who became the major figure in Victorian organised travel. His skills put the trains and hotels of Europe, the caravans of Palestine, and the steamships of the Nile at the disposal of British business men, lawyers, physicians, dons, clergymen, and spinsters and widows with private incomes. 'Cook's Tourist Agency', wrote George Augustus Sala in 1895 shortly after its founder's death,

... has opened up, not only to the London middle-class cockney but to the remotest provincial, countries and cities which ... he would never have dreamt of visiting. The devout have been able, by means of Cook, to make pilgrimages to the Holy Land; the humbler student of archaeology has had Italy and Egypt thrown open to him; and Cook at present pervades the whole civilized world.[8]

An important aspect of Cook's talent for organisation was its psychological effect. Cook's Select Parties, Popular Holiday Tours, through-tickets, hotel coupons, exchange bureaux, and uniformed agents, couriers, and interpreters in foreign parts lowered resistance to Southern travel because they tamed it. They substituted regularity and simplicity for confusion and complexity. Cook's head office in Ludgate Circus was the threshold of an ordered universe, offering a perspective on southern Europe, the Levant, and Egypt that was full of reassurance. Many very wealthy and important people made use of the firm's facilities, especially when they went to Egypt and the Holy Land; but its major market was the middle classes. This is confirmed by its advertising, which was generally designed to appeal to bourgeois snobbery. The fifteen pages of double columns listing 'Some of the Royal and Distinguished Persons who have Travelled under the Arrangements of Thomas Cook and Son' which were appended to the 1898 brochure on Egypt are a case in point. The first Thomas Cook did not intend his foreign tours for the working classes, but the occasional cheap excursions that he organised (such as that to the Paris Exhibition of 1878, which involved travel and lodging for 75,000 people) anticipated the nature of foreign travel in the twentieth century and confirmed his role in the history of British leisure as the link between Grand Tourism and mass tourism.

But the Mediterranean contingent had more to it than blue blood and bourgeois solidity; it had an intellectual patina, a cultural bloom.

---

[8] G. A. Sala, *The Life and Adventures of George Augustus Sala* (3rd edn., 1895), ii. 236.

'As we recede from the shores of our beloved Britain and get further from Boulogne and Paris and Brussels,' wrote Frances Power Cobbe in 1864, 'we leave behind us more of that class of tourists whose society cannot be said to convey any particular gratification . . . Once over the Alps, the genus 'Tourist', with its proper female accompaniment, becomes rare.'[9] The South was the haunt of the British artists, academics, and literati. It is difficult to think of a Victorian or Edwardian sculptor, painter, novelist, poet, philosopher, historian, or critic of any note who did not make at least one visit to the Mediterranean. Many made their residence there more or less permanent, as the representatives of what George Bernard Shaw called 'Victorian cosmopolitan intellectualism'; and some left their remains in Southern cemeteries, as if to stress their lasting attachment. Elizabeth Barrett Browning and Arthur Hugh Clough are buried in Florence, and the body of Sir Charles Eastlake was interred there for a year before it was transferred to Kensal Green. John Addington Symonds, Augustus Hare, John Gibson, and William and Mary Howitt are buried in Rome. Naples contains the grave of Mary Somerville; Lucca that of Ouida; Trieste that of Charles Lever; Menton those of Aubrey Beardsley and John Richard Green; San Remo that of Edward Lear; Cannes those of Henry Sumner Maine and Henry Brougham; Alicante that of Edward Freeman; Venice that of Frederick Rolfe; and that of Sir David Wilkie is the waters of the Mediterranean itself. Robert Browning died in Venice and would have been interred with his wife in Florence but for an official prohibition on further intramural burials.

An archaeologist recovering Victorian civilisation from a catastrophe like that of Knossos or Pompeii would be in no doubt about the Mediterranean sympathies of its upper and middle classes. In addition to an architecture showing the influence of Greek temples, Roman amphitheatres, and Venetian palaces, he would discover museums stuffed with treasures of Mediterranean art and private houses cluttered with the mementos of journeys to the South. By 1830 the British Museum was already one of the richest repositories of Greek and Roman antiquities in the world, and during the Victorian years it both expanded these collections and added rare specimens from Egypt, Carthage, and the Levant. Personal collections of Mediterranean memorabilia abounded, the trophies of vandalising expeditions to historic sites and ancient monuments.

[9] Frances Power Cobbe, *Italics* (1864), 375.

In 1838 William Wilde rifled the necropolis of Memphis at Saqqara and carried away six funeral urns of the sacred ibis.[10] Young Eddie Huth, in Cairo with Thomas Buckle in 1861, wrote to his mother that he had been to see the Sphinx and had 'broke[n] a bit off its neck to take home with us, as everyone else does'.[11] Lady Elizabeth Grosvenor, touring the Mediterranean in a private yacht, took a fancy to a marble altar on the Greek island of Delos and recorded in her diary that on 12 July 1841 'this was with much difficulty rolled down the ruin-covered slope of the hill, and by the united exertions of the whole crew transported into the ship.'[12] Less enterprising travellers bought their trophies from native dealers, who had looted on their behalf. Tomb robbers touted their wares in Cairo, Cyprus, and Palestine, offering ancient funerary ornaments, ceramics, and papyri, and even mummified remains, for a few piastres. Thus during his brief visit to Egypt Thomas Buckle was able to acquire enough antiquities to equip a private museum. In his poem *The Burden of Egypt*, Richard Monckton Milnes reproved the British for their abuse of Egypt's heritage:

> But who are now the spoilers? We even we;
> Now the worst fiends of ruin are unchained,
> That sons of science and civility
> May bear the fragments home, beyond the midland sea.

That reads like a pallid imitation of Byron's diatribes against Elgin; but Milnes could not lay claim to Byron's sincerity—unless, that is, he intended his poem as a confession, for he was himself guilty of the practice he deplored. When he went to Egypt in 1842 he packed a set of chisels in his baggage to assist the removal of hieroglyphics from temple walls. One thing is sure: if Milnes's poem was cant, it was not unusual. There was a strong element of Pharisaism in the Victorian solicitude for historic sites abroad, and those of Egypt especially attracted gamekeepers with a record as poachers. The amateur Egyptologists Greville Chester and Amelia Edwards were both associated with the setting up of the Society for the Protection of the

[10] W. R. Wilde, *Narrative of a Voyage to Madeira, Teneriffe and along the Shores of the Mediterranean* (Dublin, 1844), 267–8.

[11] Giles St Aubyn, *Victorian Eminence: The Life and Works of Henry Thomas Buckle* (1958), 79–80.

[12] Elizabeth Mary Grosvenor (Marchioness of Westminster), *Narrative of a Yacht Voyage in the Mediterranean* (1842), ii. 123.

Monuments of Ancient Egypt in 1888; yet each had acquired a private collection of Egyptian antiquities by less than scrupulous methods.[13]

Trunkloads of souvenirs specially manufactured for the tourist market were brought home from Italy and Palestine. In Naples, Florence, Rome, and Venice British visitors snapped up terracotta and alabaster replicas of museum sculptures; Venetian glass vases and beads; mosaic and cameo brooches; copies and photographic reproductions of old masters; bronze models of the temples of Tivoli and Vesta; paperweights in the form of the Pantheon; and marble miniatures of the tomb of Scipio and the Trajan Column. From the Holy Land they brought mother-of-pearl crucifixes, rosaries, and étuis; ornaments carved in olive wood from the Mount of Olives; and cups and vases made from the bitumen called Dead Sea Stone. Dickens's inventory, in *Little Dorrit*, of the 'infinite variety of lumber' from Egypt and Italy that encumbers the Meagles home at Twickenham owed as much to observation as to invention:

There were antiquities from Central Italy, made by the best modern houses in that department of industry; bits of mummy from Egypt (and perhaps Birmingham); model gondolas from Venice; ... morsels of tessellated pavement from Herculaneum and Pompeii, like petrified minced veal; ashes out of tombs, and lava out of Vesuvius; Spanish fans, Spezzian straw hats, Moorish slippers; Tuscan hairpins, Carrara sculpture, Trastaverini scarves, Genoese velvets and filigree, Neapolitan coral, Roman cameos, ... Arab lanterns, rosaries blessed all round by the Pope himself ... There were views, like and unlike, of a multitude of places; and there was one little picture room devoted to a few of the regular sticky old saints, with sinews like whipcord, hair like Neptune's, wrinkles like tattooing, and such coats of varnish that every holy personage served for a fly trap.

Documentary records of this contact with the South were equally multitudinous. The Mediterranean was a major inspiration of Victorian writers. In an essay of 1879 John Addington Symonds claimed that the influence of Italy was as strong in nineteenth-century as it had been in Elizabethan literature. 'As poets in the truest sense of the word,' he wrote, 'we English live and breathe through sympathy with the Italians. The magnetic touch which is required to inflame the imagination of the North is derived from Italy.'[14] Books about the

[13] James Pope-Hennessy, *Richard Monckton Milnes* (1949) i. 174; T. G. H. James, *The British Museum and Ancient Egypt* (1981), 20 ff.; M. S. Drower, *Flinders Petrie: A Life in Archaeology* (1985), 57, 168–70.

[14] J. A. Symonds, *Sketches and Studies in Italy* (1879), 185.

Mediterranean were one of the mainstays of Victorian publishing. The presses plied the reading public with *Sketches*, *Notes*, *Diaries*, *Gleanings*, *Glimpses*, *Impressions*, *Pictures*, *Narratives*, and *Leaves from Journals* about *Tours*, *Visits*, *Wanderings*, *Residences*, *Rambles*, and *Travels* in all the quarters of the South. Travel books on Italy alone were appearing at the rate of four a year in the 1840s,[15] and although the number subsequently dropped a steady flow was always maintained. Accounts of travels in North Africa and the Levant were numerous, and as early as 1845 Robert Curzon wrote of the reading public as 'overwhelmed with little volumes about palm trees and camels and reflections on the Pyramids'.[16] Some of these travel books carried distinguished names. Dickens, Thackeray, Gissing, Butler, Belloc, and Somerset Maugham all published accounts of their journeys to the South, and all, together with Disraeli, George Eliot, Ouida, Anthony Trollope, E. M. Forster, Frederick Rolfe, Norman Douglas, and Compton Mackenzie made imaginative use of their Mediterranean experiences in their fiction.

It says much for its peculiar allure that the Mediterranean continued to inspire travel books in the age of the guidebook. The countries of northern Europe had become banal as they had become familiar, and had lost much of their attractiveness as subjects for literary treatment. 'As for France and Flanders and Switzerland, our next door neighbours', proclaimed the *Eclectic Review* in 1824, 'they may serve John Bull very well for a country house; but to have seen those countries is no longer worth speaking of.'[17] In the second half of the century it was supposed that the same must now be true of the Mediterranean lands. 'The question nevertheless arises', wrote Alexander Graham and Henry Ashbee in 1887, in the Preface to their *Travels in Tunisia*, 'whether, with the present facilities for locomotion, there is sufficient *raison d'être* for books of "Voyages and Travels". Guidebooks will always be in request; but "Incidents of Travel", "Pencillings by the Way", "Sunny Memories" or "Letters" from this or that country would seem to belong to a previous generation.' The same thought occurred to Herbert Spencer when he was writing his autobiography, and he refrained from giving an account of his travels in Italy because he felt that there was nothing left to say. 'Those who

---

[15] C. P. Brand, *Italy and the English Romantics* (Cambridge, 1957), 17.

[16] Robert Curzon, *Visits to Monasteries in the Levant* (5th edn., 1865), i, p. v.

[17] Cited by W. C. Brown, 'The Popularity of English Travel Books about the Near East 1775–1825': *Philological Quarterly*, 15 (1936), 70–80.

have not seen Italy have read about it', he explained. 'The subject has been so well worn by generations of travellers that it is threadbare.' In 1914 James Bryce thought of all the books that had been written about the Holy Land and remarked: 'It may well be thought that nothing now remains to be said about Palestine except by archaeologists.'[18] And yet the travel book survived. The Mediterranean afflatus was inexhaustible, and the reason was that the journey south was a rite of passage. At the limit of olive cultivation the British traveller was conscious of crossing a frontier whose significance was far deeper than that of the Channel or the Rhine. On the threshold of the South he experienced an apotheosis. He passed from the circumference to the centre of things, and his thoughts dwelt on roots, origins, essentials, and ultimate affinities.

The names of places in the South acted like an incantation on the emotions of cultivated Victorians. 'I was looking on the Mediterranean,' breathed Frederick Faber in 1841; 'it was the first time those haunted waters had met my gaze. I pondered on the name—the Mediterranean—as if the very letters had folded in their little characters the secret of my joy.'[19] 'The name of Italy', proclaimed Mabel Sharmon Crawford in 1859, 'has for the educated world a kind of magic sound.'[20] James Sully wrote in 1912 of 'the thrill of awesome joy . . . echoed by the very names "Forum Romanum", "Colosseum", "Baths of Caracalla", "St. Peter's", "the Lateran", "the Vatican" and the rest.'[21] The British were enchanted by these names because they were familiar with Mediterranean history and infatuated with Mediterranean art, landscape, literature, and religion. 'These shores have yielded us our religion, our arts, our literature and our laws. If all that we have gained from the shores of the Mediterranean was erased from the memory of man, we should be savages', says Marmion Herbert in Disraeli's novel *Venetia*, repeating and revalidating, as it were, Dr Johnson's famous dictum of sixty years before. To Charles Kingsley it was 'the sacred sea; the sea of all civilisation and almost all history, girdled by the fairest countries in the world'; and it was his view that the Mediterranean 'should be one of the most august and precious objects of this globe' to all who valued the cause of human progress. Remembering his own travels to the South of France in 1864, he

[18] James Bryce, *Memories of Travel* (1923), 166.
[19] J. E. Bowden, *The Life and Letters of Frederick William Faber* (1869), 96–7.
[20] Mabel Sharman Crawford, *Life in Tuscany* (1859), 114.
[21] James Sully, *Italian Travel Sketches* (1912), 75.

declared that 'the first sight of it should inspire reverence and delight, as of coming home—home to a rich inheritance.'[22] For the large majority of Victorian travellers the most treasured item in this inheritance was the Christian religion, and they approached the biblical lands of Egypt and the Levant with reverential awe. To men and women so influenced by Christian revivalism a journey to the eastern shores of the Mediterranean was something more than a journey into the past; it was a journey to the meeting-place of the past and the eternal. It revealed the tremendous facts that Christianity was historical and that history was Christian. The lives and works of Byron, Shelley, and Keats had also enhanced the Mediterranean, and given a special slant to the Victorian vision of Italy and Greece. Refracted through Romantic poetry and Romantic biography these countries connoted magnified possibility, mystic revelation, and transfigured destiny. A heightened aesthetic appreciation of Mediterranean scenery was the legacy of the Italian landscapes of Claude, Poussin, and Salvator Rosa. These painters had bequeathed to eighteenth-century travellers visions of beauty and sublimity, exquisite symmetry and golden light, and awesome chaos and stupendous power. As passed on to the Victorians this inheritance was triply enriched. The Romantic poets gave the landscapes of Claude and Salvator literary equivalents. By stretching the *tessitura* of language and forging a new range of diction they encompassed their emotional resonance in poetry. Furthermore they invested these landscapes with the power of symbols. By using them as settings for psychological drama they turned them into landscapes of the mind; manifestations of the turmoil of the human spirit. And then they filled them with associations of noble purpose and tragic death. Byron's death in Greece, and those of Shelley and Keats in Italy, sanctified these Mediterranean lands and suffused them with elegiac reminiscence; while Byron's and Shelley's support of the fight for Greek and Italian independence identified the South as the home of a noble cause—a distraction which high-minded Victorians ardently desired.

'A man lives by believing in something, not by debating and arguing about many things', declared Carlyle in *On Heroes*. 'Faith in something I must have', cries Lancelot Smith, the hero of Kingsley's novel *Yeast*. In *Adam Bede* George Eliot specified 'doubts and qualms and lofty aspirations' as the characteristics of her age; and in *Middlemarch* she

---

[22] Charles Kingsley, *Prose Idylls* (new edn., 1882), 220–1.

told her readers: 'Scepticism as we know can never be thoroughly applied, else life would come to a standstill. Something we must believe in and do.' Leslie Stephen defined the malaise of his times as 'not that people find the old faiths failing them, but that they begin to doubt that there is anywhere such a thing to be found as faith in anything.'[23] By 1830 the battle for Greek independence had been won; but large areas of southern Europe still toiled under Bourbon, Hapsburg, and Papal bondage, and their rescue became one of the main objectives of all this idle idealism. In 1830 the Cambridge undergraduates who called themselves The Apostles struck a blow for civil liberties in Spain by assisting the abortive guerrilla expedition of José Torrijos against Cadiz; and in his apology for his own participation the twenty-three-year-old Richard Chenevix Trench, a future Archbishop of Dublin, uttered the cry that the poet Clough was later to adopt as the *leitmotiv* of the Victorian predicament. 'You will say', he wrote, 'that all this is very foolish; but it is action, action, action that we want, and I would willingly go did I only find in the enterprise a pledge of my own earnestness.' The liberation of Spain was the obsession of a few; but the liberation of Italy became the gospel of a generation. Dedication to this cause acted like a ferment on public, private, and literary life and roused Protestant England to its greatest moral crusade since the campaign against slavery. In the 1840s, 1850s, and 1860s the Italian Question was constantly debated in the British press, and statesmen like Palmerston, Gladstone, and Russell made it a significant issue in British politics. It inspired Elizabeth Barrett Browning, Algernon Charles Swinburne, Arthur Hugh Clough, Walter Savage Landor, and George Meredith, as well as a multitude of minor and minimal bards, to pour out poems, plays, novels, and battle hymns; and the Society of the Friends of Italy, inaugurated in 1851, linked the powerful and the humble in a common pursuit. 'In the number of members', claimed the Committee of the Society in its first Report,

are included men of all ranks and professions: members of the legislature; the chief magistrates and members of the corporations of various of the largest and most influential towns; clergymen of all denominations; distinguished professors in our universities; men of literary celebrity; men engaged in commerce; and working men. The Committee can confidently state that

---

[23] Leslie Stephen, *Essays on Plain Speaking and Free Thinking* (1873), 8–9.

rarely, if ever, has a Society of the same limited extent, formed for an object of the same nature, been composed of materials at once so various and so select.

The Victorian public venerated the rebel leader Garibaldi as a hero who, if not perhaps darkly wise, was certainly rudely great. He was greeted with huge demonstrations of welcome when he visited England in 1864, and some 800 volunteers enlisted to fight with him in Italy. Most of these were hard-drinking roughs from the slums of London and Glasgow; but the spirit of chivalry moved officers like Peard and Dunne; and women auxiliaries like Jessie White found in the Italian service a scope for heroic aspiration. Jessie White—novelist, journalist, and wife of the Italian patriot Alberto Mario—was Italy's Boadicea and Garibaldi's Florence Nightingale. She was twice imprisoned in Italy for subversive activities, and during Garibaldi's campaigns in Sicily and Naples in 1860 and in northern Italy in 1866–7 she nursed the wounded both behind the lines and on the battlefield. Here, too, if her fellow correspondent George Augustus Sala is to be believed, she struck a blow in the cause of female emancipation, for after an encounter with the Austrians at Montesuelo in 1866 she and her companion Mrs Chambers tore up their drawers to make bandages.[24]

In an atmosphere so saturated with association, suggestion, and quixotism, books were liable to crystallise around even the most slender talents. Narratives of tours round the Mediterranean and in Italy, Palestine, and Greece continued to find publishers and, presumably, readers even when written by authors who revealed little except the poverty of their experience, the triteness of their thought, and the strength of their ability to inflate anecdotes into volumes by means of digression, quotation, and tedious drollery. As always, a ready market encouraged the production of trash. But there was more in the travel catalogues of Victorian and Edwardian publishers than pulp-literature. There were substantial guides and handbooks, which dealt with the practicalities of travel and retailed expert essays on history, archaeology, and art; and there were the contributions of notable writers who gave the travel book a new function as literary portmanteau, with elements of autobiography, disquisition, and essay.

[24] J. Bromley, *The Man of Ten Talents: A Portrait of Richard Chenevix Trench* (1959), 38; Harry Rudman, *Italian Nationalism and English Letters* (1940), 308–19; *First Annual Report of the Society of the Friends of Italy* (1852), 2; *Memoirs of Signore Alberto Mario and Signora Jessie White Mario*, published by the Garibaldi Unity Committee (n.d.); Sala, *Life and Adventures*, ii. 111.

As treated by late Victorians and Edwardians like Samuel Butler,
Vernon Lee, George Gissing, D. H. Lawrence, and Norman Douglas,
the travel book was less a mirror than a window. It was a personal
testament, describing an inward as well as an outward journey and
serving as a vehicle for random fragments of description, opinion, and
erudition. In their travelogues the style is more studied, the pose less
public, the treatment more selective, the content more recondite, and
the interest more human. They wrote about the byways rather than the
highways of the Mediterranean and they focused their attention on the
transient suggestiveness of localities and encounters rather than on
the enduring magnitude of architecture and art. They aimed, in
Norman Douglas's words, 'to follow Goethe's advice about grasping
that living life which shifts and fluctuates about us'.[25] Furthermore,
they associated the travel book with the literature of disengagement
and protest. Butler, Gissing, Lawrence, and Douglas signified in their
accounts of journeys to the South a hostility towards the values of the
modern world and a desire to withdraw from its problems and
complexities. They wrote less as the representatives of their society
than as its casualties and defeated rebels. Their work proclaims the
sadness and the anger of men who were at odds with contemporary
life, and who were looking not for action but for rest.

  Nevertheless it would distort the facts to set these authors apart as
the harbingers of a new sensibility or a new motivation. There was
nothing original in the way they felt. Echoes and assonance link their
work with that of their predecessors, and their statements often merely
elaborate and refine the commonplaces of previous generations.
When, for example, Norman Douglas, in *Siren Land* (1911), wrote how
good it was to 'Mediterraneanise' oneself, 'to dream . . . to stroll . . . to
browse at leisure' away from 'the fevered North' and its perplexing
'problems of the day', he was only repeating that invitation to escape
whose appeal was as old as sophisticated, urban society and which
Eliot Warburton had addressed to the leisured British public, with
equal fervor if not with comparable eloquence, from the pages of *The
Crescent and the Cross* seventy years before:

Reader! Even *you* may some day be induced to change the feverish life of
Europe, with all its perplexing enjoyments, its complicated luxuries and its
manifold cares, for the silence, simplicity and freedom of a life on the desert
and river. Has society palled upon you? Have the week-day struggles of the

---

[25] Norman Douglas, *Old Calabria* (new edn., 1956), 290.

world made you wish for some short sabbath of repose? Has our coarse climate chafed your lungs and do they require the soothing of balmily-breathing breezes? Come away to the Nile! ... Here are sunshines that are never clouded and fragrant airs as gentle as a maiden's whisper, instead of northern gales that howl around you as if you were an old battlement. Here are nights all aglow with stars and a crescent moon that seems bowing to you by courtesy, not bent double by rheumatism. Here is the highest species of monastic retirement: you stand apart from the world; you see its inhabitants so widely differing from yourself in their appearance, their habits, their hopes, and their fears, that you are enabled to look upon man in the abstract and to study his phenomena without prejudice ... As you recede from Europe further and further on, towards the silent regions in the past, you live more and more in the past ... At last even your island restlessness softens down and merges into the universal peace around ...

Moreover there is in the work of Douglas, as in that of Lawrence, an element of overstatement and stridency, and a self-conscious determination to be shocking, which suggest the nagging persistence of inherited values. It has rightly been said of Douglas that he never killed his conscience, and it is equally true of Lawrence that he never killed his prudery. Both lived on the turbulent frontier between conformity and rebellion and both were prone to judgements that the most puritanical Victorian would not have disowned.

Generally speaking, the differences between the later writers and their predecessors were more those of emphasis and language than those of motivation, attitude, or experience. The British response to the Mediterranean in these years was not characterised by interruptions, reversals, or new departures. The same motives, attitudes, and experiences persist and recur, and they often conflict within the same individual. Chronological sequence therefore imposes a false perspective on these aspects of the subject. So too does biography, because the writers generally supposed to have been influential are shown by the wider evidence to have been either representative or disregarded. Ruskin, for example, quite clearly owed as much to educated opinion as educated opinion owed to him, and his achievement was rather to formulate and mediate current ideas about Mediterranean history and art than to create them. He was influential only in a limited sense, because his large audience was willing to be persuaded. The few Victorian works that forsook established or nascent tradition and pleaded for a reassessment of popular attitudes were respected, but ignored. John Addington Symonds's *Renaissance in Italy* is an obvious example. Symonds failed to defeat the tradition that Ruskin represented because he used archaic arguments that no one wanted to hear. The successful revolt was carried out by critics who said what people nurtured in a new cultural climate were predisposed to believe. Motivation and response are therefore better discussed in terms of categories than in terms of periods or personalities.

No understanding of the lives of the Victorian and Edwardian leisured and literary classes can be complete without some knowledge of how they travelled to the South, where they went in the South, why they went, how their experiences shaped their attitude, and how their attitudes shaped their experience. In their travel books, and in the guidebooks, letters, essays, and miscellaneous comment that the Mediterranean connection engendered we have the means to explore such questions. This documentary territory is not unknown. Biographers and anthologists have often gone there and brought back isolated samples. But hitherto it has not been surveyed and charted.

PART ONE

WAYS AND MEANS

VICTORIANS and Edwardians who travelled to the Mediterranean at leisure followed the instinct of migration. They timed their movements to avoid the extremes of hot and cold, going south in the autumn and north in the spring. In Venice, according to the popular American novelist W. D. Howells, October was 'the month of the sunsets and the English';[1] and throughout the Mediterranean it was the same—save only, perhaps, in the Holy Land, where the weather generally deterred pilgrims until Easter. In the summer British tourists avoided these countries, and British residents contrived to escape the heat by moving to higher ground. So from May until September there was little sign of a Northern presence in the popular localities of the South. Boulevards and promenades stretched desolate and dusty in the sun; villas were shuttered; boarding houses were closed; first-class railway carriages were all but empty; and the monuments of antiquity enjoyed a sabbath seclusion. On the Riviera only a few hotels remained open, and the stray visitor was liable to pay for his untimeliness. 'I would suggest to mine host of the Hotel des Anglais', protested Christopher Home Douglas after an out-of-season visit to Nice in 1874, 'that the nationality for which he specially professes to minister objects, even in the month of May, to a toilet table festooned with spiders' webs. Decayed boots and chicken bones are also objectionable in a bedroom, even though under your bed and supposed to be out of sight.'[2] In the 1860s an attempt was made to attract foreign visitors to San Remo in the bathing season. The hoteliers announced their intention to operate throughout the summer, and plans were drawn up for bathing sheds along the beach; but the project foundered and until the First World War the French and Italian Rivieras remained, in British estimation, essentially winter resorts. The Italian habit of bathing in the Mediterranean in July and August was regarded as a foreign perversity. 'To our English minds', commented Lucy Baxter ('Leader Scott') in the 1880s,

this seems inconceivable. During those two months the scorching rays of 'Sol Leone' render the sands a burning desert, the sea is as warm as the hot air above it, and the close lodgings are too stifling to endure. Of what use is a

---

[1] W. D. Howells, *Venetian Life* (2nd edn., 1867), i. 153.

[2] Christopher Home Douglas, *Searches for Summer, Showing the Anti-Winter Tactics of an Invalid* (1874), 119.

month at the seaside to us if our children cannot dig in the sands, and our boys and girls take long walks, seaweed and sea-anemone hunting?[3]

The big cities of the South, likewise, were reckoned to be unendurable during the summer. Rome was abandoned by Northern tourists and residents soon after Easter; Florence and Naples emptied; Algiers and Cairo were left to their garrisons and officials. The tourists retreated homewards, and from the 1850s those leaving Italy were followed as far as the Lakes, Switzerland, or Germany by most of the British residents. It had once been the habit of these expatriates to linger south of the Alps and seek the shade and breezes of hill and mountain resorts. The Neapolitans used to take up summer quarters at Sorrento, Castellammare, or Ischia; the Romans at Albano; and the Florentines at Lucca or Siena. But in the second half of the nineteenth century, with the increased cheapness and facility of travel, these habits changed. Many residents now chose to quit Italy altogether and join their compatriots on the Rhine or in the Swiss valleys. By the 1880s a number of Riviera hoteliers had branches in Switzerland, which they opened in the summer months with employees and equipment transferred from France.

I. JOURNEYS

During the nineteenth century journeys to the Mediterranean by land and sea were radically changed by steam locomotion, and in the first years of the twentieth century journeys by land were being changed again by the automobile. Nothing illustrates the modern revolution in transport so vividly as the experience of British travellers to the South.

In the 1830s and for most of the 1840s they relied mainly on horse power to carry them through France and Italy. Consequently the journey from London to Rome still took between three and four weeks—as long as it had taken in the days of the Roman Empire. Money could not buy greater speed—though it could buy a measure of convenience. Wealthy families could take their own vehicles and, by hiring teams of horses and *voituriers* at Boulogne, proceed on their way in well-upholstered comfort. At Abbeville in 1848 Effie Ruskin watched the departure of an English family of four and their six servants in a commodious coach. 'They are just setting off,' she

---

[3] Leader Scott, *Tuscan Studies and Sketches* (1888), 195.

reported, 'with four horses, two cages full of canary birds, and a fat sick dog in a basket.'[1] The carriage in which the Boyle family travelled to Italy in 1832 was fitted up like a miniature drawing-room, with a table, cupboards, and everything necessary for relaxation and refreshment. 'The front box,' recalled Mary Boyle, 'on which we took it in turns to take an airing and see the country, had also receptacles for different treasures of travel, while the rumble behind was occupied by the faithful Henry. In this manner we proceeded leisurely, but comfortably ... pausing in the middle of the day to bait our horses and feed ourselves, and sleeping at little wayside inns.'[2] It was in this style that the Ruskin and Dickens families made their way to Italy in the 1840s. Ease and privacy could also be secured by taking a *vettura*. A contractor, called a *voiturin* in France and a *vetturino* in Italy, undertook to convey his passengers to a stipulated destination, feeding and lodging them on the way, for a fixed sum. This was a very popular form of travel and it was still in use in southern Italy as late as the 1890s. George Eliot and G. H. Lewes travelled by *vettura* from Toulon to Florence in 1861, and George Eliot described the journey as 'the most delightful (and most expensive) ... we have ever had.'[3] Dr James Henry Bennet, writing in 1875, remembered this style of travel as 'the most comfortable, pleasant and hygienic of any for tourists not much pressed for time, or very particular about expense';[4] and Frederic Harrison counted it among the precious memories of his old age. It was like 'to have heard in their prime Rachel, Grisi and Lablache; to have read *David Copperfield* and *Vanity Fair* month by month in their early shilling numbers; to have seen the British fleet under sails; to have seen French cathedrals yet unrestored, and Rome as it was seen by Byron and painted by Piranesi.'[5]

These modes of travel were necessarily slow, even by early nineteenth-century standards, since the horses were not changed and had to be rested and baited. Thirty-five miles a day was about the most that could be expected. Any one disinclined to dally would travel post, hiring vehicles and horses from government postmasters at successive stations along the route. By this means it was possible to travel briskly

---

[1] William James, *The Order of Release* (1947), 122.
[2] Mary Boyle, *Mary Boyle, Her Book* (1901), 104.
[3] Haight, ed., *Letters of George Eliot*, iii. 410.
[4] James Henry Bennet, *Winter and Spring on the Shores of the Mediterranean* (5th edn., 1875), 683.
[5] Frederic Harrison, *Memories and Thoughts* (1906), 261.

without sacrificing comfort. In 1835 Henry Manning and his companions were able to reach Rome in twenty-five days, 'spending two at
Paris and the Sundays at Breteuil, Chalon, Nice and Civita Vecchia,
and sleeping in . . . beds every night', by travelling post.[6]

For the traveller compelled to rely on public transport the journey
to the South in these early years was something akin to torment. He
took his place in a diligence, a vehicle with the dimensions of a loaded
haywaggon carrying between fifteen and thirty passengers and
weighing up to five tons. These monstrous conveyances plied the
length and breadth of France, Italy, and Spain at little more than
walking pace, their axles hot and screaming and their passengers
prostrate from successive days and nights of relentless motion and
tight confinement. 'From Paris', wrote William Boxall to his sister in
November 1833, 'we journeyed to Chalon by diligence . . . This
journey cost us three days' and two nights' perpetual travelling,
sometimes at not more than three miles an hour, cramped, tired and
exhausted.'[7] Frances Power Cobbe looked back with nausea on her
travels by diligence in Italy. She recalled 'going four miles an hour in
the heat and dust . . . and with a full complement of Italian travellers
all ignorant of the fundamental principles of ablution . . . a journey of
perhaps thirty, forty or fifty hours'.[8] Passengers chose, according to
their means, inside seats in the *coupé* or the *intérieur*, or outside seats
on the *banquette* with the conductor; and each offered its species of
misery. 'I defy anything to render the *banquette* agreeable', wrote the
painter George Frederic Watts, who took the diligence from Paris to
Chalon in 1843. 'I never passed a more wretched night, except perhaps
on my passage to Boulogne. Fancy a cold night wind and a horrid
disgusting brute of a French conductor . . .'[9] But the penalty of taking
an inside place was a sense of asphyxiation and endless disputes with
native passengers who were determined to keep the windows closed.
Dr James Johnson, who travelled through France in 1829, described
the diligences as 'locomotive prisons . . . in which the traveller is
pressed, pounded and, what is worse than all, poisoned with mephitic
gasses and noxious exhalations evolved from above, below and
around'.[10] The artist Cato Lowes Dickinson reported that the

    [6] E. S. Purcell, *The Life of Cardinal Manning* (1896), i. 158.
    [7] Boxall MSS.
    [8] Cobbe, *Italics*, 27.
    [9] M. S. Watts, *George Frederic Watts: Annals of an Artist's Life* (1912), i. 46.
    [10] James Johnson, *Change of Air, or the Pursuit of Health* (4th edn., 1837), 29.

diligence in which he crossed the Apennines in 1850 was 'filled with the atmosphere of a cowshed impregnated with garlic'. He pulled the window down, whereupon a fellow-passenger promptly pulled it up. 'I pulled it down,' he went on, 'for I was beginning to stifle! He pulled it up again, and he rattled away in Italian ... At length, after some squabbling, I pulled it out of the frame altogether and he *couldn't* put it back again. There was a great row about it and the people began to cover themselves up as if they had been crossing the Alps.'[11] The chronicles of Continental travel are full of incidents of this kind, and Dr Thomas Madden expressed a popular British response when he wrote in 1864: 'Any fond recollections I formerly entertained of the pleasures of stage-coach travelling in the palmy days of "the road" were completely dispelled by various journeys in diligences of from eighteen to twenty-four hours each through the south of Spain and France.'[12] About the only traveller whose nostalgia survived the experience was—predictably perhaps—George Eliot, who went with G. H. Lewes from Malaga to Grenada by diligence in February 1867. 'The vehicle was comfortable enough', she declared, 'and the road is perfect.' But then they had the *coupé* to themselves, and the journey lasted only sixteen hours.[13]

The discomforts were even more acute when the vehicle crossed the Alps. It was not that the roads were bad. Napoleon had constructed two fine military roads across the Simplon and Mont Cenis passes, and a new carriage route across the St Gotthard was opened in 1841. Furthermore at the summit of the Mont Cenis pass there was, according to George Augustus Sala, 'a tolerable hotel where you could get delicious lake trout and remarkably good cheese'. It was, as Sala explained, 'the length of time consumed in the lagging diligence and the horrible jolting and creaking of the machine itself that reduced you to a condition approaching despair'.[14] The crossing took about ten hours, and in winter passengers were transferred to a conveyance called a sledge but which, as Oscar Browning recalled, was really a box, so that 'descending the lumpy slopes was ... like being precipitated downstairs in a portmanteau'.[15] Deterred by these vexations, the

---

[11] Cato Lowes Dickinson, *Letters from Italy, 1850–53* (privately printed, n.d.), 17.

[12] Thomas More Madden, *On Change of Climate: A Guide for Travellers in Pursuit of Health* (1864), 174.

[13] Haight, ed., *Letters of George Eliot*, iv. 344–5.

[14] Sala, *Life and Adventures*, ii. 88–9.

[15] Oscar Browning, *Memories of Sixty Years* (1910), 76.

traveller by diligence more often than not avoided the Swiss routes to
Italy and took instead the road to Marseilles or Aix and then
proceeded along the Cornice. The stages were sixteen hours from
Boulogne to Paris, four days and three nights from Paris to Marseilles,
and then a further three days and two nights along the Riviera to
Genoa. Even as early as the 1830s, however, it was unusual to go the
whole way by road.

Steam was already at work to relieve the passenger of some at least
of the tribulations of horse power. A regular service of river steamers
operated on the Saône and the Rhône between Chalon and Avignon,
and it was customary to transfer to one of these for the middle stretch
of the voyage. As William Boxall explained to his sister: 'The Rhône is
so rapid that the boat performs in one day what it takes by diligence
two days and two nights.'[16] By this time, too, coastal steamers were
plying regularly between the Riviera ports and Leghorn, Civita
Vecchia, and Naples, and most travellers made use of these for the last
stages of their journey to Italy, as well as for the first stages of their
journey home. When the American traveller George Stillman Hillard
boarded the steamboat for Genoa at Leghorn in 1848 he found,
besides a full complement of passengers ('most of whom were
English') three English travelling carriages strapped to the deck.[17]
The passage from Marseilles to Naples took about sixty hours and the
vessels were generally found to be clean and well maintained; but
several travellers complained of overcrowding. Charles Dickens took
the steamer from Genoa to Naples in 1853 and discovered when he
arrived on board that it was already overfilled with passengers from
Marseilles. He had to eat and sleep on deck, despite having paid a
first-class fare. 'The scene on board beggars description', he told John
Forster. 'Ladies on the tables; gentlemen under the tables; bedroom
appliances not usually beheld in public airing themselves in positions
where soup tureens had been lately developing themselves; and ladies
and gentlemen lying indiscriminately on the open deck, arranged like
spoons on a sideboard.'[18] Dr Thomas Madden, sailing from Naples to
Leghorn, arrived just before the vessel started and found not only
every berth but every table encumbered with bodies. 'I deemed myself
more fortunate than many others', he wrote, 'in succeeding, by bribing

[16] Boxall MSS.
[17] G. S. Hillard, *Six Months in Italy* (1853), ii. 267.
[18] John Forster, *The Life of Charles Dickens* (Everyman edn., 1966), ii. 134–5.

a steward, to obtain a share of a blanket on the cabin floor.'[19] Coastal steamers were a preferred substitute for land journeys in Sicily until the era of the automobile, and steamboats carried visitors up the Nile from Alexandria to Cairo (covering the distance in a day) until the opening of the railway in the 1880s.

Sea crossings under steam were an established feature of Mediterranean travel after 1830. In the 1840s a packet left Southampton on the 3rd of every month for Alexandria, and on the 25th of every month for Constantinople, via Malta, Athens, Syros, and Smyrna; while regular passenger services linked Marseilles with Algiers, Alexandria, and Malta. By the 1860s there were weekly departures from Southampton to Malaga and fortnightly departures to Alexandria. In the 1880s it was possible to embark at Marseilles, Genoa, Brindisi, Naples, or Trieste and travel by steam to virtually any part of the Mediterranean—though the smaller Greek islands were only fair-weather destinations and for some of the ports of the Levant it was necessary to change vessels at Malta or Alexandria. French, Austrian, and English companies operated these services in close rivalry, and in the estimation of most British passengers standards of comfort and courtesy were higher on the foreign than on the English vessels. The Revd Henry Christmas assured the travelling public in 1851 that in the steamships of the Austrian Lloyd Company, 'should the purse of the traveller render it advisable, he may fearlessly engage a second-class passage'. In the Peninsular and Oriental Steam Navigation Company's ships, on the other hand, the second class was 'intended only for gentlemen's servants'.[20] Frances Power Cobbe embarked on the Austrian Lloyd's *Neptune* at Constantinople in 1858 and declared it 'the most luxurious and delightful vessel' she had ever sailed in. 'It was splendidly equipped,' she enthused, 'even to a *camera obscura* on deck; and every arrangement for luxurious baths and good food was perfect.' The only drawback to the Austrian steamers came from the poor quality of their fuel. They used cheap coal from Dernis, in Dalmatia, which caused clouds of black smoke and showers of burning soot. Passengers on deck had difficulty in keeping clean and the awnings often looked as though they had been riddled with grapeshot. Sir John Gardner Wilkinson, cruising the Adriatic in 1844, one day saw the awning of his vessel on fire—something which alarmed him, but not

[19] Madden, *On Change of Climate*, 320.
[20] Henry Christmas, *The Shores and Islands of the Mediterranean, Including a Visit to the Seven Churches of Asia* (1851), p. xi.

the Captain, who 'calmly ordered it to be put out, as if it was a common occurrence'. Below decks, however, these vessels left little to be desired. Gardner reckoned that they were cleaner than any in the Mediterranean—'except British men-of-war'.[21] Such conditions were far removed from those experienced by the Revd John Aiton on the French steamers of the Messageries Impériales in the 1850s. 'The filth and vermin are worse than those of Egypt', he fumed.

The passengers are actually starved; English passengers are insulted by Frenchmen and rendered as uncomfortable as possible by the authorities on board. They are cheated on every hand and a different rate of charge [is] brought against them. They are scarcely permitted to walk the deck, far less to take up any position so as to take a view for a minute or two; and as to a Frenchman lending an English voyager a spyglass, or telling him the name of an island, he would rather spit in his face.[22]

But one suspects that the Revd Aiton was a difficult customer. The Revd Christmas rated the French vessels as only slightly inferior to the Austrian ones, and by the 1880s the Compagnie Générale Trans-atlantique was running British-built steamers of *fin de siècle* opulence on the Mediterranean routes. Thomas Wemyss Reid, who sailed on the *Charles Quint* from Marseilles to Tunis in 1881, was deeply impressed. 'Nothing more luxurious in the shape of a sea-going vessel has ever met my eyes', he affirmed. 'The saloon is a marvel of beauty and elegance. Marble walls richly gilded, luxurious armchairs, crimson couches, mirrors, carpets, pictures, silver lamps, completely destroy for the moment the notion that one is on board ship.'[23] Robert Otter, who made a habit of wintering in the Mediterranean in the 1870s, preferred the Peninsular and Oriental vessels because 'the food, the hours and the general arrangements [were] more suitable to English tastes'; but he was critical of the Company's heavy passenger load. 'In neither of the other companies have I ever been so miserably crowded for sleeping accommodation as in those of the P. & O.', he complained. 'Every little cabin is fitted up with as many berths as it can possibly hold, and is often crammed to overflowing with

[21] Frances Power Cobbe, *The Life of Frances Power Cobbe* (1894), i. 264; J. Gardner Wilkinson, *Dalmatia and Montenegro* (1848), i. 198–9.

[22] John Aiton, *The Lands of the Messiah, Mahomet and the Pope* (3rd edn., 1854), 357.

[23] Thomas Wemyss Reid, *In the Land of the Bey: Impressions of Tunisia under French Rule* (1882), 18.

passengers ... The only drawback is the chance of being crammed into an overcrowded cabin and poisoned with foul air every night.'[24]

In fact there were other drawbacks, common to all steamships of this time, in vibration and instability. The early vessels had been paddle steamers, which remained relatively steady in high seas by virtue of their deep immersion and broadness of beam; but the later ships were screw driven, drawing very little water and built long and narrow in the interests of speed. They began to roll when the sea was no more than ruffled and in bad weather their passengers suffered fearful agonies of claustrophobia and *mal de mer*. As William Flower, who made the sea crossing to Egypt in 1874, explained:

The passenger ... finds himself crowded in a dark, close cabin, with two or three uncongenial companions, lying on a narrow hard shelf, portholes rigidly closed, and the atmosphere he breathes poisoned by noisome odours, of which the sickening smell of the oil of the engines is one of the least objection-able; the rain pouring on deck makes escape from his prison, even for a few minutes, impossible ... he feels he would give all his wordly possessions for a breath of pure air or a few hours' cessation from the perpetual din of the engines within and the waves without.[25]

During a quarter of a century the steamship possessed the undisputed advantage of speed. In the 1840s, when three weeks were still required to travel comfortably overland from London to Rome, P&O steamers made the journey from Southampton to Alexandria in seventeen days. In the early 1880s the time was down to thirteen days; but by now the steamship had been superseded as the symbol of modern travel. In the intervening years steam had revolutionised transport by land, and distances once measured in days and even weeks had come to be measured in hours. The time had arrived when it was quicker and more comfortable to travel to Egypt by going overland through France and Italy and picking up the steamer at Brindisi. In this way the journey was accomplished in six days.

The middle decades of the nineteenth century were the age of intensive railway-building in France, Switzerland, and northern Italy, when the old submitted to the new with an expressive gesture of abdication. Where stretches of railway were completed, the diligence would forsake its horses and wheels and pursue its journey, with

[24] R. H. Otter, *Winters Abroad: Some Information Respecting Places Visited by the Author on Account of His Health* (1883), 92–3.
[25] Cited in Burney Yeo, *Health Resorts and Their Uses* (1882), 244.

luggage, passengers, and all, on a rolling platform hitched to a train. Private carriages too made use of this facility, with the difference that they were not hoisted minus their wheels, but driven by means of ramps on to their special trucks. By the mid-1850s the railway was open as far as Marseilles and the traveller could reach the South of France from Paris, via Lyons and Avignon, in eighteen hours. The line was then pushed steadily eastwards along the Cornice, so that by 1869 a train service was available to Monaco. Within another year the railway was open as far as the Italian frontier. A direct first-class train left Paris every evening at 7.15 and arrived at Menton at 9.32 p.m. the following day. 'Railways', proclaimed Dr James Henry Bennet in 1875, 'have all but annihilated space ... A traveller may leave the London Bridge Station at 7.40 on a Monday morning, by mail train for Paris, and be at Nice or Menton for supper the following day.'[26] Standards of comfort and service on this Mediterranean express were high. Families and groups could reserve private saloon carriages, each of which contained a sitting-room with sofas and tables, a bedroom, a smoking-room and a *cabinet*; and *coupé-lits* were available for those travelling alone. These were compartments with single rows of four seats, three of which converted into a bed for one person. Under the fourth there was a closet, confidently recommended by Dr Edward Sparks as 'well trapped'.[27] Boudoir sleeping cars, later called *wagon-lits*, were introduced into the 7.15 *rapide* from Paris in 1877, and in 1883 a weekly Mediterranean express service with *wagon-lits* was inaugurated from Calais. By the end of the century this was a daily service leaving Calais at 1.05 every afternoon and arriving at Monte Carlo at 9.39 the next morning. For the first six years the train continued to Rome; but the Cornice route to Italy was now out of favour, following improved rail facilities in Switzerland, so after 1889 the Calais–Nice–Rome Express was renamed the Calais–Mediterranean Express and terminated at Ventimiglia. This was the predecessor of the luxurious *train bleu* of the inter-war years.

Interest in the Swiss routes to Italy revived with the opening of the Fell Railway across the Mont Cenis pass in 1868. The railway was constructed with a central notched rail, which engaged a cogwheel in the engine; and according to Sala 'it did its work very well, although you usually emerged from your railway compartment as black as a

---

[26] Bennet, *Winter and Spring*, 642.

[27] Edward Isaac Sparks, *The Riviera: Sketches of the Health Resorts of The North Mediterranean Coasts of France and Italy* (1879), 146.

sweep, from the smoke of the locomotive.'[28] Oscar Browning remembered that the jolting, too, was considerable, and the descent terrifying to highly strung passengers: 'I have known delicate girls scream and nearly faint under the operation.'[29] But the Fell Railway itself was superseded in 1871, when the Mont Cenis tunnel was opened and it became possible to travel direct from Paris to Turin by train. The Italian railway was now complete to Rome, via Bologna, Florence, and Perugia, and the total journey time from London was only fifty-five hours. The old twice-daily diligence disappeared from the St Gotthard pass with the completion of the railway and tunnel in 1882 and from the Simplon after the opening of the tunnel in 1906; but no sooner had the carriage roads been consigned to oblivion than yet another innovation in transport called them back to life—for the summer months, at least. 'The new motor can claim', wrote James Sully in 1912,

as a set-off to its noise, smell and other unpleasantness, the credit of having revived many an old and moribund country road. It is reviving the Mont Cenis; for this pass is an easy one for the motorist as compared with others which have sharper turnings or which, like the Gotthard, are not open to the motorist during the greater part of the day save on the condition of his submitting to the indignity of . . . having two horses hitched to his machine.[30]

Railways did not smoothe away all the frustrations and irritations of travel. In the early years of steam especially, British passengers found plenty to complain about. Henry Alford, Dean of Canterbury, lambasted the Paris–Nice express in 1870 as 'a wretched imposture, of which any civilised nation ought to be ashamed'. 'What', he demanded indignantly, 'would the English public think of a train so ordered that . . . by its carrying only first-class passengers, it compels invalids and delicate ladies to be shut up with brutal drunken men, offending (to say nothing of other annoyances) their ears with profane and foul language during the whole night and day of the journey?' Furthermore, to speed-addicted Victorians the locomotive seemed pitifully slow. 'The pace attained by this "express" train from Paris to Nice', Alford scornfully revealed, 'is—actual stoppages being averaged — about twenty-two miles an hour.'[31] The foreign way with luggage, too,

[28] Sala, *Life and Adventures*, ii. 89.
[29] O. Browning, *Memories*, 76.
[30] Sully, *Italian Travel Sketches*, 307.
[31] Henry Alford, *The Riviera* (1870), 2–3.

sent British blood-pressure soaring. On Continental railways all
baggage had to be registered; and before 1875, when Thomas Cook
negotiated a concession from the French company, it could not be
sent in advance. This meant that it had to be claimed every time a
journey was interrupted; and claiming luggage at railway stations
abroad was an exasperating business. 'Those going abroad for the first
time', warned Mrs William Aspinall in 1869,

are not aware how much French railways differ from English ones. You
cannot, as at home, get a porter to find your luggage, put it into a cab, and so
enable you to drive off from the station a very few minutes after arriving at it.
No; you must wait till every box, basket and bag belonging to the whole train
[has] been sorted and arranged in the most leisurely manner on a long table,
and then you may go and claim your own.[32]

Foreign porters made things worse by their churlishness. 'Is there a
more civil being than the average British porter, and one more
contented with a humble fee?' demanded Henry Rider Haggard.
'Compare him to the gentleman of his profession across the Channel!'[33] Then Continental trains were horribly smutty. 'The coal in
general use', explained Dr Stuart Tidey in 1899, 'is of inferior quality,
and the engines emit dense volumes of smoke, charged with soot and
grit.' This subjected the British passenger to a teasing dilemma. He
could either open the windows and get covered in grime, or he could
close the windows and, as Tidey put it, 're-breathe breathed air,
possibly charged with all sorts of horrors in the shape of microscopic
organisms left by . . . travelling predecessors'. For Dr Tidey, as for all
his travelling compatriots, such a situation admitted of no real choice.
'The better alternative', he advised, 'is to submit to the begriming
process, which at least has the merit of being aseptic, and provide
yourself with a wet sponge in an indiarubber bag to sponge your face
and hands, and with an atomiser containing paroline with a little
menthol and eucalyptus to spray into your mouth and nostrils from
time to time.'[34] Needless to say, French and Italian passengers
invariably preferred the other option, and the familiar altercation over
windows continued with unabated acrimony throughout the age of
steam. Henry Rider Haggard voiced a common British grievance

[32] William Aspinall, *San Remo as a Winter Residence* (1865), 148–9.
[33] Henry Rider Haggard, *A Winter Pilgrimage* (1903), 37.
[34] Stuart Tidey, 'Travel in Europe', in Edmund Hobhouse, ed., *Health Abroad: A Medical Handbook of Travel* (1899), 230.

when he called Continental railway carriages 'heated infernos with every air-hole hermetically sealed'.[35]

Passengers on slower trains, which generally did not use corridor carriages, suffered from a lack of lavatories. One of the things that Lina Duff Gordon best remembered about her journey to Italy in 1890 was 'the queues of anxious people waiting at the various stopping stations for the *bonne femme* to arrive with the key'.[36] But all these lamentations really only proved that the more the travelling public got, the more it expected. No one could seriously dispute that even the poorest rail service was immensely superior to what had been offered in bygone years of public transport by road. Antonio Gallenga, Italian correspondent of *The Times*, thanked providence for the tunnel when he remembered 'the dinginess and dreariness which awaited the traveller in that damp and clammy café at the Susa Terminus, on alighting from the foul diligence at the foot of Mont Cenis'; and Marianne North lost patience with her plaintive compatriots. 'Those days of long diligence journeys are over now,' she wrote in her memoirs, 'and the tourists who abuse modern railways should remember that they have after all something to be thankful for.'[37]

During the 1860s railways were being built in southern Italy and Spain. In the 1870s a track was laid across the length of Sardinia, from Porto Torres to Cagliari. By the 1880s the main arteries of communication in Sicily, Egypt, and Algeria were served by steam and, among Mediterranean countries regularly visited by the British, only in Greece and the Holy Land did domestic transport remain dependent on horse power. When the tourist ventured beyond the environs of Athens or Jerusalem the years rolled back and he made an improvised journey whose essential features had not changed in a thousand years. 'Throughout Greece and European Turkey', we read in the 1884 edition of Murray's *Handbook for Greece*, 'journeys are made only on horseback ... As a general rule, the traveller should bear in mind that the unavoidable discomfort of travelling in Greece is so great, that it is desirable to have as few unnecessary sources of it as possible.' The tourist should dispense with tents, mattresses, and the usual travelling requisites, which were 'useless to all but their vendors', and make do with a canteen of basic pots, pans, cutlery, and

[35] Haggard, *Winter Pilgrimage*, 37.
[36] Lina Waterfield, *Castle in Italy* (1961), 29.
[37] A. Gallenga, *Italy Revisited* (2nd edn., 1876), i. 10; Marianne North, *Some Further Recollections of a Happy Life* (1893), 17.

crockery; a camp bedstead; a waterproof cloak; rugs and plaids; an indiarubber bath (with bellows to inflate it); a tin washstand basin with plenty of towels and soap; a large white cotton umbrella lined with green; and a good saddle. The last item was indispensable. 'Perhaps the next best thing to an English hunting saddle', advised Murray, 'is the large brass-mounted Turkish post-saddle used by the "Tartars" or government couriers. Or failing that, even one of the common brass-mounted saddles in general use in the Turkish army, and which can be bought second-hand in any large Turkish garrison town, will be found satisfactory.' Horses, guidance, and provisions were supplied—usually for a fixed sum—by a factotum called a dragoman, whose services were essential and who could be engaged at Constantinople, Athens, or Corfu. Only in the Edwardian years was this style of travel beginning to pass away, as the railway progressed from Athens to Lavrion in the south, to Kalamata in the west and to the border of Thessaly in the north, and the first motor cars stirred the dust of ancient highways.

In the Holy Land, where the first railway—from Jaffa to Jerusalem—was not opened until 1892 and where the roads were unsuitable for motor traffic, things changed even more slowly. Until the First World War individuals and groups travelling independently would hire a dragoman to arrange tents, horses, provisions, and escort, and then make a stately progress undistracted by mundane necessity. 'From first to last he took best care of us and our comfort in every way', wrote Marianne North of Hadji Ali, the dragoman who conducted her and her father through Palestine in 1866. 'He fed us only too well, giving what was left to any children or old people who might be near, and our tents were most luxurious. No life can be more enjoyable than the one we had with him. We had no cares, as he thought of and paid for everything for £3–10s a day.'[38] Henry Rider Haggard set out from Haifa in 1900 under the care of a dragoman who had contracted to find 'everything except wine and mineral waters', and visited Nazareth, Galilee, Mount Tabor, Nablus, Jerusalem, Jericho, and the Dead Sea. Cook's tourists travelled, like wealthy pilgrims of old, in organised caravans. In the early years of the firm these were supervised by Thomas Cook himself, whose manner was that of a benevolent but peremptory patriarch. Isabel Burton, who encountered a Cook's party of about 180 in Beirut in 1871, was deeply impressed by

[38] Ibid., 160–2.

the discipline he required, and obtained, from wayward and querulous customers. 'Mr Cook takes it all so quietly and good-humouredly, never notices or speaks of it, nor loses his temper, but goes quietly on his way, carrying out the programme, as a nurse should act towards a fractious child.' The reward of submission was a life of pampered protection. Charles Bell, the Rector of Cheltenham, who joined a Cook's tour in 1886, recorded that 16 horses, 21 mules, 17 servants, and 8 soldiers were provided for every ten members of the party.

We had seven private tents and a saloon tent for breakfast and dinner, and a cooking tent . . . Inside they had Egyptian hangings, with a pattern of scarlet and yellow and blue. The ground was covered by pieces of Persian carpet. We had everything we wanted; and indeed our tent life was wonderfully luxurious . . . Hot water was always ready at our call. Hardship there was none; and at night we had, when we asked for it, a camp fire, by which we sat under the light of the moon and stars, the red glow contrasting picturesquely with the silver lustre of the planets.[39]

During the First World War all this camp equipment was commandeered by the Turkish army, and by the time travel began again in the post-war years hotels had been built and the roads adapted to the automobile.

Travel to the Mediterranean not only became faster and more comfortable during the nineteenth century; it also became safer. The days of Corsairs and Barbary pirates on the high seas were over by 1830 and by mid-century brigandage was a thing of the past in Spain, Corsica, and northern Italy. Richard Ford, in the fourth edition of his *Handbook for Spain* (1869), scoffed at 'the fears of cockney critics and delicate writers in satin-paper albums' and dismissed reports of robbery and molestation as so much Gothic fable. 'The unexpected absence of personages who render roads uncomfortable', he wrote, 'is one of the many and not disagreeable surprises which await those who prefer to judge of [the] country by going there themselves.' The anonymous authoress of *Unprotected Females in Sicily, Calabria and on the Top of Mount Etna*, which was published in 1859, was sure that in Sicily 'the traveller [was] much more secure from violence than in England', since the local government had bought off the bandits by recruiting them on generous terms into a *gendarmerie*; while in Calabria there was no more than 'a little peppering of danger . . . to give romance'. It

---

[39] Isabel Burton, *The Inner Life of Syria, Palestine and the Holy Land* (1875), ii. 20; Charles Bell, *Gleanings of a Tour in Palestine and the East* (1887), 269.

was the Risorgimento, ironically, that revived the hazards of the road in these parts. Its associated political instability and social dislocation gave rise to lawlessness which it took several decades for the new authorities to suppress. Arthur Stanley reported in 1863 that it was 'only by encountering some risk' that he had ventured from Naples to Amalfi;[40] and ten years later John Addington Symonds wrote from Sicily that *table d'hôte* talk was 'brigands and nothing but brigands'. He complained of being 'cooped into the walls' of Palermo by the 'confounded bandits' who infested the route to Girgenti. His wife Catherine reckoned that two-thirds of the bandit stories were myths; 'but', she added, 'there is a large substratum of fact, and it is unwise to go long journeys by land.' They discovered that the only really safe methods of transport to Girgenti, fifty miles away, were coastal steamer and omnibus under military escort. They chose the steamer, which was a lot slower but more comfortable.[41] R. H. Otter, who was in Palermo in 1876, also learnt that it was hazardous to go beyond the walls of the town 'on account of the brigands';[42] and as late as 1900 Samuel Butler was warned against driving to Trapani, since it was 'not considered safe'.[43] But the 1892 edition of Murray's *Handbook for Southern Italy* assured its readers that brigandage 'properly so-called' had now been eradicated, and this was confirmed by Macmillan's *Guide to the Western Mediterranean*, published in 1901. There seems little reason to doubt that a menace which had still been real twenty years before was now only a phantom, sustained by outdated guidebooks and over-anxious hotel-keepers. In this, the age of the railway, casual highway crime was being superseded by a more sophisticated gangsterism, whose interests lay elsewhere than in the purses and watches of wandering Englishmen. Probably the only areas where rural banditry remained endemic in the late Victorian and Edwardian years were Palestine and Greece. To travel here without an adequate escort was to invite a repetition of the distressing experience of the unnamed Mr G., an early Victorian pilgrim who was stripped by Bedouin on the road to Jericho and left to find his way back to Jerusalem with nothing but his hat to hide his nudity; or the melancholy fate of Messrs Herbert, Vyner, and Lloyd, who were

[40] R. E. Prothero, ed., *Letters and Verses of A. P. Stanley* (1895), 338.

[41] Herbert Schueller and Robert Peters, eds., *The Letters of John Addington Symonds* (Detroit, 1967), ii. 285–6; Margaret Symonds, *Out of the Past* (1925), 134–5.

[42] Otter, *Winters Abroad*, 144.

[43] Henry Festing Jones, *Samuel Butler, A Memoir* (1920), ii. 329.

seized as hostages from a party of English tourists near Marathon in 1870, held to ransom, and murdered when government troops attempted a rescue.[44] This last outrage caused a sensation, and the risks incurred by travellers in Greece became a matter of concern to the British Government. In 1881 the Foreign Secretary, Lord Granville, issued a general notification that British Consular officials were under instructions not to advance money to ransom British subjects kidnapped 'in no public character but in pursuit of their own pleasure and business'. These instructions had been addressed specifically to the British Ambassador in Constantinople, since it was known that Greek bandits used Turkey's Balkan territories as a base and a refuge. The 1884 edition of Murray's *Handbook for Greece* promised travellers that the Peloponnese was safe, but it warned that their security in the border districts of the mainland could not be guaranteed. Yet even in these countries, though lawlessness was rife, it was his own imprudence that put the tourist at risk. The Greek authorities were always ready to furnish escorts, provided only that twenty-four hours' notice was given to the police; and in Palestine the Turkish Government connived at a system of blackmail which enabled travellers and tour-operators to purchase protection from local Arab chiefs.

There is no doubt that British travellers in the nineteenth century were vexed less by outlaws than by the formalities imposed by foreign governments. These were particularly exasperating before 1860, when France and the various Italian states required British visitors first to go through the tedious and expensive business of obtaining passports and visas, and then to endure repeated and prolonged customs inspections and immigration procedures. Until 1850 British passports were so difficult to obtain (they were to be had only on personal recommendation to the Secretary of State and at great cost) that most Britons found it more convenient to purchase French ones and travel, technically at least, under the protection of a foreign power. This anomaly was easily tolerated at a time when British travellers needed

[44] The story of Mr G. was often retold. It first appeared in Eliot Warburton, *The Crescent and the Cross: Romance and Realities of Eastern Travel* (1845), ii. 134–5. For the Marathon massacre see an unsigned article by Charles Lever in *Blackwood's Magazine*, 108 (Edinburgh, 1870), 240–5 and *The Illustrated London News*, 30 Apr. and 7 May 1870. A later victim of banditry in Palestine was the archaeologist Flinders Petrie, who was ambushed and plundered in the neighbourhood of Tell el Hesy in 1890. See Margaret Drower, *Flinders Petrie*, 164.

passports only as credentials of identity abroad. (Not until 1915, when the emergency provisions of the Defence of the Realm Act were extended, were they required to carry them on entering or leaving their own country.) One of Palmerston's measures as Foreign Secretary, however, was a reform of the issue of British passports. Consequently in the second half of the century these could be had either direct from Downing Street, or from approved agencies, on presentation of a letter of introduction from a banker or a certificate of identity signed by a magistrate, a mayor, a minister of religion, a physician, or a solicitor. Only a small fee was charged—initially 7s. 6d., later 2s. 6d. Right of entry to Italian and Turkish territories was conferred not by the passport, but by the *visé*, or visa, that it carried, and this had to be obtained in advance from the appropriate consulate. After the disturbances of 1848–9 the visa system was rigorously enforced in Lombardy, Venetia, Modena, Tuscany, Naples, and the Papal States, and travellers who planned to cross or stay in these territories had first to spend time and money obtaining consular signatures. Even then entry into Lombardy and Venetia was not assured, since the governing authority here was despotic Austria. 'That jealous power', wrote Edmund Spencer in 1852, 'interposes such a barrier of police laws and passport regulations around her Italian posessions for the purpose of preventing strangers from entering them, that it is almost impossible for a traveller to know when he has complied with the requisite formalities.'[45] All the Italian states save liberal Piedmont had strict customs regulations and censorship, and the peninsula bristled with venal officials who were a sore trial to British patience and a constant drain on British purses. 'The examination in the frontier *dogana* of the state being passed,' warned Mabel Sharman Crawford, 'the stranger who fancies that, as far as the Grand Duchy [of Tuscany] is concerned, all luggage troubles are at an end will find, by subsequent experience, that this idea is incorrect, since the entrance into a town of any note . . . entails the liability of having the interiors of trunks, portmanteaus and carpet bags explored anew.' But after the unification of most of Italy under the dynasty of Piedmont in 1860 these restrictions were relaxed or abolished, and the British were at last able to roam through southern Europe without passports and free of the threat of having their reading matter seized as subversive literature or their personal belongings impounded as

[45] Edmund Spencer, *A Tour of Inquiry through France and Italy* (1853), ii. 144.

contraband. No passport was necessary to enter French territory after 1860, nor to enter Egypt after 1882, when the country was occupied by the British; and in Greece a visa was required only when embarking on a tour of the interior. So amongst destinations frequented by the British only the Turkish territories of the Levant still required a visa as a condition of entry, and even here the requirement was not strictly enforced.[46]

Even more obnoxious to liberty-loving Britons than passports and customs regulations was the species of imprisonment which many Victorian travellers in the Mediterranean had to undergo in accordance with the laws of quarantine. The purpose of quarantine, which had been introduced into the Mediterranean ports in the fifteenth century, was to arrest the spread of bubonic plague. It was therefore regularly enforced against travellers arriving from areas where the plague was considered endemic—Barbary, Egypt, and the Levant; but in the nineteenth century it was used also as a prophylactic against cholera, which appeared in England in 1832, 1848, 1854, and 1866, and in southern France and northern Italy in 1835, 1855, and 1884. Hence John Henry Newman and his friends had to undergo quarantine in Algiers in 1832, on account of the cholera in England; and in 1835 travellers to Italy who had visited Marseilles, Leghorn, Genoa, or Venice found themselves liable to be detained in quarantine on arrival at Rome, Florence, or Naples. This cholera epidemic was so severe in the northern Mediterranean ports that for many years subsequently quarantine restrictions were threatened at the slightest sign of recrudescence. 'No one', grumbled the Revd Henry Christmas in 1851, 'can now eat a few plums too many in Marseilles without alarming the sanitary officers of all the southern powers.'[47]

Travellers arriving from plague areas, or even from ports in regular contact with plague areas (such as Malta and Gibraltar), were detained under medical supervision for periods varying from three to thirty days, even when their country of arrival was itself designated a plague area. Consequently on certain routes the cumulative delay could be considerable. For example, tourists visiting Egypt, the Holy Land, Turkey, and Greece in that order had a minimum of three quarantines: one at Beirut for having been in Alexandria; one at Constantinople for having been in Beirut; and one in Greece for

---

[46] Crawford, *Life in Tuscany*, 233; Gertrude Bell, *The Desert and the Sown* (1907), 328.
[47] Christmas, *Shores and Islands*, ii. 98.

having been in Constantinople. The Revd John Aiton was five times in
quarantine during his tour of Egypt and the Levant in 1851, and he
calculated that if each had lasted the stipulated period he would have
spent a total of four months in detention. Fortunately, in practice a
quarantine of more than fourteen days was rare and the full forty days
were exacted only when the plague was active (as it was in 1855).
Passengers on private vessels, and on vessels terminating their voyage
or unloading cargo, remained on board under a yellow flag for the
duration of their quarantine. Those arriving by ongoing ships
disembarked and proceeded to a lazaretto. There were lazarettos in
Valetta, Marseilles, Jaffa, Beirut, Smyrna, Marsala, Genoa, Syracuse,
Corfu, Syros, and the Piraeus, and standards of comfort and convenience varied considerably from one to another. According to the
1884 edition of Murray's *Greece* the best lazarettos were those in
Corfu, Malta, and the Piraeus; and Malta it judged 'by far the least
inconvenient and best regulated purgatory of them all'. This had been
the opinion of travellers as far back as the 1830s and 1840s, judging by
the comments of John Henry Newman, Samuel Bevan, and Sarah
Austin. The inmates of all these institutions were rigorously excluded
from physical contact with the outside world, and communications
and exchanges had to be carried on by means of fumigated letters,
shovels on long poles, and shouted conversations in *parlatorios*. These
were rooms divided by corridors of wire fencing, along which health
officials constantly patrolled. Money paid for goods received was
passed through water, in the belief that this acted as a purifying agent.
In the 1850s, in the lazarettos of Greece and the Levant, the period of
detention was reduced and personal fumigation introduced as an
alternative safeguard against contamination. 'A suite of three rooms is
prepared', explained William Beamont,

two on the outside serve as dressing rooms, while the third, the doors of which
are almost hermetically closed, except when opened for a moment to admit
the traveller, is filled with dense fumes and vapours of disinfecting smoke. The
traveller, entering the first room, strips and leaves his clothes and then
running as fast as he can through the closed room, is supposed to leave in its
disinfecting vapour all the seeds of infectious matter.[48]

Lady Eastlake was compelled to undergo a less rigorous version of this
process of expurgation at the frontier post of the Duchy of Parma
during the cholera epidemic in north Italy in 1855. She described how

[48] William Beamont, *Diary of a Journey to the East* (1854), i. 51.

she and her companions were required to stand in a closed room 'where some diabolical compound sent up its fumes'.[49]

The splenetic outburst of Mr Meagles against the quarantine restrictions in Marseilles, in the second chapter of *Little Dorrit*, sounds repeatedly in nineteenth-century travel literature. William Wilde called the system 'that abomination of travelling'. Dr John Bowring fulminated against 'the sacrifice of happiness, the weariness, the wasted time, the annoyance, the sufferings inflicted by quarantine legislation'.[50] The Revd Aiton called it 'the nightmare of horror to all travellers to the East'. The painter Penry Williams was convinced that it was not the fear of cholera itself, but the prospect of quarantine, that kept British visitors away from Rome in 1835;[51] and thirty years later Marianne North watched in some alarm as her father reacted apoplectically to the news that he was to be detained for eleven days in the harbour at Corfu. 'Signor Direttore,' he spluttered to the apologetic Austrian Lloyd agent, 'j'ai voyagé con mia figlia in tutta la terra and, hang it, I never was so shamefully treated!'[52]

But it was not all snarling and restless pacing. Some Victorian travellers, especially those on the return lap of a long voyage, found the enforced inactivity a welcome respite; and in the earlier part of the nineteenth century at least there was a general willingness to accept the system as a necessary evil. The regulations published in 1820 in Malta, by the British themselves, were some of the strictest and most elaborate on record; and in 1825 the British Parliament passed a comprehensive Quarantine Act, which gave harbour authorities power to detain in isolation vessels with foul or suspect bills of health for twenty-one days. Under this act a lazaretto was set up in Stangate Creek on the Medway and quarantine hulks were moored in the Solent.[53] Here travellers returning from Muslim countries were required to undergo quarantine, though since they were allowed to deduct the duration of their voyage from the stipulated period they were seldom detained longer than a few days, if at all. It was subsequently that intolerance of the system grew, as the conviction took root that it was not only distressing but unscientific. Quarantine

---

[49] C. E. Smith, ed., *The Journals and Correspondence of Lady Eastlake* (1895), ii. 66.

[50] Cited in John Davy, *Notes and Observations on the Ionian Islands and Malta* (1842), ii. 328.   [51] Boxall MSS.

[52] North, *Further Recollections*, 87–9.

[53] J. C. McDonald, 'The History of Quarantine in Britain in the 19th Century': *Bulletin of the History of Medicine*, 25 (Baltimore, 1951), 22–45.

was based on the assumption that plague and cholera were spread by personal contact, and Victorian medicine discarded the contagionist for the miasmatic theory of disease. The failure of elaborate inland checks to arrest the spread of cholera during the epidemic of 1832 undermined the contagionist argument and in 1848 even the conservative Royal College of Physicians proclaimed the uselessness of quarantine. The opinion grew that infection was propagated not by touch, but by poisonous effluvia in the atmosphere. Quarantine was consequently condemned as a medieval futility whose real purpose must be police surveillance. 'Under the plea of public health', complained a correspondent of the *Lancet* in 1839, 'all letters are opened, all travellers arrested, all commodities subject to costly and vexatious regulations.' When he was in Palermo in 1851 Nassau Senior insisted on enlightening the local Medical Officer about modern scientific opinion on the subject. 'The prevalent doctrine in England', he lectured, 'is that all quarantine regulations are absurdities; that plague and cholera are disorders of the atmosphere and travel in the winds, not in ships or by railways.'[54]

Anti-contagionism was at its peak in the 1850s and early 1860s. Thereafter the facts about cholera discovered by Snow, Budd, and Paccini, the germ theory of Pasteur, and then the identification of the organism *pasteurella pestis* and the elucidation of the role of fleas and droplet infection in the spread of bubonic plague, all combined to revive contagionist doctrine and bring medical opinion back to the principle of compulsory control. This was endorsed by a series of International Sanitary Conferences, which devised and recommended standard preventive procedures. The British authorities declined to reintroduce quarantine to cope with the menace of contagion, so although the Quarantine Act was not actually repealed until 1896 it was in effect superseded after 1866 by medical inspection, hospitalisation, and disinfection. In the Mediterranean ports, on the other hand, quarantine was still enforced in confirmed or suspected cases of cholera, yellow fever, or plague. The limit of detention, fixed by the Constantinople Conference of 1866 at ten days, was reduced by the Venice Conference of 1892 to five—which, although an appreciable abbreviation of the delays that the early Victorians had had to endure, was still a serious threat to the traveller's comfort and convenience.

[54] Nassau Senior, *Journals Kept in France and Italy* (1871), ii. 58–9.

2. DESTINATIONS

During the greater part of the nineteenth century, as in the eighteenth, western Italy was the most popular destination of leisured and literary Britons heading south. Statistical evidence is scanty, but what there is supports the impression gained from other sources that Italy was preferred by a majority of travellers until the late 1860s, when the appeal of the South of France was becoming paramount. In 1869 Dr Charles Theodore Williams was able to claim, with little fear of contradiction, that the Riviera had become the most popular wintering place in Europe.[1]

Richard Monckton Milnes reported early in 1834 that the number of Britons in Rome during the previous Christmas had been estimated at 5,000.[2] In the late 1840s James Whiteside quoted the number of foreign tourists visiting Florence each year as 11,000.[3] This allows for about 5,000 Britons, if we accept that Americans were by now beginning to outnumber them.[4] These figures corroborate each other, because until the 1870s the British in Italy tended to move as a herd, concentrating in the same city at the same time. The totals for Rome and Florence in any year therefore represented the same body of people, not halves of a larger aggregate. Furthermore, since the herd instinct was so strong it is unlikely that the total number of Britons in the whole country was significantly greater than the maximum of 5,000 to be found in either of these cities. By the 1880s cheap and rapid transport had brought greater variation into habits of travel. Trips were shorter and the individual was more mobile; hence when dealing with this period it is no longer safe to assume that all the British in Italy were to be found in the same place at the same time. It is safe to assume, however, that few went to Italy without visiting Rome; so the number of annual British visitors to Rome remains a useful guide to the number of annual visitors to the peninsula as a whole. In 1886 Dr David Young recorded that the number of English and American

---

[1] C. T. Williams, *The Climate of the South of France as Suited to Invalids* (2nd edn., 1869), 2.

[2] Thomas Wemyss Reid, *The Life, Letters and Friendships of Richard Monckton Milnes* (1890), i. 153.

[3] James Whiteside, *Italy in the Nineteenth Century* (new edn., 1860), 33.

[4] Nathaniel Hawthorne recorded his impression in 1858 that Americans outnumbered the British. See *Passages from the French and Italian Notebooks* (1870), 297.

visitors to Rome was officially estimated at between 18,000 and 25,000 a year.[5] Of these, allowing that the majority were American, probably between 8,000 and 10,000 were British. The value of such assessments is obviously limited; but there seems no reason to doubt that they are roughly correct, and that the number of British visitors to Italy increased from something like 5,000 to a maximum of about 10,000 a year during the half-century between the mid-1830s and the mid-1880s. During the next thirty years the rate of increase was much greater and some 90,000 British visitors are likely to have come to Italy in 1913—though not all of them were tourists.[6] The number of British residents in Italy was of course much smaller. Florence, which was the most important residential city in Italy, was reckoned by Whiteside to contain about 900 expatriates of all nationalities, and the British contingent is likely to have accounted for between a third and a half of these.

When compared with available statistics for the South of France, these figures show that Italy remained more popular than the Riviera until the late 1860s. A return of foreign visitors in Nice in March 1862 shows 473 British families, comprising perhaps 2,000 individuals;[7] and Thomas Carlyle wrote from Menton in 1867 that there were then about 800 British present in the town.[8] By allowing a further 1,000 for Cannes, which was the only other resort of any note at this time, we arrive at an annual average of something like 4,000 for the whole of the Riviera in the mid-1860s. By the end of the following decade this number had increased considerably. Hyères was then reckoned to be attracting about 300 British visitors a year and published returns for Cannes and Menton for 1878 show a total of 1,293 British families at both places.[9] Assuming an average of four individuals for each family, this figure indicates a combined total for the three resorts of five and a half thousand people, and those in Nice must have added at least as many again. By the end of the century the French Riviera had far

[5] David Young, *Rome in Winter and the Tuscan Hills in Summer* (1886), 94.

[6] Calculated from figures for 1923 and the percentages for 1927–30 given by Ogilvie, *The Tourist Movement*, 164–5. Judging by the statistics given by Ogilvie on p. 92, 1923 seems to be roughly in line with 1913 and to represent recovery point after the dislocations of the World War.

[7] Madden, *On Change of Climate*, 292.

[8] E. T. Cook and Alexander Wedderburn, eds., *The Life, Letters and Complete Works of John Ruskin* (1903), xvii. 340 n.

[9] Sparks, *The Riviera*, 197, 218, 307.

surpassed Italy in popularity. In the 1890s Nice alone was attracting 100,000 visitors a year, of whom a substantial minority were British.[10]

The number of Victorians visiting Italy was, then, small by the standards of modern and even of Edwardian tourism; but, because they were so gregarious for so long, wherever they alighted they had a considerable economic and cultural impact and created the impression that the country was swarming with English. Until well into the 1870s travelling Victorians followed the itinerary of the eighteenth-century Grand Tour, devoting their time (save for a week or so in Venice on the outward journey) to the Tyrrhenian side of the Apennines and ignoring the Adriatic coast. They spent the autumn in Florence, went to Rome for Christmas and the New Year, moved on to Naples for the remainder of the winter, and then returned to Rome for Holy Week and Easter; and these three cities brimmed with evidence of their periodic visitation. 'For one Hôtel de Paris in Italy', wrote Dr James Johnson in 1830, 'we find five Hôtels de Londres.'[11] By 1870 Rome, besides its Hôtel de Londres, boasted a Hôtel de l'Angleterre, a Hôtel des Îles Britanniques, a Hôtel Brighton and a Hôtel Victoria; and the cluster of lodging houses in and about the Via Condotti was known as the *ghetto Inglese*. In Naples there were a Hôtel Grande Bretagne, a Hôtel Bristol, a Hôtel Britannique, a Hôtel de Londres, and a Hôtel Victoria; while in Florence the visitor who did not (as was more usual here) take a villa or an apartment could choose between some half-dozen English pensions, where the maids, as Arnold Bennett discovered, wore 'the apron and cap of the English parlour maid, in plenary correctness'.[12] English churches, drawing congregations of between four and eight hundred, were operating in Rome, Florence, and Naples during the second half of the century, and in 1847 there appeared in Florence an English-language newspaper—the *Tuscan Athenaeum*. Its life was short, but it had successors: first the *Roman Times*, and then the *Roman Herald*. George Augustus Sala described the Florence of the 1860s as a curiously hybrid city, where 'English boarding houses elbow Italian *locandas*; English bakers sell you captain's biscuits and pound-cakes; and Dr Broomback's Academy for the Sons of Gentlemen is within twenty minutes' walk of the Pitti Palace.' The Pincian quarter of Rome he found full of English

[10] Thomas Linn, *The Health Resorts of Europe* (7th edn., 1899), 118.
[11] Johnson, *Change of Air*, 236.
[12] Arnold Bennett, 'Night and Morning in Florence': *The English Review*, 5 (1910), 442–55.

shops, selling Crosse and Blackwell's pickles, Brown and Polson's cornflour, Mappin's razors, Elkington's plate, Atkinson's perfumery, Savory and Moore's drugs, Guinness's stout, Parkinson and Gott's stationery, and Allsopp's pale ale.[13] In Naples in the 1890s the existence of a significant English clientele was betokened by an English circulating library, Durst the Chemist, Smith and Codrington's grocery stores, and the tourist office of Thomas Cook and Son in the Piazza dei Martiri.

Naples had too much native vitality ever to submit to anglicisation; but in the middle decades of the nineteenth century the British made Rome and Florence their own for a few months every year and the Italians melted into the background in the manner of *corps de ballet* when principals are dancing or waiters when dessert has been served. 'In Italy,' observed the American George Hillard in 1847, 'strangers seem to be at home and the natives to be exiles.'[14] No one could visit these cities during the height of the season without being constantly aware of the extravagance of English fashion, the fastidiousness of English hygiene, the chill of English manners, and the sibilance of English speech. Hillard reckoned that three-quarters of the carriages on the Cascine in Florence were English. 'They are known to be such', he explained, 'by their air of finish and good taste, the excellent condition and sleek coats of the horses, the completeness of the harness and appointments, the modest reserve of the colours, the well-fed respectability of the coachmen and the overdressed women and haughty countenances within.'[15] Twenty years later, in the area of Rome between the steps of the Trinita del Monte and the Corso, Sala was able to contemplate British spinsterhood in all its infinite variety:

There you may see, in the space of one half hour, on a fine wintry afternoon, at least sixteen varieties of English old maids; and, I delight to add, not fewer than sixty species of English young maids, arranged in the most ravishing cavalier hats, mainly with feathers in them, and with Balmoral boots whose heels are of the altitude of the Obelisk of Rhamses, with crinolines surpassing in circumference the sweep of the Circus Maximus, and with looks as lofty as the Pyramid of Caius Cestius.[16]

[13] George Augustus Sala, *Rome and Venice, With Other Wanderings in Italy in 1866—67* (1869), 347–9.
[14] Hillard, *Six Months in Italy*, i. 145.
[15] Ibid., i. 85.
[16] Sala, *Rome and Venice*, 350.

The opera, the fashionable cafés and confectioners (Doney's in Florence, Spillman's and Nazzari's in Rome), the Florentine court (in the Grand Ducal days), the pageants, and the Carnival all throve on British support. During the 1860s in fact, when the Carnival in Rome was boycotted by the Italians for political reasons, the jubilation was almost entirely the work of British and other foreign vistors.[17] The British also introduced their own social rituals and recreations, turning Florence and Rome into replicas of Mayfair. They left cards and paid morning calls; they entertained each other at *soirées musicales*, literary receptions, and glittering balls; they sketched and botanised at Vallombrosa; and they sallied into the Campagna for picnics and foxhunts. Lord Shaftesbury calculated that when he was in Rome in 1833 he devoted one-fifth of his time to card-leaving, and Charles Weld lost all sense of locality in the social whirl of the city in 1864. 'These English parties', he wrote, 'are so very similar to those given in London during the season, that it is extremely difficult to realise that you are in Rome.'[18] This was the life that Frederick Faber summarised as 'eating ices, subscribing to reading-rooms, examining artists' studios, coursing over picture galleries, reading the last novel [and] going to Mass to hear the music'.[19]

In the second half of the century similar signs of an important British presence proliferated along the Riviera. Nice had been attracting English visitors since the late eighteenth century, and when Edmund Spencer visited the resort in 1852 he found that the *faubourg* called La Croix de Marbre had become their special territory. 'Here everything is English,' he wrote,

> to the sign board over the shop door. Here we find the English Protestant Church, the residence of the clergyman, the physician and the chemist, which we may always take as evidence of the existence of an English community on the Continent; and Nice must be a favourite, since we found shops displaying English wares of every description, from the woollens of Yorkshire and the cottons of Manchester to a biscuit and a reel of cotton.[20]

The hoteliers of Nice were already flattering insular vanity with names like Victoria, Grande Bretagne, d'Angleterre, and des Anglais;

[17] A. W. Buckland, *The World Beyond the Esterelles* (1884), ii. 70–1.
[18] Edwin Hodder, *The Life and Works of the Earl of Shaftesbury* (1886), i. 181; Charles Richard Weld, *Last Winter in Rome* (1865), 239.
[19] Bowden, *Frederick Faber*, 188.
[20] Spencer, *Tour of Inquiry*, i. 151–2.

and by the 1890s they had added Westminster, Windsor, West End, and Îles Britanniques. By 1878 there were in Cannes a Hôtel des Anglais, a Hôtel Windsor, a Hôtel Bristol, and a Hôtel Britannique. Menton boasted half a dozen hotels with Anglo-Saxon names in the 1860s (de Londres, Grande Bretagne, de la Pension Anglaise, Victoria, d'Angleterre, and des Îles Britanniques) and by the end of the century it had produced five more (Balmoral, Windsor Palace, Westminster, Prince de Galles, and des Anglais). Monte Carlo, which consisted almost entirely of hotels by the 1890s, acknowledged its debt to British patronage with the Hôtels des Anglais, St James, Prince de Galles, Victoria, Windsor, Balmoral Palace, and de Londres. Even the small resort of Hyères had a Hôtel des Anglais by the 1890s. Across the border on the Italian Riviera San Remo contained a Hôtel de Londres, a Hôtel Victoria, a Hôtel Angleterre, and a Hôtel de la Grande Bretagne as early as the 1860s; and by the end of the century the list had grown to include the Windsor, the Îles Britanniques, the Savoy, and the West End. Bordighera had its Hôtel d'Angleterre in the late 1860s, and by the 1890s the Londres, the Windsor, and the Îles Britanniques had opened.

Most Riviera hoteliers tailored their services to fit British idiosyncrasies. 'English tastes', wrote Dr Edward Sparks in 1879, 'are well understood and carefully consulted in all the hotels.'[21] This amenability was especially evident in the hoteliers' constant concern to improve their sanitation. In the 1890s their advertisements regularly announced such features as 'sanitary arrangements by the best English engineers', 'modern sanitary arrangements', 'drainage executed by English engineers', 'perfect sanitary arrangements', 'complete English sanitary arrangements', and 'sanitary arrangements by George Jennings'. This insistence on the Englishness of their conveniences was a concession to the notorious mistrust of the British for any sanitation but their own—a mistrust well exemplified in 1899 by Dr Leigh Canney, in a paper comparing the merits of Algiers and Cairo. 'In the latter case', he emphasised, 'it must be remembered that the sanitation is English; in the former, French—and the two things are not identical.'[22]

English and Scottish churches were built to supply the spiritual needs of an ever-growing winter population. The Episcopal Chapel of

---

[21] Sparks, *The Riviera*, 226.
[22] See Canney's chapter in Edmund Hobouse, ed., *Health Abroad* (1899).

the Holy Trinity consecrated in Nice in 1822 soon proved too small and a bigger church was opened on the same site in 1856. In Cannes, after the laying of the foundation stone of Christ Church in 1855, Anglican churches were consecrated at the rate of one every ten years, so that by 1890 British congregations were served by Christ Church, St Paul's, St George's, and Holy Trinity, as well as by a Scottish Presbyterian chapel. By the 1890s Menton and San Remo each had two Anglican churches and a Scottish Presbyterian kirk; and at the end of the century there were English churches operating in Hyères, Grasse, and Bordighera. Supplementing these were a multitude of other amenities, including English shops, English libraries, English clubs, cricket grounds, golf courses, tennis courts, and an English newspaper (the *Cannes Gazette*).

Their English clientele shaped the character of these Riviera resorts and filled them with what Frederic Harrison called the cardinal British institutions—'tea, tubs, sanitary appliances, lawn tennis and churches'.[23] Nice, a city of hotels where the British lived very much in public, was in its early years fast and modish in the manner of a Mediterranean Brighton. 'Plenty of society—quantities of gossip—and a great deal of dressiness' is how Lady Margaret Brewster summed it up in 1857.[24] Cannes, where the British lived predominantly in villas, had the provincial and parsonical tone of English country society. 'At Cannes', wrote Lady Brewster, 'there is no Corso, no gay Boulevards du Midi, no fashionable lounges, no balls, no theatres, no fine shops, no billiard tables, no smartly dressed ladies and gentlemen ... At Cannes we have country quiet, less exciting air, tranquil companionship, and many religious privileges.' Menton was a concoction of Barchester and Baptist mission: a watering place where the atmosphere was heavy with Victorian divinity; where everyone, according to Alexander Brown, indulged in '*à la mode* church-going excess, with all its formality and display'.[25] It was the favourite resort of Anglican clergymen, Nonconformist ministers, and evangelical ladies like Mrs Dudgeon, whose villa, *les Grottes*, was a venue for prayer-meetings and Bible-classes before the opening of the Presbyterian church. 'Menton is a dull, a very dull place', wrote the Scottish publisher William Chambers in 1870; 'that is its reputation'.[26]

[23] Harrison, *Memories and Thoughts*, 241.
[24] M. M. Brewster, *Letters from Cannes and Nice* (1857), 144.
[25] Alexander Menzies Brown, *Wintering at Menton on the Riviera* (1872), 162.
[26] William Chambers, *Wintering at Mentone* (1870), 64.

Here, admitted Eustace Ball in 1888, 'social gatherings, which usually take the form of luncheon parties or "at homes", are characterised by a staid decorum which some would stigmatise as slow.'[27] Nevertheless there is a hint of Trollopian capers in Chambers's irate outburst against hotel life in the town. 'My own experiences', he growled, 'have not been very successful, particularly as regards the drawing rooms or sham *salons de lecture*, where usually some lady, with long hair hanging down her back, has, by her frantic performances on the piano, banished everything like quietude and comfort.' Throughout the 1880s Menton was the winter retreat of Charles Spurgeon, the Baptist revivalist. He and his party usually stayed at the Hotel Beau Rivage, which they filled with reminiscences of the Metropolitan Tabernacle. 'The general arrangements', recalled Spurgeon's son Thomas, 'were as homelike as possible, even to the ringing of a bell when it was time for family prayer. Not only were there guests in the house who desired to be present, but many came from other hotels and villas in the neighbourhood, and felt well rewarded by the brief exposition of the Scriptures and the prayer which followed.' He described how, at the communion service on Sunday afternoons, 'it frequently happened that the large sitting room was quite full, and the folding doors had to be thrown back'.[28]

By the end of the 1880s, when the character of Menton was being changed by what Ball called 'the Monte Carlo contingent', those in search of piety and seriousness moved on to Bordighera and San Remo, where ecclesiastical repose remained intact for another generation. At Bordighera in 1871 John Richard Green came across 'an evangelical hotel much frequented by Exeter Hall folk'. The walls of its hall were hung with exhortations to observe the Sabbath, its library was full of tracts and religious literature, and its entertainment consisted of family prayers and Gospel charades.[29] Social life in San Remo was much the same. 'I have heard it whispered', wrote Dr Edward Sparks in 1879, 'that San Remo is rather dull; that dances and lawn tennis are hard to meet with, and that prayer meetings are largely in vogue at some hotels.'[30]

The other Mediterranean country which attracted British visitors in thousands was Egypt. In the first half of the nineteenth century it

[27] E. A. R. Ball, *Mediterranean Winter Resorts* (1888), 53.

[28] Mrs C. H. Spurgeon, ed., *The Autobiography of Charles Spurgeon* (1899), iv. 215–16.

[29] Leslie Stephen, ed., *The Letters of John Richard Green* (1901), 293.

[30] Sparks, *The Riviera*, 333–4.

was usual for travellers on their way to Palestine to visit Egypt first and then proceed across the Sinai peninsula to the Holy Land; but these never amounted to more than a few dozen a year and the only Britons who came to Egypt in any numbers were passengers bound for India on the 'overland' (Alexandria–Suez) route. These generally stayed a night in Cairo and made a lightning tour of inspection, taking in, as William Bartlett put it, 'the cream of Cairo in about a couple of hours or so'.[31] Alexandria was also a frequent port of call for ships of the Royal Navy, as was evidenced by the English names and waggish inscriptions prefaced by 'HMS' that were daubed all over the obelisk known as Pompey's Pillar. It was chiefly for the edification of naval personnel, as well as for that of the small colony of British merchants, that a Scottish church was built in Alexandria in the 1860s. By the mid-1880s, however, improved communication with Europe and the establishment of the British protectorate over Egypt had caused a big increase in the number of tourists. In the late 1880s between 5,000 and 6,000 arrivals a year were being registered at Thomas Cook's offices in Cairo.[32] 'Egypt', proclaimed a pamphlet published by Cook in 1898, 'has ... become the favourite winter residence.' Cairo thus assumed its characteristic role as meeting-place of the British Empire and the British metropolis, borrowing Anglo-Saxon athleticism from the one and Anglo-Saxon sophistication from the other. The Gezireh Sporting Club offered polo, cricket, football, golf, lawn tennis, and pigeon shooting; while the renowned Cairo hotels—Shepheard's, the Gezireh Palace, the Angleterre, the Savoy, and the Grand New Continental—set standards of comfort, cuisine, and service that were unrivalled even on the Riviera. 'Cairo', declared Thomas Cook and Son, '... is in point of fact no more than a winter suburb of London.'

Egypt was unique among the British Mediterranean colonies in that it became a popular tourist resort. The others were little frequented by the travelling public. The Ionian Islands, a British protectorate until 1864, remained virtually unknown, and Gibraltar and Malta were familiar only as coaling stations and ports of call. Cyprus, acquired by the British in 1878, was persistently neglected. 'Few, except those whom duty compels, go to Cyprus', wrote Dr Edmund Hobhouse in 1899—and Henry Rider Haggard confirmed the observation when he

---

[31] William Bartlett, *Gleanings on the Overland Route* (1857), 254.
[32] Isaac Taylor, *Leaves from an Egyptian Notebook* (1888), 140; F. M. Sandwith, *Egypt as a Winter Resort* (1889), 2.

visited the island in 1901. 'Of Cyprus but few have written', he remarked. 'Travellers rarely think it worth the while to visit there.' Consequently there were no hotels. 'Until the tourist comes, it is idle to expect that conveniences for his reception will be provided.'[33]

Outside Italy, France, and Egypt, in fact, the annual muster of British travellers nowhere amounted to more than a few hundreds, and in many places they figured, if they figured at all, only as stray and eccentric individuals. Southern Spain and Greece were salient in the geography of the Romantic imagination after the publication of the first two cantos of Byron's *Childe Harold's Pilgrimage* in 1812, and the young Disraeli was a traveller who chose to follow in Childe Harold's footsteps. But Byron's itinerary in the Mediterranean had been dictated by the special circumstances of the Napoleonic domination of France and Italy, and when this had ended most British travellers returned to the familiar routes and destinations. Visiting Greece in 1880 Richard Farrer found that the country was 'off the track of the ordinary tourist', and he reckoned that visitors had been more numerous before the War of Independence. 'So rare have travellers become', he reported, 'that the entire Hellenic Kingdom only boasts four first-class guides.'[34] Since neither Greece nor Spain had been included in the Grand Tour they remained unsanctioned by habit and convention, and most Victorians and Edwardians found them vaguely intimidating and even suspect from their association with the excesses of Romantic sensibility. 'I haven't been to Greece myself', says the Revd Mr Beebe in Forster's *A Room with a View*, 'and I don't mean to go, and I can't imagine any of our friends going. It is altogether too big for our little lot. Don't you think so? Italy is just about as much as we can manage. Italy is heroic, but Greece is godlike or devilish—I am not sure which, and in either case entirely out of our suburban focus.' Spain, until quite late in the nineteenth century, still seemed as remote as it had seemed in the eighteenth. 'No country is less known to the rest of Europe', said Dr Johnson in 1761. 'There is no country in Europe so little known and yet so well worth visiting', wrote Dr Madden in 1864.[35] Cordova and Seville attracted a constant trickle of British visitors throughout the nineteenth century and in 1888 Eustace Reynolds Ball claimed that Malaga was 'rapidly coming into favour

[33] Hobhouse, ed., *Health Abroad*, 290; Haggard, *Winter Pilgrimage*, 3, 63.

[34] Richard Farrer, *A Tour in Greece* (1882), pp. v–vi.

[35] Madden, *On Change of Climate*, 70.

with a large class of visitors' who disliked 'the conventionalised and overcrowded region of the French Riviera';[36] but that fact in itself proclaims the relative unpopularity of this part of the Mediterranean. Spain, with Greece, can be classified in the third rank of the Mediterranean destinations of the Victorians and Edwardians. This is made clear by the publishing record of the three main purveyors of guidebooks to the British public in the period from the 1840s until the Great War: John Murray, Karl Baedeker, and Thomas Cook. Cook published no guide either to Greece or to Spain, while Murray and Baedeker between them issued eleven editions of handbooks for Greece and twelve editions of handbooks for Spain. These figures are modest in comparison with the twenty-five editions, contributed by all three firms, of handbooks to Egypt, and the 112 editions of their various guidebooks to Italy.

Measured by the same criterion, Algeria and Palestine rank with Spain and Greece as third-class resorts. Baedeker produced no guide to Algeria, and Murray and Cook together published only eight editions. This figure under-represents the popularity of the country, because *The Practical Guide to Algiers*, by George Harris, had already gone through ten editions with another publisher (G. Philip) before being reissued by Thomas Cook & Son in 1903 as *Cook's Practical Guide to Algiers*; so judged in quantitative terms the appeal of Algeria should probably be rated as about the same as that of Palestine, which had elicited sixteen editions of guidebooks from Murray, Baedeker, and Cook by 1914. Before the British occupation of Egypt Algiers was the favourite resort of British travellers to North Africa, and it declined only relatively thereafter. 'We hear of quantities of people going to Algiers', wrote Elizabeth Browning to her sister in 1856, 'but I don't much fancy we shall go, in spite of urgings on their part.'[37] By the end of the century a British colony was well established in the suburb of Mustapha Supérieur, served by an English Club, an English church (Holy Trinity), two winter newspapers (*The Algerian Advertiser* and *The Atlas*), and an English grocer (Dunlop and Tustes, 10, Rue d'Isly). In Palestine a British contingent mustered among the Easter crowds throughout the Victorian years. Anthony Trollope describes in *The Bertrams* how George Bertram arrived at the main hotel in Jerusalem

---

[36] Ball, *Mediterranean Winter Resorts*, 77.
[37] Leonard Huxley, ed., *Elizabeth Barrett Browning's Letters to her Sister 1846–59* (1929), 257.

in the early 1840s and 'heard such a Babel of English voices and such a clatter of English spoons that he might have fancied himself at the top of the Righi or in a Rhine steamboat'. But the number of British visitors was always comparatively small. Not even Thomas Cook could make Palestine a truly popular resort. In 1891 his firm calculated that it had organised travel to the Holy Land for 12,000 people, of whom most, but not all, were British. This figure represented an accumulation of annual totals which increased from sixty in 1868 to just under a thousand in 1891.[38]

Elsewhere in the Mediterranean trails were blazed and signposted only to be ignored. Corsica never attracted more than a few dozen British visitors a year, despite the ardent advocacy of Miss Thomasina Campbell, of Moniack Castle, Scotland, who built an Episcopal Church in Ajaccio and published *Notes on the Island of Corsica* in 1869. Macmillan's *Guide to the Western Mediterranean*, published in 1901, recorded that the total of foreign visitors of all nationalities coming to Ajaccio each year did not exceed two or three hundred. In the Balearic Islands strangers were, according to the same authority, so rare as to excite extreme curiosity. Crete remained, in the words of William Mallock, 'that country seen by so many, explored or visited by so few';[39] while Tunisia was reckoned to contain fewer than twenty Britons after the French occupation in 1881.[40] By the 1890s a few British tourists were making their way to Tunis during the winter season and in 1904 an Anglican Church was constructed in the old Maltese quarter of the town; but the country remained as Edward Lear had described the Balkans, half a century before: 'remote from the ordinary routine of English travel'.[41] Tripoli, or Libya, was even more remote; and southern Anatolia was *terra incognita*: a land of undisturbed Roman ruins, towards which British visitors in Cyprus gazed over the sea with yearning fascination.

[38] W. Fraser Rae, *The Business of Travel* (1891), 104, 272–3.
[39] W. H. Mallock, *In an Enchanted Island* (3rd edn., 1892), 41.
[40] Reid, *In the Land of the Bey*, 267.
[41] Edward Lear, *Journals of a Landscape Painter in Albania and Illyria* (1851), 397.

PART TWO

MOTIVES

BRITISH traders, colonial officials, freedom-fighters, and missionaries went south for obvious reasons. The motives that impelled the leisured, the literary, and the artistic to travel or reside in the Mediterranean were less obvious but, judging from the written record, no less serious. The Victorians, it seems, found it almost better to travel purposefully than to arrive. This was because they were conditioned to regard absence abroad—especially prolonged absence—as something suspect and subversive. Abandoning Britain meant abandoning home. It therefore threatened all the cherished values that Home implied—fidelity, obedience, connubial affection, and a stable and rooted existence. It threatened too the patriotic sentiment that underpinned national power and prosperity. 'That a long residence in foreign countries', argued Dr James Johnson in the early 1830s, 'tends to sap the foundation, or at least to weaken the force of British patriotism, is as clear as the sun at noonday'; and he reproached his expatriated countrymen for putting self-gratification and self-preservation before the national interest. Furthermore, going abroad subtracted strength from the national fight against spiritual and material destitution. In 1864 Frances Power Cobbe spoke with the stern voice of Victorian puritanism when she urged the priority of high-minded endeavour at home:

'Tis a poor choice to give up England in our manhood, and abandon for ever all its purpose and its noble strife for the lotos-eater life of the South. At this hour, when every voice and every arm are needed to grapple with error, and want, and sin . . . it is, I say, a pitiful thing to quit the field and wander away to dream, and gaze, and ponder; and live as perhaps man may have earned the right to live in centuries to come, when Giant Despair and Giant Sin are dead.

This was a message that Richard Chenevix Trench had thought worthy of verse. In a sonnet of 1834, entitled *To England: Written after a visit to Sorrento*, he rebuked himself for wishing to be free of the ties that bound him to home. 'For what is it we ask', he demanded,

> When we would fain have leave to linger here,
> But to abandon our appointed task,
> Our place of duty, and our natural sphere?

Travel, then, was not to be undertaken lightly. It needed to be justified, and this was especially the case with travel to the South, given the widely held belief that morals deteriorated as the weather improved. Charles Kingsley reminded his readers that the English were dedicated to winter sports and pastimes ('Are Englishmen hedge-gnats, who only take their sport when the sun shines? . . . We are stern people, and winter suits us'), and he attributed their special aptitude for thinking and working to this outdoor life in a harsh climate. 'Whenever all the rest of the world is indoors, we are out and busy, and, on the whole, the worse the day, the better the deed.' Ruskin, likewise, contrasted 'the industry of the tribes of the North, quickened by the coldness of the climate' with 'the languor of the Southern tribes'; and Dr Burney Yeo, in a book on health resorts published in 1882, wrote: 'Many of the best qualities of an Englishman are, to a great extent, due to the character of the climate of the country he inhabits.'[1]

This bias towards disapproval influenced the language in which Victorians and Edwardians wrote about their travels to the Mediterranean. They adopted a defensive posture and exculpated themselves by invoking solemn purposes. Only with the arrival of the rebels of the Auden generation did it become a British literary fashion to advocate travel for its own sake and to proclaim the awfulness of Home as the justification for going Abroad.[2] Before the Great War, leisured and literary Britons did not write in such iconoclastic terms. They used a different language of justification. It expressed apology and its essential concepts were pilgrimage, culture, and health. Frequently of course these were excuses or euphemisms. Plenty of Victorian and Edwardian travellers concealed their true motives, either because these were subconscious or because they were not socially acceptable. It was understandable that Mr Casaubon, in George Eliot's *Middlemarch*, should suspect aimless malingering to lie behind Will Ladislaw's ostensible reason for going to Italy. 'He wants to go abroad again', Casaubon complains, 'without any special object save the vague purpose of what he calls culture.' Nevertheless there is no reason to doubt that in many instances society's requirements influenced not only the language of travellers, but the quality of travel itself. Many if not most journeys to the Mediterranean were in fact linked to the motives declared. Pilgrimage, culture, and health were,

---

[1] Johnson, *Change of Air*, 272–3; F. P. Cobbe, *The Cities of the Past* (1863), 1; Charles Kingsley, *Yeast* (new edn., 1879), 5; Ruskin, *The Stones of Venice*, ii, Ch. VI, para. lxxv; Yeo, *Health Resorts*, 241.

[2] See Paul Fussell, *Abroad: British Literary Travelling Between the Wars* (Oxford, 1981).

as often as not, genuine reasons for going south. They are not a complete explanation for increasing British contact with the Mediterranean; but no explanation would be half complete without them.

3. PILGRIMAGE

Lytton Strachey, demonstrating a flair for the quintessential, began his sketch of General Gordon with a description of the eminent Victorian wandering in the neighbourhood of Jerusalem with a Bible under his arm. He is, we are told, pondering four questions: the site of the Crucifixion; the line of division between the tribes of Benjamin and Judah; the identification of Gibeon; and the position of the Garden of Eden. A further teasing problem, concerning the place where the Ark touched ground after the subsidence of the Flood, he has already satisfactorily resolved. This glimpse of Gordon at once identifies him as the product of a period and a culture, because among well-to-do Victorians pilgrimage to the East in pursuit of the biblical became a characteristic feature of Protestant piety.

It is arguable that during the nineteenth century British people of property and influence were more obsessed with religion than at any time before or since. 'Theology penetrated our intellectual and social atmosphere', wrote John Addington Symonds of his undergraduate days at Oxford in the 1860s. 'We talked theology at breakfast parties and at wine parties, out riding and walking, in college gardens, on the river, wherever young men and their elders met together.'[1] Most members of the Victorian upper and middle classes, whether Anglicans or Nonconformists, were deeply influenced by evangelicalism: the devout religious temper that had its origins in the spiritual revival of the middle years of the eighteenth century. The leaders of this revival—John and Charles Wesley and George Whitefield—had steered English Christianity away from the sacramentalism, ritualism, and externalised observances of the Tudor and Stuart 'High Church' settlements, and brought it closer to the Continental Protestantism of Luther and Calvin. They had made it less an outward affair of liturgy and formal works, and more an intense inward experience compounded of contrition, conversion, rebirth, and faith. Some English evangelicals moved closer than others to the central Calvinist

[1] Phyllis Grosskurth, ed., *The Memoirs of John Addington Symonds* (1984), 244.

doctrines of election and predestination. But all, whether in greater or lesser degree, received the influence of Geneva; and in their strict morality, their sabbatarianism, and their excessive reverence for the Bible we recognise the characteristic conventions of Continental Protestantism. These were the means by which religious instincts were satisfied after the rejection of auricular confession, saints' days, and ecclesiastical authority.

An evangelical dedication to moral standards explains both the obsession with 'respectability' and the increasing difficulties of religious belief that were features of the Victorian age. Many Victorians who abandoned Christianity, including George Eliot, Francis Newman, Frances Power Cobbe, Leslie Stephen, Samuel Butler, John Morley, Thomas Huxley, and Charles Darwin, were brought up as evangelicals and lost their faith because they discovered that the Bible did not match evangelical standards of justice and truth. Sabbatarianism cast the legendary chill on the Victorian Sunday, with theatres and places of recreation closed and countless households given over to church attendance and pious literature. 'Sunday was kept exceedingly strictly at Newbridge in those days', wrote Frances Cobbe of her childhood. 'No books were allowed except religious ones, nor any amusement, save a walk after church. Thus there was abundant time for reading the Bible and looking at the pictures in various large editions and in Calmet's great folio *Dictionary*, besides listening to the sermon in church and to another sermon which my father read in the evening to the assembled household.'[2] At Wellington College on Sunday all the boys were required to go to chapel at nine in the morning, repeat Bible verses to form-masters at ten, return to chapel at a quarter to twelve, attend Bible classes at half-past one and again at half-past three, return to chapel at half-past six and say prayers in their dormitories at nine.[3]

The Scriptures were a fetish. It was an age of family Bibles, Bible commentaries, framed and illuminated biblical texts, Bible classes, Bibles on lecterns in railway stations, and the Bible as an essential part of childhood experience. 'My mother forced me,' Ruskin remembered, 'by steady daily toil, to learn long chapters of the Bible by heart; as well as to read it every syllable through aloud, hard names and all, from Genesis to the Apocalypse, about once a year.'[4] The evangelical

---

[2] Cobbe, *Life*, i. 82.
[3] E. F. Benson, *As We Were* (1932), 68.
[4] John Ruskin, *Praeterita* (new edn., 1949), i, Ch. 1, sec. 8.

revered the Bible not as poetry but as history; and when Reason and Revelation clashed, foreswearing the one and accepting the other became the shibboleth of his creed. 'Perhaps', comments the autobiographical hero of James Anthony Froude's novel *The Nemesis of Faith* (1849), 'the world has never witnessed any more grotesque idol-worship than what has resulted from modern Bibliolatry.'

To a people so devoutly Christian and so deeply immersed in Scriptural lore Palestine and Egypt had a unique and sacred significance. Few Victorians would have quarrelled with Eliot Warburton when he wrote in 1845: 'What a church is to a city, Palestine is to the world';[5] or with Arthur Stanley when he claimed in 1856 that Sinai and Palestine were 'the scene of the most important events in the history of mankind';[6] or with Mrs Margaret Oliphant when she began her book *Jerusalem, the Holy City* (1893) with the assertion that Jerusalem was 'the most interesting spot on earth'. Most travellers to these lands were pilgrims in the sense that they made the journey solely for the sake of religious associations. 'Palestine', explained the Revd Charles Bell of Cheltenham in 1887,

does not offer to the stranger the charms of scenery, the beauties of lake and mountain and valley . . . Nor is there anything . . . to attract the lover of art. Its cities possess no galleries of pictures, no halls of statuary, no paintings by Raphael or Perugino, no sculptures by Phidias or Michaelangelo and no ruins so splendid and perfect as those of Athens and Rome.[7]

As Henry Rider Haggard wrote in 1901, the modern traveller to Palestine was akin to the medieval pilgrim who, 'obedient to a voice that calls in the heart of so many . . . travelled by land and sea to look upon the place where Jesus Christ was born and where the Master of Mankind hung upon His cross at Calvary'.[8] But the modern British Protestant was unlike the pilgrim of old in that he travelled Bible in hand, using the landscape and the Book to illuminate each other. 'We are now upon the borders of the Promised Land', announced William Wilde from Jaffa in 1838, 'eager to investigate its interesting localities; and with the Scriptures as our guide, to enter upon it with all the fervour and devotion of pilgrims.'[9] The medieval pilgrim had travelled

[5] Warburton, *The Crescent and the Cross*, ii.7.
[6] Arthur Penrhyn Stanley, *Sinai and Palestine in Connection with their History* (13th edn., 1862), p. xii.
[7] Bell, *Gleanings from a Tour*, 44–5.
[8] Haggard, *Winter Pilgrimage*, 2–3.
[9] Wilde, *Narrative of a Voyage*, 391.

with his imagination as his guide, weaving around the various sites identifications and attributions which the modern British pilgrim now strove to unravel in a spirit of stern evangelical literalism. His supreme object in coming to the Holy Land was to see through the accumulated layers of legend, tradition, and romance that obscured the Scriptures, and confirm their credibility by relating them to real places and real people. 'We passed through the land with our Bibles in our hands', explained the Revd Henry Tristram in 1865, 'with, I trust, an unbiassed determination to investigate *facts* and their independent bearing on sacred history.'[10] This motive is nowhere more apparent than in the missionary zeal of the British artists who came to Palestine in search of backgrounds, models, and local details. No longer content to see the land and its people through the eyes of the masters of the Italian Renaissance, they aimed to produce a biblical art of scrupulous authenticity. The pioneer in this movement was the Scottish artist David Roberts, who travelled to Egypt and Palestine in 1838–9. On his return Roberts produced a sumptuous volume of lithographs called *Views in the Holy Land, Syria, Idumea, Arabia, Egypt and Nubia*, which was the first accurate topographical record of the Holy Land to be published in England. Another Scottish painter, Sir David Wilkie, set out for Palestine in 1840 eager to inaugurate a religious art based on truthful representation. 'The traveller here must be surprised to find', he wrote from Jerusalem in April 1841,

that the great mass of Italian Scripture art is, in background, costumes and characters, so purely imaginary, or so completely Italian, that Evangelical Syria is completely unrepresented and, like a neglected constituency, seems to clamour for a fresh enfranchisement to modern art ... A Martin Luther in painting is as much called for as in theology, to sweep away the abuses by which our divine pursuit is encumbered.[11]

Wilkie did not live to carry through his projected reformation; but a leading painter of the next generation, William Holman Hunt, dedicated himself to the same cause and made three trips to the Holy Land between 1854 and 1873 in order to give his biblical pictures unimpeachable accuracy of detail. 'Truth,' he wrote in a characteristically evangelical strain, 'wherever it leads, being above price, must increase the beauty of the Divine Man.'[12] The most famous fruit of his

---

[10] H. B. Tristram, *The Land of Israel* (3rd edn., 1876), 632.

[11] W. Wilkie Collins, *Memoirs of the Life of William Collins* (1848), ii. 183–4.

[12] William Holman Hunt, *Preraphaelitism and the Preraphaelite Brotherhood* (2nd edn., 1913), i. 255.

relentless labours was *The Scapegoat*, which was exhibited at the Royal Academy in 1856 and which Ruskin appreciated as the work of a kindred evangelical spirit. 'He travels', he wrote of Hunt, 'not merely to fill his portfolio with pretty sketches, but in as determined a temper as ever medieval pilgrim, to do a certain work in the Holy Land . . . We cannot, I think, esteem too highly or receive too gratefully, the temper and the toil which have produced this picture for us.'[13]

The exponents of High Art strongly opposed this obsession with verisimilitude, and Victorian painters like William Dyce continued to treat religious subjects in the traditional idealist way; but this was no longer likely to satisfy a religious public who had been taught to regard the Bible stories as historical occurrences and who went in increasing numbers to Palestine and Syria in order to stock their minds with authentic images. When Frances Power Cobbe published her travel book *The Cities of the Past* she had lost her Christian faith; but, having been brought up as an evangelical, she well understood what the evangelical public wanted. She wrote,

It seems to me as if modern painters and sculptors have before them a field hitherto almost unworked, in giving the *real* colouring of the great scenes and parables of ancient story . . . Look at the ordinary pictures of Christ. No Oriental ever wore those pink and blue robes, or sat in those attitudes . . . Look at the painted scenes in Palestine—the deep, dark, shadowy woods, and Greek temples and Roman houses. Are these like the bare olive grove of Gethsemane, or the real edifices of Syria?[14]

Predictably, elderly clergymen and university dons figured most prominently in the excursions to the Holy Land which Thomas Cook was organising from the 1870s. Edward Freeman remarked in 1887 that 'the tendency at Oxford [was] to make the Easter vacation longer and longer (at the expense of Christmas) for the benefit of Jerusalem-gazers, and other such';[15] and Henry Rider Haggard noticed a distinct preponderance of 'folk on the wrong side of middle age' among his fellow pilgrims in 1900. 'I hardly remember noting a young and charming face, or even a pretty dress', he wrote. 'Youth flees that land; it shrinks from wandering where are no daily common pleasures, nothing but solemn sights and painful memories, which call up meditations oppressive to the spring of life.'[16] No doubt it was in order

[13] Cook and Wedderburn, eds., *Works of John Ruskin*, xiv. 47.
[14] Cobbe, *Cities of the Past*, 123.
[15] W. R. W. Stephens, *The Life and Letters of E. A. Freeman* (1895), ii. 362.
[16] Haggard, *Winter Pilgrimage*, 299.

to banish these doleful associations that the youthful Prince of Wales, travelling to Palestine in 1862 on the orders of his pious father, required his entourage to prepare for their experiences by reading not devotional literature, but Mrs Henry Wood's best-selling novel *East Lynne*.

4. CULTURE

Italy and Greece were exceptional in British estimation in that they were foreign countries where the graces of superior civilisation were acquired rather than imparted. Here the British saw themselves as pupils, rather than as teachers, absorbing lessons in art and architecture, deepening their minds, and adding the polish of taste and discernment to their rugged native genius. 'A man who has not been to Italy', Dr Johnson had once said, 'is always conscious of an inferiority, from his not having seen what it is expected a man should see'; and a hundred years later that observation was still true, because 'Italy' and 'culture' were synonymous in popular Victorian conception. Vernon Lee, writing in the 1920s, recalled that 'the word *culture* signified in the earliest 'eighties anything vaguely connected with Italy, art and, let us put it, the works of the late J. A. Symonds'.[1] Nowhere else was the Anglo-Saxon so willing to acknowledge a sense of inferiority. Victorians and Edwardians were not generally accustomed to seek elevation and enlightenment from lands other than their own. Italy and Greece, and possibly Germany, were the only countries where such a quest was admitted. Later Victorian literati might trifle with the notion of the Wisdom of the East, enthusing over Fitzgerald's translation of Omar Khayyám or Edwin Arnold's *The Light of Asia*; and candidates for the Indian Civil Service might listen patiently while Professor Max Muller lectured them on the theme *India: What Can it Teach Us?*; but few people really doubted that beyond the bounds of southern Europe the role of the British was to civilise others, not to civilise themselves. There was very little that India could teach them, and Asia generally was an area of darkness. 'It cannot of course for one moment be contended', announced the Victorian architectural historian James Fergusson, 'that India ever reached the intellectual supremacy of Greece or the moral greatness of Rome'; and it went

[1] Vernon Lee [Violet Paget], *For Maurice* (1927), p. xxxvi.

without question that her arts 'were on a lower step of the ladder'.[2]
That sort of dogmatism persisted until Roger Fry's challenging claims
for Chinese and Negro art in his Slade Lectures after the First World
War, and even Max Muller conceded, in his first lecture, that 'a study
of Sanskrit and of the ancient poetry, the philosophy, the laws and the
arts of India [was] looked upon in the best case as curious, but [was]
considered by most people as useless, tedious, if not absurd.' The
Victorians and Edwardians, in fact, preferred to take their world-view
not from the orientalists but from Thomas Buckle. Buckle had
explained, in his ponderous *History of Civilisation in England*, that the
civilisation of Europe was necessarily better and more permanent than
those of Africa and Asia, since it was based on the infinite skill of man
instead of the finite bounty of soil and climate. It represented the
subordination of nature to mind, rather than the subordination of
mind to nature. Buckle's inherently appealing volumes had acquired
added cogency from the date of their publication, for they appeared in
1857 and 1861, years that marked the outbreak and defeat of the
rebellion against European domination in India.

The ancient civilisations of Egypt, Assyria, and Tunisia were, like
the civilisations of India, curious and intriguing, and British time and
money were spent in investigating their mysteries. In the 1830s
Richard Vyse and John Perring probed the Pyramids. In the 1840s
Austen Layard opened the mounds of Nimrud and Nineveh. In the
1850s Nathan Davis excavated at Carthage and Henry Rawlinson
deciphered the cuneiform inscriptions of Babylonia. In the later
Victorian and the Edwardian years Flinders Petrie made known his
discoveries in Egypt. Public interest was strong—especially when, as
was the case in Assyria and Egypt, the archaeology had biblical
associations; but there was no inclination to pay the tribute of envy or
emulation. The remains of these ancient societies were essentially
museum specimens: the fascinating but unedifying products of alien
and inferior civilisations. 'Modern science and mechanical skill', said
a Victorian commentator on the Pyramids, 'can see in them nothing
that time and money could not now accomplish, were the end deemed
worthy of the cost and labour; while the intelligent mind will own the
evidence of more intellect and mental labour in the sculptured
pediment of the Athenian Parthenon, than in all the groups of
pyramids which still rear their lofty points towards heaven.'[3] 'What-

[2] James Fergusson, *History of Indian and Eastern Architecture* (1891), 4.
[3] Anon., *Ruins of Sacred and Historic Lands* (1850), 157.

ever partiality we may entertain for Assyrian art,' wrote the author of the volume on Nineveh compiled for the National Illustrated Library in 1851, 'we are far from putting it on a footing of equality with that of Phidias and Praxiteles.' An anonymous contributor to the *Edinburgh Review*, writing in 1861, likened the feeling aroused by the discoveries in Egypt and Assyria to 'that with which we listen to the comparative anatomist as he expounds the organisation of a mastodon or sea lizard'. All was marvellous, 'but too unlike our own day for us to do more than wonder'.

The mid-century excavations at Carthage, carried out by Davis and his French rival Beulé, did nothing to undermine the idea—vividly restated in Flaubert's novel *Salammbô*—that the Punic settlements in North Africa had been savage Asiatic despotisms possessing no indigenous culture, practising a horrific sacrificial religion, and pursuing the sordid ends of wealth and self-aggrandisement. Davis discovered some fine mosaic pavements and presented them to the British Museum as samples of Punic art; but they were subsequently identified as Roman and therefore confirmed, rather than dispelled, the theory that it was Rome that had brought the civilising influences of art to Carthage, just as it was the Roman genius of Virgil that had transformed the primitive myths surrounding her foundation into the literary epic of Queen Dido. 'It is almost painful', wrote the contributor to the *Edinburgh Review*, 'to strip off the veil with which a foreign literature enveloped the dead corpse, and discover the foul features—the superstition, the cruelty, the blind faction—which disfigured the living body.' There was justice in the Romans' obliteration of their rival, for Carthage had left 'no single legacy to posterity by which the human family has been enriched, except the moral to be derived from her fate—that a nation which has no higher aim than that of growing rich is doomed not only to certain destruction, but to as certain an oblivion'.

It was in terms of the Roman precedent that the Victorians justified modern European imperialism on the southern shores of the Mediterranean. The Islamic governments of Barbary and Egypt represented a new Asiatic darkness; and the mission of the French and the British, like that of the ancient Romans before them, was to disperse the shadows with the lights of civilisation. The British were in general harshly critical of the Muslim record in North Africa. Norman Douglas spoke for the majority when he attacked the 'apathy, improvidence, and mental fossilification' of the Arabs and held them responsible for the transformation of a garden into a desert.[4] In the description of modern Tunisia by Alexander Graham and Henry Ashbee there is an implicit comparison to ancient Carthage. 'Not a single work of literature worth recording,' they declared, 'no new development of science or industry, nor any great monument to art or utility will be handed down to future generations as evidence of a nation possessing either culture or progress.' The Muslim achievement they summarised as 'desecration, destruction, and fanaticism'. On one level the British were always ready to condemn the French occupation of Algeria and Tunisia as the work of treacherous and self-glorifying politicians and army officers; but few denied its broader historical significance as a just and legitimate exercise in European imperialism. Joseph Blakesley, friend of Tennyson and future Dean of Lincoln, visited Algeria in the late 1850s and judged the French administration 'a gain to the native population and a benefit to civilised Europe';[5] and Dr Robert Scoresby Jackson wrote in 1862 of Algeria's 'gradual emancipation from the darkness and thraldom of a nescient superstition to the sunshine and freedom of a growing civilisation.'[6] Dr James Henry Bennet congratulated the French on their 'great and noble enterprise'. He pointed out that they were doing in Algeria what the British were doing in other Muslim countries, and judged that 'the gain [was] the gain of Christianity and civilisation'.[7] Robert Lambert Playfair, British Consul-General in Algeria, asserted in 1877 that the French had done 'great things' in North Africa, and that the world owed them 'a deep debt of gratitude for having converted a nest of pirates and robbers into one of the most charming countries of the Mediterranean'.[8] Similar eulogies came from the Victorian travellers George Gaskell and Alexander Knox, and a popular Edwardian guidebook praised the French for their work in Tunisia. 'Bright days have dawned for Tunis, whatever disappointed natives think.'[9] The historian Edward Freeman rejoiced in the French occupation of Tunisia as a reprise of the Roman imperial achievement. 'The province of Africa', he proclaimed, 'is practically won back for Romania.'[10] Hilaire Belloc too saw it that way, and predicted that the

[4] Norman Douglas, *Fountains in the Sand* (1915), 215, 329.
[5] Joseph Blakesley, *Four Months in Algeria* (Cambridge, 1859), 439.
[6] R. E. Scoresby Jackson, *Medical Climatology* (1862), 92.
[7] Bennet, *Winter and Spring*, 559.
[8] R. L. Playfair, *Travels in the Footsteps of Bruce in Algeria and Tunisia* (1877), 51.
[9] Macmillan's *Guide to the Western Mediterranean* (1904), 97.
[10] Stephens, ed., *Life and Letters of E. A. Freeman*, ii. 415–16.

Muslims would eventually suffer the fate of the Carthaginians. 'Then we shall be back where the Romans were, and the Empire will be fully restored.'[11]

Britain lagged behind France in the reclamation of North Africa. By the time she occupied Egypt, in 1882, France was already mistress of Algeria and Tunisia and was poised to move into Morocco; but this did not disturb the fundamental conviction of the British that they, rather than the French, were the true heirs of the ancient Romans. In the eighteenth century, English writers had used the term 'Augustan' to describe themselves and their age; and in the nineteenth century the Roman likeness in the self-portrait became even more pronounced, since the Victorians posed against the background of a global empire. 'I felt proud', wrote Lady Eastlake after her first visit to the Colosseum in 1858, 'that my nation was more truly the descendant of that matchless race than any other in the world.'[12] In one of the most popular episodes of his career Lord Palmerston justified his gunboat diplomacy by invoking the Roman principle that all inhabitants of the empire, of whatever nationality, enjoyed the citizen's right of protection; and Latin catchphrases like *Civis Romanus sum*, *Pax Britannica*, and *Imperium Britannicum* became part of the political rhetoric of the age. Foreign observers accepted the analogy and by feeding it back to the British reinforced their sense of their Roman identity. The Duke of Sermoneta told Nassau Senior, in Rome in 1851, that the real successors of the ancient Romans were the British. 'When I read Cicero's letters', he said, 'I fancy myself reading the correspondence of one of your statesmen. All the thoughts, all the feeling, almost all the expressions, are English.'[13] The American traveller George Hillard wrote in 1853 that the British were 'the legitimate descendants of the old Romans, the true inheritors of their spirit';[14] and the idea was repeated by the French statesman Guizot in 1859, when he said to Matthew Arnold: 'You and the Romans are the only two governing nations of the world'.[15]

The idea that they were the modern Romans fortified the sense of proprietorship among British travellers in Italy. 'They stalk over the land', wrote Hillard, 'as if it were their own.' But it also reinforced

[11] Hilaire Belloc, *Esto Perpetua: Algerian Studies and Impressions* (1906), 182–4.

[12] Smith, ed., *Journals of Lady Eastlake*, ii. 107.

[13] Senior, *Journals*, ii. 99–100.

[14] Hillard, *Six Months in Italy*, ii. 210.

[15] Arnold Whitridge, ed., *Unpublished Letters of Matthew Arnold* (New Haven, 1923), 44.

their sense of humility, because the Roman genius was for technology, war and government, rather than for art and the social graces. As the Romans had acknowledged the superiority of the sculpture and architecture of the Greeks, so did the British acknowledge the superiority of the Classical and Renaissance fine arts of southern Europe, and they mediated their influence through their empire as the Romans had mediated the Greek influence through theirs. Elsewhere, to be refused deference was an insult; but on the native soil of art and civilisation to withhold deference was presumption. 'Most of us', remarked Norman Douglas, 'come to Italy too undiscerning, too reverent, in the pre-coital and prehumorous stages. We arrive here stuffed with Renaissance ideals or Classical lore . . .'[16] Treading the lands of culture with histrionic dedication, the British showed an aspect of themselves disconcertingly at variance with the characteristics by which the world had learnt to know them. Like some tropical pod in noonday heat, the dull, tight, and impervious Anglo-Saxon integument opened, to expose a soft and saccharine interior. 'The majority of English tourists', complained George Augustus Sala in 1866, 'seem to think it essential to dress themselves in their finest intellectual clothes before they pass the Alps; and nine out of ten of them . . . either gush or cant.'[17] American observers like W. D. Howells and Henry James agreed, and found it difficult to recognise in the English traveller in Italy the phlegmatic islander of legend. 'The Englishman,' noted Howells, 'so chary of his sensibilities at home, abandons himself to them abroad';[18] and Henry James was moved to ask: 'Who can say that one doesn't constantly meet the most startling examples of the insular faculty to gush?'[19]

The insular gusher makes his appearance in English fiction as Samuel Butler's George Pontifex, who falls into 'genteel paroxysms of admiration' before the masterpieces in the Uffizi; as E. M. Forster's Reverend Cuthbert Eager, who expounds the sublimities of Giotto in accents borrowed from Ruskin; and as the same author's Philip Herriton, who declares: 'I do believe that Italy really purifies and ennobles all who visit her. She is the school as well as the playground of the world.' In life the species took sundry and unlikely guises. 'Who can visit such a place of beauty and decay', intoned Gladstone about

---

[16] Norman Douglas, *Old Calabria*, 290.
[17] Sala, *Rome and Venice*, 22–3.
[18] W. D. Howells, *Tuscan Cities* (Boston, 1885), 14.
[19] Henry James, *Italian Hours* (1909), 195.

Rome, 'without feeling that it opens his mind to what he never knew
before and cannot hope to recall elsewhere?'[20] For Frederic Harrison
Rome was 'the central city of this earth ... the true microcosm,
wherein the vast panorama of human civilisation is reflected as in a
mirror'.[21] G. M. Trevelyan eulogised the city as 'the heart of Europe
and the living chronicle of man's long march to civilisation';[22] and
Frances Elliot threw herself at its feet. 'Oh rare old city! I embrace
thee and I love thee as the intellectual home of all mankind; still ...
the great parent of knowledge and art.'[23] Then there were the
quivering effusions of Vernon Lee ('We must imagine classic antiquity
full of this wonderful blond colour of marbles; arrangements of palest
lilac, green, rosy yellow and a white shimmer; colours such as we see
on water at sunset, ineffable');[24] the aesthetic antics of her friend
Clementine ('Kit') Anstruther-Thompson ('In dead silence she
advanced,' wrote Ethel Smyth, describing her reactions to an Apollo
in the Vatican, 'then retreated, shaded her eyes, and finally ejaculated:
"Look at that Johnny! How he sings! How he sings!"');[25] the mincing
flourishes of Augustus Hare ('No one has seen Italy who has missed
San Gimignano').[26] and the absurd hyperboles of Edward Hutton
('Siena ... Assisi ... Pisa ... Florence ... formed our Europe,
conserved our faith, created our civilisation and gave us nearly all that
is worth having in the world')[27]—not to mention the breathless
expatiation of the Revd Christopher Wordsworth, who littered his
description of Mount Pentelicus with italics and majuscules:

We should *here* be guilty of strange insensibility if we could regard with
indifference—nay, without a feeling of veneration—this, the *native place* of *so
many* buildings and statues, which have inspired the admiration, refined the
taste, influenced the acts, humanised the manners and elevated the thoughts,
and even added dignity to the religion of men—nay, of whole cities and
kingdoms, for hundreds and thousands of years; he would, we say, be little to
be envied ... who could behold this vast and silent chamber of rock in which
those immortal fabrics the PARTHENON, the PROPYLAEA, and the TEMPLE OF

[20] M. R. D. Foot, ed., *The Gladstone Diaries*, i. (Oxford, 1968), 514.
[21] Frederic Harrison, 'Rome Revisited': *Fortnightly Review*, 53 (1893), 702–21.
[22] G. M. Trevelyan, *Garibaldi's Defence of the Roman Republic* (omnibus edn., 1933),
Introduction.
[23] Frances Elliot, *Diary of an Idle Woman in Italy* (1871), i. 130.
[24] Vernon Lee, *The Spirit of Rome* (1906), 62.
[25] Cited in Peter Gunn, *Vernon Lee: Violet Paget, 1856–1935* (1964), 157.
[26] Augustus Hare, *The Story of My Life* (1896), iii. 343.
[27] Edward Hutton, *Siena and Southern Tuscany* (2nd edn., 1911), 30.

THESEUS were *born*, from whose recesses came forth that long train of beautiful forms which, sculpted in marbles, have made the Panathenaic solemnity, which they represent, no longer a quinquennial festival but an *eternal jubilee* ... [28]

After reading this it comes as no surprise to learn that, as Canon of Westminster, Wordsworth was notoriously long winded and seldom preached for less than one-and-a-half hours.

The cultural heritage of southern Europe attracted both tourists and students. The tourists were members of the bourgeois and landed classes in search of education and refinement; the students were intellectuals and artists who were either engaged in writing and research or training their creative talents in the Italian school of excellence.

Many of the tourists travelled heavily burdened with an evangelical conscience. It was one of the profoundest instincts of evangelicals to mistrust art and creative literature, and they arrived in the South obsessively aware that in the vestiges of Roman achievements there was an example to be avoided as well as one to be copied. In Pisa in 1843 Frederick Faber 'mused and mused and mused' until all his senses were 'wrapped in a delicious dream of art and history'—and then sharply rebuked himself. 'This voluptuous silent poetry,' he wrote, 'which Italy engenders in so many, is just what I have been arming myself against beforehand as effeminate, sensual, literary.' [29] From now on he avoided museums and galleries. The usual reaction was to enter them, but with the mind set firmly on the idea of 'improvement' and with the temptation of sensuous pleasure held at bay by the stern, mortifying spirit of *noblesse oblige*. Duty, rather than enjoyment, became the keynote of these journeys in pursuit of culture. 'It may be a duty', wrote John Henry Newman before setting out on his first trip to Italy, 'to enlarge one's ideas, to break one's studies and to have the name of a travelled man'; [30] and the elderly poet William Wordsworth, visiting Italy for the first time in 1837, dragged himself around under a heavy sense of liability. 'I never was good at sight-seeing,' he wrote wearily, 'yet it must be done.' On his return he told his daughter: 'I undertook this journey as a duty. I have gone through with it as such ... I have kept duty constantly in my eyes, and have

[28] Christopher Wordsworth, *Greece: Pictorial, Descriptive and Historical* (1840), 118.

[29] Bowden, *Frederick Faber*, 179.

[30] Ian Kerr and Thomas Gornall, eds., *The Letters and Diaries of John Henry Newman*, iii (Oxford, 1979), 99.

greatly enriched my mind.'[31] Travel writers constantly reminded tourists of the seriousness of their purpose. 'Those who journey from place to place with no object but amusement', warned Mabel Crawford in 1859, 'are not likely to derive much benefit from their wanderings';[32] and Murray's *Handbook for Greece* declared that a journey to Greece was full of interest for travellers of every character, 'except indeed for a mere idler or man of pleasure'.

Deeply impressed by admonishments such as these, many Victorian and Edwardian tourists fed on a penitential diet of erudition and then sacrificed themselves to a remorseless regime of museums, galleries, monuments, ruins, and churches. They underwent rigorous courses of reading before their departure; meekly submitted to compendious guidebooks on their arrival; and usually returned home in a state of exhaustion and guilt, 'haunted', as Hillard put it, 'by visions of churches that had not been seen and galleries that had not been visited'.[33] Richard Monckton Milnes postponed his visit to Rome in 1831 because his Cambridge tutor had told him that he might as well not go if he had not studied its topography beforehand, and Milnes advised his sister to make a full literary preparation before she ventured there. In Greece in 1847, Richard Church, tackling the sights in the spirit of a military campaign, was annoyed with himself for not being better prepared. 'I have lost some time by not getting up better my work before I came', he wrote; 'I have had to be reading when I ought to have been looking about me.' Four months later, on his return from an excursion to Delphi, he reported that on the whole his 'nine days' work' had been satisfactory, but not entirely so. 'The heat interrupted sight-seeing in the middle of the day', he explained, 'and, as usual, I have some two or three points on my traveller's conscience, as having been carelessly seen.'[34] In Edwardian times Professor James Sully warned prospective tourists that to the unprepared, Rome was bewildering and oppressive.[35]

The exhortation to 'preparation' was repeated again and again, and for the conscientious traveller this was a daunting exercise. The bibliography in the 1873 edition of Murray's *Handbook for Rome*,

[31] Ernest de Selincourt, ed., *The Letters of Dorothy and William Wordsworth* (Oxford, 1939), ii. 864, 879.

[32] Crawford, *Life in Tuscany*, 247.

[33] Hillard, *Six Months in Italy*, ii. 240.

[34] Reid, *Richard Monckton Milnes*, i. 107, 121; Mary Church, ed., *The Life and Letters of Dean Church* (1894), 89, 127.

[35] Sully, *Italian Travel Sketches*, 81.

though strictly limited to works 'chiefly of modern date, which will be the most useful in affording accurate information to our countrymen', listed some forty titles, most of which were multi-volume works in German, Italian, or French. The intending visitor was advised that Canina's *Indicazione topografica di Roma antica* and Nibby's *Roma antica* were indispensable, and warned that the controversial stance of the five-volume *Beschreibung der Stadt Rom*, by Bunsen, Plattner, Rostell, Gerhard, Ulrichs, and others, 'in unsettling the mind of the visitor, [took] away much of his interest in the sites of classical antiquity'. The 'most recent and perhaps most remarkable work' in German on ancient Rome was Alfred de Reumont's *Geschichte der Stadt Rom* (four volumes published so far), while for those who preferred to read in French the recommended work was the four-volume *Histoire romaine à Rome* by Ampère. For medieval Rome the essential work was Dr Gregorovius's *Geschichte der Stadt Rom In Mittelalter* (eighteen volumes, in progress), from which the visitor would 'derive much useful information on the principal events of the period, and many interesting topographical details'. He should instruct himself in Christian architecture from Hubsch's *Monuments de l'architecture chrétienne*, Guttensohn's and Knapp's *Die Basiliken christichen Roms*, the four volumes of Schütz's *Baudenkmaler*, and the four volumes of Fontana's *Raccolta delle migliori chiese di Roma*, bearing in mind that the five volumes of Tosi's *Descrizzioni de' monumenti sepolcrali nelle chiese di Roma* were 'a very useful supplement'. In order to understand the painting and sculpture of Rome it was necessary to consult the five volumes of Crowe's and Cavalcaselle's *History of Painting in Italy*, the two volumes of Kügler's *Handbook of Painting*, and Perkins's two volumes on *Tuscan Sculptors*. The prescribed preliminaries of a visit to Greece seem almost trivial in comparison with this Jesuitical syllabus. The 1883 edition of the *Handbook for Greece* listed only twenty works (comprising some forty volumes) as those 'which the traveller should make a point of carefully examining either prior to his visit to Greece or during his sojourn there'. The Handbook warned however that owing to their size and weight these works were 'unsuitable as travelling companions', and to supply these essentials it furnished a further list of seventeen works. This comprised twenty volumes, 'none of [which] exceed[ed] octavo size, and none of them ... very bulky'. In this knapsack library there featured Leake's *Topography of Athens*, Newton's *Essays on Archaeology and Art*, Michhöfer's *Die Museen Athens*, Müller's *Handbuch der Archaeologie der Kunst*, and the three concluding volumes of Finlay's *History of Greece*. Perhaps these formidable bibliographies were to blame for 'the enormous weight of the large trunks used by some travellers' mentioned by Baedeker in his Italian Handbooks. This, he pointed out, 'not infrequently cause[d] serious injury to the porters who ha[d] to handle them'.

Few tourists can have reached the level of academic expertise prescribed by mentors such as these; but many aimed at it and went on their way overloaded with information and judgements about art and history which determined both the things they saw and how they saw them. During the winter of 1887 members of the Toynbee Hall Travellers' Club groomed themselves for a visit to Italy by hearing lectures, examining photographs, and reading books on Italian history and Florentine and Milanese art. 'Neither', recorded Mrs Barnett proudly, 'were the conditions of the countries passed *en route* neglected, and we were further instructed on Switzerland's government and Belgium's trade.'[36] Sailing to Greece in 1900, the Revd Hugh Price Hughes 'read incessantly' so that he might understand what he was about to see. 'It was literally hot,' he recalled, 'everyone felt lazy and wanted to do nothing. I had to gird up the loins of my will to compel myself to read Herodotus, Thucydides, Pausanius, Mahaffy, and the guidebooks. Only by changing from one to the other at not too long intervals could I keep myself awake.'[37] Travel literature with no flavour of pedantry was liable to be dismissed as frivolous. Henry Neville Maugham even disparaged Stendhal's *Promenades dans Rome* because it was 'lacking the historical study necessary for Rome more than for any other town'[38]—a judgement that reveals, perhaps, why Henry was so much less successful a writer than his famous brother.

Once the tourist had reached his goal and stood face to face with his cultural inheritance in the museums, galleries, and churches of the South he had to abandon even his portable library and entrust himself to the wisdom of his guidebook. This he could do without misgiving, because the best known guides—Murray's and Baedeker's—were encyclopaedias in themselves, condensing, by dint of double columns and minute print, volumes of information into their compact octavo format. When Dickens, in *Little Dorrit*, described tourists picking their way through St Peter's and the Vatican 'delivered over to Mr Eustace and his attendants, to have the entrails of their intellects arranged

[36] S. A. Barnett, *Canon Barnett*, i. 359.
[37] Hugh Price Hughes, *The Morning Lands of History* (1900), ii, 26–7.
[38] H. Neville Maugham, *The Book of Italian Travel* (1903), 69.

according to the taste of that sacred priesthood', he was striving for historical authenticity, because at the period of the story (the early 1830s) John Chatwode Eustace's *Classical Tour Through Italy*, first published in 1813, was still in general use as a guide. What he really had in mind were the 'hundreds of English people with hundreds of Murray's Guide Books and a corresponding number of Mrs Starke's in their hands' that he had seen in Rome in Holy Week in 1845.[39] Marianna Starke's *Travels in Europe*, which alerted the tourist to the comparative merits of works of art by means of a scale of exclamation marks, had done sterling service, in its various incarnations, as the travelling Englishman's vade-mecum; but by this time it was, like Eustace's book, being superseded by the famous red handbooks published by John Murray. Murray conceded that Mrs Starke's guide was 'a work of real utility, because amidst a singular medley of classical lore, borrowed from Lemprière's Dictionary, interwoven with details regulating the charges in washing-bills at Sorrento and Naples and an elaborate theory on the origin of Devonshire cream in which she proves that it was brought by Phoenician colonists from Asia Minor into the West of England, it contained much practical information gathered on the spot';[40] nevertheless his success with new guides (written by himself) for Holland, Belgium, and North Germany, for South Germany and for Switzerland prompted him to poach on Mrs Starke's territory, and his first Italian guidebook, the *Handbook for Travellers to North Italy* by Sir Francis Palgrave, appeared in 1842. It was followed by *Central Italy* (1843), *Southern Italy* (1853), and *Rome* (1858). The *Handbook for the Ionian Islands, Greece, Turkey, Asia Minor and Constantinople*, by Sir George Bowden, had appeared in 1840. The red guidebooks published by Karl Baedeker of Leipzig were rivals with a stronger claim to impartiality, since they did not carry advertisements; but the first English-language Baedeker for Italy (the *Guide to Central Italy and Rome*) did not appear until 1869, by which time Murray was comfortably entrenched. As his son, John Murray IV, remarked in 1919: 'He built up a series which held the field against all competitors till the time when cheap travel introduced the vast horde of travellers who cared little for intellectual information and required a totally different class of *vade-mecum*—travellers to whom where to feed was a more important question than what to see.'[41] The

---

[39] K. Tillotson, ed., *The Letters of Charles Dickens*, iv (Oxford, 1977), 282.
[40] Cited in John Murray IV, *John Murray III: A Brief Memoir* (1919), 41.
[41] Ibid., 8.

popularity of Murray's guides and, by implication, the cultural preoccupations of the Victorian travelling public were attested by the constant flow of new editions, the prosperity which they brought to Murray's firm, and the notoriety which they acquired in Italy as the characteristic insignia of Anglo-Saxon tourists. Samuel Bevan complained in 1849 that a rosy *Murray* at once identified a tourist as *Inglese* and 'fair game for all kinds of imposition'.[42] One of Cardinal Manning's favourite stories concerned an Italian sacristan who, deeply impressed by the piety of the English, asked about the red prayer-book which they always carried and read so devoutly in the churches.[43]

Poking fun at 'Murrayolatry' was common; but there was no sense of fun about the practice itself. It was never less than painstaking and often it had the grim futility of a Sisyphean labour. 'Most of them', wrote James Bryce of his countrymen in Italy, 'seem to see sights for no purpose but that of verifying their Murray, which they do with praiseworthy perseverance in front of a crowd of kneeling worshippers in a church or perched on the steps of some ruined temple.' Bryce followed their example and reported in January 1865 that he had examined 'more or less carefully' some sixty or seventy churches. 'That is to say', he explained, 'I have carefully gone round them, verifying my Murray, as is the wont of the English tourist; have admired the "Sebastiano del Piombo at the third altar on the right" and anathematised the "Carlo Muretta at the fourth on the left of the entrance", and strained my eyes and twisted my neck in the effort to make something of the frescos in the cupola.'[44] The American James Russell Lowell, in Rome in the 1860s, admired the brisk efficiency with which his 'business-like British cousins' coped with the plethora of aesthetic treasures, inspecting them in 'thrifty auctioneer fashion' and checking them off in their Murrays.[45] When the brevity of his stay imposed a sense of urgency the Victorian tourist pursued his cultural education at a vertiginous pace. Oscar Browning and his mother were in Rome for only ten days in 1871, yet in that time they inspected St Peter's, the Collegio Romano, the Capitol, the Forum, the Marmorata, the graves of Keats and Shelley, San Paolo fuori le Mura, the Palatine, the Villa Ludovisi, the gardens of Sallust, Santa Maria degli

[42] Samuel Bevan, *Sand and Canvas* (1849), 201.
[43] Cobbe, *Life*, ii. 166; *Italics*, 426.
[44] H. A. L. Fisher, *James Bryce* (1927), i. 84, 89.
[45] J. R. Lowell, *Fireside Travels* (new edn., Boston, 1898), 316.

Angeli, the Lateran Church and Palace, the Scala Santa, Santa Croce, the Porta Maggiore, the Porta San Lorenzo, the Chiesa di San Lorenzo, the Villa Doria Pamphili, the Pantheon, the Farnesina frescos, the Via Appia, the Villa Borghese, the Pincian, the Baths of Caracalla, the Fountain of Egeria, the Vatican sculptures, Monte Mario, the Minerva, the Ghetto, the Castle of Sant' Angelo, and the Barberini Palace.[46] Matthew Arnold reported breathlessly from Rome in April 1873: 'We are so hard driven with sight-seeing here that it is very hard to write ... One sees far too much—and yet that is inevitable.' In one day he had been to the Farnesina Palace, the gallery and gardens of the Corsini Palace, St Peter's, the Vatican, the Ponte Molle, and the Porto del Popolo.[47]

Travellers with less than ordinary stamina were compelled to retire from the gruelling exercise overcome by frustration and fatigue. 'I am too old in head, limbs and eyesight for such hard work, such toiling and such straining', moaned the sixty-seven-year-old William Words-worth, turning homewards with an immense sense of relief.[48] Fifty years later Dr David Young, a physician practising in Rome, recorded the case of two English ladies who, ten days after their arrival, complained of exhaustion and decided that they must leave since the climate did not suit them. 'On enquiry', Young continued,

I found that their whole day was devoted to visiting places within the city, while the evening was given to reading and taking notes of the day's work ... They were thoroughly over-taxed, were sleeping badly and, at times, were so tired as scarcely to be able to take their meals; while frequently their midday meal was nothing more than a biscuit, as they could not *afford* the time to return to their hotel for lunch.[49]

Hugh Price Hughes recoiled from the exigencies of sightseeing in Italy and cried out against the ill-contrivance of providence. 'Why', he demanded, 'are all these masterpeices thus crowded together in one country, so that they come to be as silver in the reign of Solomon, and nothing accounted for because of their abundance?'[50] It is small wonder that the British in Italy struck observers as forbiddingly serious and splenetic. 'They are a people incapable of joy,' wrote Stendhal in 1828, 'and their moroseness is doubled when they see

[46] O. Browning, *Memories*, 170.
[47] G. W. E. Russell, ed., *The Letters of Matthew Arnold* (1895), ii. 96–7.
[48] de Selincourt, ed., *Wordsworth Letters*, ii. 856, 858, 859.
[49] Young, *Rome in Winter*, 197–8.
[50] *The Life and Times of Hugh Price Hughes by his Daughter* (1907), 418.

others enjoying themselves without asking their permission.'[51] The historian John Richard Green, in Rome in 1873, was dismayed by the unsmiling obsessiveness of his compatriots. 'Why are people so grave, so solemn, so afraid of laughter, of fun, of irony, of quiz, of nonsense in all its delicious forms?' he wondered. 'People pound you with picture galleries and basilicas and frown down a joke by inquiring your opinion as to the true site of the Temple of Concord.'[52] In a Florentine *pensione* in 1910 Arnold Bennett found himself surrounded by female tourists who were calm, long-suffering, and stern. 'It is impossible to believe that they are happy in Florence', he wrote. 'They do not wear the look of joy. Their gestures are not those of happiness.'[53]

Victorian and Edwardian novelists often pilloried the cultural pretensions of British tourists abroad. They mocked the guidebook connoisseurs in the manner of Molière, as clownish provincials or bourgeois philistines aping the accomplishments of high society. Thackeray laughed at 'blundering Yorkshire squires' rambling about the ruins of Greece, and scoffed: 'Men say they are enthusiastic about the Greek and Roman authors and history only because it is considered proper and respectable.'[54] Charles Lever's meandering novel *The Dodd Family Abroad* lampoons a hard-up Anglo-Irish squire and his family who wander over Belgium, Germany, and Italy 'John Murray in hand, speaking unintelligible French, and poking their noses everywhere', pursued by mishap and calamity. 'Had you come on the Continent', Lever chided the hapless Dodds, 'to be abroad what you were well contented to be at home—had you abstained from the mockery of a class you never belonged to—had you settled down amidst those your equals in rank and often much more your equals in knowledge and acquirement—your journey would not have been a series of disappointments.' The Meagles and Dorrit families in Dickens's *Little Dorrit* are *nouveaux riches* who go to Italy to acquire social recognition and prestige by joining the throng of tourists who wander through the ruins 'on somebody else's cork legs . . . straining every visible object through somebody else's sieve . . . carefully feeling their way, incessantly repeating Prunes and Prism in the endeavour to set their lips according to the received form'. Forster and Bennett

[51] V. Del Litto and E. Abravanel, eds., *Œuvres complètes de Stendhal* (Geneva, n.d.), vii. 100.   [52] Stephen, ed., *Letters of J. R. Green*, 354.

[53] Bennett, *English Review*, 5. 450, 455.

[54] W. M. Thackeray, *Notes of a Journey from Cornhill to Grand Cairo, by A. Titmarsh* (1846), 76.

satirised the middle-class Englishwomen they saw in Italy as armour-plated rearguards of Victorian virginity, trivialising great art with tiny minds. Forster's aversion for these women is expressed in *A Room With a View*, in the mildly malicious portrayal of Cousin Charlotte, a chaperon who judges the nude in Botticelli's *Birth of Venus* 'a pity' that spoils the picture. Bennett wrote sardonically of female tourists who 'nibble daintily at crumbs of art and archaeology', mistaking Golter-mann for Debussy and confusing Botticelli with Maude Goodman.[55]

When the mind is dazzled by such satire, life can easily appear to imitate art. There is always a temptation to see something because a clever writer has said it is there. When James Russell Lowell claimed in 1864 to have witnessed 'the unavailing agonies of many Anglo-Saxons from both sides of the Atlantic in their efforts to have the correct sensation before many hideous examples of antique bad taste',[56] he was probably subconsciously remembering *Little Dorrit* and making a judgement under the influence of parody. The very seriousness of the pursuit of culture, the painfulness of its excesses, and the grotesqueness of its failures, militates against the idea that it was entirely—or even predominantly—a pretence or an empty social ritual; and the broader historical context clearly indicates that while generalisations about middle-class philistinism, snobbery, and super-ficiality owed something to experience, they owed a lot more to prejudice and literary convention. The charge of philistinism, for example, is undermined by the nineteenth-century campaign to reform education, for which the middle classes were mainly respon-sible. This was concerned as much with standards of instruction as with curricula; and although it resulted in the introduction of 'Modern Sides' in the main boarding schools and endowed grammer schools it never implied a contempt for the Classics and the fine arts. The old nine endowed boarding schools (Eton, Harrow, Westminster, Shrewsbury, St Paul's, Merchant Taylors', Charterhouse, Rugby, and Winchester) remained essentially Classical institutions on the lines established by Dr Arnold even after the reforms recommended by the Clarendon Commission (1864) had been put into effect, and they certainly never lacked middle-class patronage. The Taunton Com-mission, which investigated the new proprietary boarding schools and the old endowed grammar schools, reported in 1868 that the

---

[55] Bennett, *English Review*, 5. 454.
[56] Lowell, *Fireside Travels*, 316.

mercantile and trading clases '[were] not insensible to the value of culture in itself, nor to the advantages of sharing the education of the cultured classes'; and these schools continued to teach Classical and literary subjects in conjunction with new 'Modern' curricula. The clamour from the Nonconformist middle classes for full access to Oxford and Cambridge (finally achieved with the abolition of all religious tests in 1871) was emphatically not a clamour for access to utilitarian, scientific education—which was, in any case, already available to them in the University of London and the Dissenting Academies. Even after the introduction of Honours Schools in the Natural Sciences, in the 1850s, the ancient universities remained dedicated to Classics, theology, and mathematics; and a new chair in Classical Archaeology was established at Oxford as late as 1881.

The intelligent patronage of the arts practised by many members of the Victorian bourgeoisie makes it even more difficult to sustain the general charge of philistinism. Lady Eastlake claimed that from the 1830s patronage of the fine arts in Britain was engrossed by a class enriched by commerce and trade, and it is not difficult to quote examples in support of her contention. Sir Robert Peel, William Gladstone, James Dennistoun, Sir Austen Layard, Ralph Bernal, Elhanan Bicknell, the senior John Ruskin, John Jones, John Sheep-shanks, George Salting, Robert Napier, and Sir Thomas Phillips were all unequivocally bourgeois collectors and connoisseurs of art and letters. The early Victorian years were characterised by a burgeoning of public interest in art exhibitions and a rash of subscriptions for the newly founded *Art Union Monthly Journal*; and in the great manu-facturing cities of the Midlands and the North elaborate and costly town halls, art galleries, libraries, colleges, and concert halls were commissioned and endowed by men whom the intellectuals were castigating as churlish. Manchester Town Hall, said Abel Haywood, one of the city's Victorian Lord Mayors, 'is an outward and visible sign to the world that we are not wholly given up to Mammon, and that the higher culture is not neglected among us'. And if this devotion to traditional learning and this deep interest in the fine arts do not betoken philistinism, neither do they necessarily betoken snobbery, because they were not always part of a conscious determination to mimic the aristocracy. The civic renaissance of northern England was an overt celebration of the achievements of trade and industry; and interest in the Classics and the fine arts was, as often as not, pursued by men who were contemptuous of aristocrats and only too pleased to assist, by usurping their culture and their function of patronage, in the demolition of their claim to deference and privilege.[57]

Likewise, the female tourists who were satirised by Forster and Bennett as philistines and prudes are more likely to have been assisting than impeding the campaign for the legal, intellectual, and social emancipation of women. Anthony Trollope probably depicted the type more accurately than he portrayed Sabrina Dawkins, the travelling spinster in *An Unprotected Female at the Pyramids*, as a resourceful feminist. It is clear that by the end of the nineteenth century women were outnumbering men among the tourists in southern Europe. Forster wrote of encountering 'stacks of females' in Italy in 1901 and 1903;[58] Bennett noted that in the drawing-room of his *pensione* in Florence there were fifty ladies, and a single man in a corner 'like a fly on a pin'; and women without men constantly figure in the pages of other late Victorian and Edwardian travel writers. On the culture-circuit of the South the creak of leather and the smell of cigars were receding before the rustle of silk and the scents of lavender and mothballs, and this in itself signalled a new spirit of female enterprise and independence. In early- and mid-Victorian times girls and women had travelled in the protective matrix of the family. 'Daughters can travel alone . . . occasionally,' wrote Trollope in 1866; 'but such feminine independence is an exception to the rule, and daughters are generally willing to submit themselves to . . . paternal and maternal guidance.'[59] W. D. Howells, who was American Consul in Venice in the 1860s, observed that one learnt to recognise the English by their habit of travelling *en famille*;[60] and when this was not possible the single woman usually attached herself to an obliging *ménage* of relatives or friends. The twenty-seven-year-old Florence Nightingale, for example, visited Rome in 1847 chaperoned by Mr and Mrs Bracebridge. In her autobiography Frances Power Cobbe wrote that when she set out on her solitary travels in 1857 such a journey was 'still accounted somewhat of an enterprise for a "lone woman"'; but in fact at this time a women did not need even to be alone to be

---

[57] These issues are discussed in Patrick Connor, *Savage Ruskin* (1979); Frank Davis, *Victorian Patrons of the Arts* (1963); Charles Dellheim, *The Face of the Past* (Cambridge, 1982); Katherine Sim, *David Roberts: A Biography* (1984).

[58] P. N. Furbank, *E. M. Forster: A Life* (1977), i. 85, 104.

[59] Trollope, *Travelling Sketches*, 3.

[60] Howells, *Venetian Life*, i. 152. For an account of the experience of a single woman travelling with her mother see the anonymous *Unprotected Females in Sicily, Calabria, and on the Top of Mount Aetna* (1859).

exceptional. All females abroad without male escorts, whether travelling singly, in pairs, or in groups, were classified as 'unprotected', and the term carried strong connotations of eccentricity. The unprotected female was an aberration, who found her place in fiction as either a comic or a tragic deviation from the norm. Trollope's Miss Dawkins and his Miss Todd (a character in *The Bertrams*, reckoned to be based on Frances Power Cobbe) are examples of the former; the paranoid Miss Wade, in Dickens's *Little Dorrit*, is an instance of darker singularity. The species was rare because generally women were not trained to look after themselves. Miss Cobbe made this clear when she described her own ignorance of financial transactions. 'I,' she wrote, 'who had always had money in abundance given me straight into my hand, knew absolutely nothing, when my father's death left me to manage my own affairs, of how such business is done, how shares are bought and sold, how credits are opened at corresponding branches, how, even, to draw a cheque.' By the first years of the twentieth century, in the most popular parts of the South at least, the unprotected female was the rule rather than the exception. This was partly because less enterprise was now necessary in order to go abroad—Thomas Cook had seen to that; but it was also because there was now more enterprise among women. Arnold Bennett's ladies obviously experienced none of the perplexity of Miss Cobbe. They coped with 'cheques, and cheques, and cheques always' as part of the routine of existence, and it must be true that many were intelligent and discerning. They came after all from that class of women who, having won by dint of iron determination the legal right to their own property and access to university education, were now fighting in the face of male ridicule for the right to vote.

Unlike the tourists, the students lived in close and prolonged intimacy with the artistic heritage of the South. They spent much of their time abroad and many were permanently resident in Italy, where they cultivated an easy, patronising familiarity with the local ways and language. They were chiefly critics, historians, and artists, though a few archaeologists were active on the Classical sites of the Aegean islands, Asia Minor, and Crete.

The literary figures—the art critics and historians—were the stars of George Bernard Shaw's 'Victorian cosmopolitan intellectualism'. Highly strung, bickering, and self-important, they were the prima donnas of the cultural circuit: the 'experts' who did not read guidebooks, but wrote them. Their favourite habitat was Florence, where they mustered in strength during the late Victorian and Edwardian years, after exquisite sensibility had retreated from London in the backwash of the Wilde scandal. 'Living', as Forster facetiously noted, 'in delicate seclusion, some in furnished flats, others in Renaissance villas on Fiesole's slope ... they read, wrote, studied and exchanged ideas.'[61] This colony paid homage to two matriarchs—Mrs Baxter and Mrs Ross. Lucy Baxter, daughter of the Dorset poet William Barnes, had arrived in Florence in the 1860s. Here she had married, settled at the Villa Bianca just outside the city in the direction of Vincigliata, and devoted herself so successfully to the study of Italian art and architecture that in 1882 she had been elected an honorary member of the Florentine Accademia delle Belle Arti. Under the name of Leader Scott she published popular studies of Fra Bartolommeo and Andrea del Sarto, of Ghiberti and Donatello, of Luca della Robbia, of Brunelleschi and of Correggio, as well as a more esoteric work on the medieval guild of Comacine Masons (*The Cathedral Builders*). After the death of this benign and learned lady in 1902 undivided sway passed to Janet Ross, whose erudition was slighter but whose presence, enhanced by ramrod figure and heavy eyebrows, was distinctly more imposing. As Janet Duff Gordon she had been wooed and lost by George Meredith, and she had come to Florence in the 1860s as the wife of an international banker. He cultivated orchids while she cultivated a literary reputation, publishing *Florentine Villas*, *Florentine Palaces*, and *The Land of Manfred*. Behind the towering walls of her medieval home, Poggio Gherado, she sheltered her literary niece, Lina Duff Gordon (author of *The Story of Assisi* and *The Concise and Practical Guide to Rome*) and acted as hostess to visiting celebrities from the worlds of art, letters, and high society. At the Villa Il Palmerino, Violet Paget, the waspish, lesbian bluestocking who had published *Studies in the Eighteenth Century in Italy* and *Renaissance Fancies and Studies* under the pseudonym of Vernon Lee, held court with her mysteriously paralysed brother, investigated the properties of beauty and ugliness in collaboration with 'Kit' Anstruther-Thomson, and conducted a feud with her neighbour, Bernhard Berenson, who accused her of plagiarising his own theories on aesthetics. Among the other students living and working in Florence at this time were Herbert Horne, tenant of the austere Palazzo Gondi, who collected Botticellis and laboured to produce the

[61] *A Room with a View*, Ch. 5.

definitive biography of the Master; Edward Hutton, who had published *The Cities of Umbria*, *Florence and the Cities of Northern Tuscany*, *The Cities of Lombardy*, and *The Cities of Romagna* by 1914; and Robert Hobart Cust, author of *The Pavement Masters of Siena*, who had a flat in the Via dei Bardi where he was at home at teatime on Sundays to aspirant aesthetes and tyros in art criticism.[62] Venice, too, had its resident experts in these years. They included Austen Layard (editor of Kügler and author of several articles); Horatio Brown (*Life on the Lagoons*, *Venetian Studies*); and the Hon. Alethea Lawley, wife of the Librarian of St Mark's and author of *The Story of Venice* and *The Story of Verona*. And then there were the peripatetics: students who returned to Italy again and again, roving in a state of sustained hyperaesthesia from gallery to gallery, church to church, and historic city to historic city, discovering, documenting, expatiating. Here the prominent names are John Ruskin, John Addington Symonds, and Augustus Hare, who between them produced a small mountain of monographs, essays, guidebooks, and histories. Hare was exceptional among this cultured élite in that he confessed to reading guidebooks—though only those written by himself. In 1892 he returned to Pisa using his own volume as a guide 'and', he recalled with characteristic self-admiration, 'a most delightful book I thought it'.[63] Others suggested that he read more guidebooks than he admitted and the publisher John Murray claimed to recognise whole passages from his own Handbooks in Hare's *Walks in Rome* and *Cities of Northern and Central Italy*. It is easy to find fault with these British Italophiles. They were forever striking postures and throwing tantrums, and much of their writing betrays the worst features of amateurism. It is shallow, derivative, narcissistic, and over-ecstatic, and it frequently magnifies the author by diminishing the reader. Nevertheless, taken as a whole it offers an impressive testimony to the veneration felt by the Victorians and Edwardians for the cultural inheritance of the South. As Paul Bourget remarked, when he saw the little guides and monographs that filled the library of an English hotel in Perugia: 'Quelle puissance d'activité intellectuelle supposent ces livres! Le gout du détail précis, la passion de la culture y sont admirables, et aussi l'amour intellectuel de l'Italie . . .'[64]

[62] Furbank, *E. M. Forster*, i. 84–5.
[63] Hare, *The Story of My Life*, vi. 290.
[64] P. Bourget, *Sensations d'Italie* (Paris, 1891), 136.

For most of the nineteenth century Rome was the chief resort of
British artists with the means to travel. The city was, as John Cam
Hobhouse wrote in 1859, 'one great academy for the artists of the
universe ... the metropolis of the painter, the sculptor, the architect'.[65] Edward Lear, who spent the period 1837-45 there, told his
sister: 'You have little notion how completely an artist's paradise is
Rome—and how destitute all other places would be of capacities to
study or prosper.'[66] Study in Rome formed part of the training of many
nineteenth-century Academy notables, including Turner, Lawrence,
Eastlake, Etty, Leighton, George and William Richmond, and the
sculptors Richard Wyatt and John Gibson. George Frederic Watts is a
peculiar exception among the major Royal Academicians in that he
spent only one day, out of the four years he passed in Italy, in Rome.
His training ground was Florence, where he served as resident genius
in the household of Lord Holland, British Minister to the Tuscan
court. A number of British artists made Rome their permanent
residence. These included Joseph Severn, the friend of Keats; Penry
Williams, a Welshman of humble birth whose work was favoured by
high society; and John Gibson, another Welshman who arrived in
Rome in 1817 and stayed there, save for summers in Innsbruck and
occasional trips to London, until he died in 1866.

This expatriate community lived in a style of somewhat self-
conscious bohemianism, forming what Thackeray described as 'a
broad-hatted, long-bearded, velvet-jacketed jovial colony ... who
[had] their own feasts, haunts and amusements'.[67] Their working days
were spent in the studios that filled the little streets leading from the
Corso to the Piazza di Spagna, and the focus of their social life was the
Caffè Greco, the celebrated tavern by the Barcaccia fountain in the
Piazza di Spagna where painters and sculptors of all nationalities, but
chiefly British and German, gathered in an atmosphere flavoured by
tobacco, absinthe, and ribaldry. The artists' models who touted for
hire on the Spanish Steps and who were immortalised by Dickens in
Pictures from Italy were one of the sights of Rome until the early 1860s,
when the Papal authorities mounted a campaign against prostitution
and prohibited this public form of soliciting.

The artists who made Rome their home stayed mainly in order to
take advantage of the constant demand from tourists, in the days

[65] John Cam Hobhouse, *Italy: Remarks Made in Several Visits, 1816—1854* (1859), ii. 240.
[66] Vivien Noakes, *Edward Lear* (new edn., 1979), 56.
[67] *The Newcomes*, Ch. 35.

before photography, for portraits, copies of Old Masters, and paintings of famous vistas; but most of them had come, as their predecessors in the eighteenth century had come, with the lofty purpose of perfecting their skill by studying the great works of the Classical and Christian past. Rome, said Gibson, was 'the very university of art';[68] and he signified his devotion to the Classical sculpture that he found there by striving to recapture its spirit and emulate its technique, even to the point of tinting his statues in the manner of the Greeks and refusing commissions that did not permit him to clothe his subject in antique draperies. 'He had spent his life', wrote Nathaniel Hawthorne, 'for forty years, in making Venuses, Cupids, Bacchuses and a vast deal of other marble progeny of dream work, or rather frost work: it was all a vapoury exhalation out of the Grecian mythology, crystallizing on the dull window panes of today.'[69] Gibson insisted that a Roman education was essential for a sculptor, since the antique masterpieces collected there represented a criterion of absolute excellence. 'All those men of genius in modern times', he wrote, 'who have deviated from the principles of Greek art, have left us works not superior, but greatly inferior to the ancients'.[70] Among painters much the same reverence was paid to the masterpieces of Renaissance art, and until the national collection of Italian pictures had been enlarged (chiefly through the exertions of Eastlake, as Director of the National Gallery), only in Italy could the student learn what they had to teach. It was with the object of enabling talented British artists to see these works that the Society of Dilettanti had, in 1774, endowed two travelling scholarships for students nominated by the Royal Academy. Later in the nineteenth century, with the expansion of the National Gallery, the galleries of Rome lost their unique attraction; and both Watts and Frith, when at the height of their fame and influence, declared that a visit to Italy was no longer indispensable.

There was something extra-special about the archaeologists. In contact with buried cities and lost civilisations, and initiated into the secrets of lapidary inscriptions and excavated fragments, they had a touch of esoteric mystery about them, like the 'traveller from an antique land' evoked by Shelley in *Ozymandias*. They had the mark of privilege, too. Set apart not only by the arcane nature of their craft, but

---

[68] Elizabeth Eastlake, ed., *The Life of John Gibson* (1870), 58.
[69] *The Marble Faun*, Ch. 15.
[70] Eastlake, ed., *Life of Gibson*, 87.

by their access to public money and official honours, they were the *crème de la crème* among students in the Mediterranean. They were all more or less self-taught, since there was no formal archaeological training at the British universities until the 1880s; and some were amateurs in the sense that they were men of independent means who used their own resources to finance their journeys and explorations. Charles Fellows, a gentleman of fortune, made four archaeological expeditions into Asia Minor between 1838 and 1844, in the course of which he discovered and recorded the ruins of no fewer than thirteen forgotten cities, as well as the site of Xanthus, the capital of ancient Lycia. He negotiated with the Turkish authorities for the removal of several tons of sculpture to the British Museum and was subsequently knighted 'as an acknowledgement of his services in the removal of the Xanthian antiquities to this country'. James Theodore Bent, who spent much of his time and money between 1885 and 1889 exploring and excavating in the Aegean islands of Karpathos, Samos, and Thasos, was refused permission to export his Thasian antiquities, but he published extensive accounts of his discoveries in the *Archaeological Journal*, the *Journal of Hellenic Studies*, and other reviews and magazines. Most celebrated of all these dedicated and learned amateurs was Arthur Evans, the wealthy Welshman who brought to light the legendary city of Knossos and reclaimed from the oblivion of four thousand years the civilisation of Minoan Crete. In 1894 Evans acquired the site of Knossos as his personal freehold, and five years later began systematic excavation with funds provided mainly by himself. Other archaeologists were 'professional' in the sense that they were employed by private sponsors or by the British Government to carry out investigations. Richard Pullan, a successful architect who excavated sites in Anatolia at Teos, in the Troad and at Priene in 1862, 1866, and 1869, was supported by the Society of Dilettanti, which had established a tradition of archaeological enterprise in Italy and Greece since its foundation in 1732; and further work in mainland Greece and Crete was sponsored by the British School in Athens after its foundation in 1885. The fourth expedition of Fellows to Asia Minor (1844), the explorations of Nathan Davis at Carthage and Utica (1856–8), and the work of Charles Newton at Budrum (1856–7) were all officially funded. In 1852 Newton, who was destined to become the most distinguished archaeologist of his generation, was appointed Vice-Consul at Mytilene with the special duty of acquiring antiquities for the British Museum; and with the resources thus put at his disposal he was able to excavate the site of the Mausoleum at Halicarnassus and depute Richard Pullan to conduct similar investigations at Didyma (Branchidae). Newton was appointed Keeper of the Greek and Roman Antiquities at the British Museum in 1861 and he used his powers and influence to promote archaeological surveys and digs at Cyrene and Ephesus, as well as in Rhodes, Cyprus, and Sicily. Evans and Newton were, like Fellows, both knighted in recognition of their achievements in the field of Classical archaeology.[71]

5. HEALTH

'What is it that we seek for,' asked Lady Mary Herbert, 'we English-men and Englishwomen who, year by year, about the month of November, are seen crowding in Folkestone and Dover steam boats with that unmistakable "going abroad" look of travelling—bags and wideawakes, and bundles of wraps and alpaca gowns?' Her answer was sunshine; and sunshine was sought because it meant health. 'Climate means health to one half of us; and health means power of enjoyment, for without it the most perfect of homes is spoiled and saddened.'[1] Belief in the therapeutic value of Mediterranean climates had drawn English invalids to the Riviera during the eighteenth century; and in the Victorian era 'ordering south' became a standard medical prescription for the well-to-do. In the 1870s the historian John Richard Green pondered the annual bustle of migration and the transformation of humble French and Italian fishing villages into fashionable winter resorts, and saw them as a tribute to the power of the British doctor:

It is he who rears pleasant towns at the foot of the Pyrenees, and lines the sunny coasts of the Riviera with villas that gleam white among the olive groves. It is his finger that stirs the camels of Algeria, the donkeys of Palestine, the Nile boats of Egypt. At the first frosts of November the doctor marshals his wild geese for their winter flitting, and the long train streams off, grumbling but obedient, to the little Britains of the South.[2]

---

[71] Lionel Cust and Sidney Colvin, *History of the Society of Dilettanti* (1898); Joan Evans, *Time and Chance: The Story of Arthur Evans and his Forbears* (1943); *Dictionary of National Biography*.

---

[1] Mary Elizabeth Herbert, *Impressions of Spain in 1866* (1867), 1.
[2] J. R. Green, *Stray Studies from England and Italy* (1876), 31.

Christopher Home Douglas, who accompanied his invalid wife to the Mediterranean in 1872, likened the daily express from Paris to the Riviera to an ambulance train. From a vantage point in the main hotel at Dijon he watched a 'a flow of maimed existence' arriving from the station to break its southward journey. There were

pale Oxford men who [had] broken down on the threshold of their way to the Woolsack; young ladies who [had] sickened in their first winter campaign and to whose wan cheeks the roses of an English summer [had] declined to lend their hues; gouty papas with florid faces, fondly hoping that the effects of a quarter of a century of over-feeding [would] disappear in the mellow air of the Riviera.

At the *table d'hôte* the talk was all about 'coughs and bronchial affections, climates, Nice, Mentone, Algiers and so on'.[3] Probably it was talk primed with information from one of the popular medical guides to winter stations, or from one of the many personal accounts of wanderings in search of health that were an essential part of the Victorian cults of 'delicacy' and hypochondria. It is an indication of the growing importance of health as a motive for travel to the South that more and more of the published literature on the Mediterranean was aimed at the invalid market. Dr Madden recorded in 1864 that the number of British invalids annually wintering in the South had been calculated at between seven and eight thousand;[4] but the total of visitors in the therapeutic category would be more like twice that figure, because almost all invalids travelled with a relative or companion as nurse.

The destination of the great majority of these people was the Franco-Italian Riviera, between Hyères and Genoa. In the early part of our period, until about 1860, preference was not fixed and a number of different areas were briefly fashionable and reputable as winter health resorts. Madeira and Lisbon, much in vogue during the war years, when the Continent was closed to British visitors, had already dropped out of favour with the return of peace and the reopening of the Mediterranean countries; but it was some time before the Riviera virtually monopolised invalid patronage. During the 1830s, 1840s, and 1850s Pisa, Rome, and Naples were much visited for therapeutic reasons, and Malta, Malaga, and Algiers all acquired incipient reputations as health resorts. A convalescent trip to Valetta by Queen

[3] Douglas, *Searches for Summer*, 139–40.
[4] Madden, *On Change of Climate*, 32.

Adelaide drew invalids to Malta for a while; but according to Dr Edwin Lee its popularity was waning by the late 1850s,[5] and Dr Edmund Hobhouse's *Health Abroad*, of 1899, rated it a social resort rather than an invalid station: 'A few invalids do go thither, but it cannot be recommended for such.' Marianne North, who was in southern Spain in the autumn of 1859, found Malaga 'full of invalids',[6] and its value was endorsed by Drs Scoresby Jackson and Madden; but by the 1870s it was out of favour, following its indictment by Dr James Henry Bennet. Dr William Wilde, in 1837, foresaw a promising future for Algiers as a health resort, and it did manage to attract a certain number of Victorian invalids, who liked to call it the Torquay of Africa; but comparatively few of these travellers cared to venture as far as North Africa, and those that did came to prefer Egypt, as a more familiar and sympathetic environment. This was especially the case after the British occupation in 1882.

By the 1860s, in fact, British invalids and their professional advisers were showing a marked predilection for the Riviera and habits were being formed which proved sufficiently strong to survive later modifications of medical opinion. The South of France was now adopted as their winter sanatorium by the middle and upper classes not only of Britain but of northern Europe, headed by Queen Victoria, the Empress of Russia, and the Emperor Frederick of Germany; and this remained its characteristic role until the First World War. Hotels and villas advanced further and further eastwards along the Cornice coast to the Gulf of Genoa as the demand for winter accommodation increased and cosmopolitan wealth turned quiet fishing hamlets into modish cities and chic retreats. Hyères, Cannes, and Nice were all established health resorts by 1860; by 1865 Menton, Bordighera, and San Remo had been discovered and were steadily expanding.

Invalids were the pioneers in this development and they retained something of a frontier mentality, moving on when the older resorts became too crowded. By the end of the century they were generally preferring the smaller resorts of the eastern Riviera. Henry James reported in 1881 that the hotels in San Remo were 'filled with English and German consumptives', who caused the meals to be served at impossible hours;[7] and by the early 1890s Menton had become one of the principal British sanatoria abroad. 'As a resort for English

[5] Edwin Lee, *Bradshaw's Invalid's Companion to the Continent* (2nd edn., 1861), 200.

[6] North, *Further Recollections*, 23.

[7] Leon Edel, ed., *The Letters of Henry James* (1974–81), ii. 348.

invalids', wrote A. R. Hope Moncrieff in 1893, 'this is the capital of the Riviera.'[8] Queen Victoria's choice of this locality for herself and her sickly son Prince Leopold in 1882 was a result, as well as a cause, of its rising popularity.

Assuming that supply follows demand, the distribution of British doctors practising abroad can be read as an indication of the distribution of the British invalid population. A list published in 1899 gives a total of 39 British physicians resident on the Riviera between Hyères and San Remo. This compares with 7 resident in Rome, 7 in Florence, 2 in Naples, 2 in Venice, 1 in Algeria, and 1 in Malaga. Of those on the Riviera, 14 were practising in Menton, Bordighera, and San Remo; 17 were resident in Nice and Cannes; and the rest were distributed between Hyères and Beaulieu (1 each), and Monaco (6).[9]

Invalids were a characteristic feature of winter life in all these places during the fifty years before the First World War. At Menton their Bath chairs monopolised the Promenade du Midi by day, and by night their premature retirement imparted a hospital hush to the atmosphere. In the Jardin Public at Nice they sat listening to the military band—inert figures fortified by rugs and shawls. At Cannes their infirmities pervaded social chatter, and the two subjects of conversation were (as Richard Monckton Milnes reported in 1864) 'lungs and anemones'.[10] In Venice their spectral forms haunted the Café Florian in the Piazza San Marco and glided about the canals in silent gondolas. In Rome they surveyed the ruins, either propped in carriages or walking slowly on the arms of attendants. In Florence their dry, jerking coughs started echoes in the churches and galleries. Nowhere, it seemed, was quite free from their sick-room aura and their muted sadness.

They brought to the South a wide variety of afflictions, ranging in gravity from Clergyman's Sore Throat to mortal malady. According to Dr William Marcet a considerable number were bronchitic or asthmatic; and then there were

Young people with a family disposition to consumption; ladies fatigued by the London Season; persons suffering from chronic rheumatism whose pains and stiffness of limbs are invariably increased by cold; elderly people with bladder

---

[8] A. R. Hope Moncrieff, ed., *Where to Go Abroad* (1893), 362. See also H. Coupland Taylor, *Wanderings in Search of Health* (1890), 191.

[9] Hobhouse, ed., *Health Abroad*, 356–9.

[10] Reid, *Richard Monckton Milnes*, ii. 122.

infections; other invalids undergoing general wasting and gradually losing strength from disease of the kidneys; people with weak hearts, who are utterly incapable of exerting themselves in cold weather; scrofulous children; and persons recovering from some long debilitating illness.[11]

The consumptive category was undoubtedly the largest. Until it was overtaken by bronchitis, in the 1870s, consumption was the most active killer in Victorian Britain, causing 60,000 deaths a year in the 1840s and 50,000 in the 1850s; and it was widely believed in medical circles that the only serious hope of recovery lay in transferring the patient to a Southern climate for the winter months. Phthisis therefore became the disease with which Mediterranean travel was most commonly associated.

This belief did not stem from any false ideas about the disinfecting properties of the Mediterranean atmosphere. No one pretended that Southern air acted directly on phthisis, in the way that quinine was known to do on malaria, or mercury on syphilis. Sir James Clark was at pains to disabuse the patient who believed that 'the air or climate . . . possesse[d] some specific quality, by virtue of which it directly cure[d] his disease'.[12] Dr Scoresby Jackson made the same disclaimer in his *Medical Climatology*: 'It is not pretended that the climate itself exercises any specific agency in the cure of consumption';[13] and Dr Marcet, in 1882, stressed that there was 'nothing in a Southern climate of a nature to act as a direct obstacle to the course of phthisis, nothing for instance like such medicines as quinine, which [was] pretty sure to stop an attack of ague'.[14] Not even the discovery of the disinfecting gases ozone, bromine, and iodine in the atmosphere caused a general change of opinion on this point, though one or two physicians did toy with the ozone myth and there is an intriguing mention of an 'ozonometer' in Madden's *On Change of Climate* (1864).

The use of Southern climates was in fact part of a reaction against the whole concept of pharmaceutical treatment for chronic diseases such as consumption and bronchitis. It signalled growing recognition of the impotence of specifics and local applications such as inhalants to combat these endemic afflictions, and the increasing popularity of alternative medicine. John Stuart Mill's experiences in 1854 were a

[11] William Marcet, *The Principal Southern and Swiss Health Resorts* (1883), 313.

[12] James Clark, *The Sanative Influence of Climate* (3rd edn., 1841), 9.

[13] Jackson, *Medical Climatology*, 81.

[14] Marcet, *Health Resorts*, 317.

good indication of the way medical thinking was changing. He consulted Sir James Clark about a weak chest, and Clark diagnosed lung disease. But he prescribed nothing save hemlock pills (a sedative) and mustard poultices (to raise blisters and drain the lungs of fluid)— much to Mill's dissatisfaction. 'Clark did nothing', he complained 'and thought he could do nothing but leave me to nature.' He took himself off to Dr Ramadge and his patent respirator, and was told that several of Clark's disgruntled patients had done the same.[15]

Clark's remark about leaving Mill to nature is significant, because nature-cure was the alternative medicine in question and Clark was one of its chief exponents. 'Of late years', wrote Dr Edwin Lee in 1861, 'many practitioners have more closely studied the effects of hygienic means, trusting less to the employment of pharmaceutical remedies.'[16] Nature-therapy, or 'hygiene', rested on the maxim that given his inability to treat the disease the doctor must concentrate on treating the patient. That is to say, he must assist the patient's natural powers of resistance and recuperation. 'Our attention', advised Clark, 'should be chiefly directed not to a state of disease which is incurable by climate or any other means, but to the prevention and cure of the disordered state of health which constitutes the essential element of consumption.'[17] This meant that the physician must stop thinking in terms of a cause of the sickness and think instead in terms of what modern medicine calls multiple aetiology and what the Victorians called predisposing conditions. 'There are many causes of disease', Dr H. G. Sutton told his pathology students in 1885; 'we can never say there is one cause of disease. Therefore it is exact to say, "this disease has arisen in these conditions". As much as possible, in thinking about pathology, endeavour to get rid of the word "cause".'[18] What were the conditions under which the human powers of resistance to pulmonary tuberculosis weakened? That was the question to which Victorian medicine increasingly addressed itself, as a preliminary to counter-acting those conditions and enabling the patient's body to fight infection.

Predisposing conditions were identified as psychological, environ-mental, and biological. Victorian doctors were keenly alert to the role

---

[15] Frances Mineka and Dwight Lindley, eds., *The Later Letters of John Stuart Mill* (Toronto, 1972), 129, 170, 198, 200, 202.
[16] Lee, *Bradshaw's Invalid's Companion*, 374.
[17] Clark, *Sanative Influence*, 7.
[18] Cited in J. A. Lindsay, *The Climatic Treatment of Consumption* (1887), 18n.

of stress and depression in promoting physical illness, and their books are full of warnings about such dangers as 'wear and tear . . . which results from over strenuous labour or exertion of the intellectual faculties'; 'ennui . . . , weariness of life, lassitude and langour'; 'overwork of the brain at the period of growth, prize competitions at the universities and schools, and professional struggles'; 'excessive physical or mental work, worry and disappointment'; and 'anxiety of mind'. All were conditions which, in the words of Dr Madden, 'although they do not amount to actual disease, will undoubtedly, if not controlled and counteracted in due time, merge into confirmed disease'.[19] Pulmonary weakness was increasingly associated too with density of population and an indoor, sedentary life ('confinement'). In 1867 Dr John Patterson had noted that consumption was increasing among the natives of lower Egypt *pari passu* with the introduction of large factories in connection with the cotton trade;[20] and twenty years later Dr J. A. Lindsay had in mind a mass of evidence such as this when he wrote that it was now conclusively proved 'that consumption . . . attain[ed] its maximum incidence among those whose occupation involve[d] prolonged confinement in a vitiated atmosphere'.[21] It was suggested too that the noticeably greater incidence of the disease among young females than among males was owing to the more physically confined nature of a girl's social and educational life.[22] The concept of diathesis, or constitutional tendency towards a disease, specified certain biological circumstances as predisposing towards consumption. These were defined in terms of age, heredity, and physical characteristics. It was known that the duration of the disease (implying diminished virulence) increased with age, and that young people under thirty were consequently most at risk; a family history of consumption was reckoned to be prejudicial; and features such as narrow chest, fine-textured skin, and soft hair were read as danger signals. Imperfect recovery from inflammatory diseases of the chest, such as bronchitis, pleurisy, and pneumonia, was also identified as a predisposing condition of phthisis, as was dyspepsia in young children. This was reckoned to be, in the words of Sir James Clark, 'a

---

[19] Madden, *On Change of Climate*, p. iii. The other doctors quoted are James Johnson, Edward Sparks, J. A. Lindsay, and David Young.

[20] J. A. Patterson, *Egypt and the Nile Considered as a Winter Resort for Pulmonary and Other Invalids* (1867), 6.

[21] Lindsay, *Climatic Treatment*, 8.

[22] Sparks, *The Riviera*, 104.

principal cause of that morbid state of the system which had been denominated the tuberculous cachexy'.[23]

The idea that cold atmosphere was a predisposing condition was less and less canvassed. The common belief in the eighteenth century had been that warm air conferred immunity from consumption, and as late as the 1840s there were still physicians who prescribed the notorious warm-atmosphere treatment, involving a high room-temperature and minimal ventilation. Dr William Chambers treated Elizabeth Barrett in this way, in the belief that cold air interfered with the physiology of the lungs, by weakening the pulmonary muscles and vascular system.[24] But this notion was already discredited. Statistical reports on the health of the British Army in the Mediterranean stations had revealed that troops serving in the warm climate of Gibraltar, Malta, and the Ionian Islands were in fact more liable to contract phthisis than were the troops serving at home;[25] and further study of the geographical distribution of the disease confirmed that inhaling cold air did not produce it and inhaling warm air did not prevent it. Atmospheric temperature was in itself without significance. Provided the patient himself was kept warm (for body-temperature was acknowledged to be crucial) the temperature of the air he was breathing did not matter.

The importance of predisposing conditions was underlined by the discovery that consumption was in fact more widespread than the mortality figures indicated and that spontaneous remission was going on all the time. The army statistics showed that, while phthisis was more widespread among the troops in the Mediterranean, it was less fatal than at home; and when attention came to be paid in autopsies to the lungs of patients who had died of other causes it was revealed that calcified tuberculous lesions were very common.[26] The illness was not curable in the sense that it was reversible; but in the absence of predisposing conditions it was obviously arrestable, leaving lungs damaged but serviceable.

The object of nature-therapy was to counteract the damage suffered under predisposing conditions by providing the optimum conditions for spontaneous recovery. These conditions were fresh air, exercise, and removal from the sources of stress and fatigue. Climatotherapy, or

[23] Clark, *Sanative Influence*, 13–34.
[24] Betty Miller, ed., *Elizabeth Barrett to Miss Mitford* (1954), 255.
[25] Davy, *Ionian Islands and Malta*, ii. Ch. 12, *passim*.
[26] Mineka and Lindley, eds., *Letters of J. S. Mill*, 199; Lindsay, *Climatic Treatment*, 224.

the use of climate as a curative agent, played a vital role in this form of medicine—for two reasons. In the first place, climate determined a patient's measure of fresh air and exercise. Secondly, climate operated as a depressant or stimulant. It was a natural substitute for drugs such as digitalis, laudanum, hemlock, alcohol, iron, and quinine, and the traditional 'lowering' device of phlebotomy, or bleeding. Victorian climatotherapists paid minute attention to the effects of different climates on the nervous and digestive systems and decided that, as a broad principle, climates were either tonic and exciting, or sedative and relaxing. They could be used either to liven a patient up, or to calm him down. Which type a patient required depended on whether his malady was inflammatory and feverish, or a disease of debility; and this was determined by his pulse-rate, his general temperament, and the nature of his dyspepsia. A high pulse, an irritable or hysterical disposition, and gastric or nervous dyspepsia were associated with inflammatory and feverish affections, and indicated a sedative climate; a low pulse, a gloomy or lymphatic temperament, and atonic or sluggish dyspepsia were associated with diseases of debility and indicated a tonic one. Correct classification and assortment were essential because sending an invalid to the wrong climate could, as it were, short-circuit his system. These therefore were the main functions of medical climatology—a science which was, as Dr Scoresby Jackson said in 1862, 'every day taking a stronger hold upon the minds not only of medical men, but of the general public'.[27]

The Mediterranean was used extensively by Victorian climato-therapists, first because it was comparatively warm and dry in winter. These attributes were attested to by a huge array of statistics covering the temperature, rainfall, hours of sunshine, direction and velocity of winds, atmospheric pressure, humidity, electricity, and general vagaries of the weather in all the best-known localities. Thermometers of every variety, barometers, pluviometers, aethrioscopes, hygro-meters, and anemometers were pressed into service by a host of professional and amateur observers, and all confirmed its essential suitability. The military statistics did likewise. Dr John Davy, Inspector General of Army Hospitals, concluded after studying the army reports of the 1830s that the fresh air and exercise made possible by the warm, dry weather of the Mediterranean stations counteracted the effects of poor accommodation and dissipation, and so kept down

[27] Jackson, *Medical Climatology*, p. vii.

both mortality from consumption among British troops and the incidence of consumption among the native populations.[28] Twenty years later Dr Edwin Lee spelled out what had become the classic argument for the warm Mediterranean winter in cases of this disease:

By the facility afforded for taking exercise daily the muscular system is maintained in a healthy tone; the due equilibrium of vital powers is preserved; and a pernicious concentration of activity towards the brain and the abdominal viscera is prevented. The numerous claims upon the attention from the variety of impressions received during out-of-door exercise likewise counteract abnormal predominance of the sensitive system, by giving rise to fresh ideas. The digestive, respiratory and cutaneous functions are consequently more easily performed, the sleep is sounder, the general *bien-être* is more perfect, and numerous inconveniences arising from a sedentary life beneath cloudy skies are avoided.[29]

The other reason why the Mediterranean was so frequently prescribed was because it offered a wide choice of tonic and sedative climates. Mediterranean climates ranged from relaxing (Pisa, Rome) through intermediate (Malaga) to moderately exciting (Cannes, San Remo, Menton) and very exciting (Algiers, Nice, Naples). There was a difficulty about deciding which type was suitable for consumptive patients because their symptoms were usually a mixture of the irritable and the lymphatic. 'We generally find', wrote Clark, 'a weak and relaxed state of the system accompanied very often with a morbid sensibility of the nervous system.'[30] Clark himself was guided by the irritable symptoms. He maintained that sedative therapy was indicated by the high risk and grave implications of congestion, inflammation, and fever in tuberculous dispositions, and under his powerful influence (he was Physician to the Queen and author of standard treatises on consumption and climatotherapy) Pisa and Rome became the chief resorts of this class of invalid. In 1845 Dr Chambers recommended a winter in Pisa to Elizabeth Barrett, not only as a means (as he thought) of avoiding pulmonary damage from cold air, but as a natural substitute for the large doses of laudanum that were being used to tranquilise her and which were giving rise to obvious signs of opiate addiction. In the 1850s Pisa was, in the words of Dr

[28] Davy, *Ionian Islands and Malta*, ii, Ch. 12, *passim*.

[29] Lee, *Bradshaw's Invalid's Companion*, 375.

[30] Clark, *Sanative Influence*, 245–6: See also Clark's *A Treatise on Pulmonary Consumption* (1835), *passim*.

Burgess, 'the great central depot for foreign consumptive invalids',[31] and the traditional resorts of Montpellier and Nice were, on account of their tonic climates, being neglected. In the second half of the century however the pathology of phthisis was understood in a different way and the climatic treatment reversed. Writing in 1890 Dr Coupland Taylor referred to 'the great revolution' that had been brought about in the treatment of consumption by the theory that it was 'essentially a disease of debility and malnutrition'.[32] This revolution was the work of physicians like Burgess, Bennet, and Scoresby Jackson, who questioned Clark's priorities. Burgess argued that since pulmonary tuberculosis was 'the result of a torpid and vitiated condition of one of the vital functions—nutrition', a sedative climate was more likely to hinder than promote recovery.[33] This view became common from the 1860s and opinion swung back in favour of tonic climates, as better calculated to stimulate tissue-change and promote nutrition. 'The climate of Pisa', wrote Jackson in 1862, 'is mild, damp and relaxing, and has a tendency to depress vital energies, and as such must be baneful in its effects upon consumptive patients.'[34] Bennet was quite forthright in his denunciation of the old school:

Phthisis is essentially a disease of debility . . . In such a disease . . . a bracing, stimulating climate . . . must be beneficial . . . As long as pulmonary consumption was considered a species of inflammatory disease of the lungs, a warm and rather moist winter climate was considered right for consumptive sufferers. But now the more enlightened members of the medical profession know that tubercular disease of the lungs is in reality a malady of the blood and digestive system, a disease of lowered general vitality, and that death can only be avoided by the renovation of the general health.[35]

Lindsay summed up the new mode of treatment in 1890, when he wrote: 'In consumption we naturally select tonic climates as a general rule of climatic treatment, and fall back upon the relaxing class only when the former are for some reason inadmissible, the keynote to treatment being the improvement of nutrition.'[36]

This revision in professional opinion was responsible for the revived popularity of the tonic climates of the Riviera from the 1860s,

---

[31] Thomas Henry Burgess, *The Climate of Italy in Relation to Pulmonary Consumption*, (1852), 148.   [32] Taylor, *Wanderings in Search of Health*, 64.

[33] Burgess, *The Climate of Italy*, 167.

[34] Jackson, *Medical Climatology*, 398.

[35] Bennet, *Winter and Spring*, 154, 207.

[36] Lindsay, *Climatic Treatment*, 47.

and the burgeoning of new resorts such as Menton, Bordighera, and San Remo. Menton was Bennet's own discovery. A consumptive himself, he resigned his medical duties in London and, in his own words, 'departed southwards, in the autumn of the year 1859, to die in a quiet corner . . . like a wounded denizen of the forest'. He lighted on Menton, then a small Italian town of a few thousand inhabitants, 'and under its genial sky, freed from the anxieties and labours of former life', began to rally, and then to thrive. He made Menton his permanent winter residence, attracted invalids by singing its praises in the successive editions and German translation of his *Winter and Spring on the Shores of the Mediterranean*, and built up an extremely lucrative professional practice. Among the better known consumptives who came to this resort were John Richard Green, Robert Louis Stevenson, and Aubrey Beardsley. Rome, Naples, and Pisa were all abandoned by this class of invalid, though Rome was still occasionally recommended for other chronic diseases and some functional disorders, such as throat and bronchial affections, Bright's Disease, diabetes, gout, and rheumatism.

It is not difficult to understand the popularity of medical climatology in the Victorian and Edwardian eras. It is well attested that belief in alternative treatments flourishes in times of medical impasse and low morale, and in chronic endemic diseases such as bronchitis and pulmonary consumption Victorian and Edwardian doctors confronted infections that defied the traditional methods of prophylaxis (vaccination) and cure (drugs). 'We want lights!' exclaimed Dr Scully to Elizabeth Barrett in the early 1840s;[37] and half a century later, the lights of Pasteur and Koch notwithstanding, orthodox medicine was still as helpless. The discovery of the micro-organic nature of infection had no such immediate repercussions in medicine as it had in surgery, because the search for new vaccines failed (save in the case of rabies) and no known drug had the power of destroying hostile micro-organisms once they had entered the body. 'No medical agent', admitted Coupland Taylor in 1890, 'whether taken internally or locally applied . . . by inhalation or other means, has been proved to have any specific power over the bacilli in diminishing their numbers.'[38] The discovery of those agents, the antibiotics penicillin, streptomycin, and the sulphonamides, was still over half a century

[37] Miller, ed., *Elizabeth Barrett to Miss Mitford*, 210.
[38] Taylor, *Wanderings in Search of Health*, 65.

away; and pending their arrival it was understandable that medicine should forswear pharmaceutical methods and revert to nature-therapy.

6. HIDDEN MOTIVES

Pilgrimage, culture, and health were part of the special language of Victorian and Edwardian travellers; and the function of this, as of all languages, was dissemblance as well as elucidation. The fact is that pilgrimage, culture, and health were sometimes not motives but either rationalisations of motives that were less easily defined or excuses for motives that were less readily admitted. Beyond the commonplaces there is an elusive residuum of explanation for the lure of the South.

Various writers diagnosed the annual exodus from England as a symptom of a restlessness, of a perpetual desire to be somewhere else, that was peculiar to the British; and this they attributed to special environmental and historical circumstances. Gautier, for example, suggested that the propensity of the British to wander was a result of the insular isolation of their homeland. When he visited the fortified isthmus of Cadiz in 1840 he found that awareness of being enclosed by ramparts and by the sea aroused an urge to retreat to the mainland, and he deduced that this must be the urge that was constantly impelling the British towards the Continent: 'Il me semble que la seule pensée que puissent nourrir des insulaires, c'est d'aller sur le continent.'[1] The claustrophobia experienced by the British as soon as war cut them off from Europe seems to support this idea. E. M. Forster wrote in 1915 that England seemed 'tighter and tinier than ever ... almost insistently an island', and he added: 'There are times when one longs to sprawl over continents, as formerly.'[2] The novelist and social critic William Mallock, betraying a touch of the world-weariness that he had himself so deftly satirised in his portrait of Pater in *The New Republic*, diagnosed the compulsion to travel as the malaise of a rich and sophisticated society: the craving of jaded palettes for exotic peppers, condiments, and fruits out of season.[3]

[1] Gautier, *Voyage en Espagne*, 349.
[2] Furbank, *E. M. Forster*, ii. 18.
[3] Mallock, *Enchanted Island*, 2–3.

This was certainly an element in the psychology of travellers who
were in the true sense of the word explorers—figures like Sir John
Gardner Wilkinson, whose wanderings in Dalmatia, Montenegro, and
Hercegovina in the 1840s took him to places where an Englishman had
never before been seen, and Gertrude Bell, whose pre-war excursions
in Palestine, Syria, and Asia Minor were described with poetic
perception and diaphanous prose in *The Desert and the Sown* and
Amurath to Amurath. It counted too among the motives of late
Victorians and Edwardians who were sentimental travellers in the
manner of Sterne; travellers who roamed with no object save the
pleasure of serendipity and the delectation of *genius loci*, loving, as
Mallock put it, 'change for the sake of change, taking it into their
system as a smoker inhales smoke, and finding it exhilarate them like a
kind of spiritual haschish'. Mallock himself in Cyprus, Somerset
Maugham in Andalusia, and Maurice Hewlet, D. H. Lawrence, and
Norman Douglas in Italy, resisting the tyranny of the dead and the
sclerosis of scholarship, turned away from museums, galleries,
monuments, and ruins either to observe the living or to make contact
with uncontaminated nature; while John Addington Symonds sought
the culture of Italy less for its own sake than for its human
associations. 'One cannot help thinking', he once wrote, 'that too
much fuss is made nowadays about works of art—running after them
for their own sakes, exaggerating their importance, and detaching
them as objects of study, instead of taking them with sympathy and
carelessness as pleasant or instructive adjuncts to our actual life.[4]
Even George Gissing, whose interests were primarily Classical and
who lived and travelled rough more from necessity than from choice,
rhapsodised about 'dim little *trattorie* in city byways, inns smelling of
the sun in forgotten valleys'.[5]

In the late Victorian and Edwardian years, after the railways had
been completed and before the automobile had invaded, a number of
travellers abandoned the anonymous, cosmopolitan haunts of the
tourists and connoisseurs for the deserted roads, neglected country
towns, and rural monasteries of Italy and southern Spain. The young
composer Ethyl Smyth set out in the spring of 1884 to walk from
Florence through the Casentino and across the Apennines into the
Romagna, with no luggage but 'a camel's hair Salzburg cape, a comb

---

[4] J. A. Symonds, *Italian Byways* (1883), 118.
[5] George Gissing, *The Private Papers of Henry Ryecroft* (1903), 208.

and a toothbrush, a tiny bit of soap, an iron-shod stick, an Ordnance map and a revolver'.[6] In 1901 Hilaire Belloc walked from Milan to Rome—the last stage of a 400-mile journey from his birthplace in France to the Eternal City. Three years later the novelist Maurice Hewlett published *The Road in Tuscany*, a celebration of the delights of travelling *al fresco* in Italy, with perception liberated from the upper and nether millstones of timetables and guidebooks. 'The railways, the love of towns, and the worship of art', Hewlett claimed, 'have worked together in a vicious circle which has become like a whipcord around the neck of the intelligent traveller.' Boldly defying Ruskin, Baedeker, and Berenson, he deposed art and promoted the people of Italy to the first place in his affections. 'He saw the museum,' he wrote of Baedeker, 'but I saw the *custode* of it, a very noble priest. He saw the fresco, but I saw its poor patient proprietress. He saw the inn and said it was a good one. So it is; but I saw the innkeeper's pretty daughter, and was witness to the unuttered, unutterable passion of the waiter for her.'[7]

Somerset Maugham displayed the same susceptibilities in *The Land of the Blessed Virgin*, a travel book on Andalusia which he published in 1905; and the historian George Macaulay Trevelyan, who visited Italy in 1906, 1907, and 1910 to research the campaigns of the Risorgimento, chose to follow the routes of the historic marches on foot and on a bicycle. In 1910 he cycled round the whole of Sicily and down through Calabria to the Straits of Messina, recognising and admiring in the countrypeople the robust and simple virtues that he venerated in Garibaldi. 'I have walked along the whole route traversed by Garibaldi's columns from the gate of Rome to Cesenatico on the Adriatic', he wrote,

and have visted the scenes of his adventures near Comacchio and Ravenna . . . This has taught me what cannot be clearly learnt from the pages of Ruskin or Symonds, or any other of Italy's melodious mourners, that she is not dead, but risen, that she contains not only ruins but men, that she is not the home of ghosts but that land which the living share with their immortal ancestors.[8]

More easily defined, but less willingly divulged, were the motives of social conformity and moral dissidence. It was a symptom of the

---

[6] Ethel Smyth, *Impressions that Remained* (1919), 338.

[7] Maurice Hewlett, *The Road in Tuscany* (1904), i. 11–19, 303–5; ii. 69.

[8] G. M. Trevelyan, *Garibaldi's Defence of the Roman Republic* (omnibus edn., 1933), 5; *Garibaldi and the Making of Italy* (omnibus edn., 1933), 139; Mary Moorman, *G. M. Trevelyan: A Memoir* (1980), 102–8.

ambiguity (or hypocrisy, perhaps) of Victorian educated opinion that it could condone neither of these attitudes. The idea of conformity was offensive to a society that venerated liberty, originality, individualism, and private judgement (hence much indignation when Mill dared to suggest, in *On Liberty*, that Britain was threatened by paralysing custom and tyrannical public opinion); while dissidence was reprehensible because it challenged the equally cherished notions of fixed moral categories and peremptory duty (hence the sense of outrage that followed the publication of Swinburne's *Poems and Ballads* in 1866). Yet it was likewise part of the ambiguity of British travel to the South that it signified both social conformity and moral dissidence. Anthony Trollope acknowledged the power of convention when he wrote in 1866 of families who went abroad because it was the thing to do. 'The spirit that instigates them to roam abroad', he insisted, 'is no hankering after fashion ... It is not fashion that they seek, nor is it chiefly amusement ... But it is the thing to do. Not to have seen Florence, Rome, Munich or Dresden, not to have ridden over the Gemmi or to have talked with Alpine climbers at Zermatt, is to be behind the world.'[9] Other observers were equally convinced of a hedonistic and snobbish motivation for travel, and they reproved British society abroad as a shameless parade of Vanity Fair. 'Persons coming abroad', wrote Dr William Farr of Nice in 1841, 'have commonly two motives, an avowed one and a concealed one. The avowed one is health—the concealed one pleasure.'[10] William Chambers made much the same comment in 1870. 'Fashion, *ennui* and love of gaiety', he noted, 'seem to send quite as many abroad as absolutely bad health.'[11]

There can be no doubt that these were valid appraisals. Like Bath, Cheltenham, Tunbridge Wells, and Brighton in the eighteenth century, the Mediterranean sanatoria attracted invalids of wealth and rank, only to acquire a second identity as centres of high society and dissipation. Visitors motivated by snobbery and a thirst for recreation followed where those in search of recuperation had led. This was the case with Rome between the 1820s and the 1860s ('Rome', said Elizabeth Browning in 1859, 'is like a watering place—like a Cheltenham'),[12] and with Naples, Cairo, and the Riviera between the 1870s and

[9] Trollope, *Travelling Sketches*, 7–8.
[10] William Farr, *A Medical Guide to Nice* (1841), 5.
[11] Chambers, *Wintering at Mentone*, 48.
[12] Huxley, ed., *E. B. Browning's Letters*, 305.

the First World War. 'Of late years', wrote Eustace Reynolds Ball in 1888, 'Cannes has come to be frequented by visitors who, liking to be fashionable, consider it the correct thing to spend a winter [there] ...The plutocratic element is more prominent than formerly.'[13] In the 1890s Thomas Cook & Son were openly bidding for this sort of custom by advertising Cairo as 'the chosen winter playground of the whole fashionable world'.[14] One of the most egregious snobs among British travellers of the nineteenth century was the Eton schoolmaster and Cambridge don Oscar Browning, a camp-follower of the aristocracy who might have strayed from the pages of Proust. Browning was of the tribe who do very little, but who go everywhere and know everybody. He visited Rome thirteen times between 1862 and 1871, usually with a gilded youth in tow, never without a dress suit in his baggage and always liberally provided with crested letters of introduction. 'I had made the acquaintance of Mr Layard, afterwards Sir Henry Layard, then Under-Secretary for Foreign Affairs', he explained. 'Layard conceived an interest in me and arranged that, when I went abroad, I should furnish him with a list of those places which I intended to visit, and he would send me Foreign Office introductions to Ambassadors and other officials who might assist me in my objects. In this manner I became a constant and, I hope, not an unwelcome guest in most of the chanceries of Europe.' In Rome, he claimed intimacy with the great. 'I must at that time', he boasted, 'have known nearly every one in Rome worth knowing.'[15] He embellished his memoirs with the names of important people—a compliment which the important people did not, alas, so readily return.

By the end of the nineteenth century Naples had become the foremost Italian city of fun: a warm and wicked place which was, to quote Macmillan's *Guide to the Western Mediterranean*, 'a delightful winter residence for those fond of pleasure and gaiety'. The San Carlo Opera, the theatres, concerts, and Anglo–American hospitality ensured that 'a few weeks' stay in this lively capital [was] a good cure for *ennui*'. Other delectations, not specified in the guidebooks, attracted homosexual predators like Lord Ronald Gower and Oscar Wilde. 'It is not for pleasure that I come here,' wrote Wilde mischievously from Naples in 1897, 'though pleasure, I am glad to say,

[13] Ball, *Mediterranean Winter Resorts*, 20.
[14] *Cook's International Tickets to Egypt* (prospectus, 1898–9), 3.
[15] O. Browning, *Memories*, 84, 144.

walks all round.'[16] On the Riviera revelry was less innocent. It had the mind of big business and the face of cosmopolitan sophistication. Here even the Carnival was, in the words of Macmillan's *Guide*, 'more a huge advertising speculation than a purely popular festival'. The acquisition in 1862 of the concession for the Casino of Monte Carlo by François and Louis Blanc, the highly successful concessionaires of roulette and *trente et quarante* at Wiesbaden and Homburg, inaugurated the large-scale commercialisation of pleasure in the South of France and stimulated wealthy debauchery to rank profusion. 'The larger number of winter visitors', wrote Dr Edward Sparks in 1879, 'come not for health but for pleasure, which, in other words, means gambling at Monte Carlo or playing baccarat at the clubs on the Promenade des Anglais.'[17] Dr Burney Yeo, writing in 1882, described Nice as a kind of Paris-sur-Mer. 'When you descend at the railway station,' he complained, 'especially if you arrive by one of the evening trains which go on to Monte Carlo, you find yourself surrounded by faces and costumes which irresistibly recall ... the Boulevard des Italiens at one o'clock in the morning.'[18] The Casino acted like a magnet on British travellers of every description. Those with a taste for excitement and high living, like Arnold Bennett and Arthur Balfour, tried their luck at the gaming tables. Those who enjoyed being shocked, like Charles Spurgeon and Hugh Price Hughes, relished the atmosphere of depravity and damnation, and set their pulpit talents to work on the nightmare faces, feverish gestures, painted women, spectacular losses, and hushed-up suicides. Spurgeon called Monaco 'The Serpent in Paradise'. Hughes titillated his Methodist readers with glimpses of upper-class iniquity. 'The incredible follies and vices of our countrymen at Monte Carlo', he declaimed in 1901, 'are enough to account for the contempt with which many of the best people in Continental countries now regard us. You must see the imbecilities of rich English people at Monte Carlo to understand what I am too distressed and ashamed to describe.'[19] The most prominent partaker of the pleasures of the Riviera was Edward, Prince of Wales. In the 1880s and 1890s the restaurateurs, pimps, and gaminghouse-keepers of Cannes grew rich on the recreations of this overweight satyr and his retinue of ennobled plutocrats.

[16] Rupert Hart Davis, ed., *The Letters of Oscar Wilde* (1962), 647.
[17] Sparks, *The Riviera*, 254.
[18] Yeo, *Health Resorts*, 291.
[19] Hughes, *The Morning Lands of History*, 333.

An explanation for permanent expatriation was suggested by the American George Stillman Hillard in 1874, when he wrote that one of the aspects of their own country which drove the British abroad was 'the grim exclusiveness of its society'.[20] Dr Edwin Lee had said much the same in 1861, when he specified 'the more easy and unrestricted tone of society' as one of the main attractions of the Continent.[21] The ostracised and the outrageous always figured among the Anglo-Saxon exiles in the South, and it could be argued that Victorian polite society was able to cherish its conventions and proprieties because it was able to decant its subversive elements abroad. The sadistic and the hyper-energetic went to India and the colonies; the rakish, the rebellious, and the eccentric went to the south of Europe. From the time of Byron to that of Oscar Wilde the outlawed, the unfrocked, and the black-balled made their way to Italy—Shelley's 'Paradise of exiles'. Newman wrote from Naples in 1833 of 'the wealthy English adulterers who are the attraction of the place'.[22] Richard Monckton Milnes, in Rome in 1843, found 'all sorts of blackguards and blackguardesses from London rolling about in the Borghese'.[23] Expatriate society in Florence was renowned for its tolerance of sexual solecisms and dubious principles. In *Nicholas Nickleby* Florence is the refuge of the four shady stockbrokers who involve Mr Nickleby in financial ruin; and in 1853 Robert Bulwer Lytton described it as 'a horrid scandalous place' where people did everything with impunity 'except read the Bible'.[24] Tradition has it, plausibly enough, that Florence was one of the destinations of fugitive homosexuals after the arrest of Oscar Wilde. Another was Capri, where there was a small international homosexual colony. Eloping heterosexual couples often ended up in Italy. The best known are Elizabeth Barrett and Robert Browning, who made their legendary flight from Wimpole Street in 1846 and settled first at Pisa and subsequently at Florence. Another was Lady Eleanor Butler, who as Lady Lismore had eloped with an officer of the Guards. When the painter Cato Lowes Dickinson met her at Sorrento in 1851 she was living the life of a wealthy divorcée in the sun, with a villa overlooking Naples and a handsome yacht riding at anchor in the Bay.

[20] Hillard, *Six Months in Italy*, i. 85.
[21] Lee, *Bradshaw's Invalid's Companion*, 406.
[22] Kerr and Gornall, eds., *Letters and Diaries of J. H. Newman*, iii. 298.
[23] Reid, *Richard Monckton Milnes*, i. 291.
[24] B. Balfour, ed., *Personal and Literary Letters of Robert, First Earl of Lytton* (1906), i. 38.

Rubbing shoulders with the moral exiles in the expatriate colonies of the South were the eccentrics: oversize personalities whose voices, gestures, and passions required high ceilings, strong light, and stupendous views. Walter Savage Landor, whose oddity bordered on insanity and who lived and wrote in a perpetual chaos of quarrels, litigation, eviction, and prudential flits, was in Florence from 1818 until 1835 and then again from 1858 until his death in 1864. He spellbound visitors and upset the authorities with his caustic diatribes, scintillating recollections, and freakish behaviour, and in 1859 became the central figure in a domestic melodrama when his wife, finally exasperated beyond endurance by his senile excesses, turned him out by physical force and left him wandering wild and Lear-like on the dusty highway. He was found and rescued by the Brownings, and the story goes that he repaid their hospitality by throwing one of their dinners out of the window. In 1847 the Casa Standish in Florence was leased by the novelist Charles Lever, an Irish Protestant who, with truly Hibernian volatility, interspersed furious activity and boisterous good humour with spells of somnolent lethargy and ugly fanaticism. When he first appeared on the Cascine in Florence, with his piebald horses and swarm of children, he was taken for a circus proprietor; and this was appropriate, because it was as resident impresario that he served the expatriate colonies in Florence and Bagni di Lucca during the next twenty years—the life and soul of every party, save on those rare occasions when he was obliged to be absent at Spezia in his official capacity as British Vice-Consul. The 1840s and 1850s were the years, too, when Mrs Stisted resided at Lucca. 'She was', wrote Thomas Trollope, 'one of the queerest people my roving life has ever made me acquainted with.'[25] She bullied the Duke of Lucca, carried her own crimson chair to receptions and soirées, posed with a harp that she could not play and, when her husband died in Rome, had his remains sent back to Lucca in a closed carriage that was labelled for customs purposes as *bona fide roba usata* ('genuine second-hand goods'). Lever depicted her as Mrs Ricketts in his novel *The Daltons*.

The most colourful exile of the next generation was Louise de la Ramée, an ugly spinster from Bury St Edmunds who wrote under the pseudonym 'Ouida' and who established herself as the queen of Victorian popular fiction with sensational novels of romance and high life, like *Held in Bondage*, *Strathmore*, and *Under two Flags*. In 1871 she

[25] T. A. Trollope, *What I Remember* (1888), ii. 137.

swept out of England, infuriated by the ridicule of London society, and sought abroad a more receptive audience for her peculiar talents of self-dramatisation and invective. For twenty-three years Florentine society alternately tittered and fulminated at her delusions of grandeur, her stage-managed receptions, her whiplash insults, and her grotesque passions for eligible men in public life. Her novels *In a Winter City* and *Friendship*, which purported to be *exposés* of Anglo-Saxon society in Florence ('Floralia') created a scandal and made Janet Ross her mortal enemy. In her heyday she drove around in a silk-lined victoria, dressed in expensive creations by Worth, and held bizarre literary salons at the Villa Farinola, where she proclaimed herself the greatest author of all time and guests trod warily in the presence of dozens of canine waifs and strays. In her decline at Viareggio she was a gaunt and shabby recluse, surrounded by yapping dogs, persecuted as a witch, and fighting with belligerent compassion for the welfare of animals and the rights of peasants. Ouida was rivalled if not outdone in preposterousness by her friend Lady Orford, an aristocratic eccentric separated from her husband and ferociously at odds with convention. She chain-smoked, held midnight receptions, dressed in a style thirty years out of date, and kept the English community in awe with her devastating wit and daring worldliness. Small wonder that Harold Acton, remembering his childhood in Florence before the First World War, wrote that the designer Gordon Craig, 'with his flowing hair and velveteen clothes, driving his school, a bevy of Kate Greenaway girls, round the city in a Dickensian stagecoach', seemed part of a recognised tradition.

To Venice, in 1908, came Frederick Rolfe, the whimsical and brilliantly idiosyncratic writer who called himself Baron Corvo. Here he lived until his death from heart failure in 1913, compulsively poisoning his relationships with the English colony and wistfully romanticising his relationships with the gondoliers. Half genius, half fraud, and probably more than half mad, Rolfe had solaced himself for his failure to become a priest by making himself Pope in an autobiographical fantasy called *Hadrian the Seventh*; and in Venice he struggled tirelessly, but in vain, to make a living by writing and win from the literary world the recognition that the Catholic Church had always denied him. The victim partly of incomprehension and indifference but more of his own paranoid delusions, he was reduced to humiliating and exhausting shifts and stratagems in order to keep alive. Homelessness and even starvation constantly menaced him, save during the brief interlude when he sponged an allowance from a gullible patron. Then he sailed the lagoons in a gondola like Cleopatra's barge, gorgeously carved and painted and decked with leopard and panther skins.[26]

Eccentrics of this vintage were rare even in the Anglo-Saxon enclaves of the South; but there were plenty of less flamboyant misfits—men and women who chose to live abroad from what Dickens called 'general unfitness for getting on at home'.[27] One such, Miss Raincock, is mentioned by Marianne North in her memoirs. Miss Raincock lived in Rome because 'she hated the ceremony and conventionality of ordinary English middle-class life'. Abroad she made do with arrangements that were 'delightfully primitive' and divided her time between painting, riding, and breaking in wild ponies for a local horse-dealer. At Lucca in 1883 William Howells met an ancient English couple 'who had lived so long in the region that they had rubbed off everything that was English but their speech', and he commented that they were 'types of a class which [was] numerous all over the Continent, and which seem[ed] thoroughly content with expatriation'.[28] The spiritual casualties of modern life, those classified by Henry James as 'the deposed, the defeated, the disenchanted, the wounded, or even only the bored',[29] often made their way to the South when means and circumstances permitted, and sought solace and seclusion in the sun. It was disenchantment that drove Max Beerbohm, for example, into placid semi-retirement on the Italian Riviera at the age of thirty-eight. In 1910 Max, who as essayist, critic, and caricaturist had played Puck to the *poseurs* of the English Decadence and who was about to find himself labelled, in Holbrook Jackson's book on the Eighteen Nineties, as 'the spirit of urbanity incarnate', decided that he had had enough of 'the chatter and clatter and hustle and guzzle' of literary and fashionable London.[30] He withdrew with his newly married wife, the actress Florence Kahn, to a modest villa

[26] For Landor see John Forster, *The Life of Walter Savage Landor* (1869); for Lever, E. Downey, *Charles Lever: His Life and Letters* (1906); for Ouida, Eileen Bigland, *Ouida, the Passionate Victorian* (1950); for Craig, Harold Acton, *Memoirs of an Aesthete* (1948), 46; for Corvo, Miriam J. Benkovitz, *Frederick Rolfe, Baron Corvo* (1977) and Donald Weeks, *Corvo* (1971).

[27] *Little Dorrit*, Book 2, Ch. VII.

[28] Howells, *Tuscan Cities*, 223.

[29] Henry James, Introduction to 'Browning in Venice', by K. de Kay Bronson: *Cornhill Magazine*, 12 (1902), 149.

[30] David Cecil, *Max: A Biography* (new edn., Boston 1965), 332.

on the outskirts of Rapallo, and lived there for most of the remainder
of his life. Like Elizabeth Barrett Browning and D. H. Lawrence, and
unlike writers of the Bloomsbury type, he decided that he was happier
and more creative out of society than in it. Improbable as it may seem,
Mrs Browning spoke for all three of them. In *Aurora Leigh* she
declared:

> It's sublime
> This perfect solitude of foreign lands!
> To be, as if you had not been till then,
> And were then, simply what you chose to be.

It was not only its eccentrics, rebels, and spiritual casualties that
Victorian polite society deported. It got rid of its paupers in the same
way. Among the middle and upper classes it was a common response
to straitened circumstances to go abroad to retrench; but travellers
whose principal motive was economy did not, as a rule, choose
Mediterranean retreats. Boulogne, Dinan, and Avranches, and
German towns such as Munich, Dresden, Stuttgart, Wiesbaden, and
Frankfurt were the usual destinations of financial casualties, and
expatriate society in these places had the threadbare look associated
with bankrupts, officers on half-pay, penurious spinsters, and families
making do with cut-price gentility. Cheap living was, it is true,
available in the South, and until the middle years of the nineteenth
century towns like Milan, Genoa, Pisa, Siena, and Florence had a
reputation as places where the indigent could live like potentates. 'An
English family of the highest respectability', wrote Benjamin Disraeli
from Italy in 1826, 'may live in Florence with every convenience and
keep a handsome carriage, horses, liveries, etc. for five hundred a
year.'[31] In 1837 William Wordsworth claimed that 'with three hundred
a year a man at Florence might live quite in style, and with eight
hundred like a prince';[32] and Elizabeth Browning said that for three
hundred a year one could live 'much like the Grand Duchess'.[33] (In
London £300 would just about pay a year's rent on a modest house in a
fashionable district. This is what Dickens received for his house in
Devonshire Terrace during his year abroad.) Furthermore this
reputation undoubtedly attracted some hard-up families. The
Milneses lived in Italy—chiefly in Milan—from 1828 until 1835 in

[31] W. F. Monypenny, *The Life of Benjamin Disraeli*, i. (1910), 108.
[32] de Selincourt, ed., *Wordsworth Letters*, ii. 866.
[33] F. G. Kenyon, ed., *The Letters of Elizabeth Barrett Browning* (1897), i. 373.

order to economise. The Trollopes moved to Florence in 1843 for the same purpose; and they were followed in 1847 by the Lever family. But it must be true, generally speaking, that the prospect of economy was only a subsidiary inducement. The cheapness of Italy was never such as to attract people who were not already disposed to go there.

The first reason for this contention is that it was only luxuries that were cheap—palatial residences, carriages, wine, servants, boxes at the opera, and so on. Necessities (other than food) could be very expensive. This was the case, most notably, with fuel for heating—something that British visitors found indispensable during the Mediterranean winter. Effie Ruskin reported from Venice in 1849 that she and John were 'at a dreadful expense for wood'. Each basketful cost half a crown; and rather than use charcoal ('which is unhealthy') they resorted to energetic indoor ball-games in order to keep warm.[34] Alison Cunningham, who kept house for Robert Louis Stevenson's family at Menton in 1863, was scandalised to find that firewood cost fifteen francs a week, with an extra fifteen francs for charcoal in the kitchen.[35] In Rome in the 1860s, according to Charles Weld, large fires (which were 'absolutely necessary if you would be comfortable during a cold winter') had become prohibitively expensive. 'I have known more than one Roman lady', he wrote, 'inhabiting handsome apartments, have recourse for warmth in winter days to cheerless blankets on account of the high price of fuel.'[36]

Secondly, the high cost of travel had to be offset against any economies realised through cheaper living. Samuel Palmer and his wife spent £50 on the single journey from London to Rome in 1838.[37] Ten years later Charles Lever wrote from Florence that it would cost him £100 to go alone to London and back.[38] In 1849 Elizabeth Barrett Browning calculated the price of a round trip to London for herself and her husband at 120 guineas, of which one half represented the cost of transport and the other half the charges for overnight accommodation *en route*, customs dues, and fees for visas.[39] Since the cost of travel was in excess of the savings that could be made in a single season in Italy, net reductions in expenditure could be achieved only by staying

[34] Mary Lutyens, ed., *Effie in Venice* (1965), 84.
[35] A. G. Skinner, ed., *Cummy's Diary* (1926), 69.
[36] Weld, *Last Winter in Rome*, 26–7.
[37] E. Malins, *Samuel Palmer's Italian Honeymoon* (Oxford, 1968), 64.
[38] Downey, *Charles Lever*, i. 284.
[39] Huxley, ed., *E. B. Browning's Letters*, 106.

abroad for a long period—several years, at least. During the second half of the century, when the railways had been built and the unification of Italy had abolished internal customs duties and visa fees, the cost of travel fell quite sharply. By the early 1870s the fare from London to Rome was, depending on route and class of travel, between £8 and £12. But, simultaneously, the cost of living rose. Mrs Browning reported from Florence in 1859 that prices were increasing fast and that carriages were now dearer than in Paris. Their suite in the Casa Guidi, leased in the 1840s, had cost the Browings £26 a year. In 1859 Walter Savage Landor was paying £4. 10s. a month for a modest furnished apartment in Florence.[40] By the 1890s furnished apartments were costing between £10 and £16 a month, and furnished houses between £10 and £20.

Naples was a very dubious prospect for those bent on retrenchment. James Whiteside wrote in 1848 that it was an expensive city, mainly because rents were so high, and that only those who stayed there permanently, and who knew the language and local ways, could hope to live more cheaply than in London.[41] Ruskin found in 1851–2 that living in lodgings in Venice was as expensive as living in Park Street in London;[42] while Rome, cheap in the early 1830s, became notoriously expensive from the 1840s. 'At Rome', reported Dickens in 1845, 'the English live in dirty little fourth, fifth and sixth floors, with not one room as large as your own drawing room, and pay, commonly, seven or eight pounds a week.'[43] Richard Digby Best had to pay £260 for a seven-month lease on the first floor of the Palazzo Albani in 1857;[44] and Robert Browning confirmed in 1858 that rents in Rome were prohibitive. He and Elizabeth, as a special favour, were charged £11 a month for rooms which at current rates were worth £16 to £17.[45] The high cost of provisions caused Murray's *Handbook* to warn its readers in 1872 that Rome was 'now as expensive as any city in Europe'.

The Riviera was a preserve of the rich throughout the nineteenth century; a place where it never cost less and often cost appreciably more to live in a style comparable to that enjoyed at home. At Nice furnished houses were being let for as much as £300 a year in the 1840s,

[40] Kenyon, ed., *Letters of E. B. Browning*, ii. 353.
[41] Whiteside, *Italy in the Nineteenth Century*, 418.
[42] J. L. Bradley, ed., *Ruskin's Letters from Venice* (New Haven, 1955), 5, 15, 22, 139.
[43] Tillotson, ed., *Letters of Charles Dickens*, iv. 268.
[44] John Richard Digby Best, *Nowadays* (1870), i. 283.
[45] Kenyon, ed., *Letters of E. B. Browning*, ii. 353.

and by the 1870s superior villas were fetching £1,000 for the seven-month season. High prices, which were rising higher year by year, were facts of life all along the Côte d'Azur. Villas were on offer at £1,200 for the season at Cannes in the 1880s, and the cost of essentials and services was in proportion. 'I think everyone who is sent there', cautioned Dr Edward Sparks in 1879, 'should, if not in really good circumstances,be warned that living in the South is an expensive thing';[46] and Anne Buckland confirmed in 1884 that 'the wealthy only [could] afford to seek health in the genial climate of the Riviera'.[47]

[46] Sparks, *The Riviera*, 162.
[47] Buckland, *Beyond the Esterelles*, i. 37, 46, 109.

PART THREE

EXPERIENCE AND ATTITUDE

THERE are two dimensions to the Victorian–Edwardian response to the Mediterranean. Seen from one angle, it reveals attitudes that were determined by experience. Seen from another, it represents experiences that were determined by attitude. It therefore describes two different things: the world that British travellers discovered, and the world that they invented.

Experience simplified the South. It resolved ambiguities and focused emotion, and so shaped an unequivocal attitude of adoration or of loathing. Experience of life in the Lebanon, for example, destroyed the vision of the Orient that the Edwardian poet James Elroy Flecker had distilled into his own verse and caused a violent reversal of attitude. 'I hate the East', he declared; '... but I have written the best Eastern poems in the language.'[1] Victorian travellers to Italy often fulminated against bards who sang of Southern delights. 'Poets ought to be strangled for all the lies they have told of this country', raged Lady Bulwer Lytton, scratching her mosquito bites and retching from bad smells;[2] and Mabel Sharman Crawford muttered imprecations as she nursed her chilblains in the Florentine winter: 'Oh poets and novel-writers! Great is the responsibility resting on your heads for having fostered the huge illusion which generally prevails with regard to the blessedness of an Italian winter clime ...'[3] On the positive side there is Elizabeth Barrett Browning's attitude to Florence. 'With all its dust, its cobwebs, its spiders even, I love it,' she wrote in 1858, 'and with somewhat of the kind of blind, stupid, respectable, obstinate love which people feel when they talk of "beloved native lands".'[4] Many Victorians and Edwardians wrote or thought like that about a favourite Italian city. Deep affection bound Dickens to Genoa, Gissing to Naples, Ruskin to Verona, Charles Lever to Florence, John Addington Symonds to Venice, and Samuel Butler to Calatafini in Sicily. The lovers of Rome included William Gladstone, Anna Jameson, Charles Eastlake, George Eliot, Mrs Gaskell, and Oscar Wilde. Among British painters, Frederic Leighton and William Richmond found Italy sweeter than home. 'A faithful

[1] James Elroy Flecker, *Some Letters from Abroad* (ed. Hellé Flecker, 1930), 68–9; John Sherwood, *No Golden Journey: A Biography of James Elroy Flecker* (1973), 154–5.
[2] Cited in Brand, *Italy and the English Romantics*, 173.
[3] Crawford, *Life in Tuscany*, 199–200.
[4] Kenyon, ed., *Letters of E. B. Browning*, ii. 285.

lover I return, after six years of longing absence, to the home of my inward heart', declaimed the youthful Leighton on his way to Rome in 1852;[5] and in 1919 the aged Richmond recalled the Italians as 'people with whom I have much more affinity than with my own'.[6] These are only single voices in a murmur of pleasure—isolated handclaps in a torrent of applause; but Italy, for all its popularity, did not monopolise British affection. Hardly a spot along the Mediterranean shores failed to move some Briton to lyrical enthusiasm.

Four sorts of experience shaped British attitudes to the South. First there was the purely physical experience of squalor, discomfort, and inconvenience. Tourist literature is full of complaints about weather, food, dirt, and the absence of home comforts. Victorian travellers disliked unperforated postage stamps and twenty-four-hour clocks; and for all their schooling in *laissez-faire* economics they were offended by the naked crudities of the market mechanism—haggling, importuning, touting, and extorting. These aspects of life abroad made the traveller sorry he had come. But a different mood was induced by the aesthetic experience of Mediterranean landscape and people, the social experience of the Mediterranean masses, and the sensual experience of Mediterranean sunlight and Mediterranean life. These types of experience did not merely confirm, they recreated and enlarged, the inherited idea of the South as a favoured realm of enchantment and repose. They revealed to the traveller a world that was sometimes unattractively strange, but often entrancingly familiar; they disclosed unsuspected quantities of civility, urbanity, and sobriety; and they suggested the rich possibilities of an existence unencumbered by intellectual burdens and social constraints.

7. THE LIGHT OF RECOGNITION

The South was haunted by a familiar presence. The landscape and the people seemed to greet the traveller like old acquaintances. George Gissing found that 'every spot of ground' in Italy and Greece gave off 'an absolute perfume of reminiscences and associations'. John Addington Symonds, surveying the view from Taormina, wrote: 'Every spot on which the eye can rest is rife with reminiscences.'

---

[5] Emilie Isabel Barrington, *The Life, Letters and Work of Frederic Leighton* (1906), i, 68.
[6] A. M. W. Stirling, *The Richmond Papers* (1926), 425.

Norman Douglas declared that in the Bay of Naples every footstep was 'fraught with memories'. The sense of *déjà vu* was common among British travellers visiting the Mediterranean for the first time. 'Even those who have never been there before', wrote Robert Louis Stevenson, 'feel as if they had been; and everybody goes comparing, and seeking for the familiar, and finding it with such ecstasies of recognition that one would think they were coming home after a weary absence, instead of travelling hourly further abroad.' William Somerset Maugham described the same sensation in identical language, specifying the characteristic effect of Italy as 'more than anything a joyful sense of recognition, a feeling as it were of homecoming'. Arthur Stanley found his first day in Athens, in 1840, 'like a strange dream, every single step being so perfectly familiar'; and his experience was repeated in 1847 by Richard William Church, in whose eyes Athenian localities were at once 'strangely familiar and . . . quite unreal'. In 1846 Fanny Kemble was astonished to find how perfectly she knew St Peter's, in Rome. 'I felt', she wrote, 'as if I had been there a hundred times'; and when Matthew Arnold looked for the first time on the Tuscan landscape, from the Turin–Florence train, he already knew it so accurately that the idea of predestination crossed his mind. The same sense of familiarity followed the traveller further afield, to the Balkans, the Levant, and North Africa. 'I seemed somehow to have seen it all before', wrote Edward Lear of his first experience of Turkish etiquette, at an audience with the Pasha of Monastir in 1848; and Thackeray used the same language to describe his experience of Smyrna and the Levantine ports. 'You may imagine', he assured his readers, 'that you have been in the place before, you seem to know it so well.' Lucie Duff Gordon found on arriving in Cairo in 1862 that everything seemed half remembered, and she wrote home about 'this so new, so beautiful, and yet so familiar life'.[1]

This sense of affinity with the South owed much to the Classical element in their education and their art. 'Even though a man may not

---

[1] Algernon and Ellen Gissing, eds., *Letters of George Gissing to Members of his Family* (1927), 111; J. A. Symonds, *Sketches in Italy and Greece* (2nd edn., 1879), 189; Norman Douglas, *Siren Land* (new edn., 1957), 196; R. L. Stevenson, *Virginibus Puerisque* (new edn., 1900), 132; William Somerset Maugham, *The Land of the Blessed Virgin* (1905), 25; R. E. Prothero, *The Life and Correspondence of Arthur Penrhyn Stanley* (1893), i. 274; Church, ed., *Dean Church*, 77; F. Butler (née Kemble), *A Year of Consolation* (1847), i. 130; Russell, ed., *Letters of Matthew Arnold*, i. 268; Lear, *Journals in Albania*, 57; Thackeray, *Cornhill to Grand Cairo*, 83; Lucie Duff Gordon, *Letters from Egypt* (new edn., ed. Janet Ross, 1902), 25.

have any very great classical enthusiasm,' wrote Frederick Faber in 1841, 'still from his very education he must feel himself pursued all through Greece by an indefinable feeling that "this is Greece", which smoothes every disappointment, slightly increases every pleasure, and throws a general enchantment over the whole journey.' In 1912 Professor James Sully claimed that the Classical education of the British gave them a special kinship with Rome. 'The English wanderer in Rome', he wrote, 'who remembers a decent quantity of his school and college lore will often experience little shocks of recognition which make him feel that he is not far from home.' Travellers who recognised the landscapes of Greece and Italy were seeing them with the eyes of Homer, Thucydides, Herodotus, Virgil, Theocritus, or Livy. Wandering in the hills behind the Cornice road in 1866, Symonds found a well exactly resembling the one described by Theocritus in *Hylas*. 'I recognised this fountain by his verse,' he said, 'just as if he had showed me the very spot.' Vision tutored in the antique school could easily discover the legendary settings in landscapes that had hardly changed in two thousand years. 'Everything', as Symonds wrote, 'fitt[ed] in to complete the reproduction of Greek pastoral life.' To travellers steeped in Classical lore, the scenery of southern France, Italy, and the Peloponnese suggested Arcadia, the Gardens of Armida and Alcinous, and the Gardens of the Hesperides; and the sites of historic battles were well known from the descriptions of Greek historians. Gladstone, John Stuart Mill, Edward Freeman, and J. A. Symonds all explored Syracuse with the aid of Thucydides' account of the Athenian naval siege of 415–413 BC, and Mill wrote that the surroundings of the port were as familiar to him as if he had known them all his life. The young George Curzon and his friends, visiting Greece in 1883, saw a land that had been prefigured in Classical legend and ancient history. 'The Greece we were exploring', wrote Curzon, 'was not in our eyes the Greece of King George . . . so much as the Greece of Homer and Herodotus, of Pericles and Phidias, of Aeschylus and Sophocles, of Aristotle and Plato.' Such travellers could reconstitute the past from fragments and from silence. To George Gissing the desolation of Paestum was overpoweringly evocative; and across the sea in Tunisia James Henry Bennet (in 1874) and Herbert Vivian (in 1897) communed with well-known ghosts amid the ruins of Carthage. 'We thought and talked of the past,' wrote Bennet, 'of Marius sitting on the same spot and musing over the ruins of Carthage, and of poor Dido, whose plaintive speech to Aeneas, destined to deceive her so cruelly and perfidiously, I have for many years repeated to myself.' Vivian wrote of 'plucking cornflowers whose progenitors were trodden by Dido or Hannibal', and of 'dreaming away an afternoon upon the rocks where the lidless eyes of Regulus were exposed to the fierce rays of the African sun'.[2]

Classical sources made people, as well as places, familiar. The arrival in England of the Elgin Marbles in 1806 had revitalised an old debate in the world of professional art concerning the nature of Greek sculpture. Was it real or ideal? Imitation or invention? Were those superb forms a record of vanished perfect humanity, or were they the inward visions of elevated minds? In the eighteenth century, academic opinion, following the teaching of Winckelman and reasoning from a few celebrated fragments (the Medici Venus, the Apollo Belvedere, the Farnese Hercules, and the Dying Gladiator), favoured the idealist interpretation and proposed Phidias (whose works were lost) as its chief exemplar. Blake and Byron had carried this view forward into the nineteenth century; but the Elgin Marbles (sculptures from the Parthenon in Athens, reputedly by Phidias) seemed to betray a naturalistic inspiration and to show Greek art in a new light, as a celebration of sensuous rather than of spiritual beauty. For this reason traditional connoisseurs, anxious to preserve the idealist view of the Periclean Greeks, disputed the authenticity of Elgin's plunder and talked of a decline in Greek art: a decline from the spiritual idealism of the lost works of Phidias to the decadent realism of the Parthenon marbles and the works of Praxiteles. This doctrine was given full exposition in Richard Westmacott's *Handbook of Sculpture* of 1864 and it claimed widespread support in professional circles until Edwardian times.[3]

Few Victorian travellers showed any sympathy for such fastidious discrimination. Most scorned academic prudery and followed instead those poets and critics who accepted the Elgin marbles as Phidian, and Greek statues as portraits of physically perfect beings. 'Who, save nature herself, reality itself, could conceive the form of the Fighting

[2] Bowden, *Frederick Faber*, 111; Sully, *Italian Travel Sketches*, 76; Symonds, *Sketches in Italy and Greece*, 2, 5; Schueller and Peters, eds., *Letters of J. A. Symonds*, i. 428–9; Mineka and Lindley, eds., *The Later Letters of J. S. Mill*, 384; G. N. Curzon, *Leaves from a Viceroy's Notebook* (1926), 368–9; George Gissing, *Letters to Eduard Bertz* (ed. A. C. Young, 1961), 23; Bennet, *Winter and Spring*, 571; Herbert Vivian, *Tunisia and the Modern Barbary Pirates* (1899), 183.

[3] S. A. Larrabee, *English Bards and Grecian Marbles* (1943), 151–60; Frank Turner, *The Greek Heritage in Victorian Britain* (New Haven, 1981), 45–50.

Gladiator, or of the Dying Gladiator, or of the Venus di Milo, or of the Neapolitan Psyche, or of the Praxiteles Faun, or greater than all, of the sublime forms expressed in the Elgin Marbles? These statues, one and all, are portrait statues.'[4] That was written in 1894 by the American sculptress Harriet Hosmer; but the sentiment was common among English travellers, who imbibed it, as did Miss Hosmer, from Keats, Haydon, Hazlitt, Ruskin, and John Gibson, the celebrated Victorian sculptor who lived and worked in Rome. Taught to see life in Greek statues, British travellers looked for Greek statues in life. They scanned the figures in the Mediterranean landscape hoping and expecting to find living equivalents of antique marbles, and their deepest aesthetic instincts were satisfied when they saw fishermen who might have descended from the Parthenon pediment or shopgirls apparently released from an Attic frieze. Gibson was infatuated with the people of the Mediterranean because 'it was among them . . . that the sculptor of the Dying Gladiator, and of the Boy taking a thorn out of his foot, found these statues . . . It was there Praxiteles saw his young faun leaning against the trunk of a tree, and cupid bending his bow. It was among them that the Discobolus of Myron and the same beautiful figure by Naucides were seen in living motion.'[5]

Forms and faces already familiar as statues or mental images were frequently encountered in the South. Gibson wrote of a model called Grazia, a peasant girl from Capua, whose face was startling in its Classical suggestiveness. 'Every part of her face was Greek—her eyes were large and black—her eyebrows black and strong and dropping a little where they met . . . Her mouth with the short upper lip was perfect . . .' In Sorrento, in 1864, the young J. A. Symonds was enraptured by human beings that matched his conception of Hellenic beauty. 'They seem', he wrote, 'to retain some of the old Greek loveliness of shape and dignity of carriage. Girls carrying pitchers on their heads have the neck or bust of a statue, and the young men look like Athletes with deep ardent eyes.' Ouida claimed that in Italy could still be seen faces 'beautiful as the Vatican Hermes''. George Gissing was struck by the ancient Greek appearance of the fishermen of Taranto; Roger Fry by that of the shepherds of the Roman Campagna. Both were reminded of the shapes on a Classic vase. Janet Ross, in 1889, saw a girl 'like a Greek statue' gathering olives at Leucaspide, in

⁴ Harriet Hosmer, *Letters and Memories* (ed. C. Carr, 1913), 333.
⁵ Eastlake, ed., *The Life of John Gibson*, 80.

Apulia; Norman Douglas admired the 'half naked, Praxitelean shapes of men and boys' at work among the olive mills of Sorrento; and to D. H. Lawrence the *bersaglieri* of Lerici, in northern Italy, evoked the double Classical association of Agamemnon's men on the seashore and male caryatids 'with a great weight on their heads, making their brain hard, asleep, stunned'.[6]

The painters George Frederic Watts and Frederic Leighton, both dedicated students of the works of Phidias, recognised physiques worthy of the master among the Arabs of North Africa: Leighton in Algeria, in 1857, where he reckoned he perfected his sense of form; and Watts in Egypt, in the 1880s. Watts had been persuaded that mundane modernity had everywhere erased Phidian perfection. 'The well-dressed gentleman of 1854', he wrote after his second visit to Italy, 'can bear small resemblance to the exquisite of the time of Phidias. The limbs, deprived by the fashion of modern clothing of freedom, and shut off from the action of sun and air, never acquire their natural development, texture or colour.' But on a journey up the Nile in 1887 he too was gratified by the sight of bodies that recalled the models of the Greek masters. The Arab boatmen had torsos reminiscent of antique nudity; and at Luxor, among a team excavating a temple, he saw a beautiful young workman who was 'a very distinctly Greek type ... his clothing knotted and twisted about him into a delightful arrangement of lines, the colour of it not white, but a rich low-toned ivory, and every movement of his limbs ... magnificent'.[7] Another traveller who recognised Greek features among the Mediterranean Arabs was Marianne North, who visited Beirut in 1865. The women there, statuesque and with water-jars poised on their shoulders, reminded her of the Elgin Marbles.[8]

Travellers to Greece itself had high expectations of finding the descendants of Phidian and Praxitelean models. It was with this object that John Stuart Mill 'went about the thronged market place looking at the faces' when he arrived in Corfu in April 1855. Mill managed to see 'very few' with authentic Greek features, but other travellers reported

[6] Ibid., 93; Schueller and Peters, eds., *The Letters of J. A. Symonds*, 439; Ouida, *In Maremma* (1882), 215; George Gissing, *By the Ionian Sea: A Ramble in Southern Italy* (1901), 32; Denys Sutton, ed., *The Letters of Roger Fry* (1972), i. 132; Janet Ross, *The Fourth Generation* (1912), 294; Douglas, *Siren Land*, 19; D. H. Lawrence, *Twilight in Italy* (1914), 76–7.

[7] M. S. Watts, *George Frederic Watts*, i. 149; ii. 67–8.

[8] North, *Further Recollections*, 100–1.

gratifying success in their quest for the antique type. Dr John Davy, who was in the Mediterranean with the army from 1824 until 1835, claimed authoritatively that the Ionian islanders were the descendants of ancient Greeks. 'The antique beauty is common among them', he affirmed; 'they speak the same language, use the same written character, and as far as regards person, may be considered a fine example of a European race.' Lady Grosvenor remarked on the 'antique cast of countenance' of the modern Greeks; the Revd Henry Christmas on their 'classical form and . . . flashing eye'; and Dr James Henry Bennet on 'the old Grecian statuary type' still be to be found in the archipelago. In Patras, in 1850, the Irish poet Aubrey de Vere was dazzled by his Albanian guide, 'who might have supplied a sculptor with a model for Apollo . . . His black piercing eye had that roundness which, in the ancient fresco of the head of Achilles, so marvellously unites the expression of human intellect with the audacious passion of the animal.' On her first visit to Colonna, Mrs Russell Barrington, patron and biographer of Victorian painters, craned her neck as her train pulled in at a local station on the lower slopes of Mount Hymettus, for there, hurrying through the adjacent olive groves, were two superb men, 'more magnificent in form than any statue ever made' and either of whom 'might have sat to Phidias for the Theseus'. The Irish Classical scholar John Mahaffy also played this game of recognition and repudiated the scholars, like Fallmerayer and Finlay, who claimed that the old Greek race had disappeared and been replaced by a mixture of Turks, Albanians, and Slavs. Linguistic evidence alone, he claimed, suggested that the modern Greeks were lineal descendants of the old; and visual evidence gave the suggestion striking corroboration.

Any careful observer will not fail to see through the wilder parts of the Morea types and forms which are equal to those which inspired the old artists. There are still among the shepherd boys splendid lads who would adorn a Greek gymnasium, or excite the praise of all Greece at the Olympic games. There are still maidens fit to carry the sacred basket of Athene.

To the expert eye of the archaeologist it was the details of posture, dress, and ornament that were most remarkably familiar. Charles Fellows, during his expedition into southwestern Asia Minor in 1840, was struck by the similarity between the costume, sandals, jewellery, and hairstyles of the modern Anatolians and those he had seen in Greek sculpture; and in the gestures of modern dancers he recognised 'the attitudes displayed in the fauns and bacchanal figures of the antique'.[9]

It would probably be a mistake to attribute true empathy for the Classics to more than a small minority of travellers. In the preface to his novel *The Last Days of Pompeii* (1834) Lord Lytton described his attempts to resurrect the ancient world for a modern audience as a battle against cultural hiatus and hateful memories of forced labour at school. 'The creed of that departed religion,' he wrote, 'the customs of that past civilisation, present little that is sacred or attractive to our Northern imaginations.' Thackeray, likewise, questioned the sincerity of the Classical enthusiasm of many of his countrymen. He maintained that genuine appreciation was necessarily the perquisite of an erudite few. Greece was an esoteric pleasure. He claimed to speak for his generation when he declared that ten years of Classical education had given a taste like that of castor oil to everything connected with that country.[10] Such comments suggest that many Victorians of the travelling classes were less than profoundly responsive to Classical associations. Nevertheless there was still enough in their cultural diet to create a genuine sensitivity to Southern life and landscape. Those with a knowledge of art had long been familiar with the Italian scenery depicted by Gaspard, Poussin, Claude, and Salvator Rosa and their eighteenth-century English imitators; while Gothic fiction and Romantic poetry had created a widespread taste for the sort of mountain scenery and tinted atmosphere to be found in parts of Italy and Greece. Under such influences tourists thronged the fringes and even the summits of Vesuvius and Etna, and the occasional painter roamed further afield in search of picturesque foregrounds and sublime distances. The most indefatigable of these wandering artists was Edward Lear, who scoured Sicily, the Ionian Islands, Calabria, Corsica, Albania, Crete, and the Levant, filling his portfolio with sketches that recalled the landscapes of the seventeenth- and eighteenth-century masters. One of the most avid connoisseurs of Romantic landscape was John Stuart Mill, who found that his Classical knowledge was unconnected with his intensest delight. 'The

[9] Mineka and Lindley, eds., *Later Letters of J. S. Mill*, 408, 410; Davy, *Ionian Islands and Malta*, i. 19; Grosvenor, *Narrative of a Yacht Voyage*, ii. 161; Christmas, *Shores and Islands*, ii. 250; Bennet, *Winter and Spring*, 314; Aubrey de Vere, *Picturesque Sketches of Greece and Turkey* (1850), i. 53; Barrington, *Frederic Leighton*, i. 229 n.; John Pentland Mahaffy, *Rambles and Studies in Greece* (2nd edn., 1878), 287; Charles Fellows, *An Account of Discoveries in Lycia* (1841), 94, 103, 128, 150.

[10] Thackeray, *Cornhill to Grand Cairo*, 65–7, 76–7.

more than earthly beauty of this country', he wrote after surveying the
Greek landscape from Mount Pentelicus, 'quite takes away from me
all care or feeling about the historical associations.'[11] Visitors to Spain,
North Africa, and the Levant saw much that they could identify from
The Arabian Nights. Lord Lindsay for example, in Cairo in 1836, found
the bazaars 'familiar to the imagination' because 'everything reminded
us of the Arabian Nights and Haroun Al-Raschid'.[12] The same
recollections came to Eliot Warburton, Thackeray, Lucie Duff
Gordon, Janet Ross, William Somerset Maugham, and no doubt many
more whose impressions are not recorded, as they wandered in Cairo,
Smyrna, Beirut, Damascus, and Cordova.

But most important of all in any inventory of this kind is the
Bible. It was knowledge of the Bible, far more than knowledge of
the Classics or pictures or poetry, that was the distinctive cultural
characteristic of the Victorian propertied classes; and in the Mediterranean the Bible was being recalled all the time. This was especially
the case in the Holy Land itself, where the way of life and the
landscape were so reminiscent of Scripture that they stirred the
deepest roots of a traveller's remembrance. 'The first impressions of
childhood are connected with the scenery', wrote Eliot Warburton;
and Frances Power Cobbe referred to 'the thousand tender associations' linking the Bible-bred English with Palestine. The parables of
the New Testament were constantly evoked by the sights and sounds
of the Holy Land. At Nablus, in Samaria, in 1840, Lord Francis
Egerton saw a shepherd going before his sheep, and remembered the
parable in the Gospel of St John. In the 1850s Arthur Stanley watched
the biblical stories come to life. 'The vineyards with their towers I
noticed at Hebron and Bethlehem. On the hills above Bethany, and
still more in the valley of Jehoshaphat, I saw the shepherds herding
their flocks of sheep and goats, white sheep and black sheep inter-
mingled. In the cornfield of Sechem women and children were
carefully picking out the green tares from the wheat . . .' Frances
Power Cobbe in 1858 and Henry Rider Haggard in 1900 both saw
enacted the Parable of the Lost Sheep as recorded by St Luke.[13]

[11] Mineka and Lindley, eds., *Later Letters of J. S. Mill*, 429.
[12] Alexander William Crawford, Lord Lindsay, *Egypt, Edom and the Holy Land* (3rd
edn., 1839), i. 44.
[13] Warburton, *The Crescent and the Cross*, ii. 7; Cobbe, *Life*, i. 234, 241; Lord Frances
Egerton, *Mediterranean Sketches* (1843), 93; Prothero, *Life of Stanley*, i. 456; Haggard,
Winter Pilgrimage, 246.

Such experiences were common in Palestine and Egypt; but they were not confined to the lands immediately associated with Scripture. Knowledge of the Bible gave an air of familiarity to widely scattered areas of the Mediterranean landscape. Cyprus, for example, was redolent of the Old Testament in William Mallock's eyes. Nicosia was 'exactly like a picture of Damascus, the city old in the days of Abraham'; and a peak in the Trodos Mountains had vapours about it 'which were making it smoke like Sinai'. Symonds found his mind 'carried by the force of association to Jerusalem' when he saw the Italian city of Orvieto. 'We could fancy ourselves', he wrote, 'to be standing on Mount Olivet, with the valley of Jehoshaphat between us and the sacred city.' Charles Spurgeon, the Baptist revivalist, reckoned that he saw in the French Riviera an almost exact replica of the Holy Land as it had been in the days of Jesus, and in his Sunday afternoon communion addresses at Menton he used to allude constantly to local features that he recognised from the Bible. The most prominent of these was the olive tree, which always fascinated British travellers because of its Scriptural associations. To Ruskin its grey-green foliage suggested 'the ashes of the Gethsemane agony . . . cast upon it for ever'; and Symonds noted that at the sight of the olive 'we dream of Olivet, or the grave garden of the Agony, and the trees seem always whispering of sacred things'. Spurgeon's son remembered that his father loved the olive trees 'chiefly because they told him of his Lord and Gethsemane'. In 1838 the olives near Florence brought the Hebrew Scriptures to Macaulay's mind, and he looked at them 'with the same sort of feeling with which Washington Irving . . . heard the nightingale for the first time when he came to England after having read descriptions of her in poets from his childhood'. D. H. Lawrence, at Lerici in North Italy in 1913, said that the olive groves constantly reminded him of the New Testament. 'I am always expecting when I go to Tellava for the letters to meet Jesus gossiping with his disciples as he goes along above the sea, under the grey, light trees.'[14]

Discovery, as well as recognition, made the people of the South attractive, because it was human colour, as well as human form, that appealed to the aesthetic sense of British travellers. The Victorians generally admired and envied brown complexions, which struck them

---

[14] Mallock, *Enchanted Island*, 116–17; Symonds, *Sketches in Italy and Greece*, 5, 88; Spurgeon, ed., *Autobiography of C. H. Spurgeon*, iv.4, 206; Ruskin, *The Stones of Venice*, iii, Ch. IV, para. xii; G. O. Trevelyan, *The Life and Letters of Lord Macaulay* (new edn., 1880), ii. 22; H. T. Moore, ed., *The Collected Letters of D. H. Lawrence* (1962), i. 255.

as healthy and sexually attractive; and they avoided exposing themselves to the sun because they feared it, not because they wished to
remain white. 'You can go out in the sun if it is to *do* anything, and if
mind or body are occupied and strung up,' John Stuart Mill assured
his wife Harriet from Corfu; 'but if you *lounge* you are likely to have
fever.' In the Peloponnese in 1858 it was only, as they thought, 'at the
risk of a sunstroke' that William George Clark and his companions took
a picnic lunch on a rock in the middle of a stream. One of the few sun-
tanned heroines in Victorian fiction is Little Dorrit. She returns from
the South with 'the ripening touch of the Italian sun . . . visible upon
her face', and the effect is to make her 'something more womanly'—
more sexually desirable, from the loss of pallid puberty. Clara, the
heroine of William Morris's utopian romance *News From Nowhere*,
envies the beautiful Ellen her tanned complexion. 'Look if I don't
need a little sun on my pasty white skin!' she exclaims. In India in the
1830s Emily Eden had found herself admiring the sepoys for their
brown skins. 'I am convinced', she wrote, 'that brown is the natural
colour for man—black and white are unnatural deviations, and look
shocking. I am quite ashamed of our white skins.' Lucie Duff Gordon
did not have a very high opinion of Miss Eden and judged her 'theatre
burlesque' view of India 'inexpressibly tedious'; nevertheless she
shared her preference for brown people. The Arabs of Egypt, she
explained, were not black, but brown and very beautiful. She watched
the men and boys at work among the green corn, 'the men half naked
and the boys wholly so', and admired their colour, which was 'just like
dark clouded amber, semi-transparent'. Fanny Kemble chanted the
'beauty of form and brilliancy of colouring' among the Italian
peasantry, and admitted 'the great superiority of these Southern
peoples in physical comeliness over our Northern races'. The
adjectives 'bronze' and 'bronze-like' were constantly used as tokens of
admiration. Frances Cobbe remembered the 'broad chests and bronze
limbs nearly bare' of the men of Cairo; Dr James Henry Bennet
described the men of the Greek islands as 'bronzed by the Eastern sun
. . . muscular, hardy and good-looking'. The 'bronzed' fishermen of
Capri were admired by J. R. Green; those of Burano captivated
Horatio Brown. 'Bronzed' limbs and torsos are a recurring feature in
Ouida's descriptions of stalwart Italian peasants. According to André
Gide, Oscar Wilde had a strong preference for Arab youths 'like
bronze statues', and on the Riviera in 1899 he rhapsodised about 'three
lads like bronzes, quite perfect in form'. Gissing searched for a new

metaphor and came up with 'terracotta' for the splendid limbs of the fishermen of Taranto. George Frederic Watts felt a rush of inspiration as he looked on the rich carnal tints of the peasantry in Italy and Egypt, and he deplored the way in which 'the form and colour of flesh' and deteriorated under modern conditions. 'He began', recorded his wife, 'to think the Western complexion was quite a mistake.' Many Victorian painters shared this predilection and Mediterranean models were always sure of employment in London. A number came to Britain in 1870, forced out of Paris by the Franco–Prussian War, and one of these in particular was in heavy demand. This was Alessandro di Marco, an Italian whose colour, according to William Richmond, was 'a kind of bronze-gold'.[15]

This tawny flesh suggested life and health. It was the antithesis of the waxen whiteness of sickness and death. To John Henry Newman the Sicilians and Calabrians were 'very healthy-looking' because of 'their sparkling eyes, brownish skins and red cheeks'. Gissing made the same association: the Calabrians were 'all so healthy . . . even a beggar, crawling on all fours on the pavement, has a ruddy face'. In her portrait of the Sicilian sailor, Daniello, in *In Maremma*, Ouida linked brown colouring with sexual vitality: 'His warm brown cheeks, his brilliant eyes, his elasticity of step, his rapid movements, were all the signs of a perfect health and a dauntless manhood.' To D. H. Lawrence, red-haired, pale, and dying in a long erotic dream, the swarthy complexion of the Italian peasantry likewise spoke of 'heavy health', of 'dark unblemished will' and of 'dark blood': the motive forces of erotic life.[16]

Some travellers, too, discovered an intrinsic beauty in Mediterranean scenery. Holman Hunt reckoned that 'the formation of the country, the spread of the plains, the rise of the hills [and] the lute-like lines of the mounts' made Syria exquisite, and his opinion found endorsement in the understated but deeply felt response of Gertrude

[15] Mineka and Lindley, *Later Letters of J. S. Mill*, 415; William George Clark, *Peloponnesus: Notes of Study and Travel* (1858), 182; Emily Eden, *Letters from India* (1872), i. 128; Gordon, *Letters from Egypt*, 131; Butler, *A Year of Consolation*, ii. 218; Cobbe, *Cities of the Past*, 57; Bennet, *Winter and Spring*, 314; Stephen, ed., *Letters of J. R. Green*, 345; Horatio Brown, *In and About Venice* (1905), 182; André Gide, *Si le grain ne meurt* (Paris, 1926), iii. 125; Davis, ed., *Letters of Oscar Wilde*, 784; Gissing, *By the Ionian Sea*, 32; M. S. Watts, *George Frederic Watts*, i. 149; ii. 68; Stirling, *The Richmond Papers*, 272.

[16] Kerr and Gornall, eds., *Letters and Diaries of J. H. Newman*, iii. 224; Pierre Coustillas, ed., *The Diary of George Gissing* (Hassocks, 1978), 467; Gissing, *By the Ionian Sea*, 117; Moore, ed., *Letters of D. H. Lawrence*, i. 267; D. H. Lawrence, *Twilight in Italy*, 76–7.

Bell. Browning loved to observe the insects and plants of the Italian countryside, and he described them in verse with Pre-Raphaelite minuteness. Ouida, despite her penchant for strong situations and elemental passions, was deeply responsive to the subtlety of light, colour, sound, and smell in the rural hinterlands of Italy, and accumulation of detail gives novels like *Signa* and *In Maremma* a vivid authenticity. John Addington Symonds's daughter Margaret, in her *Days Spent on a Doge's Farm* (1893) wrote with a naturalist's affection of the wild flowers and animals that throve in the fields and dykes of the Lombard plain. But such spontaneous appreciation was rare, even in creative literature. It is conspicuously absent, for example, from Lytton's *The Last Days of Pompeii*, a novel whose landscapes have no more reality than stage scenery, and from George Eliot's *Romola*, which is remarkable for its total lack of feeling for the Tuscan countryside. Generally speaking there was much more of recognition than of discovery in the way the British enjoyed the Southern landscape. With Ruskin, they might have rebuked themselves for 'forgetting nature in art'. What failed to evoke the antique, the biblical, or the well-learnt conventions of the picturesque rarely aroused their enthusiasm. Fanny Trollope probably spoke for the majority when she reproached Italy for 'the unvarying repetitions of its Apennine heights in one region and its unvarying plain in another' and preferred the landscape of Germany because it was 'more picturesque'; and many intellectuals must have agreed with Symonds when he found the neighbourhood of San Remo 'sadly prosaic' because 'the country did not suggest a single Greek idea'. Such judgements make it easy to understand Ouida's lament in *Pascarel*:

Poets of every nation have celebrated the great and the gorgeous scenery of this land that is the native land of every artist . . . but of its sweet, lowly, simple loveliness that lies broadcast on every hillside and under every olive orchard, amongst the iris lilies in the meadows and along the loose lush grasses where the sleepy oxen tread their fragrant path—of these, I say, not one in a thousand wanderers thinks, perhaps not one in ten thousand even knows.[17]

Indifference or hostility was aroused when landscapes failed to match preconceptions derived from art or literature and appeared strange when they should have been familiar. Many travellers to

---

[17] Hunt, *Preraphaelitsm*, ii. 29; H. I. Shapiro, ed., *Ruskin in Italy: Letters to his Parents, 1845* (Oxford, 1972), 164; Symonds, *Sketches in Italy and Greece*, 11; Frances Trollope, *A Visit to Italy*, (1842), ii. 173–4; Ouida, *Pascarel* (1873), ii. 164–5.

Palestine looked for the pastoral vistas of the Psalms, the Prophets, and the Song of Solomon, and registered disappointment and distaste when they failed to find them. 'Pity that truth should dispel so fair an illusion!' was William Beamont's plaintive cry. 'It has become the fashion to despise the scenery of Palestine', complained the Scottish theologian George Adam Smith in 1894. 'The tourist . . . finds the landscape deteriorate almost from the moment he leaves the orange groves of Jaffa . . . The Plain is commonplace, the glens of Samaria only "pretty", the Judaean table land revolting in its stony dryness, and the surroundings of the Lake of Galilee feverish and glaring.' In Greece the experience was similar. Captain Abercromby Trant, who travelled in the Greek islands in the winter of 1830, found that Arcady vanished under leaden skies and left nothing but 'barren rocks against which the foaming waves dashed with fury'. Classical shepherds and shepherdesses became horrible savages, and expectation issued in disappointment. 'Thus at every step a stranger makes in Greece', he sighed, 'the veil of romance is forcibly rent from his eyes.' Lady Elizabeth Grosvenor, surveying the Greek islands from her yacht in 1841, wrote them off as 'rocky, grisly and dismal'; and even John Stuart Mill, who adored Sicily, was pained to discover that the Homeric 'meadows of asphodels' had probably been dreary savannas covered with colourless daffodils, like the plain of Mazzara. 'I much fear' he told his wife, 'the flowery meads of Enna from which Proserpine was carried off were mere wastes like the one I have just crossed . . . There are no meadows properly so called in any southern country.' When the Revd Henry Christmas visited the Greek islands in 1851 he realised the paralysing effect of Northern preconception. 'All Classical preparation fails', he confessed; 'the mind will *not* be excited . . . You might as well play a symphony of Beethoven's to a child and expect admiration, as to look for it in favour of the Greek islands from one accustomed to more northern landscapes . . .' William George Clark, approaching the islands of the Aegean in 1858, tried hard to admire 'these masses of limestone and granite, infinitely varied and always beautiful in form, lit up with splendid sunshine, set in a vast circle of cobalt blue'; but he had to admit defeat because the discrepancy between the reality and the Keatsian vision of 'embowered Cyclades' that had fed his expectation was too strong. 'The sense of abandonment and desolation', he admitted, 'gives one pain . . . We have a vision of our own, and we undo it by a visit.' E. M. Forster felt that same disappointment in Greece in 1903, in both the sunshine and the rain. 'Who would expect visions from a dripping silhouette', he wrote of Cnidus, 'when, time after time, the imagination has dwelt in vain desire amidst sun and blue sky and perfect colonnades, and found in them nothing but colonnades and sky and sun?' In his short story *The Road from Colonus* he used this experience and made the failure of recognition a stimulus to imagination: 'The imagination became creative, taking wings because there was nothing to bid it rise.' But for most British travellers imagination was powerless to mould these intractable landscapes into what expectation demanded. Their satisfaction depended on recognition, and was liable to collapse as soon as recognition faltered.[18]

8. CIVILISATION

'It is the *people* that are the charm of Italy', Harriet Taylor once told John Stuart Mill, adding, 'as they are the curse of England'; and experience of Italy convinced Mill that she was right. 'The nuisance of England is the English',̇ he wrote to her from Pisa in 1855.[1] This judgement was endorsed by a large number of travellers, who found in the South a style of behaviour that enhanced their estimation of society abroad and diminished their estimation of that at home.

They came to the Mediterranean in a misanthropic state of mind, influenced by a cultural climate which was hostile to eighteenth-century optimism and which was shaping a much less generous view of humankind. In particular, it gave 'the people'—the socially inferior majority—a new and ugly identity. When Victorian intellectuals and men of substance talked about 'the people' they had in mind 'the masses'—a depersonalised manifestation of swarming nature. 'The lavish profusion . . . in the natural world appals me', confessed Tennyson; 'from the growths of the tropical forest to the capacity of man to multiply—the torrent of babies.' That shiver of horror vibrates through Victorian literature. Fear of the people no longer seemed

---

[18] Beamont, *Diary of a Journey*, i. 190; G. A. Smith, *The Historical Geography of the Holy Land* (16th edn., 1910), 93; Thomas Abercromby Trant, *Narrative of a Journey Through Greece* (1830), 22–3, 35, 69–70; Grosvenor, *Narrative of a Yacht Voyage*, i. 268; ii. 114; Mineka and Lindley, eds., *Later Letters of J. S. Mill*, 366; Christmas, *Shores and Islands*, ii. 210; Clark, *Peloponnesus*, 22; E. M. Forster, *Abinger Harvest* (new edn., 1946), 170.

---

[1] John Robson, *The Improvement of Mankind: The Social and Political Thoughts of J. S. Mill* (1968), 55; Mineka and Lindley, eds., *Later Letters of J. S. Mill*, 277.

irrational, because science had identified humanity as part of a fearful natural process. The old distinction between the state of nature and the state of society had crumbled away as the idea grew that society itself was subject to nature's laws. Victorian sociologists, led by Herbert Spencer, developed a theory of Social Darwinism whose fundamental premiss was natural selection or 'survival of the fittest', and advocates of eugenics propounded schemes of selective human breeding. Spontaneous fecundity was no longer an assurance of progress. It was a symptom of morbid repletion. 'The degree of fertility', wrote Spencer in 1852, 'is inversely proportionate to the grade of development; ... higher degrees of evolution must be accompanied by lower rates of multiplication.'[2] Deeply impressed by this equation, the fastidious recoiled from the recklessly propagating lower orders. In the novels of George Eliot and George Gissing compassion fights a losing battle with revulsion, and the people become a hideous plethora. Social critics like Mill, William Mallock, Matthew Arnold, and James Fitzjames Stephen wrote of them with feelings ranging from distrust to disgust. William Hale White ('Mark Rutherford') spoke for these and many others when he said: 'It is appalling to reflect what our future will be if the accumulation of population is not checked.'[3]

Victorian misanthropy was fundamentally religious. It was rooted in the distinctive pessimism of the Northern Protestant mind, which conceived mankind as essentially fallen and sinful; and it assumed the guise of science because in the special conditions of Victorian Britain human failures acquired a new and subversive significance. The nineteenth century in Britain was an age of towns, industry, and democracy, and each of these features set specific requirements in terms of human attributes. Towns needed civilised citizens; industry needed disciplined workers; democracy needed educated voters. There was therefore less and less tolerance of such social evils as crime, drink, and ignorance, and an increasing tendency to despise the lower classes for their addiction to them.

Far from being nurseries of civic virtues, Victorian cities were academies of crime and subversion into which the educated and the propertied peered with horror and fear; and crowds, clots within these urban densities, were especially feared as concentrations of evil intent.

---

[2] Herbert Spencer, *An Autobiography* (1904), i. 388.
[3] William Hale White, *The Deliverance of Mark Rutherford* (1893), 65.

British towns had a long history of turbulent crowds; but Victorian gatherings were particularly menacing in that they were often politically motivated. There was a world of difference between the hectic irreverence of eighteenth-century urban riots and the demonstrations of 1831, 1848, 1866, and 1886 in London, Bristol, Birmingham, Leeds, Manchester, Glasgow, and Edinburgh. It was the difference between protests against measures and protests against a system; between affronts to dignity and affronts to power. In the nineteenth century it came to be assumed that a crowd was guilty until proved innocent, and every time one gathered the collective bourgeois heart missed a beat. When the vast crowds attracted by the Great Exhibition in Hyde Park in 1851 proved law-abiding and good-tempered, everyone was moved to self-congratulation. 'I was glad that foreigners should see how completely *order*, *peace* and entire liberty could be combined', wrote Anna Jameson after the opening ceremony in the Crystal Palace.[4] Such comments have often been taken at face value, as evidence of social stability. What they really show is the sense of relief, following contrary expectations.

Drunkenness among the lower classes precluded efficient industry, and efficient industry was now vital to Britain's economic survival. Her wealth was no longer in agriculture; it was in mines and machines. By 1850 only 21 per cent of the working population were earning their living from the land, compared with 40 per cent in industry, mining, and building. And if a religious justification for industry were required, Carlyle had provided it. The Scottish sage reminded the British public of the biblical exhortation to labour and resanctified work as the mystic force that brought cosmos out of chaos. Such sentiments echoed and re-echoed in the propaganda of the Anti-Corn Law League and even found an apotheosis in paint, in Ford Maddox Brown's canvas *Work*, the fruit of thirteen years' painstaking effort.

Drink made men oblivious of this sacred ideal. It put British workers on a par with Carlyle's lazy 'niggers' and sporty aristocrats, alike contemptible in their idleness. It meant fouling up the industrial and scientific economy with rustic debauchery and feudal idiocy, of the type portrayed by Kingsley in *Yeast*. The United Kingdom Alliance, founded in 1853 to outlaw all trade in alcoholic drink, was supported chiefly by industrial manufacturers;[5] but drink as a brutish,

---

[4] Anna Jameson, *Letters to Ottilie von Goethe* (ed. G. H. Needler, Oxford, 1939), 176.
[5] Brian Harrison, *Drink and the Victorians*, (1971), 220.

boorish pleasure in a world demanding purpose and discipline drew down the anger of intellectuals too. 'Beer, gin and *fun*' went together in Matthew Arnold's estimation,[6] and whenever she thought of the swilling multitude George Eliot's heavy features hardened into grim reproval.

Mitigated democracy arrived in 1867, with the grant of the vote to all male householders and most male lodgers living in Parliamentary boroughs. The measure raised cries of alarm from the articulate classes, who had been dreading something like this since the 1830s, when the electoral system had received its first overhaul and de Tocqueville's *Democracy in America* had become a topic of discussion. What most educated Victorians feared was not democracy as such, but democracy in the particular circumstances of Victorian Britain. The masses were not ready, because they were appallingly ignorant. 'I am', said the political journalist Walter Bagehot, 'exceedingly afraid of the ignorant multitude of the new constituencies.'[7] Ignorance was fearful because it meant cultural privation; and this in turn meant incomprehension and hatred of the educated classes. The masses were in a state of cultural schism—a fact noted in 1844 by Engels in *The Condition of the Working Classes in England*, in 1845 by Disraeli in his novel *Sybil*, and in 1878 by Matthew Arnold in a lecture on equality. Arnold reminded his audience 'how often it happens in England that a cultivated person . . . talking to one of the lower classes . . . feels, and cannot but feel, that there is somehow a wall of partition between himself and the other; that they seem to belong to different worlds. Thoughts, feelings, perceptions, susceptibilities, language, manners—everything is different.' This gulf was also Gissing's major theme, and he dramatised its immensity through the sense of exile of the man of culture who finds himself trapped on the wrong side of it. It was the natural reaction of the brutalised to despise the refined; consequently the Victorian intelligentsia foresaw martyrdom as soon as democracy had armed the multitude.

Because the failings of the masses—crime, drunkenness, and ignorance—were understood as sins, the response they generated was a missionary campaign of moral reclamation. The middle and upper classes made a sustained effort to encourage obedience, sobriety, and

---

[6] Matthew Arnold, 'Equality', in Noel Annan, ed., *Selected Essays* (Oxford, 1964), 198, 203.
[7] Walter Bagehot, *The English Constitution* (ed. The Earl of Balfour, Oxford, 1928), 276.

self-improvement among the proletariat. Until the First World War they sponsored a multitude of leagues, societies, associations, and organisations for the reformation of the lower orders, all sheltering under the label 'philanthropy', but all inspired by a philosophy that was much closer to misanthropy.

A prominent aspect of this campaign was a revived interest in Christianity as a means of moral rearmament. Dickens's sardonic comment in *Hard Times* about the Coketown clique who wanted legislation that would make the masses religious 'by main force' was prompted by a real obsession among the ruling classes. In the 1830s the Church of England began, with state encouragement and support, a drive to evangelise the masses. New parishes were delineated and new churches built; and in its original form the Factory Bill of 1843 compelled all factory children to receive three hours' religious instruction a day. It was generally believed that religion and morality were inseparable. 'Wherever you find the absence of religious worship and instruction, there you find vice and evil.' So proclaimed the High-Church Anglican Sir Robert Inglis in a Parliamentary debate on church extension in 1840.[8] Even Victorian intellectuals accepted the equation, and it was widely reaffirmed as the crisis of religious belief intensified. Christian piety became fashionable even as Christian dogma became outmoded.

Since to most intellectuals impiety meant moral failure, they were anxiously alert to the religious state of the masses. In common with most of the propertied classes they read with disquiet the report of the Religious Census of 1851, which indicated 'an alarming number of non-attendants' at places of worship, and which concluded that the recusants were from 'the labouring myriads'.[9] Confronted by such evidence of mass profanity, the intellectuals forgot their secular alternatives and closed ranks with the upper and middle classes behind the banner of Christianity. Agnostics like Frances Power Cobbe, Thomas Huxley, and Henry Sidgwick became meek auxiliaries in the work of proselytisation. The Nonconformists' effort was as unremitting as the Anglicans', and they united to oppose secular education. State education was delayed mainly because state education must mean secular education; and secular education was regarded as worse than none at all. In the Parliamentary debates on the Education Bill of 1839 the examples of France and America were cited to prove that it led to an increase of violent crime. Consequently after the introduction of non-denominational state schools in 1870 there was a renewed effort at spiritual reclamation. The Salvation Army was founded in 1878; and in 1884 Toynbee Hall set the pattern for Christian social settlements in London and the provinces.

To British travellers thus accustomed to think of themselves as a beleaguered minority, worn and nervous from ceaseless watching and missionary effort, the Mediterranean offered a haven and a holiday. Here misanthropy made no sense. Morally, as well as physically, it seemed, humanity was transformed by the sunlight of the South. The behaviour, as well as the appearance, of the Mediterranean people evoked admiration and envy, because it conformed to the style that was so eagerly desired yet so relentlessly elusive at home. In the South the masses were by comparison civilised, sober, and cultured.

The common people of the Mediterranean countries were remarkably urbane. Their civility, tact, and lawfulness put the masses at home to shame. When Edward Lear was in Albania in 1848 he was deeply gratified to find that the Turks never gaped. 'I am satisfied', he wrote, 'that if you chose to take your tea while suspended by your feet from the ceiling, not a word would be said, or a sign of amazement betrayed.' In Cairo, Frances Cobbe felt deliciously unselfconscious as she sauntered through the street alone, observing without, it seemed, being observed. She noted with gratitude that there was 'no intrusive staring at strangers'. In 1874, in Algiers, the painter Frederick Walker found nothing resembling 'the impudent stare and disgusting laugh' that tormented the stranger at home; and Alexander Graham and Henry Ashbee, exploring Tunisia in the 1880s, paid tribute to the instinctive delicacy that put the European traveller at his ease in native cafés. 'There is a decorum, a self-restraint in the Arab very pleasing to contemplate,' they reported; 'no pushing, no prying, no intrusion, no molestation of any kind.' In the mountain villages near Rome the conversation might falter when English strangers entered an *osteria*; but, as the painter Cato Lowes Dickinson discovered, curiosity was pushed no further. 'Save when opportunity offers of showing some act of courtesy, no further notice is taken.' George Henry Lewes, in Barcelona with George Eliot in 1867, liked the Spaniards because they were not inquisitive. 'Even the commonest', he noted, 'look away directly they see you notice their looking at you.'[10]

George Eliot agreed, and added that the Spanish were agreeable also because they showed goodwill without servility. This trait in the Spanish character had appealed strongly to George Borrow, and Ouida recognised and admired it among the Tuscan peasantry. 'Whatever be its other faults,' she wrote of the Tuscan character, 'servility is utterly alien to it.' Here was evidence of the true art of manners—something that often attracted the admiration of Britons in the South. Lady Mary Herbert praised the Spanish for their politeness to each other, which was so different from the 'gruff, boorish intercourse of our own people'; and Arthur Stanley found them 'so thoroughly a nation of gentlemen'. 'Such courtesy!' he exclaimed. 'Such self-respect! Such generosity!' There was no impression of rudeness even when the people *did* stare—as they did at Gladstone, in Sicily, in 1838. 'Their curiosity is peculiar and intensive,' he remarked, 'but it cannot be called rude. Their general manner is courteous, kindly and respectful.' Dickens loved 'the beautiful Italian manners'; and Mary Shelley, revisiting Italy in 1844, felt bound to revise the abusive judgement of the Italians expressed in her husband's letters and poems. Extended acquaintance persuaded her that 'graceful manners—accents modulated by the kindest courtesy—suavity that is all gentleness, and a desire to do more than please, to be useful' were innate among all classes of the country. Mill, likewise, cherished the courtesy, civility, and anxiety to oblige that he found in both the northern Italians and the Sicilians.[11]

When a crowd gathered in the South, it seemed to radiate goodwill. It never became ugly and menacing, like a crowd at home. In *The Last Days of Pompeii* (1834) Lytton inferred 'a wonderful order and unquarrelsome good humour' among the crowds in the ancient amphitheatre, because such was 'now the wont with Italians in such meetings'. Writing from Florence in 1848 Mrs Browning enthused

---

[10] Lear, *Journals in Albania*, 32; Cobbe, *Cities of the Past*, 57; J. G. Marks, *The Life and Letters of Frederick Walker* (1896), 286; Henry Ashbee and Alexander Graham, *Travels in Tunisia* (1887), 65–8; Dickinson, *Letters from Italy*, 79–80; Haight, ed., *Letters of George Eliot*, iv. 340n.

[11] George Borrow, *The Bible in Spain* (Everyman edn., 1906), 185; Ouida, *Signa* (1875), ii. 25; Herbert, *Impressions of Spain*, 130; Prothero, ed., *Letters and Verses of A. P. Stanley*, 121; Foot, ed., *Gladstone Diaries*, ii. 459, 481; Tillotson, ed., *Dickens Letters*, iv. 131–2; Mary Shelley, *Rambles in Germany and Italy* (1844), ii. 106; Mineka and Lindley, eds., *Later Letters of J. S. Mill*, 289, 403.

about 'the most gracious and graceful courtesy and gentleness ... in the thickest of crowds'; and ten years later she was still sounding the same theme. 'Think of the refinement and gentleness and—yes I must call it superiority—of this people,' she exclaimed after the Carnival Ball, 'when no excess, no quarrelling, no rudeness or coarseness can be observed in the course of such wild masked liberty!' Dickens was struck by the unbroken good humour of even 'the commonest men and boys' during the Roman Carnival in 1845—an experience shared a few years later by Cato Dickinson, who remembered how different things were at Greenwich Fair. 'None of the shoving, pushing or rudeness of an English crowd were anywhere observable.' English visitors constantly harped on this difference between crowd behaviour in the South and that in the North. 'How different a thing a crowd is here to an English crowd you must come here to learn', Elizabeth Browning wrote to her sister from Florence in 1847. J. R. Green reported from Rome in 1873 on the decorum of the throng. 'Nobody crowded, nobody squeezed, nobody rushed. We all moved gravely, quietly, as if we were walking in church.' In Ouida's novel *Pascarel* (1873) there is an implicit rebuke for English crowds in the compliments paid to Italian ones. 'The crowd was unoccupied and willing to be amused', we read, 'but not impatient or out of temper, because it was a crowd of Italy.' And again: 'The Italian crowds, though often riotously mirthful, are never rough nor rude.' Canon Isaac Taylor was similarly impressed by the crowds of Cairo. 'You look in vain', he wrote in 1888, 'for any exhibition of the surliness, ruffianism and brutality of Western cities.' In 1889 Gissing warmed to the crowds of Florence and Rome, which he found 'exquisitely courteous, charmingly urbane'. What pleased him most was 'the utter absence of anything resembling English rowdyism, whether male or female ... Nowhere a giggling shopgirl, nowhere a young fellow behaving like a fool or blackguard'.

In the South there was no evidence of the ghoulish bloodlust that made public executions fair-days in London. Dickens watched a guillotining in Rome in 1845 and reported that the crowd was scanty and impassive. In 1850, in Majorca, the Revd Henry Christmas heard that the rare event of an execution would empty the town. 'It is a fact', he reported of a recent execution, 'that not only was there no gathering together of a savage and demoralised mob to witness the dying agonies of a fellow creature, but that incredible multitudes left the city till the execution was over.' What a lesson, he thought, to enlightened England.

In the view of Thomas More Madden even the Spanish bullfight was a civilised pastime in comparison with the sadism of the English prize fight 'and all its attendant evils'. Everywhere, in fact, one found delicacy and refinement. Nowhere was there an equivalent of the bestial residuum that lurked in English cities. George Gaskell, in Algeria in the early 1870s, reckoned that even the poorest Arabs, 'the *pariahs* of Algerian society', were 'in general quieter, more polite, and better behaved than our roughs at home'.[12]

Furthermore there was no sense of hypocrisy about this civility. It was rooted in a genuine respect for life and property. Crimes of the sort familiar at home—violent robbery and theft—were apparently extremely rare. 'There are crimes frequent with us and the French of which they are never guilty', wrote Mary Shelley of the Italians. In Italy there were crimes of passion, and there was plenty of cheating, especially of foreigners; but 'brutal murders committed for filthy lucre' were unknown. Even the *banditti* were 'full of redeeming traits'. In 1833 John Henry Newman had made a similar comment, and blamed the imprudence of the English victims for a recent case of robbery at Paestum. In his view foreign tourists who picnicked on large quantities of silver plate were asking for trouble; and in this instance murder had been the consequence of panic, not of cold-blooded premeditation. These reactions were characteristic in that banditry, for all the sensational éclat of one or two notorious instances, never seems to have weakened the impression that an Englishman's life and property were safer in the Mediterranean than at home. Among the British colonies in Tuscany and on the Riviera the night brought no terrors. 'There have been two murders (properly so-called) since we came, just three years ago,' wrote Mrs Browning from Tuscany in 1849; 'one from jealousy, and one from revenge . . . and the horror on all sides was great, as if the crime were some rare prodigy, which indeed it is in this country.' Thomas Adolphus Trollope, recalling life in Florence in the 1840s, confirmed this idyllic picture. 'The streets were so absolutely safe', he claimed, 'that my lady might have traversed them alone at any hour of the day or night.' The same

---

[12] Kenyon, ed., *Letters of E. B. Browning*, i. 383; ii. 257; Charles Dickens, *Pictures from Italy* (Oxford India Paper edn:, n.d.), 131; Dickinson, *Letters from Italy*, 296; Huxley, ed., *E. B. Browning's Letters to Her Sister*, 145; Stephen, ed., *Letters of J. R. Green*, 353; Taylor, *Egyptian Notebook*, 6; George Gissing, *Letters to Eduard Bertz* (ed. Arthur Young, 1961), 38; Christmas, *Shores and Islands*, i. 94–5; Madden, *On Change of Climate*, 130; George Gaskell, *Algeria As It Is* (1875), 41.

delightful state of affairs was encountered on the Riviera, where the ex-Lord Provost of Edinburgh, William Chambers, after wintering at Menton in 1869–70, reported 'an absence of crime of a serious or, it might be said, of any kind'. Further afield, on the Mediterranean islands, a utopian civility prevailed. In Majorca, according to the Revd Christmas, locks were unknown and highway robberies non-existent; and news of a murder was liable to fill the whole island with consternation. There was no avoiding the conclusion that life and property were 'far more secure in the island of Majorca than even in the island of Great Britain'. The comment in Macmillan's *Guide to the Western Mediterranean* (1901) on the Balearic Islands was: 'One does not see a policeman in any of them.' In Rhodes in the 1850s the archaeologist Charles Newton found travel safe everywhere; in Cyprus, according to the British Consul Robert Lang, brigandage was unknown and unescorted treasure perfectly safe. In Algeria the lower native orders—those who, in the words of George Gaskell, 'like naughty children [knew] no better'—were inclined to pilfer; but professional crime was unknown and 'cases of assault and robbery, such as make the environs of some European cities unsafe after dark' were seldom heard of in the neighbourhood of Algiers. The amount of crime in Cairo was, according to Isaac Taylor, 'extremely small' and the police were 'seldom seen'. In fact there were few places on the Mediterranean itinerary where this sense of contrast was not strong, and where British visitors did not feel relieved of a frightening threat.[13]

Nothing did more to convince the Victorian public of the essential civility of the Mediterranean masses than their behaviour during revolutions. British travellers deeply appreciated the calm and dignified style of the Greek revolts of 1843 and 1862, and the Italians were widely admired for their conduct during the climactic stages of the Risorgimento—the patriotic movement aimed at national unity and liberty. The Risorgimento proposed the abolition of some half-dozen sovereign dynasties and the expulsion of Austria from Lombardy and Venetia; and for this reason the British propertied classes initially regarded it with mixed feelings. In principle they supported the cause of Italian liberty. Cruel despotisms like that of the

---

[13] Shelley, *Rambles*, i, p. ix n.; Kerr and Gornall, eds., *Letters and Diaries of J. H. Newman*, iii. 229; Kenyon ed., *Letters of E. B. Browning*, i. 423–4; Trollope, *What I Remember*, ii. 106, 197; Chambers, *Wintering at Mentone*, 91; Christmas, *Shores and Islands*, i. 75–6; C. T. Newton, *Travels and Discoveries in the Levant* (1865), i. 209–10; R. H. Lang, *Cyprus* (1878), 206; Gaskell, *Algeria*, 43; Taylor, *Egyptian Notebook*, 11.

Bourbon dynasty of Naples and foreign occupations such as that of
Austria affronted some of their most cherished dogmas. But in
practice they mistrusted political subversion and they feared political
violence. The early efforts of the Italian patriots found little support in
Britain because there was always a deep anxiety that revolution might
lead to anarchy. The Italians would sow the wind and reap the
whirlwind, because they had no experience of political freedom. Their
traditions of citizenship had been forgotten during generations of
tyranny. Like over-disciplined children they were capricious and
demoralised, and liable to be wicked as soon as control was relaxed.
British talk was of 'dear Italy' and 'poor Italians'. Their pathetic
condition invited commiseration but forbade encouragement. Italian
unity, wrote Lord Shaftesbury, was a dream that must not be talked of,
'for bloodshed, violence, revolution, massacre, horror and failure at
last' would be the inevitable consequences.[14]

The first crisis of the Risorgimento, in 1848–9, served only to
confirm these misgivings. Even British liberals shook their heads
sorrowfully when the heard of the mob-rule and carnage in the Roman
Republic that was set up in the place of the toppled Papal government;
and those who witnessed the volatile and pusillanimous behaviour of
the revolutionaries in Tuscany smiled wryly and felt, like Mrs
Browning, 'a gentle and affectionate approach to contempt'. 'Poor
Rome! Poor Italy!' she sighed. 'Here there are men only fit for the
Goldoni Theatre, the coffee houses, and the sunny side of the Arno
when the wind's in the north.'[15] Revolt flared up and spluttered out in
Venice, Naples, Milan, and Palermo as the people there proved too
weak to be courageous and too vindictive to be strong; and for ten
years afterwards the Italians' charm and urbanity could never quite
dispel the memory of fickleness and fecklessness.

But in 1859–60 the Italian masses finally proved themselves, in
British estimation, distinguished graduates in patriotism. Their
civility and courage withstood the stringent tests of renewed revolution and war. They now eschewed extremism and anarchy, and
resumed the campaign of unification and liberation with precisely
those methods which the British cherished as the hallmark of their
own Revolution of 1688. They rejected the leadership of the fiery
republican idealist Mazzini for that of the royalist pragmatist Count

---

[14] Hodder, *Shaftesbury*, i. 192.
[15] Kenyon, ed., *Letters of E. B. Browning*, i. 388; Huxley, ed., *E. B. Browning's Letters*,
101, 106.

Cavour; and they forsook ignoble conduct for the phlegmatic fortitude that the English liked to regard as their own special characteristic. 'Every proceeding', commented *The Times* in April 1859, 'has been as reasonable, as orderly, and as little influenced by extravagance and enthusiasm, as if it had been directed by an English churchwarden and modelled upon the proceedings of an English vestry.'[16]

This judgement accorded with eyewitness accounts of the revolts which broke out in Tuscany, Modena, Parma, Rome, and Sicily under cover of the French invasion of northern Italy in 1859. British observers paid glowing tribute to the conduct of the Italian people both on the streets and in the field. Mary Somerville recalled that everything was so quiet and orderly during the revolution in Florence in the spring of 1859 that she and her daughters walked about the town ('as did most ladies') to see what was happening. 'Not a person has been insulted,' she was able to report, 'not a cry was raised against anyone ... No nation ever made such progress as the Tuscans have done since the year '48. Not a word of republicanism—it has never been named.'[17] Austen Layard wrote from Milan in November 1859 that 'no population in the world could have preserved order as the Italians of central Italy [had] done, without a regular government and under every provocation.'[18] The Revd William Arthur watched the victory celebrations in Milan the following year and was 'greatly impressed with the order and good temper' of the crowds. 'Thorough good nature' prevailed. At Bologna, during the first general election for the Italian Parliament, Arthur was deeply impressed by the 'perfect decorum' of the public, which put the British masses to shame. 'It appears certain', he remarked ruefully, 'that in making elections instruments of vice, no people has yet come near to us.' The decorum and urbanity of the festivities marking King Victor Emmanuel's entry into Florence he reckoned were 'almost incredible', given 'the passionate material' of which Italian crowds were made.[19] Elizabeth Browning saw evidence of a 'wonderful ripening' since 1848. 'How admirable have been the constancy, dignity and energy of this people', she exclaimed in October 1859; and a year later she was still buoyant

---

[16] M. B. Urban, *British Opinion and Policy on the Unification of Italy* (Scottdale, 1938), 279–80.

[17] Mary Somerville, *Personal Recollections* (1873), 313, 317–18.

[18] Ross, *The Fourth Generation*, 69.

[19] William Arthur, *Italy in Transition: Public Scenes and Private Opinions in the Spring of 1860* (3rd edn., 1860), 158, 259.

with enthusiasm. 'No people, however educated, could have acted better.'[20]

Mrs Browning still had reservations about the Neapolitans and Sicilians, but few of her countrymen shared them. The bravery and discipline of the Sicilian guerrillas who fought under Garibaldi in his campaign of 1860 commanded the esteem of British observers, and this was recorded with due veneration by George Macaulay Trevelyan in 1910, in *Garibaldi and the Making of Italy*.

When Garibaldi quitted Sicily and invaded the mainland, British tourists and residents in Naples were poised for flight to the British warships at anchor in the Bay; but as the drama unfolded panic seemed so inappropriate that they changed their minds and stayed to enjoy the immensely civilised excitement. An amazing proof of the self-control of the Neapolitans came soon after Garibaldi's arrival. As night descended it was announced that the hero had gone to rest, and instantly the jubilant crowds were silent. W. G. Clark remarked that a stranger might have lived in Naples without knowing that there had been a change of regime, and the only sign of revolution that John Richard Best could discover was the overnight disappearance of the Bourbon fleurs-de-lis from the tops of the lamp-posts.[21]

This admirable reticence redeemed the Risorgimento and it now garnered unqualified if belated congratulation. Frances Power Cobbe called it 'one of the grandest events in modern history'; Mabel Sharman Crawford praised its 'patriotism . . . purified of selfish aims'; and George Meredith celebrated its heroic virtues in *Vittoria*, a novel about the Milanese revolt of 1848. 'My object', he told Swinburne, 'was . . . to represent the revolt itself, with the passions animating both sides, the revival of the fervid Italian blood, and the character of the people.' To the Victorians patriotism was one of the most precious of civic virtues, because it denoted acceptance of the inherited hierarchy of rank and property. In *Hard Times*, Dickens coupled 'patriotism' and 'discontent' as incompatibles, like good and evil, love and hatred. Where the one was found, the other must be absent. Patriotism, it was now clear, existed in Italy; and this pointed an enviable contrast with Britain, where discontent was rife.[22]

---

[20] P. N. Heydon and Philip Kelley, eds., *Elizabeth Barrett Browning's Letters to Mrs David Ogilvie* (1974), 145, 158.

[21] W. G. Clark, 'Naples and Garibaldi' in Francis Galton, ed., *Vacation Tours* (1889), 295; Best, *Nowadays*, ii. 207, 219.

[22] Cobbe, *Italics*, 3; Crawford, *Life in Tuscany*, 333; Amy Foster Watson, 'Meredith

If menace was missing from the Mediterranean crowds, so too was the turpitude associated with drink. Travellers who shrank in disgust from the sottish vulgarity of the masses at home warmly approved of the sober pleasures of humble folk in the South. 'A drunkard is scarcely to be found on all the shores of the Mediterranean,' wrote John Aiton after returning from a tour in 1851; 'in Africa, Asia or in Europe eastward of the Straits of Gibraltar, such a man I never saw. But the first object which attracted my notice on my return to Scotland was a drunk porter staggering and vapouring.'[23] Sixty years later another Scot, Norman Douglas, watched the happy yet sober festivities in honour of the Madonna di Pollino, in Calabria, and thought bitterly of the 'drunkard-strewn field of battle' at the close of the Highland Games and of 'God-fearing Glasgow on a Saturday evening'.[24] Few travellers recorded their experiences without comparing the inebriety of the North with the sobriety of the South. The theme inspired something like an obsession, expressed in strong language. Nothing made the British visitor less glad to go home.

Observation in all corners of the Mediterranean confirmed that the meridional races were uncorrupted by the bottle. 'During the many years I have passed in Italy,' wrote Mary Boyle, 'I have never seen above three instances of drunkenness in the streets.' Mrs Browning noted how 'you never [saw] drunkenness nor brutality in any form in the gladness of these Tuscans'; and William Arthur and John Richard Best both remarked that not even the excitement of the victory celebrations in Milan and Naples in 1860 managed to produce public spectacles of intoxication. Lord Shaftesbury in the 1830s and J. R. Green in the 1870s watched the Carnival on the Italian Riviera and sensed no taint of drink in the enjoyment. 'As far as I saw there was nothing but innocence', remarked Shaftesbury; while Green observed that it was a rare thing to see anybody lose his temper and 'a yet rarer thing to see anybody drunk'. Italian delight was never curdled by alcohol or prolonged into tedious nocturnal debauchery. 'The sulky altercations, the tipsy squabbles of Northern amusements are unknown,' wrote Green; 'the Italian . . . doesn't care to spoil the day's amusements by making a night of it. A few hours of laughter satisfy

---

and Italy': *Fortnightly Review*, 105 (1919), 293–302; Dickens, *Hard Times*, Book The First, Ch. 11.

[23] Aiton, *Lands of the Messiah*, 330.
[24] Douglas, *Old Calabria*, 158.

him, and when evening falls and the sunshine goes, he goes with the sunshine.' The lower classes in Spain and Greece were likewise exemplary in their abstemiousness. The Revd Richard Roberts, who visited southern Spain in 1859, admired the sobriety of the peasantry. It was, he remarked, 'a circumstance greatly to their credit that, in all our wanderings through town and country . . . we never saw four men who were in the least intoxicated'. Lord Ronald Gower, in Barcelona in 1881, watched the harmless fun of the Carnival and commented that 'in London such a *festa* would end in fisticuffs, brawling and drunkenness'. John Mahaffy linked the proverbial 'bright intellect' and 'great reasonableness' of the Greeks with their habitual moderation in drink; and Maurice Hewlett, who was in Athens during the Easter Bank Holiday of 1914, observed that there was 'no disorder and nobody drunk'. Others noted the same delightful sobriety among the people of the Mediterranean islands and North Africa. Dr John Hennen, for example, reported of Malta in the 1820s that drunkenness was unknown on public festive occasions, 'unlike England and many parts of the Continent'. Thomasina Campbell, the Victorian *doyenne* of expatriate society in Corsica, compared Corsican with English fairs and commented that in the former there were 'no shows, no booths, no noise, no drunken people, no thimble-rig or Aunt Sally'. George Gaskell wrote that the Arabs of Algeria were 'sober and abstemious, perhaps more so than any other people in the world'; and Frederick Walker confirmed that there were 'no drunkenness and no policemen' in Algiers. Even the most fastidious natures found it difficult to be shocked by the lower classes in the South. George Gissing remarked in 1881 that since arriving in Italy he had not seen a drunken man; and in Calabria in 1897 he was deeply impressed to discover that café conversation was fuelled by 'a tiny cup of coffee or a glass of lemonade', and that the talk sounded refined in consequence. 'I noticed the entire absence of a certain kind of jocoseness which is so naturally associated with spirituous liquors.' Gissing was profoundly grateful for the spontaneous joy of the southern Italians because in their street music he at last heard a voice of the multitude to which he could respond. 'I forgive these people everything,' he said, 'as soon as they make music.' Among the Neapolitan crowds this most lonely of English writers no longer felt alone.[25]

[25] Boyle, *Mary Boyle: Her Book*, 108; Huxley, ed., *E. B. Browning's Letters*, 44; Arthur, *Italy in Transition*, 90; Best, *Nowadays*, 214–15; Hodder, *Shaftesbury*, i. 191; Green, *Stray Studies*, 55; Richard Roberts, *An Autumn Tour in Spain in the Year 1859* (1860), 321; Lord

The inoffensive gaiety of the Mediterranean people suggested childhood in its most endearing aspect. 'There seems to prevail', wrote Dickens of the Roman Carnival, '. . . a feeling of a general, almost childish simplicity and confidence.' Horatio Brown referred to the gondoliers of Venice as 'these children of the lagoons' and said that there was 'a gaiety, a laughter and a light-heartedness' about them that was 'very winning'. 'They are extremely clever and nice children,' wrote Lucie Duff Gordon of the Cairo Arabs, 'easily amused, easily roused in a fury which lasts five minutes and leaves no malice'; and Isaac Taylor likewise referred to them as 'these simple children of the Prophet'. Among such people the British found the same delight that they found in the company of children. They were reminded that joy could be sober and that laughter was not always the voice of the Devil; and so they felt able to relax their stern intolerance of popular revelry. They even began to lament that they had forgotten how to laugh themselves. 'To the colder, graver temperament of Northern climes,' wrote Mabel Crawford in 1859, 'the huge draughts of pleasure that can be swallowed by the impulsive, excitable natures living under Southern skies must prove a subject of surprise; and to some, perhaps, may assume the aspect of a privilege to be envied.'[26]

No less enviable was the absence of class conflict in the South. Here the visitor was spared the painful consciousness of two nations in abrasive contact, such as set the teeth on edge at home. In the Mediterranean social relationships between the classes suggested harmony and easy complaisance. 'The mixture of classes is to me one of the most delicious features of the South', declared Mrs Browning in 1852; and at the Carnival Ball in Florence in 1857 she was delighted to see her manservant Ferdinando unselfconsciously enjoying himself in the same room with the Grand Duke. In Florence in the early 1880s the composer Ethel Smyth discovered among the Italians 'a certain closeness to nature which welds all ranks together at the base'; and in her memoirs she recalled with fondness how 'that greatest of great ladies, Donna Laura Minghetti, treated her butler and was treated by

Ronald Sutherland Gower, *Old Diaries* (1902), 6; Mahaffy, *Rambles and Studies*, 21; Laurence Binyon, ed., *The Letters of Maurice Hewlett* (1926), 282; John Hennen, *Sketches of the Medical Topography of the Mediterranean* (1830), 478; Thomasina Campbell, *Notes on the Island of Corsica* (1868), 138; Gaskell, *Algeria*, 40; Marks, *Frederick Walker*, 286; Gissing, *Letters to Bertz*, 39; *By the Ionian Sea*, 125–6; *Diary*, 456.

[26] Dickens, *Pictures from Italy*, 131; Brown, *In and About Venice*, 33; Gordon, *Letters from Egypt*, 69; Taylor, *Egyptian Notebook*, 11; Crawford, *Life in Tuscany*, 88.

him as an equal at bottom'. Gissing echoed this satisfaction in his travel diary of 1889. In Florence he noted a 'democratic spirit' among the people, which meant that 'the distinctions of the North [did] not exist in anything like the same trenchant way'; and in Venice the impression was reinforced. 'Again', he wrote, 'I feel the democratic nature of Italian society. All the classes blend in the easiest way; and the working girls in their long coloured shawls and bare heads promenade among ladies without a trace of self-consciousness.'[27]

It was common for Victorian and Edwardian travellers to claim this merit of social fellowship for their favourite country. In the view of Lucie Duff Gordon the essential charm of Arab society was in the easy familiarity between social ranks that one recognised from the *Arabian Nights*. 'Great Beys sit with grocers, and carpenters have no hesitation in offering civility to *naas omra* (noble people)', she wrote from Cairo. 'This is what makes Arab society quite unintelligible to most Europeans.' In John Mahaffy's estimation the Greeks were 'the most intensely and thoroughly democratic' people in Europe. 'They will allow no distinction of classes', he explained. 'Every common mule-boy is a gentleman (κύριος) and fully your equal. He sits in the room at meals and joins in the conversation at dinner.' For similar reasons Thomas Trollope advanced the claim of Italy to be considered 'by far the most genuinely democratic country on the face of the earth.' Such spiritual democracy was envied because it implied an absence of lower-class hostility—of what J. R. Green called 'a spirit of envious levelling'. Green noted how the Italian convention of social equality precluded 'the surly incivility with which a Lancashire operative [thought] it proper to show the world that he [was] as good a man as his master'. In other words, it promised to draw the sting of political democracy. In his travel book *The Road in Tuscany* Maurice Hewlett confessed to a sense of gratitude for the cheerful labour of the young milliners whom he used to watch through a window in Arezzo:

That they should live ungrudgingly, not cursing me in their hearts; that they should be able to laugh, hum tunes, nod to the baker's boy from their prison casement high above him; that they should dress themselves prettily and turn about before the glass; that it should be possible to suck juices out of such poor husks and shreds of days, bloom like flowers in unsunned corners of the ground—all this filled me with wonder and thanksgiving.[28]

---

[27] Kenyon, ed., *Letters of E. B. Browning*, ii. 65, 257; Smyth, *Impressions*, 334–5; Coustillas, ed., *Diary of George Gissing*, 123, 128.

[28] Gordon, *Letters from Egypt*, 288; Mahaffy, *Rambles and Studies*, 23; Trollope, *What I Remember*, iii. 327; Green, *Stray Studies*, 55–6; Hewlett, *The Road in Tuscany*, ii. 303.

What they saw in the Mediterranean confirmed many travellers in the view that the fundamental malady of their own society was not economic but cultural disparity. In the South they were confronted by a cultural consanguinity that neutralised the antipathies between class and class. 'It is singular', mused James Whiteside after visiting Florence in the 1840s, 'to find oneself amidst a people all of whom seem to be equally civilised.' In his autobiography Ruskin wrote of the 'companion-people' of Italy because in that country there was no 'commonness'. The people were characterised by 'eager intellect and delicate senses, open to every lesson and every joy of their ancestral art'; and in his last years he acquired an interest in the folk-songs of Tuscany as evidence of a truly communal artistic heritage. J. A. Symonds likewise drew attention to these songs as 'the wild stock of that highly artificial flower of art'; the fruits of an inspiration shared by both Petrarch and the modern peasant. Among the lower classes in Italy the traveller found refinements which in Britain had been monopolised by the rich. It was, as Mary Boyle discovered, a country where waiters would correct quotations from Metastasio and street urchins complete couplets from Dante. 'Picture to yourself', she exclaimed, 'a waiter at a London hotel volunteering to finish for you the last lines of a sonnet by Milton or of a speech by Shakespeare!' Gissing was persuaded that the shopgirls who thronged the galleries in Florence and Rome found genuine pleasure in looking at the pictures, and William Richmond always valued the criticisms of his Italian models. 'Every Italian', he insisted, 'is in some degree an artist. A keen critic and a keen observer, he has initial good sense and instinctive good taste.' Symonds and Hewlett admired the rustic chivalry of the Tuscan peasant; and Ouida, in her novels of Italian life, wrote feelingly of his aristocratic refinement and innate sensibility. 'He will always have some delicate touch of the artist in him,' she wrote in *Pascarel*, 'and always some fine instinct of the gentleman. Let him be poor as he will, ill-clad, half-starved and ignorant even of the letters that make his name ... but he will wear his tatters with a grace; he will bring a flower to a woman with the bow of a king; and he will resent an insolence with an air to which no purple or fine linen could lend dignity.' In Florence the strolling player Pascarel, hearing a cabman expounding Donatello with possessive fondness, reflects: 'It is well—nobly and purely well—with a people when the men amongst it who ply for hire on its public ways think caressingly of a sculptor dead five hundred years ago, and tell such a tale standing idly in the

noonday sun, feeling the beauty and the pathos of it all.' A theme of
Signa, the story of a peasant boy who becomes a famous composer, is
the birth and nurturing of art in the harsh social conditions of the
Italian countryside.[29]

It seemed to many travellers that in Italy almost everyone was an
aristocrat in taste, manners, and speech. They encountered a
prevailing ease and *savoir-faire* that made it difficult, as Mrs Browning
observed, to 'discern the least difference between class and class, from
the Grand Duchess to the *Donna di faccenda*'. The cultural equality
which J. R. Green saw in the South—the 'gentleman-like stamp'
shared by 'the roughest fisher or the commonest *trasteverino*'—set him
pondering on the difference between Swiss or Teutonic democracy,
which implied equality only in the political sense, and Italian
democracy, which implied 'a development of the whole man—
political, intellectual, religious and artistic'. This form of equality was
something that the Italians shared with the Mediterranean people in
general. Frances Cobbe found grace, ease, and dignity among even the
poor of Cairo; Herbert Vivian noted a 'nobility of expression' and
'majesty of gait' among the ragged Arabs of Tunisia; Benjamin
Disraeli revered the nobility of the Spanish. It appeared that only in
the North was 'commonness' the perquisite of the mass; that, in the
words of Frances Cobbe, 'only to us ... were it possible to be
awkward, mean in countenance, and vulgar in demeanour'.[30]

Various explanations were offered for the admirable human
qualities found in the Mediterranean. Some travellers cited vague
racial influences. For example Disraeli, in *Contarini Fleming*, attributed
the dignity of the Spanish to 'the legacy of their oriental sires'. Green
spoke of the 'innate gravity of the Southern temper'. Others were more
searching. Elizabeth Browning specified the genial tolerance of the
Catholic Church and the absence of puritan constraints and censure.
'The narrowness which cuts down literature', she explained, 'and
refuses to accept art into the uses of Christian life, is more rife with
injury and desecration than you see at first glance.' Mary Shelley and
Robert Lang singled out the strength of family affection; while Ouida

---

[29] Whiteside, *Italy in the Nineteenth Century*, 23; Ruskin, *Praeterita*, ii, Ch. VI, sec. 123;
Symonds, *Sketches in Italy and Greece*, 132–3; Boyle, *Mary Boyle: Her Book*, 113, 203–5;
Gissing, *Letters to Eduard Bertz*, 39; Stirling, *The Richmond Papers*, 204.

[30] Kenyon, ed., *Letters of E. B. Browning*, i. 383; Stephen, ed., *Letters of J. R. Green*, 308–
9, 353; Cobbe, *Cities of the Past*, 57; Vivian, *Tunisia*, 46; B. Disraeli, *Contarini Fleming*,
Part V, Ch. 2.

1(*a*). 'Ordered South', 1892

1(*b*). Descending the Mont Cenis pass in winter, 1864

2(*a*). The cholera epidemic, 1884: passengers from Marseilles being fumigated at Paris

2(*b*). Cholera quarantine at Marseilles, 1884

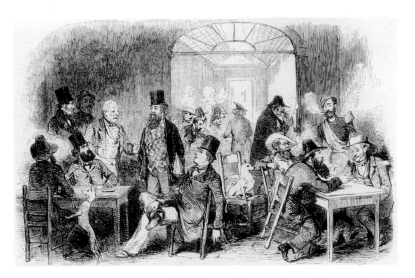

3(*a*). The Caffè Greco in Rome, 1850

3(*b*). The Campo Santo at Pisa, 1860

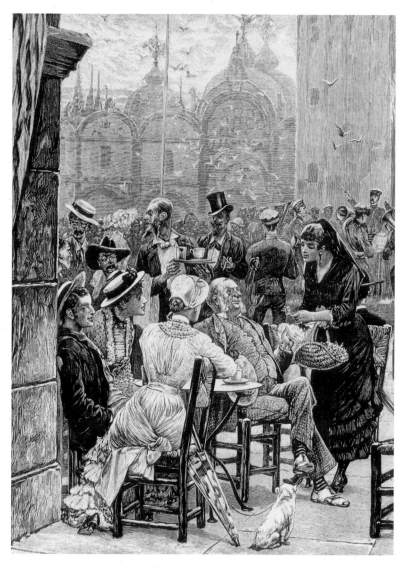

4. Tourists in Venice, 1881

5(*a*). The ascent of Mount Vesuvius, 1872

5(*b*). The Promenade des Anglais at Nice, 1866

6(*a*). The Café de Paris at Monte Carlo, *c.* 1900

6(*b*). The terrace of the Casino at Monte Carlo, *c.* 1900

7(*a*). The Promenade at Menton, looking west, *c.* 1900

7(*b*). The Promenade at Menton, looking east, *c.* 1900

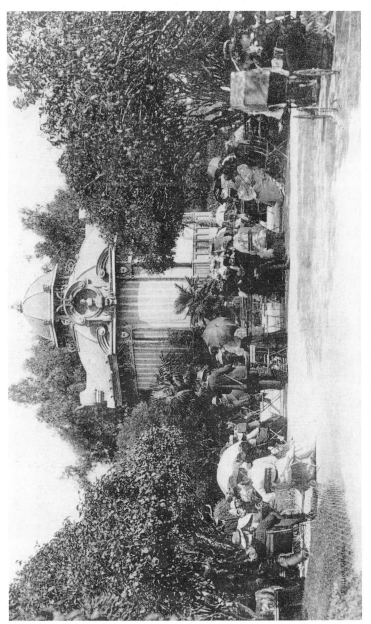

8. The Jardin Public at Menton, c. 1900

9. The Victorian vision of the Dead Sea: Holman Hunt's 'The Scapegoat' (1856)

10(*a*). 'Starting for the Pyramids', 1874

10(*b*). 'The English in Cairo: Visiting the Howling Dervishes', 1893

11(a). The Protestant Cemetery at Rome, c. 1890

11(b). British graves in the Old Cemetery at Menton

12. A Glimpse of Arcadia. (An unattributed photograph, *c.*1890, from the Italian albums of J. A. Symonds)

traced rural Italian refinement to a style of life that was 'simple, archaic, close clinging about tradition'. She was echoed by Norman Douglas, who stressed the tradition of patriarchal discipline and the 'archaic simplicity' of southern Italian life, whereas Samuel Butler thought that the Italians had been polished smooth by thousands of years of contact with sophisticated civilisation.

But the explanation which appealed to most travellers was the one that best accorded with their diagnosis of social evils at home. Southern people were superior because they were religious. The salutary effect of both Muslim and Christian influence was undeniable. William Wilde, in Cairo in 1838, listened to the antiphony of the muezzins' chants and experienced 'fervour and devotion at the thought of a nation, in many respects so far beneath our own, thus calling to the worship of our common God, and answered by her people, not with the sneer of scorn, the silence of contempt, or the apathy of indifference, but with a decorum and apparent piety that would well become professing Christian nations'. Fifty years later Isaac Taylor paid tribute to Muslim devoutness in almost identical terms, and attributed to it the endearing behaviour of the Egyptian masses. 'Religion', he wrote, 'seems to exert a greater binding moral force on the conduct of the labouring classes than in London, Paris or Berlin. It restrains men from evil, and tends to make them kindly, virtuous and moral.' The religious spirit of the masses in Spain and Italy won the admiration and respect not only of Catholics like Lady Herbert and Hilaire Belloc, but of Protestants too. 'They are externally, and really sincerely devout here in a way to which our country affords no parallel', wrote James Bryce from Italy in 1864. George Eliot paid tribute to the ardent religiosity of modern Florentine life in the Proem of *Romola*, and John Addington Symonds wrote an essay ('May in Umbria') in celebration of the affecting and edifying piety of Italian country folk. Ouida detected a truly religious feeling beneath their frivolity and casual ritualism, and in Bruno, the hero of *Signa*, she drew a powerful study of an illiterate peasant who, driven by 'the old, simple, blind faith' of Dante and Savonarola, sacrifices himself to avenge the violation of innocence by evil. Ruskin praised the Tuscan peasantry as 'a people who labour and pray'; and in 1910 Oscar Browning rejoiced to discover that 'there [was] not one of the 365 churches which Rome [was] credited with possessing lying idle'. In fact the value attached to religious influence was such that several Protestant travellers admitted anxiety about the secular tone of the modern unified Italian state. For all the anti-Catholic prejudice of their society they were unwilling to see the Catholic Church in Italy substantially weakened. Christopher Wordsworth lamented the struggle between government and episcopate which he witnessed in Italy in 1862. The unfilled bishoprics, the secularised monasteries and convents, and the taxes on Church property were all to the detriment of religion and morality. 'Religion suffers by this struggle', he warned. 'If it is prolonged, the people may lapse into irreligion; and if irreligion prevails, revolution will soon follow.' Ominous portents were already appearing, in the form of 'the number of *caricatures* which [met] the eye in the streets, where the most sacred objects of religion [were] exposed to ridicule'. Any religion, he felt, however corrupt, was better than no religion. John Richard Green was depressed by the prospect of 'Young Italy ... growing up Godless, indolent, spiritless, with little love for anything but lounging and billiards'; and Thomas Trollope sounded the same note when he deplored the declining standards of modern, secular Italy and stressed 'the advantages of even a very corrupt faith over none at all, whether in private or in public life'. Even a self-proclaimed agnostic like Frances Power Cobbe gave anxious thought to this matter and doubted that 'the downfall of a vast church, whose shadow [had] been the graveyard of religious thought for a thousand years, [could] be the signal for a resurrection of faith and piety'.[31]

This explanation was undoubtedly coloured by preconception and expectation. It says less about the religious state of the Mediterranean masses than about the Victorians' belief in the power of religion as a means of social control. But if there is reason to doubt the inference, there is less reason to doubt the premiss. It would leave out of account too much that is certain about the effect of rapid industrialisation and urbanisation on human psychology and human manners to suggest that behavioural differences between Northern and Southern populations existed only in the minds of Victorian travellers. The observation of these travellers was admittedly selective. Criminal riot

[31] Huxley, ed., *E. B. Browning's Letters*, 45; Shelley, *Rambles*, ii. 109–10; Lang, *Cyprus*, 203; Ouida, *In Maremma*, 109; Douglas, *Siren Land*, 75–6; Samuel Butler, *Alps and Sanctuaries of Piedmont and the Canton Ticino* (new edn., 1913), 123; Wilde, *Narrative of a Voyage*, 213; Taylor, *Egyptian Notebook*, 8; Fisher, *James Bryce*, i. 82; Cook and Wedderburn, eds., *Works of Ruskin*, xxxvii. 130; O. Browning, *Memories*, 83; Christopher Wordsworth, *Journal of a Tour in Italy* (1863), i. 71, 222–6; Stephen, ed., *Letters of J. R. Green*, 268; Trollope, *What I Remember*, iii. 37; Cobbe, *Italics*, 6.

was not absent from the Mediterranean, as the Victorians well knew. One instance in particular became the issue of heated public debate. This was the disturbance in Athens in 1850, when the house of Don Pacifico, a Maltese Jew with British citizenship, was sacked by a mob. Yet even without the filtering and the softening the truth would remain sufficiently attractive. The testimonies are too consistent and too extensive, and they depict characteristics too often shown to be real in old and undisturbed societies, to be attributed merely to wishful fantasy. This aspect of the Mediterranean world at least was discovered rather than created.

9. THE LIFE OF LIFE

Many Victorians and Edwardians associated the South with blessed escape from a painful state of mind and an oppressive society. The Mediterranean seemed like the realm of Keats's nightingale or Tennyson's lotos-eaters, offering oblivion from weariness, fever, fret, and the consciousness of mortality. To Matthew Arnold, thinking of his brother dying at Gibraltar worn out by service in India, the waters of the Mediterranean suggested repose in death; an incongruous grave of peace after the restless toil of English public office:

> Not by the gracious Midland sea
> Whose floor tonight sweet moonlight fills,
> Should our graves be.

To others they suggested repose in life; an intermission of the turbulence and friction of existence—'a sense of abstraction', as Elizabeth Browning put it, 'from the vulgarities and vexations of the age'.[1] In *The Last Days of Pompeii* Lord Lytton apostrophised Italy as a soothing enchantress ('whoever visits thee seems to leave earth and its harsh cares behind—to enter by the Ivory gate into the Land of Dreams'); while George Gissing, in *By the Ionian Sea*, recorded the poignant calm that Italy afforded to a life 'menaced with dreary harassment'. 'As I looked my last towards the Ionian Sea', he recalled, 'I wished it were mine to wander endlessly amid the silence of the ancient world, today and all its sounds forgotten.' Frances Power Cobbe in 1864 and Hilaire Belloc in 1902 both described the descent

---

[1] Kenyon, ed., *Letters of E. B. Browning*, ii. 285.

of the Alps into Italy as a deliverance. For Miss Cobbe it was 'like passing from winter to summer ... We feel that we have left behind the atmosphere of black frosts, moral and physical, and may expand ourselves happily in a much milder medium.'[2] Belloc 'thought to approach a softer and more desirable world'. 'I was glad', he wrote, 'as a man come home again.'[3] On his arrival in Nicosia in 1888 William Mallock was exhilarated by 'a feeling of escape from the furies of modern life—disillusion, doubt, democracy'.[4] To Norman Douglas the uplands of Sorrento were 'Siren Land', beckoning the 'perennial drudge' of the North to 'a brief period of *katharsis*, of purgation and readjustment'.[5] D. H. Lawrence revelled in a sense of emancipation in northern Italy in 1913. 'Here it is so free', he cried. 'The tightness of England is horrid . . .'.[6]

This idea of the South as a realm of peace and freedom came from a multiple experience of burdens lifted and barriers removed. One of its sources was the psychological effect of arrival in the Mediterranean at the end of the year, when the climatic contrast between North and South was extreme. The lingering warmth and light of the Mediterranean never failed to intoxicate minds numbed by the dark and cold of an English November or December, so that even a morose hypochondriac like Herbert Spencer could not resist a *frisson* of pleasure as he strolled on Christmas morning in 1879 in the garden of the Hotel des Îles d'Or at Hyères and heard the buzzing of flies in the sunshine—'a sound', as he said, 'so strongly reminiscent of a summer's day'. Nothing delighted Victorian and Edwardian tourists like the Mediterranean light, and nothing teased the ingenuity of Victorian and Edwardian writers and artists more. It entranced them and eluded them. Painters like Wilkie, Lewis, Phillip, Roberts, Turner, Watts, Leighton, and Lear pitched their palettes higher and higher, and writers like Ruskin, Hare, Vernon Lee, and J. A. Symonds ransacked the vocabularies of metallurgy, mineralogy, and horticulture in a vain attempt to encompass its magic in art. Such enchantment is of course a common Northern response to the South, but in the Victorian and Edwardian British it was intensified by the experience of living in a country that was more than naturally dark and dingy.

[2] Cobbe, *Italics*, 1.
[3] Hilaire Belloc, *The Path to Rome* (1902), 251.
[4] Mallock, *Enchanted Island*, 80.
[5] Douglas, *Siren Land*, 27–8.
[6] Moore, ed., *Letters of D. H. Lawrence*, i. 187.

Industrial pollution had thickened the gloom of Britain's cloudy atmosphere and produced effects on the face of its cities and the minds of its inhabitants that are now increasingly difficult to appreciate. When travellers like Roger Fry and Norman Douglas complained of Britain's 'hyperborean gloom' and 'Cimmerian darkness' they had in mind more than just the overcast skies of summer and the premature dusks of winter. They thought of cities of dreadful night, where everything was seen as through a dark veil, where buildings and vegetation were black, and where monstrous fogs smothered the feeble resistance of oil lamps and gaslight. Atmospheric pollution was so heavy in late Victorian London that windows were often fitted with smoke-blinds—fine wire meshes designed to trap the smuts of soot floating in the outside air. Even so public buildings would fill with smoky haze. 'Even upon a bright summer's day', wrote William Richmond, 'the interior of St Paul's is veiled by a smoke which is never absent . . . No amount of artifice will create clear light in an air so polluted with smoke.'[7] When George Gissing went to a concert in St James's Hall in December 1890 he found the atmosphere 'so thick one could hardly see the singers'.[8] *Bleak House* and *Hard Times* contain only the best-known literary testimonies to the murkiness of the great English cities. There are plenty of others. As early as 1836 Elizabeth Barrett was describing London as 'wrapped up like a mummy in a yellow mist';[9] and in *Aurora Leigh* she wrote of the 'great tawny weltering fog' which made it seem 'as if a sponge had wiped out London'. In her letters of the 1860s George Eliot referred frequently to the London fog and its depressing effect on her 'faith in all good and lovely things'; and there are similar cries of dejection in the correspondence of J. R. Green, J. A. Symonds, and Lord Ronald Gower. Gissing's journals for the 1880s and 1890s are scattered with references to the black fogs of London, which would linger for days even in the summer months; and his early novels are heavy with the symbolism of urban darkness. 'Windows glimmered at noon with the sickly ray of gas or lamp', he wrote in *Thyrza*; '. . . and only the change from a black to a yellow sky told that the sun was risen.' One man alone, perhaps, felt an oppression more intense than Gissing's. This was Ruskin, whose obsession with fog and darkness assumed the

---

[7] Stirling, *Richmond Papers*, 288, 395–6.
[8] Coustillas, ed., *The Diary of George Gissing*, 232.
[9] Kenyon, ed., *Letters of E. B. Browning*, i. 35.

quality of insanity. In 1859, in a lecture on Modern Manufacture and Design, he described his vision of Bradford, with 'the furnaces of the city foaming forth perpetual plague of sulphurous darkness, the volumes of their storm clouds coiling low over a waste of grassless fields'; and thereafter his mind was possessed by the incubus of the storm-cloud and the psychopathic fear that the sunlight would fail.

To minds brooding on nature so violated, nature in the plenitude of Southern light was a solace and a gorgeous revelation. Ruskin's comparison of the sky above modern Rochdale with the 'sacred untroubled sky' above medieval Pisa was only a heightened statement of the contrast observed more prosaically by the painter Frederick Walker in Genoa in 1868. 'When I think', he commented after describing the pellucid Italian atmosphere, 'that in poor old London one cannot place one's self or one's belongings out of doors without getting *dirty*, it seems so strange.'[10]

By the Mediterranean the burden of mortality too seemed lifted from the soul. Several travellers described how awareness of the flight of time and impending death was suspended by some trick of Southern sorcery, which unlocked the chamber of the mind containing the days disowned by memory, and summoned from somewhere beyond consciousness memories of which memory knew nothing. When John Henry Newman passed the island of Ithaca in 1832 he was reminded not only of things past, but of things outside the past. Pope's translation of Homer and its associated childhood scenes swam into his ken, bringing with them infant intimations of immortality. 'I thought of Ham', he told his mother, 'and of all the various glimpses, which memory barely retains and which fly from me when I pursue them, of the earliest time of life when one seems almost to realize the remnant of a pre-existent state.' Arthur Stanley, in Greece in 1840, found himself transported back to schooldays and to youth. 'Visions of the library at Rugby, and of the lecture room at Balliol, were constantly blending themselves with the visions of battles, and temples, and oracles.' Frances Cobbe found that experience of Egypt included assurance of realities outside time. '*Das Morgenland* it is in very truth,' she wrote, 'and the morning of our own lives comes back to us there in the same mysterious way as when we hear the half-remembered notes of our mother's songs; or, burying our faces in the moss and grass, inhale "the field-smells known in infancy".' Gissing's

[10] Marks, *Frederick Walker*, 134.

flight to the South was a flight to boyhood ('the names of Greece and Italy . . . make me young again'); William Mallock's days of excitement and discovery in Cyprus were preludes to 'nights of childhood'; and Belloc's delectation in Tuscany was the delectation of youth redis-covered and eternity glimpsed. 'The noise of the grasshoppers brought back suddenly the gardens of home, and whatever benedic-tion surrounds our childhood. Some promise of eternal pleasures and of rest haunted the village of Sillano.'[11] In *By the Fireside* Browning celebrated this experience in verse:

> We slope to Italy at last,
> And Youth, by green degrees.

The feeling of liberation in the Mediterranean was made keener by the sun's narcotic power. 'Avez vous remarqué', Oscar Wilde asked André Gide in Algeria in 1895, 'que le soleil déteste la pensée? Il la fait reculer toujours et se réfugier dans l'ombre.'[12] It was an experience that Gide understood, and he made the transition from abstraction to life one of the themes of emancipation in his novel *L'Immoraliste*. For a large number of British writers likewise, thought banished was bondage ended. It meant release from a morbid addiction. Victorian London echoed to the world's debate. Old orthodoxies expired and new ideas proliferated in the dense double columns of its quarterly, fortnightly, weekly, and daily reviews, magazines, and newspapers. A heavy diet of erudition was regularly announced in publishers' catalogues; and educated men and women grew faint and giddy from trying to follow intellectual frontiers as they advanced in all directions. 'I have been dull today,' says Gissing's Henry Ryecroft, 'haunted by the thought of how much there is that I would fain know, and how little I can hope to learn. The scope of knowledge has become so vast.' Knowledge was disintegrating—diverging beyond the angle of human vision; and for the first time man was losing his ability to perceive the universe coherently.

> The wind-borne, mirroring soul
> A thousand glimpses wins
> And never sees a whole

[11] Kerr and Gornall, eds., *Letters and Diaries of J. H. Newman*, iii. 172, 193; Prothero, *Life of Stanley*, i. 269; Cobbe, *Cities of the Past*, 2; Gissing, *By the Ionian Sea*, 6; Mallock, *Enchanted Island*, 143–4; Belloc, *The Path to Rome*, 373–4.

[12] Claude Martin, *André Gide par lui-même* (Paris, 1963), 89.

cried Matthew Arnold, in *Empedocles*. But there were sages who still strove to see a whole, straining their sight after ever wider systems, syntheses, or synopses and engaging in a superhuman effort to preserve cosmic coherence and postpone the day when academies and specialists would preside over the fragmentation of learning and bury for ever man's aspiration to comprehend the universe. There was Herbert Spencer, worn to a shadow by thirty-six years of labour on a fourteen-volume portion of work planned to subsume the whole of human knowledge in a theory of cosmic progress; Thomas Buckle, in a state of collapse after producing the first two volumes of a projected sixteen-volume *History of Civilisation*; John Ruskin, thinking—in the words of Frederic Harrison—'in encyclopaedias, comprising man and nature in one library',[13] and planning, after thirty years' unremitting literary effort, a further seventy volumes on various aspects of art, geology, and political economy.

The images of pathos and desolation presented by such men, and the feeling of exhaustion generated by cerebral ferment, set up a counter-current of anti-intellectualism within the intellectual world. The intelligentsia were prone to fitful moods of revolt against the idea of reaching light through labyrinths of thought, and to sudden sharp awareness of needs unsatisfied in a life of introspection. It was this mood which drove George Meredith, Leslie Stephen, and Frederic Harrison to vigorous physical activity like club-swinging, hiking, and mountaineering, and which inspired Clough's yearning for action and Arnold's 'ineffable longing for the life of life'. 'Congestion of the brain is what we suffer from', Arnold told Clough; 'I always feel it and say it and cry for air like my own Empedocles.' Ruskin himself said that 'the mass of society [was] made up of morbid thinkers and miserable workers'; and Kingsley told his wife: 'We may think too much! There is such a thing as mystifying oneself . . . Thinking a dozen thoughts in order to get to a conclusion, to which one might arrive by thinking one.' In *Adam Bede* George Eliot pined for 'Old Leisure', who was 'undiseased by hypothesis; happy in his inability to know the causes of things, preferring the things themselves'; and in *Middlemarch* she depicted the futility of the intellectual life in the tragic career of Edward Casaubon, a character whose most likely model was Herbert Spencer. Casaubon is mouldy with spiritual death; a casualty of the pursuit of vast and elusive synthesis. His projected work, *A Key to*

---

[13] Frederic Harrison, *John Ruskin* (1902), 158.

All Mythologies, is redundant even before it is finished, because modern scholarship has overtaken it. Knowledge grows faster than a single mind can move and a malediction rests on those who live in the realms of thought. 'In that I write at all I am among the damned', declared Samuel Butler in 1876, voicing the mood of self-disgust that accompanied much Victorian writing.[14]

In the South the intellectual rediscovered his instinctual humanity. He reverted to the emotional from the cerebral life—to the native hue of resolution from the pale cast of thought—and he divined in the unthinking existence a mode of knowing of which reason knew nothing. George Henry Lewes, in Naples with George Eliot in 1860, gazed on the mountains and felt 'a sort of yearning to be for ever living among them, without any of the intellectual strife and vicissitudes of English life'. George Eliot herself, in *Middlemarch*, used Italy as a catalyst in the emancipation of the heroine, Dorothea, from the sterile intellectualism that has consumed her husband Casaubon. During her honeymoon in Rome Dorothea's smothered sensibilities are stirred by the titanic monuments of art and history around her, and she realises from Casaubon's impoverished and banal responses to the sensuous suggestiveness of Roman life 'that the large vistas and wide fresh air which she had dreamed of finding in her husband's mind were replaced by anterooms and winding passages which seemed to lead nowhither'. In Venice in 1881 John Addington Symonds discovered an existence 'full not of literature but of vehement life'. 'The problem of what to work at', he told his friend Graham Dakyns, 'has not only retired, but seems insignificant . . . I have gained a complete blur of all merely literary preoccupations, and the entrance into a new stage of living.' Goldsworthy Lowes Dickinson found release from the suffocating intellectualism of Cambridge on his first visit to Greece in 1897. 'I felt as though my dull senses were being stimulated into life', he recalled, 'and trying, as it were, to throw off the long incubus of thought and books, to live by feeling and perception.' In the uplands of Sorrento Norman Douglas renewed contact with 'elemental and permanent things . . . casting off outworn weeds of thought with the painless ease of a serpent' under the guidance of an illiterate peasant boy called Amitrano. He spent months alone with this obliging child,

[14] Matthew Arnold, *Empedocles on Etna*, Act II, line 357; H. F. Lowry, ed., *The Letters of Matthew Arnold to Arthur Hugh Clough* (1932), 130; Ruskin, *The Stones of Venice*, ii, Ch. VI, para. xxi; Fanny Kingsley, ed., *Charles Kingsley: His Letters and Memories of his Life* (9th edn., 1877), i. 87; Philip Henderson, *Samuel Butler* (1967), 120.

'learning what is not to be learnt out of books'. Mrs Russell Barrington pursued this theme of emancipation in her *Life of Lord Leighton*, published in 1906. She described Leighton's delight in the emotional spontaneity and intuitive responses of the Italian peasantry, and added accusingly: 'There are many among modern men and women, taught by much reading, who overweight their physical vitality in the effort to develop intellect and to forward self-interest, till all simple physical enjoyment is lost, and the natural man becomes repressed into a mental machine incapable of any spontaneous emotions or joy.' That seems to anticipate Forster's *Howard's End*, and it was also the philosophy of D. H. Lawrence, whose revolt against the constraints of mind was only a late and laboured expression of an old malaise. Lawrence, whose belief that the blood and the flesh were wiser than the intellect was developed among the peasants of northern Italy, was a true heir of his Victorian literary predecessors—with this difference, that what in their work had been an undercurrent creating subtle tensions and half-hidden sadness, in his became a surface tide, relentless and strident.[15]

Delicate organisms such as these, jarred by the seismic shocks and shifts of Nothern life, relished the stillness of the South. They loved the septembrial equipoise of immemorial ruins and ancient societies, in days and nights without flux, by a sea without tides. 'There', wrote Gissing reminiscing about his days in Italy, 'there did the gods reveal to me the secret of their eternal calm.' On shipboard off Naples one night in 1897, as he watched the faint lights of Capri, he felt the silence and the immobility numb his sense of material constraint. 'The mind knew only the phantasmal forms it shaped, and was at peace in vision.' To Douglas, repose was the hallmark of Siren Land—the repose of an archaic world where social problems had long been solved and forgotten, and where a prescriptive ethical code sustained human life in settled equilibrium. Here a pervading sense of continuity tranquil-lised the ferment of psychological stress, and existence was remote from 'the wilderness of our ever-changing worldly circumstances'.[16]

And with this freedom of spirit there went social freedom; a liberty to form relationships that was unknown at home, where puritan

[15] Haight, ed., *Letters of George Eliot*, iii. 292; Schueller and Peters, eds., *Letters of J. A. Symonds*, ii. 706; Dennis Proctor, ed., *The Autobiography of G. Lowes Dickinson* (1973), 163; Norman Douglas, *Late Harvest* (1949), 74; *Siren Land*, 27–8; Barrington, *Frederic Leighton*, i. 23.

[16] Gissing, *Henry Ryecroft*, 209; *By the Ionian Sea*, 7–8; Douglas, *Siren Land*, 75–6.

disapproval and class barriers arrested the natural flow of human affections. The classic protest against 'the hostile and dreaded censorship' which weighed on the private lives of the Victorians is of course Mill's *On Liberty*, an essay published in 1859 and inspired partly by the author's own experience of vindictive public opinion, incurred as a result of his long unorthodox relationship with Harriet Taylor; but this was a grievance that found expression in fiction too—notably in the work of three novelists who used the Mediterranean as a setting for liberation from false attachments and the inhibitions of Protestant guilt. George Eliot, George Gissing, and E. M. Forster detected in the rich art and emotional life of the South an invitation to relationships based on sympathy and sincerity rather than on rules of conduct.

In George Eliot's *Middlemarch* (1871) Italy plays a crucial role in the social emancipation of Dorothea Brooke. Dorothea is a genteel provincial girl, 'brought up in English and Swiss Puritanism, fed on meagre Protestant histories and art chiefly of the hand-screen sort'. Her passionate nature, thwarted by a sterile and narrow environment, turns inwards and creates dangerous fantasies. She casts the middle-aged pedant Edward Casaubon in the role of transfiguring sage, and marries him under the illusion that she is to become the helpmate in a momentous career—a sort of Mrs John Locke or Mme Blaise Pascal.

In Italy comes the moment of truth. During the Roman honeymoon the falsity of her attachment to Casaubon is starkly exposed. In the South, contrarieties pull apart. Age diverges from youth; death from vitality; light from darkness. 'The light had changed,' we read, 'and you cannot find the pearly dawn at noonday.' Dissonant relationships dissolve and harmonious ones form. The tumultuous responses which divide Dorothea from her husband draw her strongly to Will Ladislaw, an Apollonian figure with sunlight in his hair who promises the 'fuller sort of companionship' for which she hungers. The currents of intellectual and sexual sympathy which link Dorothea and Will cut across a double prescription—her own marriage to Casaubon and, after Casaubon's death, the codicil to his will, which forbids her to marry Ladislaw on pain of disinheritance.

Before their resolution these dissonances modulate through several hundred pages, controlled by the author's strong commitment to the humanism of Spinoza, Comte, and Feuerbach and her personal conviction that we all create destiny, as well as obey it. Italy emancipates Dorothea from her illusions; but it does not give a licence for self-gratification. It initiates her into a higher form of fellowship, in which self-fulfilment comes through self-sacrifice. Her own suffering alerts her to the suffering of others and she is reborn into a state of sad but noble altruism—a secular equivalent of the evangelical experience of conversion and rebirth. Her feelings of revulsion against her pathetic husband mellow into compassion, and physical union with Will is postponed until Casaubon is dead and Dorothea is satisfied that her remarriage cannot compromise the happiness of others. Italy makes true marriages, but it also alerts the individual to the claims of his fellow men.

Another novel in which Italy figures as a liberating influence is *The Emancipated*, by George Gissing, which was published in 1889. Like Dorothea, Gissing's heroine, Miriam Baske, arrives in the South a victim of the suffocating stringencies of Northern puritanism. She averts her gaze from art, landscape, and fellow travellers, and thinks only of the Nonconformist chapel that she is to endow at Bartles, her Lancashire home. A main theme of the novel is the thawing of these numbed sensibilities under the genial alchemy of Naples and Rome. By the Mediterranean old attachments dissolve, and her affections flow with new and spontaneous energy:

The name of Italy signified perilous enticement, and she was beginning to feel it. The people amid whom she lived were all but avowed scorners of her belief, and yet she was beginning to like their society. Every letter she wrote to Bartles seemed to be despatched on a longer journey than the one before; her paramount interests were fading, fading . . .

The architect's plans for the new chapel remain undisturbed in her portmanteau, and she hungers for a relationship that will allow scope for her newly discovered responsiveness to art and beauty. This she finds with Ross Mallard, a painter whose inspiration is the Italian landscape. Her natural sympathies for Mallard triumph over the false antipathies of religious prejudice, and together they set up a home 'sacred to love and art'.

As in *Middlemarch*, physical marriage is a consummation long delayed, but in this case the postponement does not serve to accommodate the humanist theme of renunciation. By the time he wrote *The Emancipated* Gissing had lost his early enthusiasm for Comte and had fallen under the influence of Schopenhauer; and this, with his own mixed feelings about emancipated women, inspired a contrapuntal story of disappointment and despair. Italy does indeed make good alliances; but it cannot always prevent bad ones. Despite its warning signals—the destructive flashes of Vesuvius, the petrified ruins of Pompeii—Cecily Doran, Mallard's ward, elopes with the feckless Reuben Elgar and ultimately has to thank her 'liberation' for an unhappy marriage and a dead baby.

George Eliot and Gissing were agnostics, so it is understandable that they should have blamed religious bigotry for the sundering of kindred souls. E. M. Forster was homosexual, which makes it equally understandable that he should have blamed class prejudice. 'Social barriers', asserted the Victorian traveller Richard Ford, 'are more difficult to be passed than walls of brass, more impossible to be repealed than whole statutes at large';[17] and this fact was the great bane in the lives of British homosexuals. It is of course undeniable that they had religious and legal proscriptions to contend against too. Certain homosexual acts had been classified as felonies since 1533 and until 1861 these actually carried the death penalty. The notorious Criminal Law Amendment Act of 1885 introduced a new and very wide category of homosexual misdemeanour, thereby making prosecution easier and conviction more likely. This was the measure that inaugurated the era of persecution of homosexuals by blackmailers and moral-purity brigades like the National Vigilance Association. Nevertheless it remained more dangerous to sin against the prescriptions of class than to sin against the law. Heterosexual relationships that defied class barriers were no threat to hierarchy in a society where men were dominant and women subservient; but homosexual relationships that did so were potentially subversive. Hence aristocratic and bourgeois homosexuals with working-class consorts were always more gravely at risk than those practising in upper-class preserves such as public schools and universities. Inquisitorial procedures and punishments were reserved for men like Lord Henry Somerset, who was forced to flee to Florence in 1879, and Oscar Wilde, who was brought to the dock in 1895. Wilde was indicted on counts relating not to his well-known liaison with Lord Alfred Douglas, but to his connections with servants and office boys; and the heavy and hostile emphasis laid on their inferior status by both judge and prosecuting counsel made it plain that he was on trial as much for his social as for his sexual preferences. This taboo explains the ardent sympathy of homosexuals like Edward Carpenter and J. A. Symonds for the poetry

[17] Richard Ford, *A Handbook for Travellers in Spain* (4th edn., 1869), ii. 210.

of Walt Whitman, with its celebration of social democracy and comradeship transcending class. 'I could not understand, and I've never been able to understand,' wrote Symonds in his secret memoirs, 'why people belonging to different strata in society—if they love each other—could not enter into comradeship.'[18] The same protest informs Forster's novel *Maurice*, which he finished in 1914 but never published in his lifetime. This is as much about the cruelty of class barriers as about the intolerance of sexual inversion. It depicts the suffering of a young middle-class man who shocks and outrages society not so much because he is homosexual—for certain homosexual relationships society can ignore—as because he is a homosexual who loves someone of inferior rank.

In the Mediterranean, where society was much less rigidly hierarchical, this caste-mentality was missing. Consequently it was easy for rich and educated Englishmen to make and maintain contact with complaisant young fishermen, gondoliers, *facchini*, *cocchieri*, urchins, sailors, and boulevard boys. In the large cities and seaports of the South such intimacies were socially acceptable. 'He knows everybody,' wrote Symonds of Lord Ronald Gower in Venice in 1892, 'from the cabbies, corporals and *carabinieri*, up to the painters, princes and plenipotentiary envoys.' Roger Fry met Gower, Symonds, and Horatio Brown in Venice, and learnt something of their double lives. Gower he recognised as the model for Lord Henry Wotton in Wilde's *The Picture of Dorian Gray*, his fine aristocratic face 'not yet quite brutalised by debauchery' and his conversation 'weird and remarkable without ever being other than perfectly proper'. Symonds, whom he found in 'a tiny pub . . . sitting boozing with a lot of Italian workmen', he described as 'the most pornographic person' he had ever seen— 'but not', he added, 'in the least nasty'.[19] Symonds, as his own letters make clear, was deeply appreciative of the democratic spirit of Italian society, and pitifully grateful for the companionship he could buy from 'bright-eyed, sleek-necked sailors' and gondoliers like sea-gods. In a crucial sense Italy was cruel to him. It exposed both the hopelessness of his sexual psychology and the futility of his poetic aspirations. Every visit yielded the same sad vintage of frustrated longing and aborted verse, and again and again he returned to his home in Switzerland with his soul like a dead chrysalis. But while he could not

[18] Grosskurth, ed., *Memoirs of J. A. Symonds*, 116.
[19] Sutton, ed., *Letters of Roger Fry*, i. 146–7.

satisfy his longings in Italy, he could at least exhaust them. The same was true of Oscar Wilde, though Symonds refused to recognise in Wilde a kindred spirit and saw him as a liability in the campaign for greater tolerance and understanding. This was because Wilde hid the pathos of homosexuality behind a mask of cynicism and triumph, goading society with an impersonation of blatant and dangerous vice and mocking its proprieties with freakish laughter—the laughter that so disconcerted André Gide on the occasion when he pursued lascivious Arab boys with Wilde and Alfred Douglas in Algiers. Symonds was a puritan. He was repulsed by the sordid and in his homosexual encounters he was always looking for connubial sanctity. This is why his daughter Katherine protested so strongly when she learnt of Roger Fry's use of the word 'pornographic' to describe him.[20] Wilde had no such refining instincts. Influenced by the French Decadents, he celebrated the sordid by dressing it up in the language of the sublime. Even his years of destitution and exile he chronicled in letters of titillating irony, parading mudlarks, gigolos, and adolescent riff-raff from the Mediterranean towns as Classical heroes and truant divinities. Only at the end of his life, when he indulged in self-recrimination, did he reveal his debauchery in its true light, as the harmless platitude of a penitent with a vivid sense of sin. 'How evil it is to buy love!' he wrote from Rome in 1900, 'and how evil to sell it! And yet what purple hours one can snatch from that grey, slowly moving thing we call Time!'[21]

Most of the Englishmen who frequented those 'strange places of the most varied description' that enticed Symonds to Venice year after year will never be identified; but enough is known about A. E. Housman, Edward Lear, Oscar Browning, Theo Marzials, Frederick Rolfe, Simeon Solomon, Somerset Maugham, Norman Douglas, and E. M. Forster to warrant the assumption that they took advantage of such opportunities during their travels in the Mediterranean. Indeed Forster's experience of sexual emancipation in the South was an obvious and important influence on his fiction. It suggested the theme of his first two novels, which is the effect of Italy on 'the undeveloped heart' of the English.[22]

---

[20] There is a correspondence on this topic between Katherine and Virginia Woolf (Fry's biographer) in the Symonds Archive, University of Bristol.

[21] Davis, ed., *Letters of Oscar Wilde*, 828.

[22] Forster, *Abinger Harvest*, 8; Furbank, *E. M. Forster*, i. 90–1.

On his first visit to Italy in 1901 Forster, then twenty-two, found a new world of human warmth and spontaneity. Italy both revealed to him his own sexual deviance and suggested possibilities and opportunities to be reclaimed from the twin demons of class prejudice and guilt. One evening, as he watched two youths walking in the Campagna with arms across each other's shoulders, he recalled Orestes and Pylades and had his first intimation of the power of friendship to link, and thereby cancel, the prose and the passion, the monk and the beast, in humankind. He felt inspired to explore both imaginatively and in his own life relationships based on affection and sincerity; and in his first published novel, *Where Angels Fear to Tread* (1905), he celebrated Italy's redemptive power over both the body and the soul. The central character is Philip Herriton, a middle-class twenty-four-year old from Sawston (Tonbridge), who is obviously a wry self-portrait. 'At twenty-two', we are told, 'he went to Italy with some cousins and there he absorbed into one aesthetic whole olive trees, blue sky, frescos, country inns, saints, peasants, mosaics, statues, beggars. He came back with the air of a prophet who would either remodel Sawston or reject it. All the energies and enthusiasm of a rather friendless life had passed into the championship of beauty.' But beauty has not the holiness of the heart's affections, and rebirth is delayed until he returns to the South and discovers human love.

His contact with Italy is renewed as a result of his widowed sister-in-law's marriage with a petty-bourgeois Italian youth called Gino. Philip is sent to Italy by his bullying mother to retrieve first her and then, after her death, her baby. The South generates a purgative flux of emotion, which leads to the death of the baby and a violent quarrel between Philip and Gino, described with vivid—though apparently unconscious—sado-masochistic suggestiveness. As a result of his injuries Philip undergoes conversion. He experiences the redemptive power of love, and the spell of Sawston is broken. But the love that possesses him is ambiguous. It is love not only for Caroline Abbott, the young English girl who nurses him, but for Gino, the handsome son of a servants' dentist. Philip finds himself 'bound by ties of almost alarming intimacy' to Gino; and together they realise that 'vision of perfect friendship' that had haunted Forster since his first visit to Rome.

In his second Mediterranean novel, *A Room With a View* (1908), Forster was more careful to dissimulate the homosexual inspiration and chose a suppressed woman as his fictional surrogate. Lucy

Honeychurch is a young heroine in the tradition of Dorothea Brooke and Miriam Baske, with the difference that it is class prejudice, rather than religious guilt, that weighs down her soul. She arrives in Italy emotionally trussed and socially compliant, in the tow of Cousin Charlotte, who personifies the shackles of bourgeois respectability. Abroad, they are claimed by the freemasonry of English snobs that links rural parishes in the Weald of Kent with *pensioni* in Florence, and rivets fetters on human hearts even as it makes the world small. But Lucy is rescued by pagan, democratic Italy. In Italy the idea of class is an absurdity, because here even the gods are proletarian. Phaethon is a cab-boy, who drives them to Fiesole 'recklessly urging his master's horses up the hill'. Lucy receives back her soul and attains to a new concept of life. 'Her senses expanded; she felt that there was no one whom she might not get to like; that social barriers were irremovable, doubtless, but not particularly high. You jump over them, just as you jump into a peasant's olive yard in the Apennines, and he is glad to see you.'

She returns to England spiritually pledged to George Emerson, the son of a lower-class socialist, and submits to engagement to the aesthete Cecil Vyse inwardly rebelling. George reappears, Michael-angelesque; the sun-god Apollo smiles; and Italy triumphs over Tunbridge Wells. George and Lucy return to Florence for their honeymoon and realise that it was Cousin Charlotte who had brought them together. Even her frozen sympathies had thawed in the South; and they think of her as they listen to the river 'bearing down the snows of winter into the Mediterranean'—a clear echo of the passage in *Middlemarch* where Dorothea's ideas and resolves seem 'like melting ice floating and lost in the warm flood of which they had been but another form'. Forster's novel is an extended and refined treatment of an idea first sketched in a short story, *The Story of Panic*, in which the god Pan mocks Anglo-Saxon proprieties by wreaking havoc with a picnic party near Florence and reclaiming the soul of Eustace, an inbred, feckless English youth. Eustace defies the barriers of class and nationality, and forms a close and mystic brotherhood with an Italian fisherboy.

Forster's dissimulation is of course partly explained by the fear of heterosexual prejudice. He was writing in the shadow of the Wilde tragedy, at a time when fashionable literature (that of Shaw, Kipling, and Wells) was in strident reaction against the moral ambivalence of the Decadents; but it is equally well explained by the paramount importance of class prejudice as a restriction on the homosexual's freedom. It is noteworthy that even André Gide, a much less fastidious writer than Forster and one who wrote in a cultural climate which made open confession of homosexuality possible, chose to reverse sexual inversion in *L'Immoraliste*, his own semi-autobiographical Mediterranean novel. Furthermore he even de-sexualised the emancipation experience. The protagonist is male ('Michel'), but the Arab prostitutes he encounters are changed from male to female and petty larceny is substituted for homosexuality as the 'immorality' which signals liberation from puritan values. Michel's voyage of self-discovery does not end in sexual heresy, but it does end beyond the barrier of his social class. He finds fulfilment in the social stratum remotest from his own, among the stevedores, vagrants, and foreign sailors of Syracuse, and among the street urchins and jail birds of Biskra, in Algeria. For Gide, too, the democracy of the South mattered at least as much, and probably more, than its moral licence.

PART FOUR

ATTITUDE AND EXPERIENCE

THE other world described in the record of Victorian and Edwardian travellers to the South is the world that they invented. Attitude determined experience, and added a second dimension to their response.

Attitude complicated the South. It created a chaos of stricken beauty and moral decay, of religious inspiration and religious pain; and it invited death to a sumptuous banquet. It matched splendour with intimations of peril and treachery, and it evoked the image of Circe: a radiant sorceress surrounded by shadows, offering a benediction that was poisoned with regret. This experience inspired a response that was ambivalent and deeply troubled. 'What little pleasure I still look for', said Ruskin in 1871, 'will be in Italy, mixed with bitter pain.'[1] Twenty-six years later Gissing remarked of Italy: 'Its unspeakable beauty is inseparable from the darkest thoughts.'[2] Visiting Rome for the first time in 1882, the aged Richard Church, now Dean of St Paul's, 'almost hated the place' as he tried to make sense of its clashing attributes of divinity and diabolism. 'I had the feeling', he told Lord Blachford, 'that it is the one city in the world, besides Jerusalem, on which we *know* God's eye is fixed, and that He has some purpose or other about it—one can hardly tell whether of good or evil. A good deal of His purpose is visible—and what of the rest? I cannot tell you how this kind of uncertainty about what the real meaning of the whole thing was, tormented and vexed me.'[3] One of the most sustained expressions of this sort of fragmented response is the verse dialogue *Dipsychus*, written thirty years previously by Church's friend, Arthur Clough. In this work, which is a Faustian scenario of temptation and fall, the poet's two selves interpret the promise of Venice alternately as deliverance and damnation, and the note of ambiguity is amplified by a serio-comic style. Torment and vexation were the keynotes too of the response of the Decadent poet Arthur Symons, who went mad in Venice in 1908. 'Inexplicable soul of Venice,' he wrote a few days before his breakdown, 'Satan threw dice with God and won half the game.'[4]

[1] John Ruskin, *Letters to Charles Eliot Norton* (Boston and New York, 1904), ii. 41.
[2] John Halperin, *George Gissing* (Oxford, 1982), 259.
[3] Church, ed., *Dean Church*, 295–6.
[4] John M. Munro, *Arthur Symons* (New York, 1969), 110.

Victorian experience of the Mediterranean was shaped by emotional, intellectual, and moral attitudes. Nostalgia made its beauty
seem ravaged and its heritage betrayed; an obsessive concern to
preserve the credibility of the Bible invested the topography of the
Holy Land with vivid suggestions of fulfilled prophecy; an attitude to
painting and architecture that was rooted in the concept of Christian
Art filled the works of early Italian masters with new meaning and
consolation; Protestant prejudice steeped the modern religions of the
Mediterranean in evil; evangelical values gave its political and
cultural decline the flavour of retribution and helped to fill its English
graveyards. The tension created by these conflicting attitudes
precluded Flaubertian or Byronic visions of transcendent harmony,
and the South disintegrated into antithetical meanings. For the
Victorians it represented both the world they longed to enter and the
world they must strive to leave. It was at once a golden city of the
Beyond and a forbidden city of the Plain.

10. A WRECK OF PARADISE

In the South sensitive Britons often felt, like Alfred de Musset, that
they had come too late into a world too old. The breathless meridian
was fading, the Sphinx had lost its immemorial calm, and delight kept
time to the numbered pulses of mortality. They found everything
lovelier than it would soon become, nothing as lovely as it once had
been; and they pined for something unknown and irrecoverable. 'I
find one of the effects of Rome is to set one longing,' sighed Anne
Thackeray; 'I don't know for what, exactly . . .' Horatio Brown defined
Rome, Siena, and Venice, as 'cities of the soul' with 'the fatal gift to
touch the imagination, to awaken a permanent desire'. In the young
John Addington Symonds 'a continual, unsatisfied desire' was evoked
by the splendours of Sorrento; and twenty years later he was still
wondering why it was that Italy troubled the spirit in a way that
Switzerland never did. What was 'this sense of want evoked by
Southern beauty'? Ruskin's joy in the art of Italy was embittered by the
conviction that he was writing its epitaph, and every visit intensified a
sense of loss and impending bereavement. Even his celebrated
evocation of the beauty of the sea-city in the opening of the second
volume of *The Stones of Venice* is a threnody, for we are told that the
bygone city was 'more gorgeous a thousandfold than that which now

exists' and that it is only 'the hurried traveller' who can 'shut his eyes to the depth of her desolation'. For forty years he waged a feverish battle against the flight of time and the failure of memory, striving to fix in words and drawings some record of Italy's fugitive glory, until at last his overstretched mind disintegrated and he turned with insane loathing against the Italian people. He despised them as a brutish residuum amidst the ruins of Paradise; incarnations of the evil that had brought the curse of death on man's beatitude. Here, he raved, was 'mere Caliban bestiality and Satyric ravage, staggering, drunk and desperate, into every once-enchanted cell where the prosperity of kingdoms ruled and the miraculousness of beauty was enshrined in peace'. His private diaries, loaded with vituperation and imprecation, are a terrible testimony to the toxic power of art on famished affections.[1]

Ruskin's misanthropy was extreme, but not unique. With George Gissing, Edward Hutton, and Norman Douglas likewise, love of art was apt to express itself as hatred of man. In 1889 the English tourists in the galleries of Rome filled Gissing with aggressive resentment. 'Every day', he wrote, 'I saw people whom I should like to have assaulted. What business have these gross animals in such places?' Hutton fulminated against 'these days when there are so few things left that have escaped the universal deluge of democratic barbarism', and Douglas showed the ugly side of the aesthetic temperament in outbursts of savage intolerance. He abused the Italian Government for spending money on 'feeding, clothing and supervising a horde of criminals, every one of whom ought to be hanged ten times over', instead of retrieving the buried treasures of Herculaneum; and during the Second World War some compassionate editor who had suggested that 'a single child's life is more valuable than all the historical monuments of the world' drew down his scathing contempt. 'England', sneered Douglas, 'used to be known as the home of cranks, and one is glad to find that the breed is not yet extinct.'[2]

The growth of tourism was partly responsible for this state of mortified sensibility, because tourism was robbing the South of its

---

[1] Hester Ritchie, ed., *The Letters of Anne Thackeray* (1924), 136; Schueller and Peters, eds., *Letters of J. A. Symonds*, i. 440; Symonds, *Italian Byways*, 5; Brown, *In and About Venice*, 1; John Ruskin, 'Mornings in Florence': Cook and Wedderburn, eds., *Works of Ruskin*, xxiii. 414.

[2] Gissing, *Letters to Bertz*, 33; Hutton, *Siena and Southern Tuscany*, 280; Douglas, *Late Harvest*, 6.

bouquet and its bloom. In the wake of the tourist, it seemed, came
bathos and vulgarity. Thackeray found the Pyramids trivialised by the
mundane bustle and noisy instrusions inseparable from the presence
of Europeans, and he yearned in vain for that sense of the sublime
expressed by Shelley. Lucie Duff Gordon complained that the
Europeans ruined everything in Cairo, making Muslim festivals like
Derby Day. In Athens in 1850 Aubrey de Vere was distressed by

that universal nuisance, the all-seeing English traveller—the traveller of that
class who scribble their names on the walls of temples, write witty criticisms in
the stranger's book at inns, are always paying too much and raving about
extortion, depreciate everything that is not like what they are used to, swallow
an infinite quantity of dust, and return home with as much knowledge and
worse morals than they took with them.

Ruskin grieved over the corpse of Florence, cursing 'the wretched
Germans, English and Yankees busy upon it like dungflies'; and
further afield, in Baalbek, Wilfred Scawen Blunt winced at the
solecisms of the Americans. 'There are the usual American tourists
here,' he grumbled, '. . . the most senseless type of human nature,
being quite insensible to beauty or decorum and with the manners of
shop-boys, who ramble through the gardens of the ancient world with
as little knowledge of their value as beasts have, defiling all and
trampling all . . . They should be kept at home, for they have no
business in these ancient lands.' The organised tour particularly
menaced the fragile magic of art and atmosphere, and despising
Cook's tourists (or 'Cookites') became a mannerism of the cultured
élite. Charles Lever wrote in horror of 'cities of Italy deluged with
droves of these creatures' and of 'the Continental bear-leader who
conducts tribes of unlettered British over the cities of Europe', and
Gissing referred with pain to 'the Cook's Tourist type' who made the
exquisite precincts of Italy unbearable. Frederic Harrison conceded
that 'railways, telegraphs and circular tours in twenty days' had
'opened to the million the wonders of foreign parts'; but, he asked,
'have they not sown broadcast disfigurement, vulgarity, stupidity,
demoralisation?' The blighted landscape of the Riviera was a tragic
witness to the destructive impact of the tourist invasion. Rapid and
uncontrolled development had, in the view of William Chambers,
ruined Menton by 1870. 'The most genial as well as the most beautiful
spot on the Riviera was architecturally spoiled', he complained.
'There was no attempt to construct buildings in harmony with the

surrounding scenery.' In 1882 an article in the *Pall Mall Gazette* deplored the flow of cosmopolitan wealth to Cannes, since this was 'destroying the natural beauties of the place and making scorching, sunbaked boulevards where were formerly olive-shaded lanes'. Nice bristled with hideous hotels, like the Hotel Regina, which in Lord Ronald Gower's opinion looked like 'some monstrous stage decoration, with grotesque pinnacles and ugly, bloated, white-domed towers'. In 1904 Maurice Hewlett found the Riviera full of 'trash, vulgarity and dust, that ma[de] even the roses an eyesore and the orange flowers to stink'; and two years later Frederic Harrison mourned the arrival on the Riviera di Levante of 'American Grand Hotels, Monte Carlo villas, Parisian boulevards ... and ... that new disease, *motoritis*'.[3]

But tourists were not entirely to blame for the desolation. Commercial and political contacts, and the circulation of ideas, all helped to convey the banalities of the North into the Mediterranean world, setting up utilitarian values and modern technology in place of the quaint, the romantic, and the picturesque. 'Wherever the steamboat touches the shore', observed Thackeray gloomily, 'adventure retreats into the interior, and what is called romance vanishes ... Now that dark Hassan sits in his divan and drinks champagne, and Selim has a French watch and Zuleika perhaps takes Morrison's Pills, Byronism becomes absurd instead of sublime.' In 1850 the Revd Henry Christmas discovered that the exotic aspects of Spain were rapidly vanishing. 'Warren's Jet Blacking is advertised on the walls, Rowland's Macassar Oil dresses the hair of the Senora, while Mechi's razor trims the beard of the Don.' And he added the exhortation that was to become a refrain: 'Those who wish to see Spain while it is worth seeing must go soon.' The narratives of travellers to the Levant and North Africa frequently modulated into valediction. 'We have need to make haste', warned the Revd Andrew Thomson on his return from the Holy Land in 1869, 'if we would catch the old picture of the East entire. The colours are fading, the forms are changing.' Looking back

---

[3] Thackeray, *Cornhill to Grand Cairo*, 293–7; Gordon, *Letters from Egypt*, 296; de Vere, *Picturesque Sketches*, i. 145; Joan Evans and John Whitehouse, eds., *The Diaries of John Ruskin* (Oxford, 1956–9), iii. 1031; Wilfred Scawen Blunt, *My Diaries: Part Two* (1919), 93; Rae, *The Business of Travel*, 150, 152; Coustillas, ed., *Diary of George Gissing*, 71; Harrison, *Memories and Thoughts*, 233, 259; Chambers, *Wintering at Mentone*, 58; Anon., 'A Drawback to Southern Sunshine': *Pall Mall Gazette*, 4 Jan 1882; Gower, *Old Diaries*, 289; Hewlett, *The Road in Tuscany*, i. 90.

in 1865 to his visits to the Levant, Robert Curzon reckoned that those countries had been much better worth seeing thirty years before. 'They were', he explained, 'in their original state, and each nation retained its own particular character, unadulterated by the levelling intercourse with Europeans, which always, and in a very short time, exerts so strong an influence that picturesque dresses and romantic adventures disappear.' Frances Power Cobbe, after being offered Bass's Ale in the shadow of the Pyramids and dining off willow-pattern crockery by the grave of Abraham, felt moved to protest: 'It is almost too much, this Anglicizing of the world.' Lucie Duff Gordon bewailed the modernisation of Cairo. 'All is exquisite', she wrote, 'and, alas, all is going. The old Copt quarter is *entamé*; and hideous, shabby French houses, like the one I live in, are being run up.' The Pasha was carrying out sweeping 'improvements' on the French pattern—'long, military straight roads cut through the heart of Cairo'. Alexander Knox sorrowfully observed in 1881 that in Algiers the French had made a clean sweep of 'well-nigh all the old buildings which might recall the vanished greatness of the place'; and eighteen years later Herbert Vivian complained of the persistent efforts being made in Tunis to 'mould the old-world town upon the ordinary commonplace European pattern'. Henry Rider Haggard noticed in 1900 that some of the women of Nazareth had discarded their ancient narrow-necked earthenware pitchers and were fetching water in paraffin cans, and on the Sea of Galilee he saw the boatmen 'pause to refresh themselves with copious draughts of the lake water, drunk from out of an old meat tin'.[4]

In Italy enchantment was fleeing before remorseless progress. By the early 1840s a railway viaduct was being built across the lagoon between Mestre and Venice, to cries of remonstrance from English travellers. 'It is impossible not to repine at this innovation', wrote Mary Shelley. 'The power, the commerce, the arts of Venice are gone; the bridge will rob it of its romance.' To Ruskin, its railway, gas pipes, and patent ironwork made Venice as prosaic as Liverpool or Birmingham; and nearly forty years later Robert Browning echoed his lament, angrily rebuking the Venetians for 'their obstinate determina-

[4] Thackeray, *Cornhill to Grand Cairo*, 93; Christmas, *Shores and Islands*, i. 219; Andrew Thomson, *In the Holy Land* (1886), 74; Curzon, *Monasteries in the Levant*, p. vii; Cobbe, *Cities of the Past*, 3–4; Gordon, *Letters from Egypt*, 63, 360; Alexander Knox, *The New Playground, or Wanderings in Algeria* (1881), 53, 184; Vivian, *Tunisia*, 158; Haggard, *Winter Pilgrimage*, 210, 228.

tion to Liverpoolize' their city. Anne Buckland imagined Shakespeare and Byron turning in their graves, and wailed: 'Is romance to be thus driven from her last resting place in Europe by the discordant shriek of the railway whistle and the light of modern science, dispelling that darkness or dim moonlight which she loves?' Ouida and Augustus Hare were among a host of travellers who deplored the urban development of Florence in the later nineteenth century. 'They have tacked on to her venerable palaces and graceful towers', complained Ouida, 'stucco mansions and straight hideous streets, and staring walls covered with advertisements, and barren boulevards studded with toy trees . . .' Maurice Hewlett found Edwardian Florence, with its telegraph poles, tramways and kerbed pavements, no longer an enchanting old town, but a 'botched parody of a new one'.

The changes carried out in Rome after it had become the capital of Italy raised a chorus of regret. Oscar Browning gave up his annual visit for twenty years because he was assured by many who knew the city that it was 'entirely altered and in every way spoiled'. In 1893 Frederic Harrison was dismayed by its 'avenues, tramcars, electric lighting and miles of American hotels'. Rome had become like any other European city—'big, noisy, vulgar, overgrown, Frenchified and syndicate-ridden'. It was 'striving to become a third-rate Paris'—a mournful spectacle to those who remembered it of old. 'He who visits Rome today,' he wrote, . . . having known the Eternal City . . . in the torpid reign of Pio Nono, cannot stifle the poignant sense of having lost one of the most rare visions this earth had ever to present . . . The light and poetry have gone out of it for ever.' He fondly recalled the 'quaint old Papal pageantry' and 'the medieval absurdities of Papal officialism . . . the grotesque parade of cardinals and *monsignori* . . . the swarm of monks, friars and prelates of every order and race . . . with all the historic glamour, all the pictorial squalor, all the Turkish routine, all the magnificence of obsolete forms of civilisation which clung around the Vatican.' This note of nostalgia frequently recurs, for the temporal power of the Papacy and the ceremonials of the Roman Church were, like so much else, enhanced by death. No sooner had they passed away than they ceased to be outrageous and sinister and became the innocent casualties of a new barbarism. Arthur Stanley was saddened by the abolition of the Pope's temporal power. 'It is', he wrote, 'rather a grief to me. It had been so much reduced that it did very little harm.' Its extinction, in his view, marked the lapse of Rome from the quaint to the commonplace. Anne Buckland missed the ungainly Papal processions in the Roman streets; and in his autobiography Augustus Hare reminisced elegiacally about the days when the Pope was king:

Those who visit Rome now that it is a very modern city can have no idea of the wealth and glory of picturesqueness which adorned its every corner before 1870, or of how romantic were the passing figures—the crimson cardinals; the venerable generals of religious orders with their flowing white beards; the endless monks and nuns; the *pifferari* with their pipes . . .; the handsome, stalwart Guardia Nobile in splendid tight-fitting uniforms; and above all the grand figure and beneficent face of Pius IX, so frequently passing, seated in his glass coach, in his snow-white robes, with the stoic self-estimation of the Popes, but with his own kindly smile and his fingers constantly raised in benediction.[5]

Travellers of the next generation, such as Gissing, Norman Douglas, Maurice Hewlett, Edward Hutton, and D. H. Lawrence, had never known these idyllic archaisms; but they were no less convinced that a stable, hierarchic, and innocent world was perishing under foreign influence. Factory chimneys, deforestation, railways, urban development, cosmopolitan dress, and emigration all betokened enslavement to new and false gods. Italy struck Gissing as 'swamped in the ignobleness of modern life', and he was swept by 'a mood of anger with the modern Italians, who ruin all the old associations'. Lawrence detested modern city Italians ('all socks and purple cravats and hats over the ear') and sensed 'a queer, sad, gnawing restlessness' among the peasantry. Douglas blamed emigration for the degeneration of Italian youth into 'gamblers, wine-bibbers and flashily dressed mezzo-signori', because emigration, 'a continual coming and going', was eroding parental control and encouraging a speculative spirit. Edward Hutton bewailed the infatuation with progress that motivated the modern Italian. 'Having turned nearly all the cities of Italy into a kind of pandemonium . . . he is now busy infesting the country byways with the same infernal machines.' In 1914 Hewlett, finding that large areas of the Peloponnese were virtually depopulated as a result of emigration, approved a recent government edict which forbade young people to leave the country. 'They not only

[5] Shelley, *Rambles*, ii. 104; Harold I. Shapiro, ed., *Ruskin in Italy; Letters to his Parents, 1845* (Oxford, 1972), 198–202; T. L. Hood, ed., *The Letters of Robert Browning Collected by T. J. Wise* (1933), 224; Buckland, *Beyond the Esterelles*, ii. 114–15, 208; Ouida, *In a Winter City* (1876), 3; Augustus Hare, *Florence* (3rd edn., 1890), 3; *The Story of My Life*, iii. 100; Hewlett, *The Road in Tuscany*, 160; O. Browning, *Memories*, 82; Harrison, *Fortnightly Review*, 53. 702–21; Prothero, *Life of Stanley*, ii. 383.

went to America to the tune of a thousand a week,' he explained, 'but when they came back they brought phthisis with them.'[6]

The anguish caused by vandalism was more intense even than that caused by tourism and the cult of progress. The artistic and the architectural heritage of the South were subjected to abuses that made British travellers weep and wring their hands. They saw the precious legacy being destroyed by ill-treatment, neglect, and grossly insensitive restoration.

Sir Francis Palgrave, in the first edition of Murray's *Handbook for Travellers to Northern Italy* (1842), alerted travellers to the sorry state of many paintings, frescos, and monuments in Tuscany, and castigated the Italian authorities for their culpable indifference. Lord Lindsay concluded his *Sketches of the History of Christian Art* (1846) with 'an appeal to the rulers of Italy on behalf of the grand old frescos . . . either perishing unheeded before their eyes, or lying entombed beneath the whitewash of barbarism, longing for resuscitation'. Precious works of the early masters were 'flaking off the walls, uncared for and neglected', and scarcely one, he predicted, would survive the century. In 1845 Ruskin reported from Lucca that he saw 'nothing but subjects for lamentation, wrecks of lovely things destroyed, remains of them unprotected, all going to decay'—and it was the same in Pisa and Florence. 'I do believe', he wrote in despair, 'that I shall live to see the ruin of everything good and great in the world, and have nothing left to hope for but the fires of judgement to shrivel up the cursed idiocy of mankind.' Cato Lowes Dickinson was distressed and angry to discover that the *loggie* of Raphael in the Vatican were, in 1850, 'deliberately scribbled over, effaced with knives, covered with Italian names'; and he wondered that 'anything [was] left at all in Italy, so carelessly [had] all the great works been preserved'. Lady Eastlake saw rare pictures in the churches of Florence 'all defiled and bespattered, stuck through with hundreds of nails and even of pins, with the dust and drought of centuries upon them'. Austen Layard, writing in the *Quarterly Review* in 1858, detailed the successive onslaughts suffered by the early masterpieces of fresco: first repainting by Mannerist academicians; then whitewashing by Catholic puritans; and finally the knocks and rubs resulting from foreign military occupation. And the

---

[6] Coustillas, ed., *Diary of George Gissing*, 471; Gissing, *Letters to Bertz*, 49, 245; *By the Ionian Sea*, 25; Moore, ed., *Letters of D. H. Lawrence*, i. 232; Douglas, *Siren Land*, 75; *Old Calabria*, 49; Hutton, *Siena and Southern Tuscany*, 221; Binyon, ed., *Letters of Maurice Hewlett*, 226.

few odd frescos that had survived this triple ordeal were fair game for improvised embellishment on religious holidays:

Workmen hurry about with tinkling chandeliers, and acolytes with jugs of fragrant lilies and roses. The ponderous ladders are raised against the painted aisles, and huge nails are driven in with remorseless hands. Flakes of yielding plaster fall in showers to the ground, and things that have cost years of earnest thought and loving labour are gone for ever.

'The fumes of incense and the smoke of a thousand tapers' added their effect, and the work of mutilation was complete. 'Talk of London smoke!' he stormed. 'Why, Italian neglect, indifference and ignorance have done more to deprive the world of some of its noblest and most precious monuments of art than the atmosphere of ten Londons.'

In both Italy and Greece ruins and architectural treasures were defaced by mundane obscenities. John Cam Hobhouse found in 1854 that the Forum and the Basilica of Constantine in Rome were 'almost inapproachable from filth, and from the purposes to which the unhidden nooks of these ruins, crowded as they were by visitors, were unblushingly applied'. In 1851 Ruskin reported that the arcades of the Ducal Palace in Venice were serving as a latrine; and thirty years later, when Gissing went in search of the well of the Eumenides, at the foot of the Areiopagos near Athens, he discovered that the locality was 'a vast *lieu d'aisance* for the public'. The air was poisoned and the ground covered with human excrement. According to Mahaffy the Greek habit of insulting ancient monuments was carried to the point of physical assault. In Athens he heard that the Greeks themselves had bombarded the Acropolis during the War of Independence, and he personally watched a young marksman using fragments of the Theatre of Dionysus for target practice. Such behaviour caused him grave misgivings about the repatriation of the Elgin Marbles. Could it, he wondered, expiate Elgin's crime to commit another—that of surrendering the precious fragments to unfit custodians?[7]

The mania for restoring and excavating that succeeded the earlier offences of ill-treatment and neglect merely added insult to injury. The abominable practice of 'restoring' impugned the genius of great

[7] Shapiro, ed., *Ruskin in Italy*, 51, 52, 61, 71, 72, 88; Dickinson, *Letters from Italy*, 37–8; Smith, ed., *Journals of Lady Eastlake*, ii. 73; Austen Henry Layard, *Autobiography and Letters* (ed. W. N. Bruce, 1903), ii. 205; Hobhouse, *Italy*, ii. 158; Bradley, ed., *Ruskin's Letters from Venice*, 32; Gissing, *Letters to Bertz*, 89; Mahaffy, *Rambles and Studies*, 43–4, 90–3.

painters and replaced authentic art by shameless forgery; while excavation shattered the dignity and repose of ancient buildings and historic sites.

In Layard's view, when the Italian authorities decided to repair their omissions

they let loose upon the devoted monuments a plague more terrible than any that had as yet swept over them. An army of restorers was raised in every city of Italy and recruited by every dauber who had interest or means to obtain the privilege of earning a miserable pittance by repainting and repairing. Their work has proved more mischievous than even that of time and neglect.

John Stuart Mill and Thomas Hardy were other travellers who fretted at this practice. 'To me', wrote Mill from Florence in 1857, 'most of the Raphaels and Correggios in the Tribune are spoilt in a great measure because they have so evidently been repainted.' Thirty years later Hardy felt aggrieved and disappointed because 'pictures by Giotto have been touched up so thoroughly that what you see is not a Giotto at all but the over-lying renovations'; and he added a lament for the 'wronged great soul of an ancient master'. With Ruskin, restoration became an obsessive grievance. In 1845 he was filled with anguish as he watched the workmen busy on Giotto's Campanile in Florence, 'perpetually . . . chipping and cleaning, and putting in new bits, which though they [were] indeed of the pattern of the old ones, [were] entirely wanting in the peculiar touch and character of the early chisel'. What he witnessed in Venice left him distraught. 'They are repairing the front of St Mark's, and appear to be destroying its mosaics', he told his father; 'I cannot draw here for the tears in [my eyes]. Tyre was nothing to this.' He worked restlessly to copy elaborate carvings and elusive contours before they vanished for ever, and on one occasion struggled to draw a palazzo (the Ca' d'Oro) 'while the workmen were hammering it down' before him. 'Fancy trying to work', he cried, 'while one sees the cursed plasterers hauling up beams and dashing in the old walls and shattering the mouldings.' It was these unhappy experiences that inspired his ardent plea against the restoration of buildings in *The Seven Lamps of Architecture*.[8]

[8] Layard, *Autobiography*, ii, 206; Mineka and Lindley, eds., *Later Letters of J. S. Mill*, 481; Florence Emily Hardy, *The Early Life of Thomas Hardy* (1928), 249; Shapiro, ed., *Ruskin in Italy*, 119, 199, 200, 209.

Ruskin's aversion was shared by many eminent Victorians. Edward Freeman described the erection of scaffolding around old buildings as 'a process ... which always makes one tremble'. Augustus Hare, Edward Burne-Jones, William Morris, and a number of political figures all admonished and implored in the crusade against restoration. The Catholic statesman Lord Ripon bought the convent of San Damiano, near Assisi, and donated it to the monks on the sole condition that it was never to be restored; and a loud cry of alarm arose in 1877 when Battista Meduna, supervising repairs to St Mark's in Venice, announced his plans for the great western façade. Morris mobilised the recently founded Society for the Protection of Ancient Buildings and wrote letters to newspapers; at Oxford in 1879 Burne-Jones, for the first and only time in his life, addressed a public meeting; and the British press gave the topic extensive coverage. Morris and Burne-Jones drew up a Memorial of protest to the Italian Government which was signed by Gladstone and Disraeli, among many others, while Ruskin contributed a circular written in wrath and despair. In this instance the fuss was to some effect, because the Italian Government intervened and laid down a rigorous code of standards for the repairs; but this offered little consolation to conservative temperaments who felt that all renovation, however sensitive and even though necessary, was loss. Englishmen who revisited Rome after 1870 regretted the ill-kempt, fern-clad ruins of the old days even though removal of the vegetation was declared essential for the structural survival of the buildings. 'The spoliation of Rome continues every day', moaned Augustus Hare in 1874. 'Its picturesque beauty is *gone*. Nothing can exceed the tastelessness of all that is being done—the Colosseum, the Baths of Caracalla and the temples are scraped quite clean and look like sham ruins built yesterday.' In 1884 Mrs Buckland mourned for the Colosseum of twenty years before, 'beautiful in its clinging, graceful drapery of living green'. Now, like the Baths of Caracalla and other spots once romantically evocative, it was stripped, swept, and emptied, and reverie was banished by barriers, gates, and disfiguring excavation. Archaeologists were arraigned as major culprits in this work of devastation, because what they recovered was deemed a pitiful compensation for what they destroyed. Ruskin found the Italian capital dismal from antiquaries' quarrying, with 'the ground torn up in every direction, yawn[ing], dusty and raw'; Frederic Harrison complained that well-stocked museums were no substitute for the Salvator Rosa ruins of old; and Wilfred Blunt was deeply upset by Schliemann's activities at Mycenae, which were 'disturbing ancient ruins virgin of all meddling for three thousand years'.[9]

There is no doubt that Victorian and Edwardian travellers experienced the Mediterranean at a time when social and physical change was accelerating; but there is no doubt either that they were morbidly predisposed to interpret change as loss and to see wreckage and deterioration wherever they looked. This afflicting awareness of moving through a world that was being torn apart owed something, obviously, to outward circumstance; but it also owed much to inward neurosis. Perception of decay caused depression; but it is true too that depression caused perception of decay. Over and above the perennial human sadness at the flight of time and the impermanence of things, the Victorians suffered from that Romantic sense of rootlessness which de Musset called 'la maladie du siècle'. They felt severed both from the past and from the future. 'Tout ce qui était n'est plus; tout ce qui sera n'est pas encore.' That cry of pain in de Musset's autobiographical novel *La Confession d'un enfant du siècle* was almost exactly repeated in Matthew Arnold's depiction of the modern soul as 'Wandering between two worlds / One dead, the other powerless to be born'. Sensitive minds mourned the loss of ancient sanctities. The French Revolution, the Industrial Revolution, and the corrosive cults of Reason and Utility had sundered connection with what had gone before. They had cancelled an immemorial dispensation in human affairs and cast man adrift into a world dominated by his worse rather than his better self. 'The age of chivalry is gone,' ran Burke's famous lament; 'that of sophisters, economists and calculators has succeeded; and the glory of Europe is extinguished for ever.' The signs of the times were the Cheapness, Nastiness, and Mammonism castigated by Carlyle; the dehumanisation of labour bewailed by Ruskin; the ugliness hated by Morris. A better future was powerless to be born because the new scientific dispensation suggested by the concept of Evolution seemed to many cultured Victorians to preclude the possibility of ethical behaviour. Evolution prognosticated a higher life for the race; but it also implied that death was personal extinction. Not even Tennyson, with all his power of strident celebration and wishful

[9] E. A. Freeman, *Sketches from the Subject and Neighbour Lands of Venice* (1881), 152; Hare, *The Story of My Life*, iv. 171; vi. 293; Cook and Wedderburn, eds., *Works of Ruskin*, xxiv, pp. lviii–lxii; xxxvii. 99; J. W. MacKail, *The Life of William Morris* (new edn., 1907), i. 342–3, 368–9; ii. 6–7; G. Burne-Jones, ed., *Memorials of Edward Burne-Jones* (1904), ii. 95–6; Buckland, *Beyond the Esterelles*, i. 240–1; ii. 111; Blunt, *My Diaries, Part One*, 12.

mystification, could fit death into the evolutionary scheme. The essential note of continuity was lost in the wrench and shock of bereavement:

> But thou art turned to something strange,
>   And I have lost the links that bound
>   Thy changes . . .[10]

Death was a hiatus—a leap; and evolutionary nature, as Darwin was to remind the Victorians, does not make leaps. To troubled intellectuals like Matthew Arnold and Arthur Clough this loss of personal immortality nullified the assurance of progress, because without the promise of an afterlife and the sanctions of reward and retribution man was incapable of right action. He became a slave either to sense or to thought. Evolution therefore spelled the end, as well as the beginning, of man's post-Christian hopes.

At such a time, when thoughtful people despaired of the present and felt deeply pessimistic about the future, they longed all the more acutely for the irrecoverable past. Then, it seemed, human achievement had matched human potential.

> And we shall fly for refuge to past times,
>   Their soul of unworn youth, their breath of greatness[11]

wrote Matthew Arnold. Even thinkers reckoned to be radical constantly looked backwards with regret, combining an intellectual assent to the idea of progress with an emotional attachment to the days that were no more. Thus George Eliot used fiction as a means of connecting characters with a modern agnostic outlook to the past of her childhood, while Frederic Harrison combined Positivist philosophy with active membership of the Society for the Protection of Ancient Buildings.

In the case of the Victorians this Romantic nostalgia was complicated by a further, distinctive influence. To Romantic misgiving about the present and the future they added misgiving about the past itself. The traditional focus of European nostalgia—the Platonic Golden Age—was being demolished by modern scholarship and science. History was dissolving into myth; and myth was being transmogrified into the mental effusions of savage and barbaric races. Richard

---

[10] *In Memoriam*, XLI.
[11] *Empedocles on Etna*, Act II, lines 383–4.

Farrer's soulful reflections in the Peloponnese, in 1880, show how Victorians found it increasingly difficult to idealise the remote past:

It is the country of the Golden Age, wherein gods walked with men as friends long before the growth of wealth and pride and wrong caused these manifestations to cease from off the earth. Such indeed is no more than the popular belief of every civilised and self-conscious age; although unhappily Science tends to prove it groundless by showing primitive man to have been in reality but a very wretched and unloveable creature.[12]

The idyllic image of Classical Greece bequeathed by Winckelmann and the German Romantics fell victim to modern critical inquiry. Victorian Hellenes like Matthew Arnold, Benjamin Jowett, Frederic Leighton, and Max Muller all tried, in their various ways, to perpetuate this image; but theirs was labour in vain, because scientific investigation had by the end of the century laid bare the shocking perversities of Greek society. The major statement of the comparative-anthropological interpretation of Greek myth was James Frazer's *The Golden Bough*, and in his preface to the 1900 edition of the complete work Frazer wrote as the demolisher of redundant fable:

It is indeed a melancholy and in some respects thankless task to strike at the foundations of beliefs in which, as in a strong tower, the hopes and aspirations of humanity through long ages have sought a refuge from the storm and stress of life. Yet sooner or later it is inevitable that the battery of comparative method should breach these venerable walls, mantled over with the ivy and mosses and wild flowers of a thousand tender and sacred associations. At present we are only dragging the guns into position: they have hardly yet begun to speak. The task of building up into fairer and more enduring forms the old structures so rudely shattered is reserved for other hands, perhaps for other and happier ages. We cannot foresee, we can hardly even guess, the new forms into which thought and society will run in the future. Yet this uncertainty ought not to induce us, from any consideration of expediency or regard for antiquity, to spare the ancient moulds, however beautiful, when these are proved to be outworn.

Yet, like Darwin's *The Origin of the Species*, *The Golden Bough* was the product of a cumulative process of intellectual reassessment. It was a result, as much as a cause, of the ideas and the spirit it expressed. Consequently Frazer was aiming his artillery at an almost empty citadel. His victims had had due warning. Just as those emotionally committed to Christianity had shifted their ground in anticipation of

[12] Farrer, *Tour in Greece*, 165.

Darwin, so those emotionally committed to the past had shifted theirs in anticipation of Frazer. They had compensated for loss of ability to idealise the remote past by focusing their vision on the intermediate past: a past identified not by Classical architecture in pristine perfection, but by medieval buildings and by Classical monuments transformed by age into beautiful ruins. Like the Golden Age, this past had no existence in space or time. It was located, like a dream, in the mind; and like a dream it lay athwart the planes of outward and inward history, beginning with Byzantium and ending with the loss of youth.

Nostalgia distorted the perception of Victorian travellers, as it distorted the perception of poets and painters, because the phantom past of their reminiscence created illusions of regression and decay. These illusions are exposed clearly in Ruskin's diaries and letters. In 1875 he wrote of Florence: 'The wreck of it is now too ghastly and heartbreaking to any human soul that remembers the days of old';[13] and the following year he told Count Zorzi, a leading opponent of the restoration of St Mark's:

Of all the happy and ardent days which, in my earlier life, it was granted to me to spend in this Holy Land of Italy, none were so precious as those I used to pass in the bright recesses of your piazzetta, by the pillars of Acre . . . I pass the same place now with averted eyes. There is only the ghost—nay, the corpse— of all that I so loved.'[14]

But his diaries and letters of those earlier years contain no record of any such happiness. In them Ruskin is still choking with indignation, still fighting back his tears, still yearning for a paradise that is lost. Clearly, the image of ravaged beauty that so oppressed him in Italy was a reflection of something that he carried within himself. It was produced by a blight of vision that moved with him through life, always darkening what he saw and always transfiguring what he remembered.

II. THE GIFT OF PROPHECY

Like General Gordon, most Victorian pilgrims sought and found in the Holy Land a justification for belief in the literal truth of Scripture. 'All that I have seen', declared the Revd Bell of Cheltenham on his

---

[13] Cook and Wedderburn, eds., *Works of Ruskin*, xxiii. 413.
[14] Ibid., 405–6.

return from Palestine in 1887, 'confirms the truth of God's Holy Word and gives its wondrous story a reality for which I am most thankful.'[1] 'A visit to Palestine', proclaimed Hugh Price Hughes in 1901, 'confirms and illustrates the Bible . . . in a way which nothing but a visit can explain.'[2] Testimonies such as these, and the tone of religious enthusiasm often adopted by archaeologists and explorers, suggest that increasing familiarity with the eastern Mediterranean helps to explain the survival of evangelical Christianity as the typical religion of the governing classes.

This survival requires explanation, because informed opinion was increasingly hostile to the sort of uncritical, fundamentalist belief that evangelicalism implied. The Victorian modern mind accepted that truth was indivisible; but it did not accept that undivided truth was in the Bible. The modern mind rejected catastrophe and creation in favour of gradualism and evolution, whereas evangelicals remained committed to the biblical explanations for geological phenomena and organic variety. Furthermore, evangelical belief in the Verbal Inspiration of Scripture conflicted with modern biblical scholarship, which was exposing inconsistencies and anachronisms in the sacred texts. By the mid-Victorian years the case against the Bible seemed so strong that prominent intellectuals were diagnosing their age as a period of religious eclipse. 'In England', commented Harriet Martineau in 1855, 'the lamentations of the religious world, and the disclosures of the recent census, show how even outward adhesion to Christianity . . . is on the decline; and if they did not, the chaotic state of religious opinion would indicate the fact no less reliably.'[3] James Anthony Froude, surveying the world of the 1860s from the editor's desk of *Fraser's Magazine*, saw 'a general doubt . . . coming up like a thunderstorm against the wind, and blackening the sky'.[4] George Eliot counted her age among the 'eras of religious decay';[5] and Matthew Arnold, in his poem *Dover Beach*, lamented with elegiac cadences the ebbing of the Sea of Faith.

This diagnosis was, however, wrong. The Victorian crisis of belief was deep, but it was not wide. Beyond a narrow circle of writers and

---

[1] Bell, *Gleanings from a Tour*, 256.

[2] Hughes, *The Morning Lands of History*, 18.

[3] Harriet Martineau, *Autobiography* (3rd edn., 1877), ii. 459.

[4] J. A. Froude, 'A Plea for the Free Discussion of Theological Difficulties' in *Short Studies on Great Subjects* (1888).

[5] Haight, ed., *Letters of George Eliot*, iv. 472.

intellectuals Christianity did not decline—not yet, at any rate. On the contrary, it survived and even prospered; and no variety of Christianity survived and prospered so well as evangelicalism. Despite the loss to agnosticism of some of its brightest lights, the popular appeal of evangelicalism grew stronger rather than weaker in the middle decades of the Victorian age. The year 1859 marked the beginning of a religious revival which brought thousands of converts to the evangelical churches, and in 1860 the Evangelicals in the Church of England won an important battle. They thwarted the theologians who adopted a double standard of truth and interpreted the supernatural elements in the Bible in a moral and poetical rather than literal sense. The manifesto of the group, called *Essays and Reviews*, was condemned by twelve thousand clergymen; two of its authors were prosecuted for heresy; and general intolerance of 'Broad Church' opinion prevailed in the Establishment for another generation. Travel and archaeology contributed to this evangelical survival because they seemed to show that the Bible was true not only in essentials but in details. Victorian pilgrims found in the topography and ruins of the Near East confirmation of scriptural prophecy, while Victorian archaeologists discovered in the buried cities of Syria and Mesopotamia a wealth of authentication of the scriptural record. Pilgrims and archaeologists produced evidence that enabled both themselves and evangelicals at home to fortify their convictions, confute their critics, and recruit their spiritual strength.

The traditional focus of Christian interest in the Levant was the Holy Places of Palestine—the alleged sites of the Nativity, Crucifixion, and entombment of Christ and all the related gospel occurrences. Victorian Christians found a deep interest in these localities as shrines hallowed by centuries of pilgrimage and veneration. Nevertheless after the publication of Dr Edward Robinson's *Scriptural Researches* in 1841 they were generally sceptical about their authenticity. They preferred to locate Calvary, for example, not in the Church of the Holy Sepulchre but outside the medieval walls of the city. General Gordon's theory, that it was the Hill of Jeremiah's Grotto, an ancient quarry just outside the Damascus Gate, seemed particularly plausible because the Hebrew term for execution-ground was *golgotha*, or 'place of a skull', and seen from a certain angle and in a certain light this hill resembled a human skull. Less open to dispute, and therefore doubly edifying, was the testimony to the truth of Scripture in the ruins and landscapes of Palestine, Egypt, and Asia

Minor. This corroboration was especially welcome since it seemed to strengthen the evangelical position where the sceptics were concentrating their attack. The fallibility of biblical prophecy was one of the main arguments of critics like Francis Newman; so it was an immense comfort to defenders of the faith to be able to reaffirm this traditional proof by citing visible evidence of the fulfilment of biblical oracles.

Victorian travellers read in the desolation of much of modern Egypt, Syria, and Mesopotamia a clear sign of the judgement promised in the Bible. When Lord Lindsay rode into the Valley of Ammon in 1837 and found the air full of the stench of dead camels and the ruins covered with camel dung, he at once recalled the prophecy of Ezekiel: 'I will make Rabbah a stable for camels, and the Ammonites a couching place for flocks; and ye shall know that I am the Lord!' 'That morning's ride would have convinced a sceptic', he declared.[6] The Irish traveller Eliot Warburton described in 1844 the 'utter desolation' that everywhere prevailed in Judea and saw in it the seal of malediction. 'No other landscape in the world is like this', he asserted. 'It resembles rather some visionary sketch ... than anything in nature; distorted piles of cinderous hills, with that Dead Sea lying among them like melted lead, unlighted even by the sunshine that is pouring so vertically down as to cast no shadow'.[7] Thackeray, in the same year, found 'a landscape unspeakably ghastly and desolate'. 'After a man has seen it once', he wrote, 'he never forgets it; the recollection of it seems to follow him like a remorse, as it were to implicate him in the awful deed which was done there.'[8] Presbyterian Scots in particular seem to have been amenable to this sort of suggestion. John Aiton, a Presbyterian minister, toured the Bible lands in 1851 and recorded his sightings of confirmatory signs and signals. 'What rendered this country so close to my heart', he wrote of Egypt, 'was the frequent mention which is made of it in the Scriptures ... and the degraded state to which this, the richest district and finest climate in the world, has been reduced according to fulfilment of prophecy.' In Palestine he surveyed the deserted coast of Samaria and the ruins of Caesarea, the site of Jericho and the shores of the Dead Sea, and recognised with grim satisfaction the unmistakable imprint of divine anathema. As he put it, 'the sight was grand in its own way, from the picture everything presented of the country of a reprobate people cursed by the

[6] Lindsay, *Egypt, Edom and the Holy Land*, ii. 110.
[7] Warburton, *The Crescent and the Cross*, ii. 142.
[8] Thackeray, *Cornhill to Grand Cairo*, 212.

Almighty.'[9] John Ruskin, after viewing the Dead Sea landscape depicted in Holman Hunt's *The Scapegoat*, affirmed: 'Of all the scenes in the Holy Land, there are none whose present aspect tends so definitely to confirm the statements of Scripture as this condemned shore.'[10] But not even Hunt's Palestine was as portentous as that of Dr John Kelman, a Scottish theologian who made his pilgrimage in 1901. Kelman described a land that was 'sinister', 'petrified', 'uncanny', 'spectral', 'deathly', and 'ghostly', and whose every aspect suggested preternatural uniqueness. He told his readers: 'Something has happened here, you feel, which never happened elsewhere'; and he heard the sob and the groan of an awful chastisement. 'It is not merely stony', he explained; '. . . it seems to have been *stoned*—stoned to death for its sins . . . Any one can see that every part of the land is being judged and is bearing the punishment of sin.'[11]

The present condition of the wicked cities of Scripture—Nineveh, Babylon, Jerusalem, Samaria, Tyre, and Ephesus—was likewise deeply impressive. Stricken and abandoned, they were mute witnesses to the power of God and the miraculous prescience of the Hebrew seers. Austen Henry Layard, the most famous explorer and excavator of his generation, described for the Victorian public how minutely the ruins of Nineveh and Babylon vindicated the predictions of the prophets. The fate of Nineveh matched exactly the words of Ezekiel and Zephaniah. She was a desolation and dry like a wilderness; flocks and all the beasts of the nations lay down in the midst of her; and the voice of the cormorant and the bittern sang in her windows.[12] Of Babylon, Isaiah had proclaimed: 'The wild beasts of the desert shall lie there, and their houses shall be full of doleful creatures; and owls shall dwell there; and satyrs shall dance there'; and Jeremiah had prophesied: 'The wild beasts of the desert with the wild beasts of the island shall dwell there, and the owls shall dwell therein, and it shall be no more inhabited for ever'. When Layard surveyed the site of the city in 1850 he found everything as foretold. Not even the detail of the owls was missing. 'A large grey owl is found in great numbers,' he noted, 'frequently in flocks of nearly a hundred, in the low shrubs among the ruins of Babylon.'[13]

[9] Aiton, *Lands of the Messiah*, 102, 191.
[10] Cook and Wedderburn, eds., *Works of Ruskin*, xiv. 47.
[11] John Kelman, *The Holy Land* (new edn., 1912), 246–70.
[12] A. H. Layard, *Nineveh and its Remains*, (2nd edn., 1849), i. 71.
[13] A. H. Layard, *Nineveh and Babylon* (new edn., 1882), 270, 294, 310.

Mesopotamia was beyond the reach of the ordinary Victorian traveller; but evidence of fulfilled prophecy was just as plentiful in the ancient cities of Palestine and Anatolia. The fate of Jerusalem, for example, seemed to betoken dire calamity. Lindsay found the city still fair of aspect but, 'like the bitter apples of Sodom', filled with rottenness. It was filthy, depopulated, and politically insignificant. Aiton saw the city in the same light. 'Everything within the range of my eye', he wrote, 'was evidently drear and forsaken, blighted and cursed by the Almighty for the enormous wickedness of which it had been the scene . . . This Holy City, once the joy of the whole earth . . . is now the deserted capital of a Turkish Pashalite.' Eliot Warburton and Anthony Trollope both stood on the Mount of Olives and saw that Christ had wept there with good reason. The Temple had indeed been over-thrown, and Jerusalem was steeped in an atmosphere of retribution. Colonel Sir Charles Wilson's description of Jerusalem from the Mount of Olives, published in 1888, avoids explicit reference to the New Testament prophecy but it paints a picture in harmony with this prediction and its language is loaded with implication. 'Looking down from his vantage point on Olivet', wrote Wilson,

The spectator is at once struck by the appearance of ruin and decay which the city presents . . . The extensive cemeteries which hem in the city on almost every side give a mournful aspect to the view, and this effect is heightened by the oppressive silence which broods over the place during the greater portion of the day, and by the sober grey of the dome-roofed houses. How strangely changed from that Jerusalem which the Psalmist once described in loving terms as 'beautiful for situation, the joy of the whole earth'!

Kelman's picture was characteristically lurid. 'As we stand amid the deepening shadows on the spot where Christ was crucified,' he intoned, 'a change seems to come as the blood-red sky crimsons the minarets and domes. It is no longer Christ that hangs upon the Cross, but Palestine.'[14]

The city of Samaria, too, recalled and confirmed biblical utterance. It had become 'an heap in the field' precisely as the prophet Micah had said it would. 'We confess', wrote the Revd Andrew Thomson after his visit of 1869, 'to our having been startled when we read those ancient prophetic words and saw with what minuteness they had

[14] Lindsay, *Egypt, Edom and the Holy Land*, ii. 61; Aiton, *Lands of the Messiah*, 131, 136; Warburton, *The Crescent and the Cross*, ii. 98; Charles W. Wilson, *Jerusalem the Holy City* (1888), 4; Kelman, *The Holy Land*, 277.

photographed the living picture that lay before us.'[15] When the pilgrim reached Tyre he found confirmation of Scripture even more arresting in its exactness. 'The prophecy of Ezekiel against Tyre', announced William Beamont after visiting the ruins in 1855, 'has had an awful accomplishment.' According to Ezekiel, Jehovah had warned the proud city: 'I will make thee like the top of a rock. Thou shalt be a place to spread nets upon.' The modern traveller arrived, and found— nets! Fishermen's nets, spread to dry on rocks that were the site of ancient palaces! William Wilde saw them in 1838, as did Alexander Keith in 1844 and John Aiton in 1851. When Canon Tristram of Durham visited the site in 1864 the nets were not actually spread because the sea was too high and rough; 'but', he hastened to assure his readers, 'they were hanging about'. By 1900, when Henry Rider Haggard came to Tyre, the nets had resumed their usual position, causing him to exclaim: 'What a place it is now, when the curse of the Almighty is at work within its shattered walls!'[16] Ephesus, the city that had spurned Christ in the name of the pagan goddess Diana, had become a malarial wasteland whose every feature suggested chastise- ment. 'It is not only barrenness we look upon,' reported the Revd Thomson, 'but something that is awfully desolate and judgement- ridden.' When the Revd Henry Christmas took up his pen to describe his visit to the site in 1851, he became greatly excited and bombarded his readers with pulpit exhortation. 'Look around', he urged. 'The splendours of paganism are crumbled into ruin! Not a country, not a city, where the Christian martyrs have met their fate, that has not been visited by a doom still direr . . . The sword, the fire, the wild beast and pestilence have held sway over the once proud abodes of their persecutors.'[17] To the evangelical mind such arguments were as peremptory as geometry. 'No proposition in Euclid', declared Aiton exultantly, 'comes out more faithful to the facts than the accomplish- ment of these predictions.'[18]

The enthusiasm of these fundamentalists received a magisterial rebuke in 1856, when Arthur Stanley published his *Sinai and Palestine in Connection with their History*. Stanley, who was Professor of Ecclesi- astical History at Oxford and a future Dean of Westminster, made two

[15] Thomson, *In the Holy Land*, 244.

[16] Beamont, *Diary of a Journey*, ii. 183; Haggard, *Winter Pilgrimage*, 200; H. B. Tristram, *The Land of Israel* (3rd edn, 1876), 46.

[17] Thomson, *In the Holy Land*, 343; Christmas, *Shores and Islands*, iii. 147.

[18] Aiton, *The Lands of the Messiah*, 216.

trips to Egypt and Palestine: the first in the winter of 1852–3, and the second in the spring of 1862, when he acted as cicerone to the Prince of Wales. *Sinai and Palestine*, which was based on material gathered during his first visit, was different from the run of Protestant travel books in that it was objective and dispassionate. Stanley suggested that those who went looking for confirmations of Scripture tended to see what they wanted to see and were 'often tempted to mislead themselves and others by involuntary exaggeration or invention'. Discarding subjective interpretation for empirical inquiry, he investigated the influence of geography and topography on the history and religion of ancient Palestine. By identifying 'local influences', Stanley aimed to separate 'Fancy or Feeling' from 'Fact and Truth'; and he confronted his readers with a stupendous anomaly. There were, he decided, *no* local influences to account for the sublime biblical literature. Palestine was small, barren, and supremely unremarkable:

There is little in these hills and valleys on which the imagination can fasten . . . Shiloh and Bethel . . . almost escape the notice even of the zealous antiquarian in the maze of undistinguished hills which encompass them. The first view of Olivet impresses us chiefly by its bare, matter-of-fact appearance; the first approach to the hills of Judaea reminds the English traveller . . . of the least striking portions of the mountains of his own country.

All the attributes of desolation and damnation were suggested not by the scenery itself, but by the imaginations of over-expectant tourists. They were at one with the exploded figments concerning the Dead Sea—the notions that its noxious surface did not reflect the blue sky and that no bird could fly across it. And if the first feeling was disappointment, the second might well be thankfulness, because the nature of this landscape proved that Scripture was something more than mere mythology. Mythology required suggestive scenery, such as the 'rustling forests or the clefts of mysterious precipices' of Greece and Italy. Its absence from Palestine could indicate therefore only that Scripture was based not on Fancy, but on Fact.

Fact—yes; but Fact of the philosophical and moral, rather than of the historical kind. It was back to the division of truth. Stanley was a Broad Churchman: disciple and biographer of Thomas Arnold and defender of the authors of *Essays and Reviews*; and like them he insisted that the language of much of the Bible was figurative. Those who interpreted the whole of Scripture as a chronicle not only diminished its glorious and universal message, but imposed on it standards of evidence which—as modern German scholarship had shown—it could not meet. For this reason Stanley strongly disapproved of those who would see the fulfilment of prophecy in the present condition of specific localities. Prophecy had to do with moral, not political, vicissitudes. The accuracy of the Bible as a guidebook might well indicate that the historical passages did not require 'the latitude of poetry'; but it was imperative that 'the poetical imagery of the prophetical books' be not 'measured by the value of prose'. When Isaiah and Ezekiel prophesied the overthrow of Tyre, Sidon, Askalon, Damascus, and Petra, they spoke of the transience of worldly greatness, and fulfilment should be looked for in a 'moral and poetical' rather than 'literal and prosaic' sense. Common sense and piety, and the historical record itself, warned against 'staking the truths of Christianity and the authority of the Sacred Records on the chances of local and political revolutions'.

As a guidebook, *Sinai and Palestine* met with immediate and lasting success. It went through thirteen editions in six years and few Victorian pilgrims felt properly equipped without its 600 octavo pages somewhere in their baggage. But it did not kill the prophetic fallacy. In 1859 Dr Alexander Keith, of the Free Church of Scotland, brought out the thirty-seventh edition of his *Evidence of the Truth of the Christian Religion Derived from the Literal Fulfilment of Prophecy*, and this he subtitled 'A Refutation of the Rev. A. P. Stanley's Poetical Interpretations'. Keith's treatise, which was first published in 1828 and which had gone through forty successively enlarged editions by 1873, had immense authority in evangelical circles. 'It is recognised', said Thomas Chalmers, 'in our halls of theology as holding a high place in sacred literature, and it is found in almost every home and known as a household word throughout the land.' Its message was uncompromising and its tone hectoring. The prophecies concerning Jerusalem, the Jews, the land of Israel, the cities of Israel, Samaria, Ammon, Moab, Edom, Philistia, Tyre, Egypt, Babylon, Nineveh, and the Seven Churches of Asia had all had a literal fulfilment, and this was 'sufficient to illustrate the truth of Christianity'. The mode of accomplishment was irrelevant, because the fact was incontestable. 'THE PROPHECIES ARE TRUE', bellowed Keith; 'they may be overloooked; but no ingenuity can pervert them.' To ensure that they were not overlooked, he quoted them extensively and showed how closely they matched not only accounts of modern travellers (including Stanley), but the impartial photographic record. The thirty-sixth and subsequent editions included engravings from daguerrotypes taken by Keith and his son during their visit to Palestine in 1844.

Keith's use of photography was part of an attempt by the evangelicals to strengthen their position by enlisting the resources of science. The idea that religion and science were fundamentally opposed was a product of Victorian scepticism, not of Victorian belief. Like most Christians, evangelicals regarded science as an amplification of Revelation; and in this instance science was being used to fortify the faith of those who could not go to the Holy land by bringing the Holy Land to them. This was also done by means of art. Evangelical painters like David Wilkie and Holman Hunt went to Palestine in search of authentic backgrounds, persuaded that an accurate depiction of the Palestinian landscape would supply, in Wilkie's words, 'a collateral evidence of the truth of the sacred writings'.[19] The work carried out by Hunt during the three visits that he made between 1854 and 1873 was sustained by a religious zeal which in Ruskin's view excused its artistic shortcomings. Thus Ruskin approved of *The Scapegoat*, even though he judged it a technical failure, because its Dead Sea setting, with 'the purple mountains of Moab and . . . the pale ashes of Gomorrah', was 'exactly the scene of which it might seem desirable to give a perfect idea to those who [could] not see it for themselves'.[20] But art was a less reliable means than science to this end. Even Pre-Raphaelite painters like Hunt, for all their profession of fidelity to nature, were not entirely beyond accusations of distortion, whereas it was supposed that the camera could not lie. It was immune from the charge of seeing what it wanted to see. Photographs taken in the Holy Land in the 1850s and 1860s therefore became important auxiliaries in the evangelical campaign to refute critics like Stanley.[21]

In the longer term of course, as Mrs Cameron and her school revealed the artistic possibilities of the camera, the objectivity of the photographer seemed less well assured; so it was important for the evangelicals' pretensions to science that they find another ally in their campaign—an ally whose scientific credentials were less liable to be impugned. This ally they found in the archaeologist.

Evangelicals had always had high expectations of archaeology. 'I am convinced', said Lord Shaftesbury in 1838, 'that Providence has laid

[19] D. and F. Irwin, *Scottish Painters at Home and Abroad 1700–1900* (1975), 183.

[20] Cook and Wedderburn, eds., *Works of Ruskin*, xiv. 47.

[21] Michael Bartrum, *The Pre-Raphaelite Camera* (1985), Ch. IV.

up in store many riches of testimony to the authenticity of the Bible, to be produced in these evil days of apostasy and unbelief . . . Egypt will yield largely in confirmation of Jewish records; and Palestine, when dug and harrowed by enterprising travellers, must exhibit the past with all the vividness of the present.'[22] Charles Spurgeon, the Baptist revivalist, made a similar prediction in 1870, after noticing that the bas-reliefs on the Arch of Titus in Rome confirmed the biblical account of the siege of Jerusalem. 'The more discoveries that we make of ancient cities,' he wrote, 'especially in Palestine, the more will the truth of the Book be confirmed, and the record upon stone will be found to tally with what is written on the tablets of God's word.'[23] These expectations were dramatically justified in Mesopotamia, where Layard brought to light the buried cities of Nimrud (the biblical Calah) and Nineveh, and retrieved the civilisation of ancient Assyria from the penumbra of legend. The immense hoard of bas-reliefs and cuneiform inscriptions that he and his successors sent to the British Museum corroborated the Old Testament narrative of the wars between King Hezekiah of Judah and Sennacherib of Nineveh, and yielded besides a sensational Chaldean account of the Deluge and the Ark. The huge interest generated by Layard's first discoveries prompted an enterprising evangelical publisher, the Scottish Free Churchman Thomas Nelson, to issue a popular digest of archaeological and topographic researches throughout the world. *Ruins of Sacred and Historic Lands*, published in 1850, stressed the 'evidence of remarkable fulfilment' and the 'unexpected confirmation to the most remarkable declarations both of fulfilled and unfulfilled prophecy' in recent discoveries; and it held out the enticing prospect of yet further corroboration in Palestine itself.

Excavation made in Jerusalem in 1840 for the foundations of a new missionary church of the London Jewish Society had already revealed something like forty or fifty feet of ancient debris beneath the modern city. This had caused Dr Andrew Bonar, of the Church of Scotland, to recall the utterances of David and Jeremiah about Jerusalem becoming heaps of stones: 'Truly, the prophets spoke with a divine accuracy when they said, "Jerusalem shall become heaps" . . . The fact that these heaps of ruins are of so great depth, suggested to us a literal interpretation of the words of Jeremiah, "Her gates are sunk into the

[22] Hodder, *Shaftesbury*, i. 233.
[23] Spurgeon, ed., *Autobiography of C. H. Spurgeon*, iii. 214.

ground". The ancient gates mentioned by Nehemiah are no longer to be found, and it is quite possible that several of them may be literally buried below the feet of the inquiring traveller.'[24] In 1865 the Palestine Exploration Fund was launched, with the excavation of Jerusalem as a major objective. Queen Victoria became its Patron and the original committee contained laymen and churchmen of every denomination. Even Sir Moses Montefiore, the patriarch of Britain's Jewish community, was co-opted, as a pledge of religious impartiality. During the first twenty years the Fund's subscribers averaged about 4,000, and these were kept informed of work in progress by the regular *Quarterly Statement*, three exhibitions (two in London and one in Liverpool), and a sequence of occasional publications which culminated in 1881–4 with the monumental *Survey of Western Palestine*. The most thrilling undertaking was Captain Charles Warren's excavations in Jerusalem between 1867 and 1870. Stratigraphical methods were unknown and area clearance was impracticable, so Warren and his team of nine Royal Enginners used the shaft-and-tunnel technique and mapped the foundations of the old city by opening galleries and following ancient passages, often on their stomachs and with candles in their mouths. It was highly dangerous work. The mine shafts were threatened by tons of loose debris and the galleries were often flowing with sewage too viscous to float a duckboard. But when they had finished there could be no doubt about the accuracy of Jeremiah and David. Jerusalem was builded on her own heap true enough—to the depth of a hundred feet in some places. 'The words of David are accomplished to the letter', proclaimed the Revd Bell of Cheltenham after his visit of 1886.[25] The dedicated labour of Warren and his Engineers filled the Revd Andrew Thomson with pious anticipation. 'Those green mounds,' he reflected, 'which every traveller may see in Palestine and in the Lebanon valleys, in all likelihood preserve ruins which only need the divining rod of Science to bring them to the surface, startling expectation, confirming faith, [and] casting new gleams of light upon many an inspired sentence.'[26] It was in this mood of evangelical elation that the work of the Fund was initially sponsored and accomplished . In his survey of its first nine years the Honorary Secretary, Sir George Grove, wrote that the work of the Fund must enhance the credibility of the Bible and facilitate belief:

[24] Anon., *Ruins of Sacred and Historic Lands* (1850), 106.
[25] Bell, *Gleanings from a Tour*, 77.
[26] Thomson, *In the Holy Land*, 147–8.

We know nothing for certain, till we can prove it by excavation . . . and yet
when we do know, with what fulness of light the history comes upon us! . . . It
is by such realisation . . .that faith is strengthened and reverence increased . . .
To help everyone who cares to read the Bible intelligently; to lead those who
care for it little to care for it much; to give light to dark places; to make things
hard become things easy; to narrow the bounds of controversy—these are
some of the aims of the Palestine Exploration Fund.[27]

The PEF was set up in the atmosphere of excitement created by the
spectacular finds of the Assyriologists and there is no doubt that the
great éclat of the discoveries in Mesopotamia bedevilled the cause of
archaeology in Palestine. It created an appetite for similar hauls of
museum treasures and, in their eagerness to uncover these, early
excavators disturbed sites, confused strata, and overlooked less
ostentatious but no less important evidence. Furthermore when the
expected trophies failed to materialise they compensated by making
extravagant claims and identifications. In 1874 the rule limiting the
publications of the PEF to factual statements was relaxed, to enable its
officers to express opinions concerning their own results, and under
this dispensation discoveries were announced which later experts
were compelled to reject as fanciful. These included the walls of the
Temple of Solomon, the tombs of the House of David, and the tomb
of Christ, no less. When in 1878 Captain Charles Conder claimed to
have found the true Holy Sepulchre he dragged the PEF into a
controversy that was neither scientific nor edifying. British pilgrims
generally sponsored another location, known as 'Gordon's Tomb',
because they reckoned that this best fitted the biblical specifications
(as Hugh Price Hughes pointed out, it even had seats for the angels
mentioned by St John); and after 1901, when this so-called 'tomb' and
its garden were acquired by an English committee of trustees, the
debate concerning its authenticity was pursued with less regard for
truth than for Protestant prestige.[28]

The scientific pretensions of Victorian pilgrims and biblical
archaeologists were largely specious. The true spokesman of most of
these people was not a scientist but the Christian mystic General
Gordon, who wrote in his *Reflections on Palestine*: 'The root principle of
the right study of Jerusalem is that we should first know our Bibles,
and with this knowledge examine the localities.' Officers of the PEF,

[27] Committee of the Palestine Exploration Fund, *Our Work in Palestine* (1874), 12–13.
[28] Kelman, *The Holy Land*, 277.

like Thomas Cook's tourists, followed that precept. They began with the assumption that the Bible was literally true, and confirmed it by forcing the evidence to match the Book. They were therefore still open to the charge of finding what they wanted to find, and in 1894 Stanley's accusation was repeated by the eminent theologian George Adam Smith. In his *Historic Geography of the Holy Land*, Smith chided the 'rash proposals' of the Fund's *Quarterly Statement* and Old and New Testament Maps. 'Our surveyors', he warned, 'have been tempted to serious over-identification, perhaps by the zeal of a portion of the religious public, which subscribes to exploration according to the number of immediate results.' Like Stanley, he argued that the failure of the evidence to explain the larger fact was much more significant than its confirmation of details:

A large portion of the religious public, and of writers for them, habitually exaggerate the evidential value of the geography and archaeology of Palestine, and by emphasising what is irrelevant, especially in details, miss altogether the grand, essential contents of the land's testimony to the divine origin of our religion.

During the first years of the twentieth century the income of the PEF was declining and its activities were slackening. The tendency, both among the public and in professional circles, was to write off Palestine as archaeologically impoverished,[29] and interest reverted to Mesopotamia, where Leonard Woolley's sensational discoveries at Ur recalled the great days of Layard and Nineveh. Subsequent research in Palestine, pursued on sounder principles and with more sophisticated techniques, revealed that this judgement was unjustified. Fresh and more reliable identifications of biblical places were made; excavations at Jericho, Hazor, Bethel, Gibeah, and Debir corroborated events narrated in Exodus, Joshua, Samuel, and the Second Book of Kings; the site of Lachish yielded evidence of the Assyrian invasion recorded by Jeremiah;[30] and the discovery of the Dead Sea Scrolls confirmed the antiquity of the Hebrew Bible and confuted those nineteenth century critics who had attributed much of its composition to Roman and even Christian times. Archaeology did

---

[29] The archaeologist R. A. S. Macalister, for example, expressed this view in *A Century of Excavation in Palestine* (1925).

[30] For recent work in Palestine see W. F. Albright, *The Archaeology of Palestine* (revised edn., Harmondsworth, 1960); Kathleen Kenyon, *Archaeology in the Holy Land* (1960) and *Digging up Jerusalem* (1974).

therefore ultimately reward evangelical expectations. Yet in the long run it did not fulfil the role that the Victorians had envisaged. It weakened rather than strengthened the evangelical position, because it revealed that countless Near and Middle Eastern settlements were built on their own heaps and that obliteration and abandonment had recurred with such frequency that no divine intervention was necessary to account for them and no prophet could fail who predicted them. Furthermore this appeal to archaeology undermined fundamentalism because it allowed science a voice in the debate. Science had much to say about many things, and it could not be silenced selectively. It could not be given the right to determine the age of the Bible and at the same time denied the right to determine the age of the rocks or the age of the race. Where archaeology entered, geology and anthropology were bound to follow; and in the presence of geology and anthropology miracles reverted to myths or natural causes. This was a consequence that Canon Tristram had foreseen in 1865, when he deplored the current craze for scientific corroboration of the Bible. 'If every occurrence in Sacred History is to be thus tested and accounted for,' he warned, 'the whole question of miraculous intervention has been surrendered to the enemy, and modern scientific knowledge . . . is made the test of Scriptural authenticity.'[31] In fact, by invoking science the evangelicals ultimately made belief not easier, but more difficult for themselves. In their anxiety to demonstrate a synthesis, they exposed a choice: either Reason, or Revelation; and flavoured by this stark alternative evangelicalism lost much of its appeal. Orthodoxy became 'broad' rather than 'low', as more and more Protestants looked for history in the historical parts of the Bible, and for a wisdom transcending history in its poetic and prophetic books. Truth was divided in the end.

12. SACRED ART

There was nothing new about the idea of Prophetic Evidence; but there was everything new about the idea of Christian Art. Christian art was a discovery of the German Romantics, and one which profoundly influenced the Victorian interpretation of Italian painting and architecture. Seen through Romantic eyes these too became a source of religious uplift and reassurance.

---

[31] Tristram, *The Land of Israel*, 352.

Inherited wisdom knew no such thing as Christian art. To the eighteenth-century mind art was pagan. It was the legacy of Periclean Greece and Augustan Rome, where political freedom had stimulated physical, moral, and intellectual excellence. Most pre-Victorian intellectuals denied that art might have a Christian inspiration and regarded the medieval Christian era as a 'Gothic sleep' or 'Dark Age'. A few—Shelley, most notably—suggested that Christianity was a 'blight'. Modern art, as the term 'Revival' (later 'Renaissance') implied, dated from the rediscovery of Classical culture and the re-establishment of political liberty, first in the Italian republics and then in eighteenth-century Britain. The only post-Roman art worth consideration was therefore that produced during and after the High Renaissance, when Classical canons were adopted. In painting this meant the work of the early sixteenth-century Roman and Florentine masters (Leonardo, Michaelangelo, and the later Raphael); the Mannerists of Bologna (the Carracci, Guido Reni, Domenichino, Guercino, and Correggio); and the Venetians Titian and Veronese. Anything earlier than Raphael was deemed quaint and naïve. In architecture admiration was lavished on the Classical design and pagan embellishment of St Peter's in Rome, but only faint praise or even contempt was attracted by earlier buildings such as St Mark's in Venice and the cathedrals at Florence and Siena.[1]

Enthusiasm for the Classical inheritance persisted into the nine-teenth century. The pages of Victorian travel literature are scattered with lyrical responses both to authentic pagan sculpture and ruins in Greece, Sicily, and mainland Italy, and to the Classically inspired art and architecture of the Renaissance. Moreover, the enthusiasm was no less ardent among orthodox Christians like Gladstone, William Wordsworth, John Henry Newman, Hurrell Froude, Macaulay, Thackeray, and Arthur Stanley, than it was among sceptics like J. S. Mill, J. A. Symonds, George Gissing, and Samuel Butler. All admired, for example, the interior of St Peter's (the façade was generally rated a failure) in terms that stressed its Classical properties of harmony, simplicity, and immensity. Gladstone in 1832 judged it 'a most powerful exemplification of the laws of harmony in the relative magnitude of its parts'. In 1833 Newman 'felt quite abased' standing in the basilica, 'chiefly by [its] enormous size, which added to the

---

[1] See Larrabee, *English Bards and Grecian Marbles*; J. R. Hale, *England and the Italian Renaissance* (1963); J. R. Hale, ed., *The Italian Journal of Samuel Rogers* (1956); W. E. Mead, *The Grand Tour in the Eighteenth Century* (New York, 1914).

extreme accuracy and grace of [its] proportions makes one seem quite little and contemptible'. In 1838 Macaulay was 'fairly stunned by the magnificence and harmony of the interior'; and Mill, Fanny Trollope, J. R. Green, and a host of others were equally fulsome in their approval. The colour in Italian churches both enlarged their understanding and heightened their delight, because they had been accustomed to think of Classical architecture as monochromatic and austere, appealing to the intellect rather than the emotions. 'Before I came here I had no idea of the effect of coloured stone in architecture', wrote Hurrell Froude from Rome in 1833. 'The plain stonework has all the simplicity of a Grecian temple, and the marble sets it off just as a fine scene or a glowing sky would.' To Newman it was 'a realisation of the skill and power of Daedalus, who was beautiful while he was stupendous'. Macaulay, who had drawn all his notions of Classical interiors from 'the cold, white and naked walls of such buildings as St Paul's or St Genevieve's', felt that he had entered another world when he stepped inside his first church in Genoa and saw that 'one harmonious glow pervaded the whole of the long Corinthian arcade from the entrance to the altar'. Everyone frankly acknowledged that the inspiration behind all this magnificence was pagan rather than Christian. 'The thing which most takes possession of one's mind', wrote Froude, 'is the entire absorption of the old Roman splendour in an unthought-of system; to see their columns and marbles and bronzes ... all diverted from their first objects and taken up by Christianity.' Newman made the same observation; and the Revd M. Vicary, in Rome in 1846, swooned to see the beauty of 'the pillage of the Roman temples' which the early Christians had incorporated into their churches.[2]

In painting, likewise, the continuing homage paid to the High Renaissance masters showed a persistent tendency to trace great art to Classical origins. In Florence, Rome, and Venice in 1832 Gladstone admired pictures by Raphael, Guido, the Carraccis, Guercino, Domenichino, Michaelangelo, Titian, Tintoretto, and Veronese. Disraeli, in *Contarini Fleming* (1832), relished 'the grace of Raffaelle, the twilight tints of that magician, Guercino'. In *Pictures from Italy*, Dickens singled out Guido, Domenichino, and Ludovico Carracci among the noteworthy painters represented in the Academy at

² Foot, ed., *Gladstone Diaries*, i. 462; Kerr and Gornall, eds., *Letters and Diaries of J. H. Newman*, iii. 231, 234; Trevelyan, *Lord Macaulay*, ii. 21, 29–30; Richard Hurrell Froude, *Remains* (1838), i. 298–9; M. Vicary, *Notes of a Residence in Rome in 1846* (1847), 16.

Bologna, while he admired Raphael in Rome and Titian and Tintoretto in Venice. In 1847 Florence Nightingale rhapsodised over Michaelangelo's Sistine Chapel ceiling;[3] and in 1851 Elizabeth Browning celebrated in verse his sepulchral monument in the church of San Lorenzo in Florence.[4] And cropping up again and again there is adoration of Murillo—the darling of almost every Victorian traveller to Spain.

Implicit in all these responses was the traditional idea that the ethos of great art was heathen rather than Christian and that the role of Christianity had been to annex, rather than create, aesthetic excellence. Its positive contribution to the history of art had been the worldly one of patronage, not the spiritual one of inspiration.

This thesis was given exhaustive exposition in John Addington Symonds's *Renaissance in Italy*, which was published in seven volumes between 1875 and 1886 but which is really the last and overblown fruit of eighteenth-century thinking. In one sense it is an appendix to Gibbon's *Decline and Fall of the Roman Empire*. The two works are poles apart stylistically, with Symonds's tremulous cadences contrasting strongly with Gibbon's forensic irony; but they were written in the same frame of mind. Both men had a profound distaste for Christian mysticism and asceticism; and what Gibbon had argued from the rationalist's standpoint, Symonds endorsed from the aesthete's. He insisted that Christianity was inherently hostile to art ('the spirit of figurative art and the spirit of Christianity are opposed'), and that the Church's role as a benevolent foster-parent was only a brief interlude in a long career of repression and discouragement. The Renaissance was an area of light encompassed by darkness; a time when art, 'severing itself from the religious tradition, became the exponent of the majesty and splendour of the human body', and when there arose 'a new and vital perception of the dignity of man as a rational being'. One of the most ardent of Victorian Hellenes, Symonds traced the European artistic impulse to the free and joyous celebration of mind and body in ancient Greece; and he attributed its decline to the victory of Christianity over antique civilisation. When Christianity triumphed the gods were sent into exile. The mind was imprisoned in dogma, the flesh entombed in 'hair shirts and cerements', and pleasure smothered by the concept of sin. 'Statuesque tranquillity' was gone; and in its

---

[3] Edward Cook, *The Life of Florence Nightingale* (1913), i. 71–2.
[4] *Casa Guidi Windows*, Part I, lines 74ff.

place were the morbid contortions of self-mortification. The Renaissance, the resurrection of mind and body, was brought about by the defiant aesthetic instincts of the Italian people; by their irrepressible addiction to beauty, which paganised 'the standards of moral and aesthetic taste'. It flourished because the corrupt and worldly Popes of the second half of the fifteenth century defied their own religion and bade the pagan gods return; and it collapsed because their iniquities brought down the inevitable retribution of Christian bigotry, in the shape of Jesuitry and the Spanish Inquisition.[5]

Renaissance in Italy was old fashioned even as it came from the press, because its basic premiss had already been overtaken. Since the early 1830s taste had been changing; and with the change had come a major reassessment of the role of Christianity in the history of art. Victorian travellers, including Gladstone and Manning in the late 1830s, Sir Francis Palgrave in the 1840s, the Brownings in the 1850s, and then the Eastlakes, the Layards, Augustus Hare, and a host of others from the 1850s onwards, were noticing with mounting admiration and delight the architecture and painting of the fifteenth century and before. They were leaving the beaten tourist track and making their way to churches and galleries in sleepy medieval towns like Padua, Assisi, Volterra, Perugia, Orvieto, Pavia, Vicenza, and San Gimignano, disturbing the dust and gloom of centuries in order to peer at frescos and altar-pieces and sepulchral monuments with the aid of tallow-candles and opera-glasses. In well-frequented towns like Turin, Milan, Florence, Lucca, Rome, Pisa, Siena, Verona, and Venice they were changing the pattern of tourist inspection, stopping and gazing where previous generations had merely glanced or hurried on, enraptured by soulful countenances in old, old pictures of angels and saints, madonnas and martyrs. They were earnestly discussing artists like Fra Angelico, Perugino, Botticelli, Bellini, Mantegna, Lippi, Memmi, Ghirlandaio, and even Giotto and Cimabue. In 1848 three volumes on *Sacred and Legendary Art* were produced by Anna Jameson to satisfy this growing interest in the early masters. Noting that medieval art had now become 'a reigning fashion', Mrs Jameson set out to explain its themes and motifs. Her book was in effect a sort of directory of saints, archangels, and evangelists and a glossary of symbols and emblems as they appear in European painting from the Byzantine era, with extensive exegesis

---

[5] J. A. Symonds, *Renaissance in Italy*, iii, *The Fine Arts* (new edn., 1899), 18; i, *Age of the Despots* (new edn., 1904), 11; ii, *The Revival of Learning* (new edn., 1904), 52, 287; vi, *The Catholic Reaction, Part One* (new edn., 1904), *passim*.

of the fifteenth-century masters. From 1856 the Arundel Society, at the instigation of Austen Layard, began to publish chromolithographed reproductions of medieval masterpieces, with accompanying memoirs of the artists. Taste in architecture was changing too. There was growing appreciation of the unselfconscious and edifying beauty of early buildings. The great pointed Gothic cathedrals of Milan and Seville attracted praise that was more and more fulsome; and medieval buildings in the less familiar Romanesque styles—buildings like San Marco in Venice, the Campanile in Florence, and the cathedrals of Siena, Orvieto, and Pisa—were being seen with new eyes.

The corollary of this new preference was a tumble in the reputation of the Cinquecento heroes. Raphael (in his later style), Michael-angelo, and the Bolognese were increasingly reproached for either mannered imitation of the Classical tradition or meretricious mimicry of the medieval one. Neither their power nor their serenity now seemed authentic. Dickens found Correggio's frescos in the cathedral at Parma repulsively delirious—'such a labyrinth of arms and legs; such heaps of foreshortened limbs, entangled and involved and jumbled together'; and in Michaelangelo's *Last Judgement* in the Sistine Chapel he could not see 'any general idea or one pervading thought in harmony with the subject'. Mrs Jameson reproved 'admiration wasted on the flimsy mannerists of the later ages of art; men who apparently had no definite *intention* in anything they did, except a dashing outline, or a delicate finish, or a striking and attractive management of colour'. In *Old Pictures in Florence* (1855) Robert Browning heaped scorn on tourists '. . . in ecstasies / Before some clay-cold, vile Carlino' (i.e. Carlo Dolci). Lady Eastlake summed up Michaelangelo's Sistine Chapel ceiling as 'coarse and ungraceful' and his *Last Judgement* as 'a daub'. In the same year (1858) Layard, in an article in the *Quarterly Review*, attacked the 'theatrical groups of muscular apostles and anatomic saints' which the Cinque-cento had produced—another dig at Michaelangelo, obviously. Michaelangelo's merit as a sculptor was frequently disputed and in Augustus Hare's *Florence* (1884) the San Lorenzo tombs are stigma-tised as pitiable failures. In *Middlemarch* George Eliot impugned another old favourite when she wrote of 'smirking Renaissance Correggiosities' and in *The Newcomes* Thackeray wrote dismissively of Raphael's late *Transfiguration* in the Vatican. High Renaissance architecture, likewise, was severely condemned. Elizabeth Eastlake reckoned that St Peter's was 'like a clubhouse, with balconies and entresols and every kind of mixed ornament which the worst upholstery and taste could invent'. Cato Lowes Dickinson was sure that it lacked the impressiveness of a Gothic church; and in 1871 Edward Burne-Jones wrote that he did not even feel it to be vast, but merely 'pompous and empty'.[6]

The British interest in medieval art and architecture did not of course originate with religiously minded Victorians. It took its rise in the secular tastes of the eighteenth century, as part of a wider 'Gothic Revival'—a craze for the antiquarian, the whimsical, and the Romantic which by the first decades of the nineteenth century was broad enough to include medieval painting and Italian Gothic buildings (such as the cathedral at Siena) as well as those in the more familiar Northern, or pointed, Gothic style. Even in Victorian times there were always those who liked medieval art for reasons profane rather than sacred. Symonds was the most obvious of these; Swinburne, Pater, Leighton, and Watts were others. What they saw and admired in early painting was the Greek spirit struggling to reassert itself. The function of the religiously minded was refinement and redefinition. They refined medieval painting and sculpture because they promoted them from the category of decoration to the category of art. They elevated them into achievements worthy of serious study and meriting comparison to those of Greece and Rome. They redefined them because they preferred the label 'Christian' to 'Gothic' or 'Ecclesiastical'. This implied a purely religious inspiration as opposed to a heathen one that had been tamed and patronised by the Church. Such an interpretation was possible because they experienced art in a new way. The question they asked themselves of a picture or building was not: 'How does it look?' but rather: 'What does it say?' The technical criteria of eighteenth-century aesthetics—'chiaroscuro', 'Correggiosity', 'handling', 'composition', and so on—were of secondary importance. What mattered most was 'Expression'. 'As poetry only have I considered them', wrote Mrs Jameson of the works discussed in her book. Her contention was that they could speak of something other than 'flowing lines and correct drawing and gorgeous colour'. They had 'another, a deeper significance than ha[d] been dreamed of by picture dealers and picture collectors, or even picture critics'.[7] 'Just sit

[6] Dickens, *Pictures from Italy*, 69, 147; Anna Jameson, *Sacred and Legendary Art* (1848), i. p. xxii; Smith, ed., *Journals of Lady Eastlake*, ii. 108; Layard, *Autobiography*, ii. 205; Dickinson, *Letters from Italy*, 23; Burne-Jones, *Edward Burne-Jones*, ii. 25.

[7] Jameson, *Sacred and Legendary Art*, i. pp. xii, xxiv.

down before your Perugino', Aubrey de Vere advised Mrs Villiers in 1848, 'and look on it, not as a picture, but as a poem . . . and then ask yourself what it has been saying all this time.'[8]

And there was only one answer. What this language of expression spoke of was Christianity. Pointed arches and soaring spires in architecture, and static postures and impassive countenances in painting, all spoke of Christian virtues, which de Vere listed as 'dignity, sweetness, purity, strength, pathos, elevation, sublimity'. They registered a spiritual inspiration superior to the purely intellectual and sensual content of both Classical and modern art.

Coleridge, in the first decade of the nineteenth century, had developed the idea that 'Gothic' art was different from 'Grecian' art by virtue of Christian influence; but it was Augustus Pugin who first gave this Christian element a concrete identity. He specified the pointed arch as its peculiar manifestation—which was as good a feature as any, because a long and tedious controversy had failed to provide a more convincing explanation for its emergence. In *Contrasts* (1836) Pugin explained how pointed architecture bore the imprint of Christian faith and devotion. 'In it alone', he wrote, 'we find the faith of Christianity embodied and its practices illustrated'; and it was this Christian element, rather than 'mere beauty or antiquity', that constituted its claim to admiration and imitation. The same was true of Italian painting of the thirteenth to fifteenth centuries, which was 'the beau ideal of Christian purity'. It was Pugin, furthermore, in his second edition of 1841, who introduced the English public to that unfavourable estimate of the High Renaissance which had been formulated by the French critics Montalembert and Rio. In their view the Renaissance was a resurgence not merely of paganism, but of debased paganism; a betrayal of the intellectual for the sake of the merely sensual in art. As Pugin summed up, in a footnote:

Almost all the celebrated artists of the last three centuries instead of producing their works from feelings of devotion and a desire of instructing the faithful, merely sought for a display of their art and an increase of fame; hence they not unfrequently selected the least edifying subjects from sacred writ . . . simply because they afforded a better scope for the introduction of pagan nudities . . . which form striking contrasts to the humble piety of the ages of faith.

[8] Wilfred Ward, *Aubrey de Vere: A Memoir* (1904), 150.

Lord Lindsay and John Ruskin adopted this thesis and embellished it with monumental erudition and eloquence. Lindsay projected an enormous five-part treatise, whose themes were to be the rise of the Christian spiritual principle in the arts from the sixth to the mid-fifteenth century, its struggle with the pagan principles of intellect and sensuality in the second half of the fifteenth century, the triumph of paganism in the first half of the sixteenth century, the sterile reign of the pagan principles until the end of the eighteenth century, and the resurgence of the Christian principle in the nineteenth century. Of this grand design only the first part was ever written, but it filled two copious volumes and was published in 1846 as *Sketches of the History of Christian Art*. It traced the development of the Christian spirit in art and architecture from the Romanesque (or 'Lombard') period until the middle of the fifteenth century; and it claimed that this spirit achieved its fullest expression in the pointed Gothic style north of the Alps. Lindsay based his argument on the evidence of moral temper and *Zeitgeist* recorded in pigment and stone. 'It is from the settlement of the Lombards', he wrote, '. . . that the life of modern Europe, civil and ecclesiastical, properly dates; and we find, accordingly, in the Lombard architecture and sculpture, the earliest voice and expression of that life.' In architecture this modern life was registered in 'new combinations and a more ample development of the spirit of symbolism'; in sculpture, in 'a profusion of imagery'. For Lindsay the Gothic styles recorded the vicissitudes of Christian principles in conflict with pagan principles. Hence 'the gradual dying away of the Christian and chivalric spirit throughout Europe' was 'visible in the gradually lower and lower depression of the pointed arch'. In the painting of this first period he found 'a holy purity, an innocent naïveté, a child-like grace and simplicity, a freshness, a fearlessness, an utter freedom from affection, a yearning after all things truthful, lovely and of good report'; and the more Christian, so necessarily the more excellent, was art. 'It is not . . . symmetry of form or beauty of colouring . . . that is required of us and that constitutes our prerogative; but the conception of the artist and expression to the spectator of the highest and holiest spiritual truths and emotions.'[9]

The ideas that art expressed moral qualities, and that moral qualities were the essence of beauty, were taken by Ruskin from the

---

[9] Alexander William Crawford, Lord Lindsay, *Sketches of the History of Christian Art* (1846), i. 4, 297–8, 317.

works of Pugin, Rio and Lindsay and made the fundamental premiss of a massive critical exegesis. After reading Rio's *De la poésie chrétienne* in 1844 he rushed back to Italy to examine the expressive content of paintings in Pisa, Florence, and Venice, and he published the results of his observations in 1846 in the second volume of *Modern Painters*. This marked the beginning of a life-long mission to awaken the English public both to the Christian virtues of the primitives and the Venetians, and to the pagan iniquities of the Roman and Florentine Cinquecento heroes. It was a mission underpinned by a strong sense of revelation and special destiny. In 1883, recalling his visit of 1845 to the Scuola di San Rocco in Venice, Ruskin wrote: 'I . . . felt . . . that I had seen that day the Art of Man in its full majesty for the first time; and that there was also a strange and precious gift in myself enabling me to recognise it, and therein ennobling, not crushing me. That sense of my own gift and function gathered strength as I grew older.'[10] It was then that he began to see Michaelangelo as a harbinger of decadence rather than as a summit of excellence—a view that had fully developed by 1871, when he published *The Relation between Michaelangelo and Tintoret*. In this essay he arraigned Michaelangelo for his obsession with violence rather than peace, with dead anatomy rather than living humanity, with bodies rather than faces, and with expression that was evil rather than benign; in all of which he read the Satanic principles of vanity, dishonesty, insolence, artificiality, and carnality.[11]

Lindsay's influence was clearly at work in Ruskin's most important architectural treatises—*The Seven Lamps of Architecture* (1849) and *The Stones of Venice* (1851–3). In *The Seven Lamps* Ruskin lists the moral attributes of Sacrifice, Truth, and Obedience among the characteristics of great architecture; and in the second volume of *The Stones of Venice* he is clearly indebted to Lindsay when he defines the 'Savageness' of Gothic architecture as 'an index not of climate, but of religious principle', and when he traces the 'strength of will, independence of character, resoluteness of purpose, impatience of control and that general tendency to set the individual reason against authority and the individual deed against destiny' of the Northern tribes in the 'rigid lines, vigorous and various masses, and daringly projecting and independent structure of the Northern Gothic

---

[10] Cook and Wedderburn, eds., *Works of Ruskin*, iv. 354.
[11] Ibid., xii.

ornament'. Lindsay had summarised the Second Period of his projected treatise as that when 'Christianity battled with the pride of Intellect and resuscitated Paganism', and this description obviously buried itself deep in Ruskin's mind, because 'pride' is one of the central moral qualities in *The Stones of Venice*. Pride and Infidelity he found written all over 'the plain cross-beam from pillar to pillar, . . . the round arch, [the] square or circular shafts and [the] low gabled roof and pediment' of High Renaissance architecture; while the 'pointed arch, shadowy vault, . . . clustered shaft [and] heaven-pointing spire' of earlier styles bore the cachet of humility and devotion. Such architecture was 'Christian' as opposed to merely 'Ecclesiastical'. With his vision thus finely attuned to evidence of sin and virtue in stone Ruskin scrutinised the architecture of Venice and read there a petrified record of the Republic's moral history. 'Venice, as she was once the most religious, was in her fall the most corrupt of European states; and as she was in her strength the centre of the pure currents of Christian architecture, so she is in her decline the source of the Renaissance.'[12]

It was mainly guilt that made Ruskin become an art critic instead of an artist. His strong aesthetic instincts—what Kenneth Clark called 'his passionate sensibility'—clashed with his evangelical conscience. They therefore demanded justification; and it was in order to justify them that he wrote. When he told his father 'I do not feel any romance in Venice. It is simply a heap of ruins trodden underfoot by such men as Ezekiel describes in xxi, 31', he was vindicating his response to Venice, not describing it.[13] The truth is that he did feel romance in Venice. It was with Venice as with all his preferred art. He loved it because it was beautiful—just as he hated poverty because it was ugly. His rhapsodic evocation of its lights and colours, and his passionate solicitude for its mortal frailty, show clearly that he responded ardently to its sensuous loveliness—just as his relentless moralising shows that he felt guilty for doing so. As with most evangelicals, his mind was a tribunal where self-indictment alternated with self-acquittal. 'My love of art has been a terrible temptation to me,' he confessed to his father in 1853, 'and I feel that I have been sadly self-indulgent lately . . . I think I must cut the whole passion short off at the roots, or I shall get to be a mere collector . . . I am sure I ought to take

[12] Ruskin, *The Stones of Venice*, ii. Ch. VI, paras. ix, lxxvi; iii. Ch. I, para. xviii; Conclusion, para. xxxvin.
[13] Bradley, ed., *Ruskin's Letters from Venice*, 185.

that text to heart "covetousness which is idolatry", for I do idolize my Turners and missals.'[14] In Volume Two of *Modern Painters* he justified his idolatry by arguing that beauty was the signature of God upon His works—a trick of self-vindication practised by the evangelical Dorothea, in George Eliot's *Middlemarch*, as she gazes on beautiful gemstones. 'All the while her thought was trying to justify her delight in the colours by merging them in her mystic religious joy.'

Ruskin's obsessive concern to explain his dedication to art in religious terms—'to prove', as he put it, 'the nobleness of delights'[15]— caused him to enlarge the repertoire of Christian art. Since his definition of what was Christian was dictated by beauty and not by history, it could change as his likes and dislikes changed; and as his preferences widened, so he annexed more and more territory to the Christian domain. As inherited from Rio, Pugin, and Lindsay, 'Christian art' comprised Northern Gothic architecture and the fourteenth and fifteenth-century painting of Florence, Siena, and Bologna. To these Ruskin added Tintoretto (in the second volume of *Modern Painters*), the Lombardic Romanesque architecture of Tuscany (in *The Seven Lamps of Architecture*)—a style which Lindsay had reproached for 'confusion of ideas' and 'metaphysical untruth'[16]— and the Byzantine Romanesque architecture of Venice (in *The Stones of Venice*). In 1860, in the fifth volume of *Modern Painters*, he recruited Veronese and Titian, deciding that seriousness and piety were not to be found merely in weakness and dullness, but in fervent celebration of the world and the flesh as well. These Venetian painters 'saw that sensual passion in man was not only a fact, but a Divine fact'.[17] In 1870, in a lecture at Oxford, he proclaimed the Christian excellence of Carpaccio. If he had liked Greek art he would probably have found the means of annexing that too.

Ruskin's taste ebbed as well as flowed, and in his last years it retreated from the gorgeous sixteenth-century Venetians back to the fifteenth-century Venetians and Florentines (Giovanni Bellini, Filippo Lippi, Botticelli) and to Giotto and the primitives. But the tide left its harvest, in the form of his printed opinions, and these were treasured as guides and oracles by a huge travelling public. Ruskin provided a litany of responses for two generations of British visitors to

[14] Cook and Wedderburn, eds., *Works of Ruskin*, xii. p. lxxvii.
[15] Ibid., iv. 43.
[16] Lindsay, *Christian Art*, i. 317n.
[17] Cook and Wedderburn, eds., *Works of Ruskin*, vii. 296.

Italy. Early disciples included Tennyson, Mrs Gaskell, and George Eliot. Later these were joined by Oscar Browning and Edward Thring. Browning relates how in 1867 he and his friend Marchie Gosselin worked their way through *The Stones of Venice* 'verifying each illustration on the spot, so that in three weeks we saw the place thoroughly'. Ruskin's *Mornings in Florence* persuaded George Gissing, in 1889, that medieval Florentine art was 'Christian' and therefore something he disliked; and in Venice, as he told Eduard Bertz, 'one thinks first of all of architecture, and Ruskin's divine work thereon.' Hugh Price Hughes relied heavily on Ruskin's guidance during his visit to Italy in 1894, and the young Somerset Maugham explored Florence as his obedient apprentice. 'I admired according to instructions', he recalled, 'the tower of Giotto and the bronze doors of Ghiberti. I was properly enthusiastic over the Botticellis in the Uffizi and I turned the scornful shoulder of extreme youth on what the Master disapproved of.'[18] William Monypenny, writing the first volume of his life of Disraeli in 1909, acknowledged Ruskin's sway by adding, after noting Disraeli's early preference for Salvator and Guercino: 'but those were the days before Ruskin.' The extent of his influence was satirized by E. M. Forster in *A Room with a View* (1908), in the episode where Lucy Honeychurch is perplexed because, abandoned in Santa Croce in Florence, she has no one to tell her 'which, of all the sepulchral slabs that pave the nave and transepts, was the one that was really beautiful, the one that had been most praised by Mr Ruskin'.

It was Ruskin, more than anyone else, who transformed the art treasures of Italy into a Christian preserve; a source of edification and reassurance for Christian travellers. As the rapt, evocative melody of his prose coaxed more and more loveliness from canvas and stone, so did the sonorous pulpit counterpoint coax more and more evidence of Christian inspiration. Italian art and architecture became vivid testimonies to the power and truth of the Christian religion. Reminiscing in 1883, Ruskin wrote that in 1845 the Campo Santo of Pisa had become for him 'a veritable Palestine';[19] and it was under his guidance that droves of British travellers detected the odour of sanctity in the artistic heritage of Italy. In the early decades of the nineteenth century the evangelical instinct was to exclude art from the

---

[18] W. Somerset Maugham, *The Painted Veil* (Pocket edn., 1936), pp. viii–ix.
[19] Cook and Wedderburn, eds., *Works of Ruskin*, iv. 350.

scheme of salvation and moral reclamation. 'Would it preserve me from one sin, or enable me to overcome one temptation?' demanded Richard Chenevix Trench in Rome in 1835.[20] Ruskin made that question redundant. It was as a result of his teaching that Maria Hare was able to remark to her adoptive son Augustus in 1870: 'I always think that walking through the Roman picture galleries is like walking through the Old and New Testament, with the blessed company of the Apostles and martyrs beside one.'[21]

Inevitably, by the turn of the century a reaction against this way of experiencing art was setting in. Late Victorian and Edwardian intellectuals were the disciples of other gurus. From Walter Pater they learnt that art was not religious, but a religion—the child and the parent of passionate experience. Bernhard Berenson, in the late 1890s, defined excellence in terms that nullified Ruskin's moral viewpoint, discarding emotional expression as redundant and religious idealism as superseded and substituting the 'purely artistic' qualities of Tactile Values, Movement, and Space-Composition as the only possible criteria of permanent greatness in painting. Another American expatriate, Henry James, lost patience with Ruskin's headmistress mentality and 'the pedagogic fashion in which he pushes and pulls his unhappy pupils about, jerking their heads towards this, rapping their knuckles for that, sending them to stand in corners and giving them Scripture texts to copy'.[22] Art, insisted James, was meant to be enjoyable, not edifying. 'Art is made for us, not we for art.' Younger British critics, like Roger Fry, Clive Bell, and Geoffrey Scott, turned their backs on the old prophet, discarding the 'ethical fallacy' in favour of 'pure art' and 'significant form'. Even Ruskin's own biographers and editors became apologetic. In 1902 Frederic Harrison published a biography in which he chided Ruskin for his blatant disregard of history, whose clear lesson was that great art had no kinship with morals. In the Introduction to the Everyman edition of *The Stones of Venice*, issued in 1907, the editor, L. March Phillips, confessed that Ruskin's 'substitution of the ethical for the aesthetic standpoint' had rendered many of his judgements valueless.

These new ideas accompanied increasing numbers of British tourists to Paris, alerting them to an art that Ruskin had never even mentioned; but they took longer to percolate into the Italian guide-

---

[20] Bromley, *The Man of Ten Talents*, 56.
[21] Hare, *The Story of My Life*, iii. 395.
[22] James, *Italian Hours*, 129.

books. Until the First World War, received opinion about Mediterranean art remained Ruskinian. It was still accepted that ancient art was perfect within its limits but spiritually impoverished; that it had died in the moral anarchy of the last years of the Roman Empire; that medieval art represented the highest level of creative genius; and that it had arisen because Christianity had brought about moral regeneration and a new awareness of the intense inner life. The medieval cloister was not a tomb (as Symonds had insisted), but a cradle. This interpretation was not extinct even by 1928, as the Epilogue to the youthful Kenneth Clark's *The Gothic Revival* makes plain.

What the critics of Ruskin and his disciples overlooked was the nature of the expectations of most Victorians. Edification and improvement, rather than enjoyment, were what these travellers were seeking, and by interpreting art in these terms Ruskin made it both accessible and spiritually satisfying. He also enlisted it in the defence of Christianity against rationalism. Under his powerful scrutiny medieval Italian art disclosed what Aubrey de Vere called 'an ideal of holiness, of moral beauty, and of . . . Divine Humanity which [had] never revealed itself in Northern regions or in modern times to the spectacled muse of Biblical criticism'.[23] There was, almost certainly, deception at work. It was with the medieval paintings and sculpture of Italy as it was with the landscape of Palestine. Evangelical teachers were seeing in it what they wanted to see. They turned stylistic conventions into evidence of divine inspiration, just as they turned the accidental contours and political misfortunes of the Holy Land into evidence of fulfilled prophecy. The ethical fallacy and the prophetic fallacy were twin products of the same subconscious concern to rehabilitate Christianity in a hostile age. But the deceived were not unwilling. Ruskin satisfied a need when he offered a formula that legitimised art in terms of religion and religion in terms of art.

13. ABOMINATIONS OF THE EARTH

The feelings of British travellers about the religions of the South were mixed. Islam generally left them fascinated but emotionally unengaged. A few eccentrics, like Edward Lane, Lucie Duff Gordon, and Wilfred Scawen Blunt, took it to their hearts; but for the majority it

[23] Ward, *Aubrey de Vere*, 149.

was too exotic to stir a deep response and too impotent to justify alarm. Viewed from a vantage point of cultural detachment and political superiority it signified no more than a picturesque and vaguely defined orientalism, composed of arabesques and odalisques, bazaars and caravans, hot palm groves and pungent perfumes, marbled gardens and enigmatic spices. It belonged to the world of light literature, parlour songs, and ornamental architecture; the world of Walter Scott, William Jones, Washington Irving, the expurgated *Arabian Nights*, and Regency Brighton. Reaction, accordingly, was relaxed and nonchalant. One of its forms was the sentimental tolerance adopted by Richard Monckton Milnes in *Palm Leaves*, an anthology of verse published in 1844. Milnes celebrated the mosque as an oasis of simple piety and spiritual brotherhood—

> The Holy place,
> Where faithful men of every race,
> Meet at their ease, and face to face—

and the harem as a sanctuary of ideal womanhood:

> Thus in the ever-closed Hareem,
> As in the open Western home,
> Sheds womanhood her starry gleam
> Over our being's busy foam;
> Through latitudes of varying faith
> Thus trace we still her mission sure,
> To lighten life, to sweeten death,
> And all for others to endure.

Another form of this reaction was impish badinage. 'You find but a waning power and a faded splendour that inclines you to laugh and mock', wrote Kinglake.[1] This was the note struck by Thackeray, in his depiction of the Muslim paradise as a seedy Vauxhall where the fountains of eternal wine are running dry and sad houris sit darning faded muslins under roasted–meat trees without gravy.[2] More earnest commentators, like Eliot Warburton, William Beamont, Alexander Graham, and Henry Ashbee, were coldly contemptuous of the puerilities of the Koran and the credulous but waning fanaticism of its votaries.

Southern Christianity was different. It was too remote to be

---

[1] A. W. Kinglake, *Eothen* (Everyman edn., 1908), 24.
[2] Thackeray, *Cornhill to Grand Cairo*, 143–4.

familiar, yet too familiar not to be disturbing. It was a face within a face; a travesty of features well known and deeply cherished. By commanding recognition and at the same time forbidding affection it generated an emotional turmoil that was expressed in violent language and bad behaviour.

Nothing in the Mediterranean was so enticing, nor yet so repulsive, as the religion of Papal Rome. Year after year British Protestants flocked to the Easter and Christmas ceremonies in St Peter's, the Sistine Chapel, and St John Lateran; and year after year it was obvious that it would have been better for their own peace of mind, and for the national reputation for sang-froid and graciousness, if they had stayed away. They pulled every string and used every ruse (a uniform, of whatever type, was reckoned to work wonders) to gain entry to the various events, and then, in the words of Charles Weld, 'rush[ed] frantically from church to chapel, and chapel to church, desirous of seeing every ceremony that season'. They jostled and elbowed for the best places; avidly observed and busily noted; and then felt a rage and disgust which demanded an outlet in ostentatious misbehaviour. They refused to uncover for the Pope, or to kneel to receive his blessing. At Mass they remained seated or standing when the Host was elevated, and Mrs Trollope was told that on one occasion the popping of champagne corks was heard from the English tribune during the silence of the sacred moment. During the music they would scoff and snigger and make loud pejorative comments—to the great embarrassment of more sensitive compatriots. 'I had no conception English women could be such brutes, or exhibit themselves so contemptibly', wrote Ruskin after attending a service in the Chiesa del Gesu in December 1840. Fanny Kemble, in St Peter's during Holy Week in 1846, was dismayed by

their indecent curiosity and eagerness to satisfy it; their total apparent forgetfulness of the sacred purposes to which the place . . . was dedicated; the coarse levity of their observations and comments upon what was going on; their determined perseverence in their own flirtations and absurd conversation in the midst of the devotions of the people whose church they were invading; [and] their discussions of their own plans of amusement.

John Addington Symonds winced at the 'open-mouthed bad taste' of his countrymen; and Robert Curzon resented their 'behaving as if they were not in a church, but at the opera or any other exhibition'. George Augustus Sala reported that during the Christmas ceremonies of 1866 'neither sanctity nor solemnity ... deterred a large number of foreigners, presumably Protestants and ... mostly of the Anglo-Saxon race, from behaving in the Gesu with extreme indecorum'. He observed with shame the contrast between their 'pushing, jostling, stamping on bystanders' toes or digging elbows into their chests, the whole accompanied by very free-and-easy remarks in the English tongue' and the 'ten times better conduct observed in the body of the church ... where the people who are ordinarily termed *canaille* [were] to be found thick clustered'.[3]

The British hurried away fretting with indignation and burning to communicate what they had seen. In their books, letters, and table-talk they retailed long descriptions of the Roman services in various styles of shock and outrage. Extreme Protestants reacted with a note of hysteria. 'I had seen the filth of Smyrna, of Cairo and of Constantinople,' screamed the Presbyterian John Aiton, 'with the dead dromedaries mortifying in the burning sun; but these were nothing to the corruptions and carnalities of Popery on the banks of the Tiber ... Here Satan has been loosed out of his prison to deceive men, that he might cast them into the lake of fire and brimstone. Verily has this Babylon ...'—and so on. Charles Spurgeon the Baptist boiled with blood pressure as he surveyed the iniquities and blasphemies of 'this city of Babylon', and he prayed 'that another Luther might arise and thunder forth the fact that men are not justified by works, but by faith alone'. The Methodist William Arthur was too appalled to be enraged, and could only murmur faintly: 'The feeling is awe; deep awe and horror.' Lay tourists, like Gladstone, Fanny Kemble, Nassau Senior, and Frances Elliot, blustered and snapped, making ample use of words like 'ridiculous', 'absurd', 'pitiful', 'puerile', 'childish', 'hideous', 'grotesque', and 'ludicrous'.[4]

Sala saw perverted pleasure in all this invective, and 'a pride of conscious rectitude' in the condemnation. There is perspicacity in his judgement; but much of the pain was authentic, nevertheless. Religious ritual was genuinely offensive to many Britons because it was an affront to the antithetical idea at the root of their Protestantism.

[3] Weld, *Last Winter in Rome*, 474; Trollope, *A Visit to Italy*, ii. 273; Evans and Whitehouse, eds., *Diaries of Ruskin*, i. 131; Butler, *A Year of Consolation*, i. 239; J. A. Symonds, *Sketches and Studies in Italy* (1879), 29; Curzon, *Monasteries in the Levant*, 182; Sala, *Rome and Venice*, 388–9.

[4] Aiton, *The Lands of the Messia*, 387; Spurgeon, ed., *Autobiography of C. H. Spurgeon*, iii. 218–19; Arthur, *Italy in Transition*, 385–6.

They accepted the Reformers' definition of sacred and profane, faith and works, as mutually exclusive categories and found it difficult to credit people outwardly devout with inward holiness. 'Ceremonial cleanness is all,' wrote W. G. Clark of the Greeks in 1858; 'inward purity is not thought of. The Pharisaism which our Lord denounced could not be more abominable than the Pharisaism which the Greek Church enforces in His name.' To the Protestant mentality, therefore, Papal symbolism was a meretricious pretence which usurped, in an ineffably preposterous way, the reverence due only to the ultimate Reality. It linked Christianity with the theatre; and the theatre, as a simulacrum, an illusion, was by implication the antithesis of truth. A stage production of Saint-Saëns's *Samson and Delilah* (1887) was delayed in England because of widespread objection to religious opera, and during thirty years the work was performed only as an oratorio. The speciality in Rome was operatic religion, which was doubly profane. A constant theme of British complaint against Catholic liturgy was that it was operatic, or theatrical. 'The music was fine,' wrote Lord Shaftesbury in Rome on Christmas Day 1833, 'but, as usual, precisely like an opera. In such rites as these the soul has no share.' Fanny Kemble attended the funeral of Gregory XVI in 1846, and found that the décor in St Peter's reminded her 'of nothing so much as the operatical representations of the tomb of Ninus in the *Semiramide*'. The Revd M. Vicary, following his visit to St Peter's the same year, felt 'contempt for those who [could] introduce into the house of God forms, accompanied with music and military display, little, if anything, removed from the representations of the opera'. Thackeray remembered visiting a church in Rome which was 'like a shabby theatre'. Bishop Christopher Wordsworth referred to St Peter's as 'a religious theatre' in which the central character was the Pope; and Frances Elliot, present at a ceremony of canonisation in 1870, found the whole thing redolent of the opera. 'I have seen the Scala at Milan', she wrote, 'and many other gorgeous opera houses, but I never beheld one to compare with this, which resembled nothing else, however—the choir being the stage, and the Pope and the cardinals the actors, with ourselves, the mighty mass of spectators, the audience.'

Such travellers were shocked by the inappropriate demeanour of the clerical part of Roman congregations. Priests chatted, cardinals took snuff, and monks laughed, banishing solemnity and reinforcing the impression of a casual *divertissement*. How much more suitable, thought James Whiteside, was the conduct of congregations in the humble Protestant church outside the city boundaries. 'Grave in aspect, serious in spirit, a congregation of Christians here meet to worship God with the homage of the soul.' The Revd Michael Seymour summed up the Protestant aversion to Papal ceremonies in 1848, when he decided that they were 'an attempt at the religious drama—a continuation of those tawdry shews and scenes that had their original in the vicious taste and depraved notions of religion that belonged to the Middle Ages, and that ought long since to have been flung aside'. Other profane entertainments suggested by the decorations and rites included Guy Fawkes festivities (Dickens), the promenade in Kensington Gardens (Seymour), and 'a Crystal Palace flower show, a Lord Mayor's feast, a royal ball, or a review' (William Arthur). Henry Christmas and G. M. Trevelyan, judging by their reference to 'millinery', 'petticoats', and 'black skirts', were put in mind of sinister transvestism.[5]

Popular Christianity in the South—both Roman Catholic and Greek Orthodox—was no less abhorrent than Popery. Its characteristic vices were sacerdotalism and superstition. Aubrey de Vere (while still a Protestant) identified 'priestcraft' as one of the essential elements of Catholicism. He defined it as 'the spiritual supremacy of the few and the servile condition of the many', and he reckoned that no one who had not been in Italy could imagine its 'extraordinary power and innumerable ramifications'. J. R. Green agreed that the peasantry were 'devout and priest-ridden to a man'; and these and similar testimonies to the power of the priesthood troubled the Victorian imagination like a midnight menace. Because they were conditioned by their education and their literature to associate Catholic clergy with the Inquisition, martyrs, cunning sophistry, and stifled lights of science, whenever they encountered priests Victorian travellers saw images of evil, dredged from the depths of Protestant prejudice. 'Slinking noiselessly about in pairs, like black cats', runs Dickens's well-known description of Jesuits in Rome. 'Deep, dark and designing', thought Cato Lowes Dickinson when a priest entered his railway

[5] Sala, *Rome and Venice*, 313–14; Clark, *Peloponnesus*, 184; Hodder, *Shaftesbury*, i. 184; Butler, *A Year of Consolation*, ii. 167; Vicary, *Residence in Rome*, 86; Thackeray, *Cornhill to Grand Cairo*, 216; Wordsworth, *Tour in Italy*, ii. 226; Elliot, *Idle Woman in Italy*, i. 12, 38; Whiteside, *Italy in the Nineteenth Century*, 462; Michael Hobart Seymour, *A Pilgrimage to Rome* (1848), 339; Christmas, *Shores and Islands*, i. 175; Trevelyan, *Garibaldi's Defence of the Roman Republic*, 62.

carriage at Turin. 'Dark, haughty, inscrutable', wrote Frances Power
Cobbe of the Jesuits. 'Dark and lonely men, isolated tools of Rome,
watchmen who walk in the dark and spy out all men's ways', was
William Arthur's assessment of the priestly cavalcade in Rome. In
Sala's description of the Vatican entourage the priests figure as Grand
Guignol grotesques: 'cadaverous parties in shovels, with ... sallow
faces and gallow looks ... whispering behind their bony hands'. If
Roman priests were fearsome for their subtlety, Greek priests were
despicable for their ignorance. 'The ignorance of the clergy is
deplorable', reported Abercromby Trant in 1830; and John Hennen
echoed this in his account of the Ionian Islands. 'Their clergy', he
wrote, 'are taken from the very scum of the population and are, with
few exceptions, illiterate, superstitious and immoral.' Charles Newton
found the priests on Rhodes 'generally mere clowns, tilling their land
like the rest, and knowing just enough Greek to read the services of
their church', and the Catholic Sir Thomas Wyse confirmed the gross
inadequacy of the clergy of the Greek mainland.[6]

The religion over which these ministers presided was riddled with
'superstition'—a word that constantly recurs in the British accounts of
Mediterranean Christianity. By superstition, the Victorian traveller
meant belief in the magical properties and supernatural powers of
relics, saints, indulgences, and images—something which seemed a
gross affront both to Scripture and to human reason. It was a survival
from the era of black art; a frightful incongruity in an age, as Vicary put
it, 'of greater light, when knowledge [had] advanced with rapid
footsteps and science unravelled many intricacies in things hitherto
unknown'. Seymour found it 'strange that amidst all the light of this
nineteenth century—an age in which knowledge runs to and fro
through the earth—the pretence to this power in issuing Indulgences
should still be made'. He felt 'distress and disgust' at the liturgical use
made of human remains, and indignation at the 'unblushing impu-
dence' with which spurious mementos (fragments of the Cross, nails
from the Crucifixion, thorns from Christ's Crown, and so on) were
foisted on a naïve laity. All was characterised by 'dark superstition'.
Many travellers were both allured and repelled by the necrolatry of

    [6] Ward, *Aubrey de Vere*, 43; J. R. Green, *Stray Studies from England and Italy*, 2nd Series
(1903), 263; Dickens, *Pictures from Italy*, 46; Dickinson, *Letters from Italy*, 16; Cobbe,
Italics, 279; Arthur, *Italy in Transition*, 210; Sala, *Rome and Venice*, 382; Trant, *Journey
through Greece*, 206; Hennen, *Medical Topography*, 174; Newton, *Travels and Discoveries*, i.
210; Thomas Wyse, *Impressions of Greece* (1871), 149, 237.

the Roman Church. Vicary described with ghoulish relish the ceremonial exposure of the remains of a saint, and whispered: 'We feel, as we gaze on the cold and inanimate object, that we are in the charnel house, and not in the church.' During the Festival of the Dead in November 1851, Cato Lowes Dickinson walked through the rows of bedizened corpses in the crypt of the church of Sant' Agnello near Sorrento, and then turned into the air 'sickened, and with a blessing on my lips that we were saved in England such religious ceremonies as these'. The reverence paid to relics left Charles Spurgeon gasping with disbelief. 'I have seen them adoring thigh-bones, skulls, arms and hands—yes, actually *adoring* these things as if they were divine!' Others derided such practices as morbid imbecilities. 'If there were no other and weightier reason to congratulate ourselves on our Protestantism,' the Revd Henry Christmas assured his readers, 'it would be enough that it preserves us from solecisms so ridiculous.' Browning, in the report of a suppositious Venetian visitor to Rome, poked fun at the shrine of Santa Maria, which contained

> The blessed *Umbilicus* of our Lord
> (A relic 'tis believed no other church
> In Rome can boast of).[7]

The superstition that was rife among Greek Christians betokened minds enthralled by black magic and conjuring tricks. According to John Davy the Greeks of the Ionian Islands believed in the evil eye, ghosts and apparitions, charms and spells, possession by the Devil, and like phenomena; and Alexander Kinglake shuddered at the combination of grotesque coiffure and obnoxious credulity that characterised the devotions of the Smyrna Greek. 'As you see him thus with shaven skull, and savage tail depending from his crown, kissing a thing of wood and glass, then cringing with base prostrations and apparent terror before a miserable picture, you see superstition in a shape which, outwardly at least, is sadly abject and repulsive.' But it was the visitor to the Holy Land who saw Greek superstition at its most dreadful. Robert Curzon was present in the Greek chapel of the Holy Sepulchre in Jerusalem in 1834, when the annual Good Friday 'miracle' of the Holy Fire triggered a stampede in which hundreds of

[7] Vicary, *Residence in Rome*, 157, 166; Seymour, *Pilgrimage to Rome*, 437, 461–3, 496; Dickinson, *Letters from Italy*, 219; Spurgeon, ed., *Autobiography of C. H. Spurgeon*, iii. 220; Christmas, *Shores and Islands*, ii. 41; Robert Browning, *The Ring and the Book*, xii, lines 184–6.

pilgrims were trampled to death or suffocated; and his description of the carnage and pandemonium, in which he had to fight for his own survival, drew the horrified gaze of subsequent travellers to this ecclesiastical trickery. William Wilde called it 'the grand climacteric of credulity and superstition'; and Warburton, Kinglake, Arthur Stanley, and Hugh Price Hughes all denounced it as a monstrous fraud, explained only by crude fanaticism. 'It is a remarkable instance', said Stanley, 'of great, it may almost be said an awful, superstition.' Both he and Hughes took comfort from the argument that such a blasphemous imposture was an irrefutable moral argument against the authenticity of the site on which it occurred. The Latin monks had long since repudiated the miracle as a trick, with unhappy consequences for their relations with the Greeks. Hence a further deplorable effect of the strategem was bitter animosity between the rival sects and the presence of Turkish guards to keep the peace. 'What a conception of Christianity must this fact give the Mohammedans!' groaned Hughes.[8]

The most blatantly anti-Scriptural form of superstition was idolatry, which was shamelessly practised in the Latin Church. Vicary watched the veneration of the statue of the Virgin in the church of the Augustines in Rome and felt the self-righteous anger of a witness to a crime. 'To accuse them of idolatry I should be sorry,' he wrote, picking his words with forensic nicety to enhance his effect; 'I will mention only patent facts ... The act of worship was undoubtedly paid to an image, a correct resemblance of the human form, chiselled by human art.' Cato Lowes Dickinson fulminated against 'the disgusting idolatry' perpetrated by the crowds who knelt before a gorgeously dressed statue of the Virgin borne in procession through the streets of Sorrento; and the Mariolatry practised in the church of San Donato in Murano drew forth one of Ruskin's most bitter diatribes: 'With rouged cheeks and painted brows the frightful doll stands in the wretchedness of rags, blackened with the smoke of votive lamps at its feet.' Hugh Price Hughes declared that when he saw the gigantic statue of the Virgin erected in Marseilles after the Franco–German War, he understood at once why France had been defeated.[9]

[8] Davy, *Ionian Islands and Malta*, ii. 100–1; Kinglake, *Eothen*, 44; Curzon, *Monasteries in the Levant*, 197–202; Wilde, *Narrative of a Voyage*, 417; Stanley, *Sinai and Palestine*, 469; Hughes, *Morning Lands of History*, 225.

[9] Vicary, *Residence in Rome*, 112; Dickinson, *Letters from Italy*, 167–8; Ruskin, *Stones of Venice*, ii, Ch. III, para. xl; Hughes, *Morning Lands of History*, 7.

The British justified their hostility towards the rituals of Popery and the practices of popular religion on the grounds that these were so much evidence of 'corruption'—a crucial concept in Protestant thinking. Corruption, in the sense of deviation from the authentic Christianity of the early Church, was the traditional and fundamental article of impeachment levelled by Protestants against Romanists, and Victorian travellers used it as a label for almost everything that they found unfamiliar or distasteful. 'The Christian system there', wrote Newman of Rome in 1833, 'is deplorably corrupt'; and he lamented 'the superstitions [and] ... the solemn reception of them as an essential part of Christianity'. In his published writings of the 1830s he specified the 'popular beliefs and usages' of the Roman Church, as he had witnessed them in the streets of Naples, as the chief disqualification of Rome's claim to represent the ancient, or Apostolic Church. Gladstone, during his second visit to Rome in 1838, deplored 'the fearful corruptions ingrained by long practice' which disfigured Catholic worship; and Seymour wrote of 'the evils and corruptions which now defile the Church of Rome'. Whiteside arraigned Papal worship on the grounds that it did not conform with ancient practice. 'Did the primitive Christians worship as I beheld the multitude worship in St Peter's? That would be impossible for any man to believe.' Christopher Wordsworth appealed for a 'purification and restoration' of the Church of Rome. 'Let the work of renovation be pursued with wise deliberation', he counselled, 'and by gradual, regular and well considered measures, according to the laws and usages of the primitive Church.' The Methodists joined with the Anglicans on this issue. William Arthur tried to convince his Italian acquaintances in Turin of the error of their ways, urging 'that we ought to learn religion from Christ's own words, the words of His Apostles, the faith and forms of the first age ... and [that] the duty of all was to discover the ancient truths and forms, to adhere to them, and to let all the accretions of the middle and modern ages fall way.' Hugh Price Hughes disparaged 'the inventions and corruptions of the papacy' and looked back nostalgically to the purer Christianity of medieval Florence and Venice.[10]

[10] Kerr and Gornall, eds., *Letters and Diaries of J. H. Newman*, iii. 241, 287; J. H. Newman, *Apologia Pro Vita Sua* (new edn., 1874), 105–6; Foot, ed., *Gladstone Diaries*, ii. 430; Seymour, *Pilgrimage to Rome*, 610; Whiteside, *Italy in the Nineteenth Century*, 445, 462; Wordsworth, *Tour in Italy*, ii. 230; Arthur, *Italy in Transition*, 39; *The Life of Hugh Price Hughes by his Daughter*, 424–5.

The theory was that these corruptions and accretions were remnants of paganism. They signified a supine surrender on the part of the churches of the South to pre-Christian, heathen traditions. 'I think the popular and exoteric religion as nearly pagan as you can fancy', wrote Newman from Naples in 1833; and a year or so later Bulwer Lytton, engaged in writing *The Last Days of Pompeii*, remarked that in modern Italy 'idolatry [had] never thoroughly been outrooted'. It had merely changed its objects of worship. 'It appeals to innumerable saints where once it resorted to divinities; and it pours its crowds, in listening reverence, to oracles at the shrines of St Januarius or St Stephen, instead of to those of Isis or Apollo.' Seymour commented in 1848 on the 'Christianizing [of] the heathen traditions of the ancients'. 'It looks', he wrote, 'as if the religion was essentially the same, and the names alone have changed.' Thackeray referred to the ceremonies of St Peter's as 'a huge heathen parade'; and Sala mocked 'the impudent plagiarisms from pagan rites' which the Roman religion presented. They were, he claimed, 'plagiarisms so close and literal that, with the assistance of a Dictionary of Antiquities, nothing [was] easier than to keep a register of these mummeries by double entry, the Romish ceremony in one column, the heathen ceremony from which it [had] obviously been copied in the other'. The poet Aubrey de Vere speculated at some length on this theme during his visit to Rome in 1839, and decided that Latin Christianity had tried and failed to digest ancient Roman imperialism, ancient Greek idolatry, and ancient Egyptian sacerdotalism. 'In proportion as the Christian faith lost its first fervour', he explained, 'these heterogeneous elements held in solution by it began to assert themselves again in their proper and peculiar characters.' The corruptions of the Greek Church were likewise explained by what Arthur described as 'the adoption of heathen or semi-heathen practices from the imperfectly Christianized multitudes who had flocked into the ranks of the Church'; and Arthur Stanley pointed to the notorious miracle of the Holy Fire in Jerusalem, forced on the Greek clergy by 'the weakness and fanaticism of its members', as a classic example of the abominations produced by incomplete assimilation.

This interpretation of the blemishes of the Southern churches did not of course mean that the British regarded all pagan culture as noxious. Their Classical education precluded such a drastic inference. The alien element in Mediterranean Christianity represented, in the words of James Bryce, 'a paganism unredeemed by the virtues of the ancients; a paganism which [was] superstitious without faith, and sceptical without philosophy'. It was not, that is to say, 'healthy' paganism—a concept much in vogue until the last decades of the nineteenth century, when the new science of cultural anthropology made it redundant.[11]

The Victorians amplified their indictment of Southern Christianity with two further charges. They claimed that it was morally and socially subversive, and that it was hostile to art and the march of mind.

The charge of subversion rested chiefly on the old supposition that plenary indulgence and auricular confession must encourage sin, by offering easy remission. 'A few words of contrition', wrote Vicary, 'and the receiving the Sacrament, joined to the absolution of the priest, is reckoned a passport to paradise. So clear is this that many, perhaps the majority [of Italians] lead the life of a Nero.' The imagination of Victorian travellers dwelt with prurient obsession on the supposed erotic vices of Mediterranean Christians—especially those locked away in convents and monasteries. 'There is in every mind a feeling called forth by mystery, and especially by mystery concerned with female life; and the world presents no deeper mystery than a nunnery.' Thus wrote the Revd Seymour, breathing rather heavily. He went on to fantasise in a sado-masochistic vein about the 'harshness and ill-usage, even to the most dreadful of injuries', which 'young, feeble and confiding females' endured in such establishments. Monasteries were associated with homosexuality—something the Victorians were very adept at suggesting without actually naming. 'More pleasing in the sight of the Almighty I really believe,' declared Edward Lear after visiting the monastery of Mount Athos in Greece, 'and more like what Jesus Christ intended man to become, is an honest Turk with six wives.' Maurice Hewlett admitted ignorance, but nevertheless drew conclusions about the morals of Greek monks. 'I hate these sexless novices extremely, and don't inquire into the morals of the business. Better not, I am sure.' Innuendos and imputations such as these were the commonplaces of Protestant invective against celibacy, which was popularly understood to be a sanctification of fornication and sodomy.

[11] Kerr and Gornall, eds., *Letters and Diaries of J. H. Newman*, iii. 294; Lord Lytton, *The Last Days of Pompeii* (Knebworth edn., n.d.) 194–5; Seymour, *Pilgrimage to Rome*, 132, 607–8; Gordon Ray, ed., *The Letters and Private Papers of W. M. Thackeray* (1945–6), iii. 326; Sala, *Rome and Venice*, 331; Ward, *Aubrey de Vere*, 41–5; Arthur, *Italy in Transition*, 433; Stanley, *Sinai and Palestine*, 470; Fisher, *James Bryce*, i. 76.

'As for the celibacy of this immense army of monks, priests and friars,' wrote Edmund Spencer knowingly in 1853, 'every man who has resided for any length of time in Roman Catholic countries must be perfectly cognisant of the frightful abuses to which it tends.'[12]

Equally subversive was the religious convention of mendicancy. This violated the two golden rules of Victorian philanthropy. It removed the salutary stigma of shame from begging, and it encouraged charity for the able-bodied—what Charles Kingsley called 'the merely sentimental charity to which superstitious nations have always been prone ... Charity which effects no permanent good ... because it breaks the laws of social economy'. Its consequences were to divert resources from the deserving poor, interrupt the supply of labour, and encourage idleness—for it went without question that all monks were idle. 'Take a spade and dig, you big beggar!' muttered Cato Dickinson when a jovial monk sat beside him in the Turin train. Effie Ruskin, as a well-schooled young lady of the propertied classes, knew that that religion must be bad which enjoined charity for the malingerers she saw swarming in Venice in the 1850s. A further consequence of mendicancy was dirt. This was something the British always identified as Roman Catholic after travelling through Switzerland, where, as the youthful Ruskin observed, 'all the Catholic cantons ... [were] idle and dirty, and all the Protestant ones busy and clean'. It seemed that national revival was impossible where religion fostered such blatant defiance of civilised standards. 'I think,' wrote Dickinson in 1852, 'and the more I see I am convinced of it, that there is no chance of freedom in Italy, no hope for her regeneration, till the power of the worst church that ever cursed humanity be knocked on the head.' After the French defeat in 1870 Elizabeth Eastlake blamed the tribulations of the Latin race on the Church of Rome. 'If we could see the one tried without the other, I think the race would do itself better justice.'[13]

The theory that religion was responsible for the decline of art and learning in Italy was based on the idea that Roman Catholicism had undergone a drastic change towards the middle of the sixteenth century. The creative era in Italian history was identified as the

---

[12] Vicary, *Residence in Rome*, 132; Seymour, *Pilgrimage to Rome*, 222; Noakes, *Edward Lear*, 142; Binyon, ed., *Letters of Maurice Hewlett*, 271; Spencer, *Tour of Inquiry*, i. 312–13.

[13] Kingsley, *Sanitary and Social Lectures and Essays*, 218; Seymour, *Pilgrimage to Rome*, 180–1; Dickinson, *Letters from Italy*, 16; Lutyens, ed., *Effie in Venice*, 306–7; Ruskin, *Praeterita*, ii, Ch. 1, sec. 8; Dickinson, *Letters from Italy*, 268; Smith, ed., *Journals of Lady Eastlake*, ii. 218.

fourteenth and fifteenth centuries. Why it had been so creative was a matter of dispute. Ruskin argued that it was because the religious impulse had been strong; Macaulay and Symonds that it was because the religious impulse had been weak. All accepted, however, that favourable conditions had ended in the turmoil of the Reformation and the Counter-Reformation. 'Our firm belief is', asserted Macaulay, '. . . that the decay of the Southern countries of Europe is to be mainly ascribed to the Great Catholic Revival.' 'Romanism,' wrote Ruskin, 'instead of being a promoter of the arts, has never shown itself capable of a single great conception since the separation of Protestantism from its side.' Symonds echoed this. 'Protestantism . . . has, on the whole, been more favourable to intellectual progress than Catholicism.' Ruskin attributed the metamorphosis of Catholicism to the Renaissance. Spiritual and intellectual bankruptcy had followed the infusion of pleasure, infidelity, and pride. Macaulay and Symonds, following von Ranke, saw the change as essentially political, originating in the alliance of the Papacy with Spain and the importation of the implements of Spanish religious tyranny—the Jesuits and the Inquisition. Both interpretations were serviceable in that they justified the Reformation; but Ruskin's was the more attractive, because it enabled Protestants to enjoy medieval painting and architecture without paying homage to the modern Catholic religion. Medieval art was the legacy of what Ruskin called 'the purity of the former Catholic Church'. Reassured by this teaching, Dr Robertson, a Presbyterian minister, was able to conduct Hugh Price Hughes and his daughter over San Marco in Venice pointing out 'how intensely evangelical and how essentially Protestant this ancient building was', even though 'defaced and damaged by vulgar and gaudy mosaics, illustrating Mariolatry and the extravagance of modern Romanism'.[14]

An obvious question poses itself. Was the dark image of Italian religion presented by travellers one of the causes of the anti-Catholicism that disfigured Victorian public life? The answer is probably no. The reverse is more likely to have been the case. It was anti-Catholicism that caused the dark image. Victorian travellers were horrified by something they expected to find, rather than by some-

---

[14] Thomas Babington Macaulay, 'Von Ranke's History of the Popes', in *Critical and Historical Essays* (Everyman edn., 1907), ii. 66; Ruskin, *The Stones of Venice*, i, Appendix 12; Symonds, *Renaissance*, vii: *The Catholic Reaction, Part Two* (new edn., 1904), 253; vi: *The Catholic Reaction, Part One, passim*; Ruskin, *Praeterita*, ii, Ch. 1, sec. 9; *The Life of Hugh Price Hughes by his Daughter*, 425.

thing that was there. 'No person who has not been abroad', wrote
Frederick Faber, 'would credit the extensive system of lying pursued
by English travel writers, religious tract compilers and Exeter Hall
speech-makers, respecting the Roman Church abroad.'[15] Robert
Curzon specified the depiction of monks as 'a set of idle dissolute
drones, either fanatical hypocrites or sunk in ignorance and sloth' as
an egregious example of British misrepresentation. 'Probably there
are few persons living', he claimed, 'who have been so much in
monasteries, both of the Latin and Greek Churches, as I have, [and]
... I do not remember having ever seen a monk whom a New
Zealander [i.e. cannibal] would think worth looking at. Quietness,
simplicity, and a complete ignorance of the world are the usual
characteristics of all monks.'[16]

The prejudice responsible for these distortions was compounded of
the traditional Protestant convictions and aversions, together with a
large measure of envy. The first half of the Victorian era especially was
a time of acute religious consciousness, when sensibility was
measured by the intensity of belief or the agony of doubt and when
contention between political parties was often an echo of contention
between religious denominations. Under these circumstances the
Roman Church was enviable because of its tremendous proselytising
power. It was fascinating and alluring in a way that the Anglican and
Nonconformist churches could not rival (though the Anglicans
involved in the Oxford Movement did their best to poach its
attributes). Men and women whose religious susceptibility had been
heightened by the Romantic Movement and evangelicalism, and
whose thirst for authority had been stimulated by the collapse of old
certainties and the withdrawal of old shibboleths, saw it beckon and
heard it sing—in the gargantuan person, more likely than not, of
Nicholas Wiseman, English Catholicism's star preacher and first
Cardinal Archbishop of Westminster after the restoration of the
hierarchy in 1850. Week after week, in the early 1850s, this scarlet
siren attracted congregations of two and a half thousand to his Sunday
night sermons. 'She alone,' wrote Newman of the Roman Church in
1841, 'amid all the errors and evils of her practical system, has given
free scope to the feelings of awe, mystery, tenderness, reverence,
devotedness, and other feelings which may be especially called
catholic.'

---

[15] Bowden, *Frederick Faber*, 166.
[16] Curzon, *Monasteries in the Levant*, 18–19.

Among British visitors to Italy, Gladstone, Macaulay, Ronald
Gower, Aubrey de Vere, Frederick Faber, Henry Manning, Ruskin,
Stanley, Symonds, and Beatrice Potter all acknowledged the allure of
the Church's barbaric splendour, ascetic piety, and ecumenical ideal.
These disturbed the subconscious mind with secret yearnings and
strange fantasies. Ruskin once dreamt that he had become a Francis-
can friar; Stanley that he had been elected Pope. Gower imagined
himself as a cardinal. There was concrete evidence of the appeal of
Romanism in the growing number of Catholics in Victorian Britain.
Figures are uncertain, but even the most cautious estimates indicate
an increase from under half a million in the 1830s to over a million by
the 1880s. Most of this was due to Irish immigration; but conversion
from the Anglican Church—including that of Newman, Faber,
Manning, and de Vere—played its part; and if statistically less
significant this was nevertheless much more impressive, because it
signified the power of Rome to divide families, sunder friendships,
and overthrow lifelong loyalties. And the success of Catholicism in
Britain was all the more galling because elsewhere it was apparently in
decline. In the 1830s George Borrow reported confidently from Spain
that Popery was tottering to its downfall; and it was a common conviction among travellers in Italy that the Roman Church was losing its
hold. Gladstone, in 1832, called it 'a machine that continues for a little
space to work, though the hand of the machinist, its principle of life,
has left it'. William Arthur confirmed that 'the people [were] weary
of the priests [and] alienated from the Church'; Edmund Spencer
declared that Popery had 'lost for ever its influence over the minds
of the people of Italy'; James Bryce wondered how much longer
the Papal pageantry would last, since everything indicated that 'no
educated man in Italy any longer believe[d] in anything at all'; and
George Augustus Sala proclaimed that in the hearts of most Italians
Romish idolatry was 'DEAD . . . as dead as any dog that ever hung'.[17]

Victorian travellers were abroad, then, at a time when Roman
Catholicism was filling many British minds with a confusion of envy
and uncertainty; and these feelings both clouded their vision of

[17] E. R. Norman, *Anti-Catholicism in Victorian England* (1967), 16–17, 68; Purcell,
Cardinal Manning, i. 211–12; Joan Evans, *John Ruskin* (1954), 350; Prothero, *Life of
Stanley*, ii. 359; Lord Ronald Sutherland Gower, *Reminiscences* (1884), i. 232, 275; Hare,
The Story of My Life, ii. 486–7; George Borrow, *Letters to the British and Foreign Bible Society*
(ed. J. H. Darlow, 1911), 155–6, 177; Foot, ed., *Gladstone Diaries*, i. 473; Arthur, *Italy in
Transition*, 264; Spencer, *Tour of Inquiry*, ii. 112; Fisher, *James Bryce*, i. 80; Sala, *Rome and
Venice*, 245.

Roman worship and created an almost manic sensitivity to converts and to ritualists with Roman sympathies. It was customary to portray converts (or 'perverts' as they were called) as deluded and naïve, the pathetic victims of a baited snare. 'They can have but one of two effects on Englishmen,' wrote James Johnson of Catholic ceremonies, 'that of turning the Romish religion into ridicule in strong minds, or that of overpowering and converting minds that are weak.' Vicary described the Easter ceremonies in St Peter's as 'very apt indelibly to impress weakly constituted minds ... The senses are fascinated and the reason becomes with them a willing victim.' Seymour wrote of the tragic credulity of converts to Rome, and added grimly: 'It will be terrible when the awakening comes.' Ruskin lambasted the 'imbecility' and 'treachery' of those who were 'lured into the Romanist Church by the glitter of it, like larks into a trap by broken glass; ... blown into a change of religion by the whine of an organ pipe; stitched into a new creed by the gold threads of priests' petticoats; jangled into a change of conscience by the chimes of a belfrey.' It was Bryce's view that 'Rome, if it influenced men's religion at all, would make of the strong sceptics, and Catholics only of the weak'; and Sala sneered at the 'silly women and sillier men' who were running crazy on ritualism. 'It is, after all, only a matter of music and millinery, which are both things very dear to the feminine mind.' Lady Margaret Brewster, authoress of an edifying series of tracts called *Work: or, Plenty to Do and How to Do It*, announced that only those could go to Rome who had lost 'all sense of the ludicrous and all purity of taste'.[18]

So British visitors to the South brought much of their sense of sacrilege with them. They arrived already deeply hostile to the Roman Church and constructed an image of her from the ingredients of old prejudice. Nevertheless, the religious state of mind in which they returned was not always the same as that in which they had come. Some found that while they were abroad a degree was added to their burden; a nuance to their sorrow. For while they did not see Rome in a new religious light, their religious view of themselves did not remain unchanged. The sins of Rome they had learnt in England; but in Rome they were reminded of the sins of England. 'In entering such a church as this,' wrote Gladstone after his first visit to St Peter's, 'most deeply does one feel the pain and shame of the schism which separates

[18] Johnson, *Change of Air*, 276; Vicary, *Residence in Rome*, 107; Seymour, *Pilgrimage to Rome*, 15–16; Ruskin, *The Stones of Venice*, i, Appendix 12; Fisher, *James Bryce*, i. 76; Sala, *Rome and Venice*, 328–30; Brewster, *Letters*, 25.

us from Rome'; and he added a heartfelt prayer: 'May God bind up the wounds of His bleeding Church!' The ideal of unity and universality took on a special resonance for Aubrey de Vere when he was in Rome, and it lingered in his mind. Thackeray, in the person of his hero Clive Newcome, confessed to feeling chastened as he surveyed Christ's mandate to his Apostle spelled out round the dome of St Peter's in colossal letters of gold. 'There must be moments, in Rome especially, when every man of friendly heart, who writes himself English and Protestant, must feel a pang at thinking that he and his countrymen are insulated from European Christendom.' No amount of fervent disclaiming of responsibility for schism could change the fact that it existed. In Italy the Anglican found himself among Christians who regarded him as an outsider and a heretic; and his pain was all the more acute because by proclamations of innocence he implicitly admitted that he had a case to answer. Those who, like Newman and de Vere, tried to transfer the stigma of schism to the Roman Church found the task intellectually impossible. Newman never satisfied himself that the Roman Church was not Catholic and that the Anglican Church was not schismatic; and twenty years after he had gone over to Rome, when he was writing about the origins of his conversion, it was St Augustine's interdiction of schism that he remembered most vividly: '*Securus judicat orbis terrarum* ['the universal judgement is infallible'] . . . These words kept ringing in my ears . . . [They] struck me with a power which I had never felt from any words before.'[19]

Protestant scholars have always maintained that when Newman wrote this he was projecting back into his Anglican period convictions belonging to his Catholic years; that as an Anglican he had never been unduly perturbed by such intellectual inferences. But this argument ignores the emotional impact that the idea of Catholicity acquired in Rome. It is clear from the accounts of other Anglicans that in the Eternal City the fact of schism became something much more than an intellectual proposition. It became an accusation that made the heart sick; an experience with the power to modify attitude.

[19] Foot, ed., *Gladstone Diaries*, i. 462; Ward, *Aubrey de Vere*, 46–7; Thackeray, *The Newcomes*, Ch. XXXV; Newman, *Apologia*, 116–17.

14. DECLINE AND FALL

History predisposed the British to be hostile, because history showed the South to be in decline. The shores of the Mediterranean were strewn with carcasses of dead empires and encumbered with museums of extinct art. The ancient supremacies of Tyre, Greece, and Rome had vanished, and the successor states of Turkey, the Italian republics, and Spain had in their turn become effete. Political, economic, and cultural power had shifted to the North; and the North was now encroaching on the South, scattering the phantoms and the dust. In the nineteenth century Spain, Italy, and North Africa were all subjected to humiliating visitations of Austrian, French, and British imperialism. There were, it was true, signs of national revival in Greece and Italy, and by 1867 the Austrians had been expelled from south of the Alps; but it was difficult to interpret these events as a true reversal of the Southern decline. It seemed that deliverance came to Greece and Italy as it had come earlier to Spain, rather as fortune's gift than as a hard-won reward. The idea was common that the Greeks had achieved their independence from Turkey not through their own efforts, but through the benevolent intervention of the great powers of the North. In 1861, George Finlay, one of the original Philhellenes, endorsed this view in his *History of the Greek Revolution*, and depicted the Greek revolt as a religious, rather than a national uprising. Similarly, it was argued that the Italians had gained unity and freedom only as a result of the assistance of France, the benevolent neutrality of England and, subsequently, the collapse of Austria before the armies of Prussia. Matthew Arnold, in his pamphlet *England and the Italian Question*, published in 1859, had foreseen, and feared, freedom as a gift bestowed by France. Bishop Christopher Wordsworth was more appreciative of the Italian effort, but he took pains to point out that the leaders of the Risorgimento were the northern Italians of Piedmont— 'one of those vigorous races which has not been enfeebled by the enervating influence of southern Italy, and seems to have been nerved and braced to deeds of heroic valour by the bleak winds which blow upon it from the Alps'.[1] Then there was the case of France herself— half Northern, but weaker than her Northern neighbours by virtue of her strong Mediterranean component. Her swift defeat by Prussia in

[1] Wordsworth, *Tour in Italy*, ii. 244.

the Franco–German War of 1870 was widely interpreted in Britain as a further stage in the capitulation of the South to the North. 'There is great talk here of the superiority of the Teutonic over the Latin races', reported Lady Eastlake from London in October 1870.[2]

The cultural decline of the South was equally manifest. A comparison between the artistic achievements of the past and those of the present revealed a pitiful decay of creative and intellectual power. 'The roots of thought here in Italy seem dead in the ground', lamented Elizabeth Browning in 1846. 'It is well that they have great memories— nothing else lives.' A visit to the ruins of Pompeii in 1850 convinced Nassau Senior that the modern Italians were put to shame by the attainments of their ancestors. 'When we recollect that Pompeii was a second rate country town,' he wrote, '. . . and compare its temples, its public palaces and its theatres with those which the Italians now erect . . . one can scarcely avoid inferring that the civilization of Italy has gone woefully back.' In Florence, fifty years later, Henry Rider Haggard was teased by the riddle of tawdry modern art at the very source of Renaissance excellence. 'Why is it?' he wondered. 'Who can explain the mystery of the change? Where has the genius flown, and will it ever return?' Several English painters, including Boxall and Leighton, were dismayed by the state of art in modern Italy and disputed the value to British artists of an environment which fostered only repetitive mediocrity and insipid Classicism. Boxall, who was in Italy for two years from 1834, was deeply depressed by endless 'Cupids and Psyches and Venuses and . . . peasant girls kneeling before the Madonna and . . . bandits *almost* ravishing the captive women'; and he realised that Rome was not the place for a painter 'who would do anything original, or who [had] a feeling in his mind that he would wish to work out'. Frederic Leighton, in Italy between 1854 and 1855, declared that Rome was 'the grave of art' where a young painter was starved of 'actively suggestive surroundings'—a stimulus that he found only in Paris. A prominent critic who shared this view was Austen Layard, who denied that modern Rome could ever generate a school of art, either of architecture, sculpture, or painting.

The place belongs to the past, and if art . . . consists in the embodiment of the feelings, opinions and manners of the day, as I think it ought, I should just like the student to have a look at the great works here, and then drive him away to

[2] Smith, ed., *Journals of Lady Eastlake*, ii. 218.

some place where there is life, national aspiration, and progress. Smoky London is infinitely better in this respect than this cloudless sky and desert waste.[3]

During the Victorian era the opinion took root that even in the art of opera—a field where the Italians had traditionally been regarded as supreme—the modern Italian contribution was second rate. In 1847 the Covent Garden Theatre was renamed The Royal Italian Opera; but the designation 'Italian' referred to the language of performance, not the repertoire. The conviction persisted that the best language for singing was Italian; but the idea that the best vocal music was Italian was taken less and less for granted. Charles Grüneisen, music critic of the *Morning Chronicle*, explained that the policy of the Royal Italian Opera was to widen the repertoire beyond 'the wishy-washy Italian masters' and perform 'the works of all masters, without distinction of country'; and it was a policy that met with both critical and popular approval. From the 1850s the works of Rossini, Bellini, and Donizetti were increasingly supplanted by French and German importations, and operas by Meyerbeer and Gounod became the mainstay of the Covent Garden seasons. In 1852, for example, out of a total of sixty-eight performances, Meyerbeer's works occupied twenty-three, whereas Donizetti's occupied only sixteen. By the 1870s Wagner's early works were being heard in London; and during the next decade the cult of the Wagnerian music-drama reinforced the notion that the Italians were superseded. In 1884 the Royal Italian Opera was wound up; and when opera seasons were restored on a regular basis to Covent Garden four years later the policy of singing everything in Italian was abandoned. Works were now performed in their original language; and with the renaming of the theatre as the Royal Opera House the Italians were ritually deposed as leaders in the lyric art. The 1891 season was almost entirely French; and of the sixty-five performances in the 1898 season thirty-two were of works by Wagner. Only nine were of operas from the traditional *bel canto* repertoire.

It is certainly not the case that Italian opera was ever in danger of disappearing from the London stage. In fact in the late Victorian and in the Edwardian years, with the arrival of works by Mascagni, Leoncavallo, and Puccini, it enjoyed a revival. But it is equally sure

[3] Kenyon, ed., *The Letters of E. B. Browning*, i. 310; Senior, *Journals*, ii, 9; Haggard, *Winter Pilgrimage*, 16; Boxall MSS; Barrington, *Frederick Leighton*, i. 147, 188, 191; Layard, *Autobiography*, 232.

that throughout most of the Victorian era and during the first decades of the twentieth century Italian opera was regarded as little more than a vehicle for fine voices. Its popularity owed more to the reputation of singers like Grisi, Patti, Melba, Tetrazzini, Destinn, and Caruso, than it did to the reputation of Italian composers. Even Verdi's place in the London repertoire was assured by connoisseurs of voices rather than by connoisseurs of music, who persistently denigrated his work as crude and meretricious. 'There is no music worth having published in Italy', wrote George Henry Lewes in 1861, at the end of the decade that had seen the publication of *Rigoletto*, *Il trovatore*, *La Traviata*, and *Un ballo in maschera*. Neither he nor George Eliot had any esteem for Verdi. The music of *Rigoletto* they reckoned 'poor' and that of *Traviata* 'hideous'. (Gounod's *Faust*, on the other hand, they adored.) And this sort of reaction was common. Charles Lever expressed a widely held prejudice when he berated Verdi with heavy humour in his novel *The Dodd Family Abroad*, accusing him of cracking voices and breaking blood vessels. Professional critical opinion was perhaps best summarised by the review in the *Morning Post* of the London première of *Il trovatore* in 1855. 'If Signor Verdi be really the "speranza di Italia",' it scoffed, 'we cannot congratulate that once favoured land of song upon its expectations, for a more uninspired or uncultivated composer never yet succeeded in attracting public notice.' With the advent of *Aida* in London in 1876 the critical tone changed to one of patronising tolerance; but not until the London production of *Otello* in 1889 did Verdi even begin to rival Wagner in professional estimation, and full recognition of his genius was delayed until after the First World War.[4]

If the contrast between past and present was painful in Italy, in Greece it was excruciating. 'Behold the first fruits of resuscitated Grecian art!' groaned Eliot Warburton after seeing the royal palace and other modern buildings in Athens. He went on:

Full in the sight of the Acropolis, in the same plain with the Temple, and in the solemn presence of that Olympian Jove, there stands a huge, white, cubic edifice that would disgrace Trafalgar Square . . . On the hill of the Museum, within a stone's throw of the Acropolis, there has just been erected an observatory that stands in as hideous contrast to the Parthenon as Caliban to Ariel. Such are the first and most prominent objects that strike a stranger's eye, and they are characteristic of all modern Greece.

[4] Harold Rosenthal, *Two Centuries of Opera at Covent Garden* (1958), 68, 100, 288; Haight, ed., *Letters of George Eliot*, iii. 419, iv. 37, 92; Dennis Arundell, *The Critic at the Opera* (1957), 335.

This lament over the unworthiness of modern Athenian architecture constantly recurs in Victorian and Edwardian accounts of Greece.[5]

Palpable evidence of decay was everywhere in the South—in ruins, deserts, tombs of potentates without posterity, and palaces to let. It was in the monuments of Egypt; the wastes of Arcadia; the prostrate Roman columns of North Africa; and the silent quays, weedy battlements, fissured walls, peeling stucco, and tarnished gilt of towns like Pisa, Siena, and Venice. Dickens especially was sensitive to the visual and tactile qualities of decrepitude, and his descriptions of the spectral cities of Parma, Ferrara, and Mantua in *Pictures from Italy* alerted countless travellers to Italy's cornucopias of cobweb and mould. His descriptions of Venice in *Little Dorrit* likewise stress the physical symptoms of decay (ancient scaffolding, blotched walls, polluted canals), whereas earlier writers, like Byron and Rogers, had read the message of decline in things more abstract and less prosaic, such as departed freedom and silenced revelry. The idea of Venice as a city that was literally dying became particularly vivid to the Victorians, because in the middle of the nineteenth century it was calculated that her foundations would soon give way, and that her long predicted entombment in the sea was now little more than fifty years away.

There was a difference, too, between the emotional response of the Victorians and that of their predecessors. The emotion registered by Gray, Hervey, Gibbon, and Byron in the presence of tombs and ruins had been sentimental sadness. They were primarily conscious of pathos in the transience and futility of human achievement, and they established a ritual of rumination whose chief conventions were the rhetorical question ('Where are its golden roofs? Where those who dared to build?'), the tear, and the sigh. Some Victorian travellers continued to experience decline and decay in this manner, influenced by the attitudes and the melancholia of earlier generations. Thus Disraeli's hero Contarini Fleming muses in Rome in imitation of Byron ('Where are the spoils of Egypt and Carthage? Where the golden tribute of Iberia? Where the long Gallic trophies?'). William Wilde, in Rhodes in 1838, adopted the Gibbonian posture ('I rested on some mouldering buttress or prostrate pillar, while the shroud of twilight closed around me . . .') and Frances Elliot did likewise in Rome, in 1871 ('I seated myself on the capital of a fallen pillar, and gazed on the ruins, the long grass, and waving reeds . . .'). Graham's

---

[5] Warburton, *The Crescent and the Cross*, ii. 307. For a further example of this disparagement see Murray's *Handbook for Travellers in Greece* (5th edn., 1883), 176–7.

and Ashbee's description of the ruins of Sbeitla in Tunisia is indebted
to Gray ('The moon was up in all its splendour, and the stillness of the
air was broken only by the bubbling waters of the river . . . and the
occasional screech of an owl, whose "ancient solitary reign" we were
disturbing') and Herbert Vivian drew inspiration from the same
source for his evocation of the ruins of Carthage ('What a sermon
upon the vanity of human glory! Surely none may be so callous as to
refuse the tribute of a sigh'). In Cyprus Mallock penned elegant
cadences reminiscent of Gray ('A feeling of sadness rose up out of the
earth, with hints of remote races and the splendours of forgotten
history') and Henry Rider Haggard meditated in the manner of Byron
('Perhaps this was the Burlington Arcade of Salamis—but oh! Where
are the Arcadians?').[6]

But the reaction of most Victorians to decay and decline was
resolutely anti-sentimental. Newman refused to mourn over the ruins
of the Colosseum; Ruskin admonished those who would treat the
record of the fall of Tyre as a lovely song; and from many other tourists
decay and ruins evoked not sadness, but horror; not sighs, but
shudders. 'We shuddered in the State dungeons', recalled Samuel
Bevan after a visit to Venice in 1842, 'and crept through the damp and
tortuous passages, gazing with feelings of awe and horror . . .' Under
Dickens's scrutiny the 'dream' city of Venice became a nightmare,
compounded of water like a coiling, slimy serpent and sensations of
suffocation in subterranean darkness. Rome weighed like an incubus
on the soul not only of Dickens, but of a host of British visitors.
Clough's sojourn there was troubled by 'a tyrannous sense of
superincumbent oppression'. Ruskin acquired a dread of the city on
his first visit in 1840, and never lost it. In 1856 he wrote of 'the sense of
despair which there is about Rome'. Browning found the place 'ill-
starred, under a curse seemingly'; and Frances Cobbe was conscious
of 'a sense as if the crimes which have been committed therein have
left an indescribable miasma, a lurid impalpable shadow, like that of
the ashes of the Polynesian volcano, which darkened the sun for a
year'. Bishop Wordsworth doubted that Rome could ever become the
capital of united Italy. 'Can any human power revive the spirit within?'
he asked. In the 1880s, according to Anne Buckland, visitors to Rome

[6] Byron, *Childe Harold's Pilgrimage*, Canto IV, Stanza cix; Disraeli, *Contarini Fleming*,
Part VII, Ch. 1; Wilde, *Narrative of a Voyage*, 307; Elliot, *Idle Woman In Italy*, i. 224;
Graham and Ashbee, *Travels in Tunisia*, 138; Vivian, *Tunisia*, 183; Mallock, *Enchanted
Island*, 79; Haggard, *Winter Pilgrimage*, 170.

were still shuddering. 'It is with a shudder you enter the shadow of these great piles and look up at the strong barricaded windows ...' Even James Joyce caught the neurosis and complained of 'horrible and terrifying dreams' in Rome. In Egypt, Herbert Spencer recoiled from all the evidence of death and decay; and in Algeria Hilaire Belloc sensed lurking evil amid the ruins of the Roman city of Timgad.[7]

All this shivering and shuddering was to some extent a symptom of sensibilities formed by the Gothic romance and the tale of terror. But it was new in that it contained a predominant element of moral disgust. It signified an increasing tendency to deplore political collapse for moral reasons. It had been a cardinal article in the Whig creed of previous generations that political and civic virtues withered among a degraded and enslaved people; that loss of liberty entailed turpitude and cowardice. This had been the burden of Byron's threnody on Greece in the second canto of *Childe Harold*, and it was echoed by other Philhellenes such as Hobhouse and Finlay. Whig attitudes influenced later travellers too. Mary Shelley, for example, doubted that the Italians would be able to profit by independence even if they won it, since they were 'too demoralised and degenerate' after years of petty tyranny; and similar reasoning made many self-styled friends of Italy initially doubtful about the Risorgimento and ambivalent about the Austrian presence in Lombardy and Venetia. As Lady Eastlake said, 'when people can't govern themselves, they must be governed'. Britain's own experience as a protecting power first in the Ionian Islands and then in Egypt seemed to confirm that people who had been subservient for centuries were morally inferior and politically irresponsible. The new element in the Victorian attitude was the idea that decline was a result, as well as a cause, of moral failure. Heavily influenced by the Old Testament, the Victorians read in decline the stigma of punishment, and they venerated Carlyle for having proclaimed, in *The French Revolution* (1837), that the collapse of the *ancien régime* had been a consequence of infidelity and iniquity. If people were oppressed, it was therefore their own fault. 'Italy's

[7] Kerr and Gornall, eds., *Letters and Diaries of J. H. Newman*, iii. 249; Ruskin, *The Stones of Venice*, i, Ch. I, para. i; Bevan, *Sand and Canvas*, 314; Arthur Hugh Clough, *Amours de Voyage*, Canto I, line 36; Evans and Whitehouse, eds., *Diaries of Ruskin*, i. 171; Ruskin, *Letters to Norton*, i. 28; W. C. de Vane and K. L. Knickerbocker, eds., *New Letters of Robert Browning* (1951), 77; Cobbe, *Life*, i. 224; Wordsworth, *Tour in Italy*, ii. 189; Buckland, *Beyond the Esterelles*, ii. 40; Richard Ellman, *James Joyce* (new edn., 1982), 225; Spencer, *Autobiography*, ii. 341–2; Belloc, *Esto Perpetua*, 162–70.

true oppression is all her own', declared Ruskin; 'Spain is oppressed by the Spaniard ... Greece needs to be saved from the Greeks.' Writing from Venice in 1849, he insisted that the Italians were suffering 'partly for sins of past generations, partly for follies of their own'. It was a constant habit of evangelicals to attribute political events to moral causes, so whenever they detected political collapse they at once smelt crime and iniquity. 'What a lesson it is to meditate upon Syracuse!' sighed Newman, reminded afresh of the fatal flaw in human majesty. 'The sun of Venice is set', announced Lord Shaftesbury in 1833. 'Her own crimes and the powerful ambitions of her neighbours would have wrought their effects, had the Cape of Good Hope remained in obscurity.' Young Arthur Stanley's judgements on Venice in 1840 sounded a note that Ruskin was later to amplify into a sermon of three volumes. 'Even in the very gorgeousness of the Piazza', he wrote, 'there is a look of resolute, hardened pride that seems to call for the vengeance that has visited it.' Frederick Faber found Venice 'beautiful beyond compare, but stricken, and decrepit, and wasted and almost lifeless'; and he saw written there the righteousness of God. Lady Eastlake drew the chilling lesson of the city's blighted greatness: 'It seems to say that righteousness and justice were not in these wondrous palaces and that, therefore, destruction is come upon them.' Nathan Davis, the excavator of Carthage, read a grim warning in 'the remains of her once sumptuous buildings, which [had] become the abode of the hyaena and the jackal'. Modern empires should learn 'the profitable lesson' afforded by the fate of that once powerful state. 'To avoid that destiny they must seek to avoid her errors and failings, otherwise their fall and their ruin will not only be doubly merited, but they will lack that sympathy which, for want of having an example before her, is so readily extended to the empire of Dido.' Matthew Arnold enunciated the general principle that 'moral causes govern the standing and falling of states', and the defeat of France in 1871 triggered a homily about 'the want of a serious conception of righteousness' discernible in the history of the Graeco–Latin nations. 'The fall of Greece, the fall of Rome, the fall of the brilliant Italy of the fifteenth century, and now the fall of France, are all examples.' Ruskin, likewise, saw the Franco–Prussian war as a moral conflict ('on the one side the French—the purest and intensest republicanism ... joined to vanity, lust, and lying—against, on the German side, a Personal, Hereditary, Feudal Government as stern as Barbarossa's, with a certain human measure of modesty, decency and veracity'); and Browning, Meredith, Freeman, and Stanley all attributed France's defeat to her pride and vainglory.[8]

In the Victorian conception therefore, political decline was doubly deplorable. It was linked to moral collapse not only as a cause, but as an effect; and sentimental melancholy faltered in the presence of retribution. British historians and British travellers approached the South expecting to encounter turpitude; and, predictably enough, what they expected to find, they did find.

Historians found it in the public crimes and private vices associated with the later Roman Empire, the Borgias and the Medicis, the Renaissance Papacy, and the Republic of Venice. Ruskin dismissed two-thirds of the iniquities attributed to the Venetian Government as so much Gothic fable; but he did so the better to expose 'the darker truths of its history and its being', and in *The Stones of Venice* he was uncompromising in his indictment:

. . . the evidence which I shall be able to deduce from the arts of Venice will be both frequent and irrefragable, that the decline of her political prosperity was exactly coincident with that of domestic and individual religion . . . The final degradation of the Venetian power appears owing not so much to the principles of its government, as to their being forgotten in the pursuit of pleasure . . . That ancient curse was upon her, the curse of the Cities of the Plain: 'Pride, fulness of bread and abundance of idleness'. By the inner burning of her own passions, as fatal as the fiery rain of Gomorrah, she was consumed from her place among the nations; and her ashes are choking the channels of the dead, salt sea.[9]

There is another extended exposition of the theme of retribution in John Addington Symonds's *Renaissance in Italy*. This work shows the emotional power of evangelical prejudice even in an author whose intellectual allegiance was to the liberalism of Mill's *On Liberty*. In his first volumes (*The Age of the Despots* and *The Revival of Learning*) Symonds justifies the Renaissance in the terms of Mill's argument. By initiating 'a philosophical acceptance of variety in fashion, faith and

[8] Shelley, *Rambles*, ii. 260–1; Smith, ed., *Journals of Lady Eastlake*, i. 293, 298; Taylor, *Egyptian Notebook*, 18; Davy, *Ionian Islands and Malta*, ii. 10–22; Cook and Wedderburn, eds., *Works of Ruskin*, xxviii. 539; xxxvi. 104; Kerr and Gornall, *Letters and Diaries of J. H. Newman*, iii. 291; Hodder, *Shaftesbury*, i. 176–7; Prothero, *Life of Stanley*, i. 266; Bowden, *Frederick Faber*, 107; Nathan Davis, *Carthage and her Remains* (1861), 461; Russell, ed., *Letters of Matthew Arnold*, ii. 48; Ruskin, *Letters to Norton*, i. 24.

[9] Ruskin, *The Stones of Venice*, i, Ch. I, para. viii; ii, Ch. I, para. i, Ch. VIII, para. cxxviii; iii, Ch. III, para. lxxvi.

conduct', it stimulated social and cultural progress. If individual freedom generated private vice, this was merely a condition of public benefit. Hence Savonarola's mission of moral regeneration was misguided and retrogressive. Yet the Protestant moralist in Symonds was constantly pulling him in another direction. 'The historian of this epoch,' he wrote in *Italian Literature, Part Two*, 'though he feels its splendour and fain would bless, finds himself forced to insist upon the darker details of the subject.' Having accepted the moral laxity of Humanism as a small price to pay for social and cultural advance, he cannot resist the urge to deplore it as a cause of political decline. As his book proceeds, political collapse and loss of liberty take on the aspect of just punishment for moral delinquency. In the two volumes of *Italian Literature* a mood of prudish censure and evangelical revulsion inflates the satirical ballads and carnival ribaldry of Medicean Florence into 'loathsomeness' and 'leprosy', and hints of impending political tragedy are pointedly juxtaposed:

Such were the songs that reached Savonarola's ears, writing or meditating in his cloister at San Marco. Such were the sights that moved his indignation as he trod the streets of Florence . . . Yet Florence, warned in vain by the friar, took no thought of the morrow; and the morrow came to all Italy with war, invasion, pestilence, innumerable woes . . .[10]

Historians found evidence of depravity in past behaviour; travellers found it in the behaviour of the people around them. If Southern society had urbanity, sobriety, and culture to its credit, the debit side of the balance sheet was also heavily itemised. Victorian and Edwardian travellers, like censorious schoolteachers, peppered their reports with animadversions on the Mediterranean character. The Greeks were mendacious and perfidious; the Arabs were idle, abject, and sensual; town Italians were frivolous, vicious, and scheming; Italian peasants were shifty, cunning, and shameless. Southern institutions like carnivals and lotteries were signs of general addiction to vulgarity, profligacy, and superstition. The same judgements occur again and again; and if there were need of further proof of inveterate idleness the British found it in the poverty that afflicted Mediterranean society. It was generally admitted that the plight of the poor in

---

[10] J. A. Symonds, *Renaissance in Italy*, i, *The Age of the Despots* (new edn., 1904), 382; ii, *The Revival of Learning* (new edn., 1904), 10; v, *Italian Literature, Part Two* (new edn., 1904), 456; iv, *Italian Literature, Part One* (new edn., 1904), 342.

the South was less pitiful than the plight of the poor at home, because travellers found little evidence of absolute destitution or starvation; but this relatively fortunate condition was attributed mainly to the benevolent climate and indiscriminate charity. It was not assumed to signify a greater dedication to the ideal of work. Most observers, it is true, acknowledged the existence of 'deserving' poor among the peasant classes of the South, and in the Italian novels of Ouida these attain to a sort of feral dignity by dint of relentless labour and prudent management; but the British also carried with them the conviction that poverty was inseparable from the presence of an 'undeserving' majority of malingerers and parasites. This conviction derived from the religious concept of retribution—a concept which flavoured most Victorian analysis of social problems. Even the so-called 'Social Darwinists' were influenced by it. They were typical of their time in that they owed much more to Malthus, who explained human suffering in terms of sin and human betterment in terms of 'moral restraint', than they did to Darwin, who depicted a struggle for survival that had no reference to moral attributes and in which suffering and extinction were the penalties not of wickedness but of weakness. The nihilism of science was in fact alien to the mentality of the age, which was suffused with the ideas of reward and punishment. The Evangelical Conscience read an assurance of progress in moral reform. For this reason, in the South as at home, most Victorians were disposed to blame the poor for their misery; to see them as culprits rather than as victims and to deplore their penury as an unnecessary affront to delicate sensibilities and civilised standards. It is a measure of the depth to which their assessment of the poorer Greeks and Italians could sink that they frequently compared them to the Irish. Thackeray wrote that Athens reminded him of Carlow or Killarney— 'the streets swarm with idle crowds, the innumerable little lanes flow over with dirty little children'. Lady Eastlake reckoned that the Venetians, 'in their indolence, their dirt and their quickness' would make excellent Irish; and Frances Power Cobbe found an unwelcome reminder of her birthplace among the Neapolitans: 'They resemble more closely in ignorance, squalor and degradation the most wretched Irish who dwell in mud cabins amid the bogs, than any other people in Europe.' Anne Buckland made the comparison even more scathing. 'They form the element of national discord, the Irish of Italy', she wrote of the Neapolitans; 'quick, gay, careless, noisy and impulsive; but vindictive, cruel, discontented, indolent; a people always ready to give trouble to their rulers, but never likely to improve their own condition.'[11]

Again and again, in all parts of the Mediterranean, British visitors were revolted by the prevailing cruelty to animals, and their reports prompted the RSPCA (founded by evangelicals in 1824 and granted a Royal Charter in 1830) to extend its activities abroad—most notably to Naples—in the 1850s. Spanish bullfighting especially evoked horror and disgust and, despite Richard Ford's reminder (in Murray's *Handbook for Spain*) that English field sports were just as cruel, many travellers insisted that the bullfight was a symptom of Spanish depravity. 'They are a ferocious and frivolous people', Lady Eastlake decided, 'and show their decline, as the ancient Romans did directly they began to be such cowards as to delight in seeing the danger and suffering of others without sharing them.' The Revd Richard Roberts blamed the bullring for 'the indifference to human life so commonly exhibited by Spaniards'.[12]

The growth of corruption, militarism, and imperialism in the modern Italian state was watched with despair by British writers and intellectuals, and it kept alive the idea of a fatal moral taint in the Mediterranean character. Ouida, outraged at the tyranny exercised by gangster-ridden syndics over the village communes of rural Italy, attacked corruption in barbed language and made herself in consequence an object of hatred and even physical menace in the land of her adoption.[13] Her detestation of Italian conscription was shared by George Gissing, who, in a passage of remarkable prescience, foretold that the patriotic idealism of the Risorgimento would be betrayed and that Italy herself would become a bloodstained oppressor:

That sweet and sounding name of *patria* becomes an illusion and a curse; linked with the pretentious modernism, civilization, it serves as a plea to the latter day barbarism, ravening and reckless under his civil garb. How can one greatly wish for the consolidation and prosperity of Italy, knowing that national vigour tends more and more to international fear and hatred? Those who perished that Italy might be born again, dreamt of other things than old savagery clanging in new weapons.[14]

---

[11] Thackeray, *Cornhill to Grand Cairo*, 74; Smith, ed., *Journals of Lady Eastlake*, i. 293; Cobbe, *Life*, i. 226; Buckland, *Beyond the Esterelles*, ii. 164.

[12] Brian Harrison, 'Animals and the State in Nineteenth Century England' in *English Historical Review*, 88 (1973), 786–820; Smith, ed., *Journals of Lady Eastlake*, ii. 125; Roberts, *Autumn Tour*, 423.

[13] Bigland, *Ouida*, 158–62.

[14] Gissing, *By the Ionian Sea*, 162.

In 1911 Italy embarked on her imperial adventures by seizing the Turkish possessions of Tripoli [Libya] and Rhodes; and in Tripoli the Italians perpetrated atrocities that revolted British liberal opinion. 'The Italians are a cowardly people,' fumed Wilfred Scawen Blunt, 'utterly vicious and corrupt, and this cruelty is a part of their nature.'[15] In the early summer of 1911 George Macaulay Trevelyan was working on the final pages of *Garibaldi and the Making of Italy*, the last volume of his trilogy on the Risorgimento. 'The Power of this great national movement', he wrote, 'has fortunately been directed only to the securing of Italian liberty, and not to the oppression of others'; and he lauded 'the unstained purity and idealism of patriotic emotion there, from the time of Mazzini's Young Italy to our own'. Later the same year, in the Introduction to his *English Songs of Italian Freedom*, he bitterly acknowledged his error:

Even while I write these words the prospect is arising that Italy will of her own accord throw away the one inestimable advantage that she has hitherto had over the other Great Powers, of being the conqueror of no other race and mistress only in her own house.

15. DEATH AND RESURRECTION

When Thomas Mann published *Death in Venice* in 1911 the idea was already old among the British that the gorgeous lands of the South were the abode of the Angel of Death. As early as 1830 Dr John Hennen had written of the Mediterranean littoral as 'immersed in the noisome vapour of untrodden marshes, and fanned by no zephyrs but those which scatter disease and death from their wings'. Many travellers were conscious of being stalked by deadly fevers. Newman almost died in Sicily in 1833. In the 1850s the family of the poet and novelist John Richard Best were ravaged by disease in Italy. Within a year, no fewer than three of the six children abroad with their parents died and a fourth fell seriously ill. 'So many of my poor countrymen commit the egregious folly of coming abroad with their families,' moaned the distraught father, 'that I would warn them of the dangers of the treacherous climate to which they entrust themselves.' Lord Ronald Gower reckoned in 1879 that a traveller took his life in his hands when he stayed for long in Rome or Naples, since 'both resemble[d] beautiful corpses, outwardly yet lovely, but internally full of death, decomposition and decay'. In 1882 an article in the *Pall Mall Gazette* asserted that 'fever, in one form or other, [was] never out of nearly all the hotels on the Riviera'. Two years later John Addington Symonds was crying out against 'this poisonous coast' and 'the foul sewer of this detested Italy' as his daughter Margaret fought for her life in San Remo. Gissing was laid low by feverish illness in Calabria in 1897, and an infection known as 'Jericho Fever' took its toll of visitors to the Holy Land. Until late in the nineteenth century most of the major cities and seaports of the Mediterranean were notorious among British medical men for their defective sanitation. Dr James Henry Bennet declared in 1875 that he would 'rather spend the winter in the pure air of Dartmoor than in the contaminated atmosphere of large, filthy southern towns like Naples, Rome and Malaga'; and other Victorian physicians were equally scathing about Hyères, Cannes, San Remo, Florence, Pisa, Venice, Algiers, Tunis, Cairo, and Valetta— chiefly on account of their powerful stench, which according to the miasmatic theory was itself a cause of disease. In these towns even sewers, the Victorian panacea, were a dubious advantage, because the sluggish rivers and tideless sea made dispersal a problem and discharged sewage would merely accumulate on the beaches and in the harbours—a potent source, as it was thought, of poisoned effluvia.[1]

If Mann's novella had been written by an Englishman its title would almost certainly have been *Death in Rome*, because in British experience Rome rather than Venice was the dread city of pestilence. 'It is more like a sepulchre than a city,' commented Shelley in 1819; 'beautiful, but the abode of death.' William Boxall, writing in 1834, described the Roman Campagna as a vast plain 'where the Angel of Death awakens with the summer heat'; and Dickens envisaged Rome as a city besieged by sickness. 'Imagine this phantom', he wrote, 'knocking at the gates of Rome; passing them; creeping along the street, haunting the aisles and pillars of the churches; year by year more encroaching and more impossible of avoidance.' Sir James Clark detailed essential precautions for all visitors to Rome, including the avoidance of accommodation near 'damp courts or gardens or standing water' and of outdoor exposure in the hour after sunset. These warnings were repeated in successive editions of Murray's

[1] Hennen, *Medical Topography*, 1; Best, *Nowadays*, ii. 63; Gower, *Reminiscences*, ii. 240; Schueller and Peters, eds., *Letters of J. A. Symonds*, ii. 899–900; Bennet, *Winter and Spring*, 197.

Handbook for Rome, and it is small wonder that the place acquired a sinister reputation. 'No city', wrote Dr David Young in 1886, 'is more dreaded for its supposed unhealthiness ... While thousands of visitors every year apparently throw aside their fears, yet it is a fact that there is no city in Europe which they enter with so many disquieting feelings and so much trembling.' Dr Aitkin, a physician resident in Rome, attributed the speed and intensity of the sightseeing of British and American tourists to their fear of disease, which made them anxious to quit the city as soon as possible. The main source of this alarm was called 'Roman Fever'—a term that continued in popular use until the First World War, though it was discarded by the medical profession in the 1880s, when the infection was identified as typhoid. The other pestilence was malaria, which was endemic not only in Rome but in large tracts of the western seaboard of Italy, in the plains of Catania in Sicily, in Algiers, in the Ionian Islands, and in the plain of Ephesus in Anatolia. It was said of the ruins at Paestum, Syracuse, and Ephesus that no one lingered there after sunset without contracting malaria; and sleeping at Paestum was regarded as almost certain death.[2]

The nefarious reputation of the Mediterranean as a hotbed of fatal disease owed more to imagination and fear than to actual mortality. In a setting such as Rome or Venice even banal death became dramatic, and the enigmatic nature of malaria intensified its frightfulness. For a hundred years and more the medical profession followed the false trail of miasmata, tracing the infection to such sources as rotting vegetation, stagnant water, mineral deposits in the soil, and ancient cesspools and tombs. Even after the parasitic nature of the affliction was discovered, in the 1880s, it was another generation before the mosquito was identified as vector. The deaths caused by these diseases were comparatively few. With the publication of regular Italian health statistics in the 1870s it was revealed that typhoid, despite its reputation as 'Roman' fever, in fact claimed far fewer lives in Rome than it did in Palermo, Milan, Florence, Naples, and Venice, and that the record of Italian towns generally was no worse than that of other large European cities—Paris especially. London, it is true, was

[2] F. L. Jones, ed., *The Letters of Percy Bysshe Shelley* (Oxford, 1964), ii. 159; Boxall MSS; Forster, *Life of Dickens*, ii. 140; Clark, *Sanative Influence*, 230–4; Young, *Rome in Winter*, pp. vii, 74, 92–3; Marcet, *Health Resorts*, 194–5; Hobhouse, ed., *Health Abroad*, 286; Bennet, *Winter and Spring*, 579; Dickinson, *Letters from Italy*, 190, 284; Jackson, *Medical Climatology*, 376.

comparatively healthy in this respect; but the English countryside was not, and it was the opinion of Dr Edward Sparks that the risk of death from typhoid was in fact greater in villages and country houses at home than it was along the Riviera. Malaria seldom affected foreign visitors since the risk was high only in the summer months, when they retreated to the rural uplands or to the North. Moreover quinine, body covering, and window gauzes were well known to be prophylactics— though of course for a long time nobody knew why they had a preventive effect. When malaria did attack foreigners it usually took the mild, intermittent form and responded quickly to treatment with quinine. The more serious, remittent form occasionally infected British troops in the Ionian Islands, causing high mortality; but death from malaria among visitors to the large Mediterranean cities was extremely rare.[3]

Yet even when magnified by legend and mystery Southern pestilence still seems inadequate as an explanation for the widespread image of the South as a necropolis. It was not the experience or the fear of infection that made most travellers think of the Mediterranean in this way; it was rather the large number of casualties among invalids who had been enticed there by false hopes and promises of cure—'the long and melancholy list', as Sir James Clark described it, 'of ... countrymen who [had] sought with pain and suffering a distant country, only to find in it a grave'. So many Protestant tombstones in the South, as Murray's *Handbook for Rome* sadly acknowledged, bore the names of Britons who had travelled in search of health. The presence of this moribund clientele turned the hotels of the Riviera ('built', in the words of Symonds, 'for as many consumptive foreigners to live or die in as can be packed into their formless parallelograms') into annexes of graveyards, and made the tourist centres of Italy ghastly and depressing. 'If there be on earth a spectacle of human misery utterly deplorable,' wrote James Whiteside in 1848, 'it is that of consumptive patients, in an advanced stage of their disease, wandering through Italy in search of health.' Dr T. H. Burgess observed these 'spectacles of human misery' in the 1850s in Milan and Rome. He saw 'compatriots in the advanced stages of phthisis, with *pallida mors* visibly stamped upon their countenances, crawling along the street, or dragged in invalid chairs, to see sights perhaps the last they will ever

[3] Young, *Rome in Winter*, 92–9, 117–18; Sparks, *The Riviera*, 87; Hennen, *Medical Topography*, *passim*; Davy, *Ionian Islands and Malta*, ii. 218–28.

witness'. Pisa he described as the city of the dead alive, 'for who can walk through its streets, especially in the English quarter, without mourning over the traditionary delusion which has enticed so many natives of England to seek a renewed lease of life in a foreign country, and find only an Italian grave?' Alexander Knox saw more of these cadaverous exiles in Algiers in 1880. 'It filled me with sadness', he wrote, 'to see the poor creatures who were sent to Algiers in search of health, and who could not reasonably hope for anything but an aggravation of their ailments, and a last resting place in the English Cemetery.'[4]

Burgess was a climatotherapist; but he demurred from the ideas of most of his professional colleagues and in *The Climate of Italy in Relation to Pulmonary Consumption* (1852) he attacked the use of Southern resorts in the treatment of tuberculosis. He testified to 'the misery, nay the positive evil, which patients of this class incur[red] by migrating from England to those countries when labouring under confirmed phthisis'. While admitting the value of Mediterranean climates in other afflictions (especially 'dyspepsia, nervous affections, rheumatism and scrofula'), he maintained that in cases of consumption they were useless. These misgivings were shared by an increasing number of physicians whose faith in Southern climates in consumptive cases was shaken by discouraging experience. Drs John Hennen and James Johnson were expressing doubts as early as 1830. Hennen detailed 'the fearful odds' encountered by phthisical patients when they embarked on a pilgrimage of health to the Mediterranean. 'There can be little, if any doubt', he warned, 'that many lives have been sacrificed in this way. Physicians, judging from latitude, have supposed that many situations *should* be favourable to phthisical patients which, on trial, have proved remarkably the reverse.' Johnson was even more emphatic. He arraigned the advocates of Italy and the South of France as irresponsible. In cases of confirmed phthisis a Southern climate was known to be 'not only useless, but injurious', while its use as a preventive treatment incurred huge expenditure on mere speculation and involved the risk of sending south patients with lungs already tubercular. Diathesis was too imperfectly understood; and even with a stethoscope it was often difficult to determine whether 'tubercular cachexy' had passed into actual disease. 'I have lived too long, and

[4] Clark, *Sanative Influence*, 52; Schueller and Peters, eds., *Letters of J. A. Symonds*, ii. 406; Whiteside, *Italy in the Nineteenth Century*, 2; Burgess, *Climate of Italy*, 74, 135, 148; Knox, *The New Playground*, 478.

seen too much, not to know the errors of discrimination and the fallacies of hope that send pulmonary invalids from the gloomy skies but comfortable abodes of England to lands where comfort is unknown, even by name, and whose atmosphere cannot work miracles, whatever their saints may do.' Dr Scoresby Jackson, in his *Medical Climatology* of 1862, admitted that 'thousands had died' under the climatic treatment; and Dr Coupland Taylor, in his *Wanderings in Search of Health* (1890), wrote of invalids in the South dying 'almost immediately after their arrival, not having sufficient strength even to survive the fatigues of the journey or voyage'.[5]

There is a strong hint of doubt and misgiving even in the writings of the most ardent advocates of these resorts. They insisted that in appropriate cases the right climate could work wonders, but always took care to add that it could do nothing unless the patient helped himself. A punishing rubric of regulations therefore formed an essential part of their treatment. The patient must not leave for the South too late, nor return too early. He should avoid streets running from north to south and verify the southward aspect of his room with a compass and its dryness with a hygrometer. Flannel underwear and woollen top clothing must be worn throughout the winter, extra wraps always carried, a light umbrella used against the sun, and shoes with cork or indiarubber soles put on when visiting buildings with cold floors. The diet must be strictly controlled to match the properties of the climate. The invalid should not be out on wet and gloomy days, or after sunset. He must avoid sudden transitions from sunshine to shade. Ventilation was essential, but draughts fatal. Windows should be open all day but closed at night and the company of Germans avoided, since they hated fresh air and vitiated the atmosphere. Evening amusements like dinners, parties, theatre, concerts, and balls were forbidden, and exhausting pastimes like visiting museums, art galleries, and churches strictly discouraged. Distraction should be sought in books, music, sketching, and the study of nature, and the truth constantly borne in mind that recovery and pleasure were incompatible. Above all, the patient must persist. He must return to the South and to this rigorous discipline again and again, forswearing family ties, professional duties, and social position. The key to cure was heavy sacrifice.

[5] Hennen, *Medical Topography*, pp. xxxv, 606; Johnson, *Change of Air*, 262–5; Jackson, *Medical Climatology*, 81; Taylor, *Wanderings in Search of Health*, 7.

When doctors sent consumptive invalids to the Mediterranean burdened with requirements as demanding as these they were implicitly admitting that the chances of recovery were slight, and probably the treatment continued in use only because it shifted the blame for failure to the invalid. For it was a characteristic of this form of alternative medicine that it reversed the postures of doctor and patient. It put the self-discipline of the patient rather than the skill of the physician on trial, and the doctor could assume the aggrieved attitude that had been the patient's prerogative under the orthodox system. Doctors who wrote on the Mediterranean frequently adopted an accusatory tone and helped to create the popular image of the consumptive as a wilful, intractable invalid.

The dissenters took a different line, and blamed the resorts rather than the patients. Tubercular invalids, they decided, were being sent to the wrong area. Nature-therapy was better served in the mountainous and desert hinterlands. Dr John Davy was suggesting as early as 1842 that a mountain climate, judging by 'the robust health and fine forms commonly witnessed in the peasantry of the higher Alps', was likely to offer the best check to the tuberculous diathesis. An article in the *Fortnightly Review* in 1865 drew attention to the rarity of consumption among the inhabitants of arctic and mountainous regions, and by the late 1860s British doctors were following the lead of the Germans and experimenting, with remarkable success, with winter resorts in the Swiss Alps. Dr Burney Yeo, himself a consumptive, passed the winter of 1868–9 at St Moritz with beneficial results, and it was St Moritz that he recommended to the notice of the British medical profession. But it was the bleak valley of Davos Platz that was destined to become the Swiss sanatorium *par excellence*. First mentioned by Dr Alexander Spengler in the German medical journal *Deutsche Klinik* in 1862, Davos rapidly increased in popularity. Its number of winter visitors grew from about 70 in 1868–9 to some 700 ten years later. Articles by Dr Clifford Allbutt in the *Lancet* in 1877 and by John Addington Symonds in the *Fortnightly* in 1878 made Davos celebrated among British consumptives, who helped to swell the winter population to 13,000 by the end of the century. Symonds made Davos his home and became one of its most prominent citizens.[6]

---

[6] Davy, *Ionian Islands and Malta*, ii. 320–1; Yeo, *Health Resorts*, 113–14, 242; Marcet, *Health Resorts*, 385–6; Otter, *Winters Abroad*, 184; Phyllis Grosskurth, *John Addington Symonds* (1967), 181–96; W. H. Vorman, ed., *Davos, its Local, Physical and Medical Aspects* (1882), *passim*.

Almost simultaneous with the growth of interest in the Swiss Alps was the discovery of the therapeutic effects of the interiors of Egypt and Algeria. By the 1860s the Nile Voyage was being recommended to consumptives wealthy enough to afford it, and its benefits were being tested by broken-down Indian officials on their way home—like General Sir James Outram, in 1861. Egypt's most famous invalid was Lucie, Lady Duff Gordon—daughter of a distinguished mother (Sarah Austin), mother of a distinguished daughter (Janet Ross), cousin of Harriet Martineau, and friend of George Meredith; brilliant, literary, and highly unconventional, like a figure from Bloomsbury out of her time. Lucie Duff Gordon began her seven years' exile at Thebes in 1862 and her sensitive and moving *Letters from Egypt*, published in two collections in 1865 and 1875, did for Upper Egypt what Symonds was to do for Davos. At first invalids hoping to benefit from the desert climate were forced to live on the Nile, making a long boat journey from Cairo to the First Cataract and back; but by the 1890s this itinerant cure had been made superfluous by the opening of the railway to Aswan and the development of Luxor and Aswan as health resorts with luxury hotels and resident English physicians and nursing staff. By this time too the Mena House Hotel and the Grand Helouan Hotel, both near the Great Pyramid, were available to those who wished to enjoy the desert air without travelling far from Cairo.[7] The Algerian desert resort of Biskra, on the edge of the Sahara, attracted some attention in the 1890s,[8] but English invalids continued to prefer Upper Egypt, for social and cultural reasons.

The Swiss and desert climates were classified as tonic and stimulating, and consequently qualified as suitable now that pulmonary tuberculosis was regarded as a disease of debility arrestable through improved nutrition. Writing in 1887, Dr J. A. Lindsay detected a decline in the popularity of the marine resorts of the Mediterranean 'in the presence of the modern drift of medical opinion in favour of the view that they afford on the whole less favourable results in consumption than the mountain sanatoria [and] the dry inland resorts'. He judged that the resorts of the Riviera were surviving only by virtue of 'their long-famous name, their ample and often luxurious accommodation, and the patronage of wealth and fashion'.[9]

---

[7] See Leigh Canney's chapter in Hobhouse, ed., *Health Abroad*.

[8] Arthur Griffith, 'An Algerian Winter Resort: Biskra': *Fortnightly Review*, March 1895.

[9] Lindsay, *Climatic Treatment*, 40–1.

Several supplementary explanations were advanced for the disappointing record of the Mediterranean resorts as sanatoria for consumptives. Conservative climatotherapists, and those with vested interests to defend, used special pleading to retrieve their reputation and insisted that the disappointments were the consequences of success. The proven effectiveness of Southern climates in many cases had raised impossible expectations and encouraged doctors to prescribe the Mediterranean indiscriminately, sending out patients either too late or to the wrong resort. 'If in individual instances the experiment of change egregiously fails', wrote Professor Walter Walshe in his *Practical Treatise on the Diseases of the Lungs and Heart* (1860), 'the failure depends either on inappropriateness in the spot selected, or more commonly on the very advanced condition of the local and general suffering when the change is effected.'[10] In view of these professional lapses it was not surprising, as Clark observed, 'that success [had] not more generally attended the practice of sending invalids abroad, nor even that the result should have been such as to bring the remedy into unmerited discredit'.[11] In 1862 Dr Scoresby Jackson urged practitioners to refuse to sanction journeys 'which would all but add another grave to one of those foreign cemeteries visited so often, and with such compassionate interest, by that class especially which affords in most ample numbers victims to their silent tombs'.[12] The plea was often repeated, especially by those who, like Dr Henry Blanc, had lucrative practices to protect. In 1893 he grumbled:

I believe if unsuitable cases had long ago been warned away, that the reputation of Cannes as a health resort would stand much higher than it does. A large number of cases which would be greatly benefitted by a winter at Cannes are not sent ... in ignorance of its advantages or because an unfavourable report has been made regarding it by those who should never have gone there at all.[13]

But if this argument explained the failures of the Mediterranean, it did not explain the successes of Switzerland and Egypt, and increasingly it was debated whether the conditions offered by the marine resorts were in fact those most propitious for nature-therapy in consumptive

[10] Cited in Lee, *Bradshaw's Invalid's Companion*, 404.
[11] Clark, *Sanative Influence*, 2–3, 50.
[12] Jackson, *Medical Climatology*, 137.
[13] Henry Blanc, *Advice to Intending Visitors to Cannes* (1893), Preface.

cases. Climatically, environmentally, and morally they appeared less and less appropriate.

With regard to climate, it seemed increasingly doubtful that warmth and low rainfall were really paramount requirements. Experience suggested that absolute dryness and atmospheric calm, rather than relative dryness and mean temperature, were crucial. Humidity, in the form of either damp soil or absolute moisture in the atmosphere, came to be recognised as a predisposing condition of phthisis. Even in 1842 Dr John Davy was suggesting that 'a very cold and dry atmosphere' was indicated in pulmonary consumption, and this was echoed by Dr James Allen in the *Edinburgh Medical and Surgical Journal* in 1844. Allen recommended the 'pure, dry, tonic atmosphere' of Upper Canada as eminently suited to consumptive patients. Edwin Lee's *Invalids' Bradshaw* of 1861 pointed out that phthisis was prevalent in temperate climates with much humidity, whereas in Russia and Sweden, 'where the cold is extreme but the air sharp and dry', it was comparatively rare. Dr Charles Theodore Williams, one of the most eminent Victorian authorities on consumption, drew attention in 1869 to the work of the Swiss physician Hermann Weber, who maintained that cold air, when dry, was not injurious to consumptives, but beneficial. He also noticed the researches of 'Doctors Bowditch and Buchanan in England and America', which had 'beyond doubt established that wetness of soil is a cause of consumption to the population living on it'. Few specialists agreed that the matter was as simple as that; but there was a general feeling that damp soil and damp atmosphere favoured the disease, and that the therapeutic effect of the climates of Switzerland and Upper Egypt was connected with their high degree of absolute dryness. This was assumed to act beneficially by inducing loss of moisture from the lungs. The dryness of the Riviera on the other hand was merely the relative dryness associated with absence of rain and fogs; and relative dryness was clinically insignificant, since it induced loss of moisture not from the lungs, but from the skin.[14]

Moreover not even their staunchest champions could pretend that the Mediterranean resorts enjoyed calm winter weather. They were turbulent to an extreme, afflicted alternately by the northern mistral or tramontana, and the southern sirocco; and turbulence was

[14] Burgess, *The Climate of Italy*, 4; Lee, *Bradshaw's Invalids' Companion*, 372–3; Williams, *The Climate of the South of France*, 63, 134; Young, *Rome in Winter*, 29–30; Hobhouse, ed., *Health Abroad*, 34–5; Lindsay, *Climatic Treatment*, 3–4, 41; Jackson, *Medical Climatology*, 483; Marcet, *Health Resorts*, 215–16.

increasingly recognised as a major disqualification in cases of pulmonary consumption. Turbulence not only made for wide and distressing fluctuations of temperature; it was also the great hindrance to outdoor life. It was wind, not cold, that kept the patient indoors. In the still atmosphere of Davos invalids could sit outside without wraps, and exercise in the fresh air, enjoying the solar heat even though the temperature of the atmosphere was 30° Fahrenheit below freezing. The hot atmosphere of Upper Egypt likewise was remarkably calm, and the invalid experienced nothing like the exhaustion caused by the sirocco in Italy. This was an advantage enjoyed by Egypt over the interior of Algeria, which was much more windy. Atmospheric temperature, it was clear, was irrelevant to the fresh-air treatment. Great heat, like great cold, was easily supportable in the absence of absolute moisture and wind.

Thirdly, the rarefied atmosphere of mountain resorts was reckoned to have a beneficial effect on the physiology of the lungs. Clark, in his *Treatise on Pulmonary Consumption* of 1835, had pointed out that tubercles tended to accumulate at the apex of the lungs, where respiratory motion was slight; and Davy, in 1842, suggested that the rarity of tubercles among alpine people was connected with the greater respiratory activity occasioned by rarefied atmosphere. By the 1880s this was medical orthodoxy. 'Davos', wrote Dr Lindsay in 1887, 'cure[s] consumption ... mainly by the rarefaction of its air, which stimulates respiratory activity, promotes healthy expansion and soundness of tissue in the lungs, and hence aids them to resist the spread of morbid deposits.' The old prejudice against tenuous atmosphere, as liable to promote haemorrhage, was now abandoned.[15]

The environmental drawbacks of the Mediterranean littoral were the increasing density of population and the rapid growth of urban conditions. Pulmonary tuberculosis had long been identified as an urban disease, a disease of crowds, and the large cities of the Riviera and Italy were merely reproducing in the South the conditions in which it was known to thrive. 'Large centres of population are uniformly and radically ineligible as sanatoria for consumption', declared Lindsay in 1887; 'the evidence that the disease is essentially one of civilised life in large communities is overwhelming.' Yet the chief sanatoria of the Mediterranean—Cannes, Nice, Malaga, Algiers,

[15] Clark, *Pulmonary Consumption*, 27, 31, 128, 300; Davy, *Ionian Islands and Malta*, ii. 321–2; Marcet, *Health Resorts*, 334–7; Yeo, *Health Resorts*, 136; Lindsay, *Climatic Treatment*, 32, 199.

Palermo—were all big cities by this time, and even the smaller resorts, such as Menton and San Remo, became tightly crowded when swollen by their winter populations. The micro-organic theory of disease, and the discovery that tuberculosis was a bacillary infection spread by droplet infection, made such places seem even less eligible as health resorts. Preference was therefore transferred to sparsely inhabited areas and sterile atmospheres. As Dr David Young put it in 1886, 'the existence of these active agents in the atmosphere gives additional importance to medical climatology, and until we know how to destroy them, our next care must be to place susceptible patients beyond their reach.' Such patients could nowhere be safer than in the Swiss Alps or Upper Egypt, where the biological purity of the air was attested by the absence of putrefaction.[16]

Finally, but very significantly, the Mediterranean resorts were condemned for moral reasons. British medical opinion insisted that dissipation and sensual indulgence were detrimental to health, and in the South the patient was tantalised by incitements to fatal pleasure— warmth, natural beauty, art, and fashionable and brilliant society. 'Where climate supplies constant stimulation for the senses,' warned Dr James Johnson in 1830, 'passion will predominate over reason; and where the passions are indulged, the range of existence will be curtailed.' Consumption was often linked to loose living and reckless enjoyment. Davy blamed sexual promiscuity for the high incidence of phthisis among the British troops in Malta. 'That dissipation,' he wrote, 'by injuring the general health and debilitating the constitution, conduces to tubercular disease, can hardly be doubted.' Dr John Patterson, writing in 1867, cited the increase of syphilis among the natives of Alexandria and Cairo as 'a very powerful predisposing cause' of the spread of consumption. The cosmopolitan socialising and gaslit gaiety of Italy and the Riviera were anathema to doctors anxious to submit their patients to the healing influences of nature. Dr Scoresby Jackson condemned 'those pernicious raree shows which, ... especially throughout Italy, ... exercise[d] an insidious and baneful influence upon weakly constitutions'; and in the opinion of Dr Lindsay 'the numerous incitements to perilous amusements' were one of the chief drawbacks of the Riviera as a winter sanatorium. 'Undue excitement, heated and crowded rooms, over-exertion and late

[16] Lindsay, *Climatic Treatment*, 29–30; Young, *Rome in Winter*, 25–6; Otter, *Winters Abroad*, 225; Yeo, *Health Resorts*, 245; Taylor, *Wanderings in Search of Health*, 68; Marcet, *Health Resorts*, 216.

hours—the usual accompaniments of life at the fashionable sanatoria—are ... in the last degree noxious to the sufferer from pulmonary disease.' Stories were current of the awful termination awaiting those who turned their cures into carnivals. Ex-Provost William Chambers passed the winter of 1869–70 at Menton and learnt of 'a young gentleman of fortune with lungs much gone who, ... contrary to advice, attended a dancing party'. He collapsed, was carried out, and died in the passage. 'In that Dance of Death', reflected Chambers mournfully, 'he had finished the last atom of lung ... gaily ending his days in the revelry of a waltz.' Aghast, Chambers observed the hectic vanity of invalids with one foot in the grave. 'Ladies bring enormous boxfuls of fashionable attire,' he reported, 'and wish to show it off somehow.' The previous season the young lady 'considered to be the reigning beauty' had had only one lung, 'which it was alleged she was doing all in her power to get rid of'. The Casino of Monte Carlo was widely condemned by medical men as a threat to healthy living. Dr Burney Yeo deplored 'the dangerous seductions of the gaming tables', and Dr James Bennet refused to recommend invalids to settle in Monaco. 'I cannot but think', he wrote, 'that the immediate proximity of a gaming table, in the absence of all other occupations, is dangerous to many who would never positively seek its excitements and risks.' Dr Edward Sparks complained that its noxious influence was infecting even Nice, Menton and San Remo, 'both in the class of unwelcome visitors which it attracts and in the ruin which it brings on respectable families'.[17]

The allurement of art was hardly less pernicious than that of gregariousness and gambling. Nemesis lurked in galleries, museums, and churches, in the form of sudden changes of temperature, fatigue, crowds, polluted air, and chilly pavements. Burgess was horrified to see invalids in the Tribuna at Rome among a crowd of spectators in a small chamber, 'jostling each other from want of room, gazing for hours together upon the immortal works of art around, whilst breathing all the time a heated, confined and impure atmosphere'. Scoresby Jackson warned against 'the imminent peril to which all visitors invariably expose themselves in Rome', in churches, galleries, and ruins; and Charles Theodore Williams deplored 'the temptations

[17] Johnson, *Change of Air*, 195–6; Davy, *Ionian Islands and Malta*, ii. 316–7; Patterson, *Egypt and the Nile*, 40; Jackson, *Medical Climatology*, 126; Lindsay, *Climatic Treatment*, 182; Chambers, *Wintering at Mentone*, 66–7; Yeo, *Health Resorts*, 295; Bennet, *Winter and Spring*, 179–80; Sparks, *The Riviera*, 299.

offered by the treasure houses of ancient and modern art', where invalids endured 'cold, fatigue and other dangers'. These physicians, writing in the 1850s and 1860s, argued that the temptations of art and society in the large Mediterranean cities should be recognised as a therapeutic disqualification. Doctors could not evade responsibility for dire consequences by blaming their patients, who were but human in their susceptibilities. 'Patients able to accomplish so long and so fatiguing a journey as that from London to Rome or Pisa', said Burgess, 'are not likely to display such abnegation as to resist the powerful attractions by which they are surrounded.' He and Scoresby Jackson implied that the doctor's function was to adapt the cure to the patient, not the patient to the cure; and both insisted that the purposes of nature-therapy would be better served by a judiciously selected climate in the south of England. Had they been writing twenty years later, they would almost certainly have recommended a Swiss resort.[18]

When Victorian doctors thus arraigned the pleasures of the South they were drawing on the deep reservoir of Protestant puritanism that fed the mentality of their age, and which represented salvation in terms not of self-fulfilment, but of self-denial. The idea that luxury and ease were devitalising and that austerity and combat were 'bracing', which owed much to biblical imagery and to Bunyan's religious allegories, was frequently stressed in the works of lay authors like Charles Kingsley, Thomas Hughes, and Leslie Stephen; and it was widely expressed or implied by travel writers too. Charles Wood, the roving son of the popular novelist Mrs Henry Wood, serves well as an example. Wood liked to lace his travel books with pulpit platitudes, and in his turgid peroration on the fatality of the charms of Majorca he adopted a conventional pose. 'Certain it is,' he wrote to his sister in 1887, 'the happiness that here falls upon me, the ecstasy that enfolds my senses, is strange and powerful . . . All that is emotional within me would ask nothing better of life than to pass it here, steeped in this voluptuous Southern dream and influence.' He feared however that 'the doom of the Epicurean' must await him if he yielded to this inclination to linger. 'But afterwards?' he went on in a style worthy of his mother's son, 'And the ending? And the awakening, when custom has marred and age has staled the infinite variety of these charms— what then? Dead Sea fruit, my sister! The apples of Sodom; the waters

[18] Burgess, *The Climate of Italy*, 135, 137; Jackson, *Medical Climatology*, 406; Williams, *The Climate of the South of France*, 102.

of Meribah; the bitterness of Marah!' His final exhortation is traditional and predictable: 'Give me the colder, healthier influences of the North, companionship with a race that resolutely fights the battle of life, pressing onward and upward.'[19]

Sentiments such as these make it clear that when Victorian doctors sent them into the mountains and the desert, they were working with their patients rather than against them. They were endorsing a deeply embedded conviction that worldly delights were a lethal snare, and thereby reversing the unfavourable psychosomatic response that the traditional associations of the Mediterranean were liable to induce. The personal records of two well-known consumptives certainly suggest that the rejection of the sybarite South and the retreat to the barren reaches of the Alps operated psychosomatically, by satisfying a religious urge to rebuke the senses and mortify the passions. John Addington Symonds interpreted his divided life as an alternation between incrimination and atonement; as an expiation in the Alps of guilt incurred in Italy. 'Italy', he wrote, 'devours the body and the soul of me'; and he reproached himself for the 'sordid passions', 'crimes', 'bad habits', and personal unworthiness that he indulged there.[20] His life in Davos, on the other hand, he apostrophised as

> . . . solemn hours of high-souled solitude,
> Health and composure of the passionless mind;[21]

and his wife Catherine summarised his as well as her own attitude and experience when she wrote of Switzerland: 'I love it better than the South really; one feels a better human being physically and morally among the snows.'[22] Like Symonds, Ruskin was a consumptive who found no relief in Italy but whose health improved dramatically in Switzerland. Sir James Clark ordered him to Rome; but it was in the Alps that the disease left him. 'The doctors had been entirely mistaken about me', he recalled. 'I wanted bracing air, exercise and rest from all artificial excitement. The air of the Campagna was the worst they could have sent me into—the life of Rome the worst they could have chosen.' Again, improvement was accompanied by a sense of religious elation, for the evangelical in Ruskin interpreted severe, coldly tinted landscape as a symbol of spiritual resurrection, and soft contours and

---

[19] Charles W. Wood, *Letters from Majorca* (1888), 298–9.

[20] Schueller and Peters, eds., *The Letters of J. A. Symonds*, ii. 797, 805, 824; iii. 53.

[21] A Sonnet from the sequence 'The Alps and Italy', in *Old and New* (1880).

[22] M. Symonds, *Out of the Past*, 298.

glowing colours as a symbol of spiritual death. He cleaved to the sterility and silence of mountains, snow, ice, and clouds, and shrank from the incitements to pleasure and to art that throbbed in the atmosphere of the South. 'I felt on the Simplon', he told his father in 1845, 'as if I were escaping to the mountains out of Gomorrah'; and in the fourth volume of *Modern Painters*, published in 1856, he recapitulated in a mood of ecstatic piety the biblical allusions which signified mountains as refuges from judgement, signs of redemption, and altars of sanctification and obedience. The Ark had come to rest on the mountains of Ararat; God had commanded Lot to 'escape to the mountain'; Divine Law had been revealed on Mount Sinai; and the Psalmist had sung: 'I will lift up mine eyes unto the hills, from whence cometh my help.' Thirty years later, in remotest Scotland, he finally broke his truce with the Mediterranean and with art. 'I was justly and finally impressed', he wrote,

with the sadness and even *weakness* of the Mediterranean coasts, and the temptation to human nature there to solace itself with debasing pleasures; while the very impossibility of either accumulating the treasures, or multiplying the dreams of art among the Northern waves and rocks, left the spirit of man strong to bear the hardships of the world and faithful to obey the precepts of Heaven.[23]

Clearly, to minds steeped in evangelical Christianity the journey to the wasteland acquired a sacramental significance. The likelihood is therefore strong that the therapeutic successes in the Alps and the desert were achieved partly through a faith and a hope that had been fortified by biblical associations. Here, medicine and religion met; for when the Victorian doctor sent his patients into the wilderness he became identified—if only subconsciously—with the Old Testament Deity, summoning his votaries from the fleshpots to a new life.

[23] Ruskin, *Praeterita*, ii, Ch. III, sec. 57; iii, Ch. IV, sec. 70; Shapiro, ed., *Ruskin in Italy*, 228; Cook and Wedderburn, eds., *Works of Ruskin*, vi. 458–66.

CONCLUSION

WHEN Victorians preferred not to contemplate the darker possibilities of human destiny they found distraction in the stir and bustle, the coming and going, of the age of steam. This they read as evidence that man was less a moral pygmy than an intellectual giant, sustaining progress through his aptitude for technology and science. 'There are hundreds of parrots who will declaim to you in speech and in print by the hour together', exclaimed an exasperated Charles Dickens in 1845, 'on the degeneracy of the times in which a railroad is building across the water to Venice! Instead of going down upon their knees, the drivellers, and thanking heaven that they live in a time when Iron makes roads instead of prison bars.'[1] Macaulay argued impressively that 'every improvement in the means of locomotion ... tends to remove national and provincial antipathies',[2] and Buckle went so far as to declare that railways and steamships had done more to diminish the warlike spirit among mankind than countless years of preaching by divines and moralists. 'Of all the causes of national hatred,' he explained, 'ignorance is the most powerful. When you increase the contact, you remove the ignorance, and thus you diminish the hatred.' To support this contention he cited the example of England and France. Here were two nations who had 'by the mere force of increased contact, learned to think more favourably of each other and to discard that foolish contempt in which both ... formerly indulged.' Warming to his theme, Buckle asserted: 'Every new railroad which is laid down, and every fresh steamer which crosses the channel, are additional guarantees for the preservation of that long and unbroken peace which, during forty years, has knit together the fortunes and the interests of the two most civilised nations of the earth.'[3]

This enviable optimism was shattered in the first half of the twentieth century, when modern methods of communication, far from inhibiting war, intensified its destruction; but even to the generation that did not live to witness Europe's agony it was apparent that Buckle's two basic assumptions (that contact diminishes ignorance and that less ignorance means more sympathy) must be false. Winwood Reade, a visionary writing shortly after the carnage of the

[1] Tillotson, ed., *Dickens Letters*, iv. 220.
[2] Thomas Babington Macaulay, *The History of England from the Accession of James II* (Popular edn., 1889), i. 182.
[3] Henry Thomas Buckle, *A History of Civilisation in England* (2nd edn., 1858), i. 202–3.

Franco–Prussian War, felt bound to concede that the theorem was unsound. 'In Europe itself', he predicted, 'it is not probable that war will ever absolutely cease until science discovers some destroying force so simple in its administration, so horrible in its effects, that all art, all gallantry, will be at an end, and battles will be massacres which the feelings of mankind will be unable to endure.'[4] Victorians and Edwardians who observed the behaviour of tourists abroad realised that modern facilities for travel were increasing contact in the quantitative, but not in the qualitative sense. More people visited foreign countries; but there was no evidence of more understanding and less suspicion between nations. In fact it seemed that national self-consciousness and jealousy were enhanced, rather than diminished, as a result. 'Time was', reminisced Frederic Harrison in 1887, 'when travellers who supped at the same table could talk quite naturally to each other in any language that served best . . .; when Frenchmen and Germans discussed the beauties of the Rhine, and when it was not an impertinence to address to a stranger a remark about the weather. All this is over.' Now, he lamented, tourists consorted only with their own compatriots:

Germans, Frenchmen, English, Russians or Italians take their pleasure sadly in foreign parts, and in strict national lines. There are English, German, and French resorts; English, German, and French hotels in the same place; English, German, and French tables in the same room. You may see English, German, and French families pass many weeks together in the same house, eat twice a day at the same table, and sit for hours in the same *salons* without ever exchanging a chance word.[5]

This exclusiveness was, apparently, especially pronounced at health resorts. Dr James Henry Bennet described how people of the same nationality would hang together at Menton, bound by 'the same feeling of union, of common origin and object, that exists among the passengers of a ship on a long voyage'.[6]

Judging by the British record, communication failed not only between visitors of different nationalities; it failed too between visitors and natives. The only local people with whom the majority of British travellers had contact were shopkeepers and servants, and even with these contact was kept to a minimum. According to Edward Sparks,

      [4] Winwood Reade, *The Martyrdom of Man* (22nd edn., 1923), 415.
      [5] Harrison, *Memories and Thoughts*, 235.
      [6] Bennet, *Winter and Spring*, 201.

on the Riviera in the 1870s many Britons were choosing to live in hotels in order to avoid the dealings with local tradespeople and domestics that residence in villas entailed.[7] Villas, it is true, remained popular—but only among those wealthy enough to bring English servants abroad. It seems that imported servants became a feature of life in villas, and that it was by and large their function to make the necessary communication with natives. There are of course exceptions to this general observation. British visitors did occasionally become deeply attached to native servants and involve themselves in their affections and worldly affairs: The relationships between Lucie Duff Gordon and her Egyptian manservant Omar, between Frederick Faber and his Greek guide Demetri, between Edward Lear and his Suliot valet and factotum George Kokalis, and between John Addington Symonds and his gondolier Angelo Fusato were of the kind that generate great power for good. But it was very seldom that association with people from the lower classes transcended the exchanges of domestic routine or the barter of commerce and prostitution; while contact with the higher classes—on the rare occasions when it occurred—was limited to niceties and formalities that expressed politeness rather than sincerity.

This was the case even in Italy, a country whose pulse the British claimed they could feel, and whose heartbeats they were supposed to hear. 'How many, even among our settlers in the land, have managed to get into sympathetic touch with its people?' demanded James Sully in 1912[8]—and it is easy to understand why. The observation was frequently made that British and Italians never associated socially. 'I know no more of the character of the better sort of the Italians than you do', wrote William Boxall to his sister in 1834. 'Neither am I likely to do so—they and the English residents never associate together.' He described how he had recently attended one of the celebrated evening receptions of the Roman banker Torlonia and found some eight hundred 'Italians, English, French, Germans, Russians, Greeks and Turks all huddled together'. Yet, he explained, 'this all ends with the night, and the Italians and the English make no friendship'.[9] Thackeray reported from Rome in 1854 that in the houses he visited he never saw an Italian, and he claimed not to know a single Roman except his housemaid and his landlord. He wrote in one of his letters

[7] Sparks, *The Riviera*, 153.
[8] Sully, *Italian Travel Sketches*, 66.
[9] Boxall MSS.

that he did not believe that Romans existed, and he put the same quip into the mouth of his hero, Clive Newcome.[10] Anna Jameson, Frances Power Cobbe, and James Bryce all said much the same, and in the hundreds of published letters of Elizabeth Barrett Browning there is mentioned only one Italian whom she met socially. This was the patriot and historian Pasquale Villari, 'an accomplished Sicilian' encountered at Mrs Lytton's villa in Bagni di Lucca in the summer of 1853. It is one of the myths of English literary history that the Brownings cultivated a special and intimate relationship with Florentine society. Elizabeth lived more or less as a recluse, wrapped up in her baby, her dog, and the exploits of her hero, Louis Napoleon of France; while Robert found his true milieu in the salons of Anglo-American hostesses in cosmopolitan cities like Rome, London, and Paris. As soon as Elizabeth was dead he left Florence for good and slipped easily into the role of literary lion of the North. He returned to Italy only for autumn holidays in Venice, where he looked at the sunsets, fussed over his feckless son, and was doted on by the wealthy American expatriate Katherine de Kay Bronson. Mrs Bronson recalled, significantly, that during these vacations 'Browning never failed to read the London daily papers, but seldom found time to look at those published in Venice'.[11] In the years before Italian unification a few British residents in Florence (the Thomas Trollopes, most notably) opened their houses to liberal writers and intellectuals; but after the victory of the liberal Italian cause in 1870 even this bond of sympathy became redundant.

Intermarriage seems to have been rare throughout the period, and chiefly restricted to servants. 'Here it is by no means an uncommon thing for English ladies' maids to marry Italians and settle happily', wrote Elizabeth Browning from Florence in 1848.[12] Her own maid ('Wilson') married an Italian manservant (after being jilted by a soldier of the Grand Ducal bodyguard) and both the Dickens and the Ruskin ménage lost female domestics in this way. Among the higher reaches of society a few English women acquired Italian titles by marriage (these included the Marchioness Pasqualino, the Duchess of Sforza-Cesarini, the Duchess of Sermoneta, the Princess Santa Croce, the Princess Doria, the Countess Gigliucci, and the Countess Pisani) and there are scattered references to English men who found Italian brides

[10] *The Newcomes*, Ch. XXXV; Ray, ed., *Letters of Thackeray*, iii. 333, 339, 351.
[11] Bronson, *Cornhill Magazine*, 12. 161.
[12] Huxley, ed., *E. B. Browning's Letters*, 96.

(including Frederick Tennyson, the poet's brother); but such liaisons were few, and they were not necessarily either a result of, or a means to, understanding and sympathy. Antonio Gallenga, who as an expatriate Italian living in England knew something of both nationalities, suggested that Anglo–Italian marriages were generally business transactions ('the exchange of a high-sounding Southern title for a comfortable Northern dowry'),[13] and E. M. Forster, the only novelist of any stature to attempt a fictional treatment of the theme, used such a marriage to illustrate not the affections that drew nations together but the disparities that kept them apart. In *Where Angels Fear to Tread* the marriage of Lilia and Gino is doomed by the incompatibility of temperaments formed by different cultures. 'No one realised', we are told, 'that more than personalities were engaged; that the struggle was national; that generations of ancestors, good, bad or indifferent, forbade the Latin man to be chivalrous to the Northern woman, the Northern woman to forgive the Latin man.'

If the British touched Southern life too lightly to receive its imprint or extract its essence, this was due partly at least to omission and evasion on the Mediterranean side. Southern society offered nothing equivalent to the professional, financial, and industrial bourgeoisie of Victorian Britain, so it was difficult for middle-class travellers to find abroad a social group with whom they could readily identify and associate. The aristocracies of Italy and Spain tended to hold aloof from bourgeois foreigners, and members of the lower classes saw the British only as representatives of wealth and power. Consequently in the Mediterranean the Victorians experienced again the perennial tribulation of the mighty. They had ample access to services and things; but the deeper satisfactions of human relationships were denied them, because in their presence people ceased to be themselves and became what wealth and power were supposed to require. Even John Addington Symonds, who lived much of his life in close proximity to Italians and who longed to be accepted by them, once complained that it was difficult to know them—to feel that one had been admitted to their confidence. 'Italians', he said,

have an ineradicable habit of making themselves externally agreeable, of bending in all indifferent matters to the whims and wishes of superiors, and saying what they think *Signori* will like. This habit, while it smoothes the

---

[13] Gallenga, *Italy Revisited*, i. 71.

surface of existence, raises up a barrier of compliment and partial insincerity, against which the more downright natures of us Northern folk break in vain efforts.[14]

Horatio Brown, likewise, reproached the Venetians for 'that fatal desire to find out what you want them to say, and to say it'.[15] Somerset Maugham reckoned that the southern Spanish were even more inscrutable than the Italians, and he was dismayed because after prolonged acquaintance he still felt like an outsider in their presence. 'I cannot', he complained, 'realise their thoughts or their outlook. I feel always below the grace of their behaviour the instinctive, primeval hatred of the stranger.'[16]

Formalities and conventions were liable to hinder personal contact in all quarters of the Mediterranean. They were of course especially evident in Asia Minor and Palestine, where Oriental etiquette prevailed and where circumstances—such as lack of maps and political insecurity—obliged even the independent traveller to encumber himself with guides and escorts. These usually made it their duty to enhance his dignity and preserve his privacy, even at the cost of creating misunderstanding and ill-feeling on the part of the local people. The explorer and archaeologist Charles Fellows, who described himself as 'always enjoying the attention and kindness natural to humanity rather than the respect commanded by authority', was upset by the constant intercession of his courier (*cavass*) during his second trip into Anatolia, in 1840. 'I fear', he wrote rather sadly,

I am represented as a very different character with regard to my feelings towards the people to what I really am. They wish to offer flowers and presents of all kinds, but the Cavass, perhaps properly, keeps them aloof, and when anything is purchased by me, they name no price, but expect a present. This the Cavass discountenances, and fixes a price upon everything, probably lower than I should be induced to give. He demands hospitality where I before received it voluntarily, and our room is always kept free of the people.[17]

Murray's *Handbook for Greece* reckoned that the traveller who had some knowledge of Modern Greek, or at least a Greek servant, would do well to dispense with the services of a professional guide and improvise his travelling arrangements from day to day. 'He will then',

[14] Symonds, *Italian Byways*, 252. See also *Letters*, iii. 376.
[15] Brown, *In and About Venice*, 33.
[16] Maugham, *Land of the Blessed Virgin*, 149.
[17] Fellows, *Discoveries in Lycia*, 177.

assured the *Handbook*, 'learn far more of the character of the country and people.' In the Western Mediterranean the equivalent impediment to informal contact was the big, modern hotel. This reduced exchanges to an impersonal ritual and sifted every vestige of local flavour from the visitor's experience. It was possible for him to stay in one of these institutions without learning anything of the country he was visiting, and in 1887 they earned this scathing rebuke from Frederic Harrison:

After a month of foreign hotels we sicken of tinned vegetables, bottled sauces, packed meat, spurious wines, canned fruits, gaudy menus, and the whole apparatus pretending to mimic the Café Riche on the tops of the Alps or the shores of the Mediterranean . . .Nowadays it is the horrid sameness of one bad standard which haunts us from Calais to Palermo . . . We go abroad, but we travel no longer. We see nothing really of the people among whom we sojourn. We never touch their lives. They are not even our caterers or our servants. We lodge in sham Grand Hotels, we take our meals of sham Paris dishes, our food is a foreign import, we are served by sham French waiters and supplied by sham French cooks.[18]

The counter-argument was of course that this was what the average tourist wanted. 'So long as he gets his money's worth of gilded and gaudy rooms, or rich food, lifts, electric apparatus and other follies,' insisted Edward Hutton, 'he is better content to put up with being a number like a convict and with being robbed like any poor devil on the road.' Hutton distinguished between 'tourists' and 'travellers'. The latter were those who, like himself, stayed in country inns, where they found 'friends, a soft bed, well-cooked food, a good wine, and a welcome'.[19] This attachment to the ethnic, the local and the homespun, which marked a contrast with the urbanity of earlier visitors, became the keynote of travel writing in the age of popular tourism. But the claim to be a 'traveller', as opposed to a 'tourist' or an 'excursionist', was in most cases only a special kind of snobbery. Primitivism was merely the obverse of sophistication. It implied revulsion from the British masses rather than new-found sympathy for Mediterranean people. As first the lower middle classes, and then, after the Second World War, the working classes began to imitate the upper reaches of society, by taking holidays in the South and bringing with them their own style of life, so the élite of birth, wealth, and intellect reacted by moving on to

[18] Harrison, *Memories and Thoughts*, 249.
[19] Hutton, *Siena and Southern Tuscany*, 245.

undeveloped localities and switching to native food and drink. Travel writers and, later, travel agencies flattered this exclusiveness with the image of the Discerning Traveller, whose special attributes are contact and affinity with local society abroad; but their real function was to annex a new no man's land in the sun, out of earshot of the playground of·the multitude but equally impervious to the sounds and influences of native life.

Whether they stayed in Grand Hotels, in country inns, or under canvas, the British were almost all alike in that they had little interest in the idea of close contact with Mediterranean people. 'We had come to Majorca to see the place,' wrote Charles Wood in 1887; 'our stay was too limited to attempt to make acquaintance with its people'—a remark that summarises the way most British travellers thought. They regarded the countries of southern Europe, North Africa, and the Levant primarily as museums, sanatoria, and asylums, not as living societies. Their main concern was with art, ruins, climate, and release from social duty and responsibility. Mallock defined one of the objects of the true traveller as disengagement from the trammels of personal relationships. Abroad, he said, one finds 'men whose aims and characters one cannot despise, not knowing them'; and he defined the spell.cast by Cyprus on the traveller in terms of the dehumanisation of its people. 'The men and women he sees are no longer fellow citizens, but figures moving in a magician's crystal.' This attitude of detachment was common. The historian Edward Freeman was a self-proclaimed 'true traveller' who fled from 'the gabble of English tourists' in the late 1870s to explore the Adriatic towns on the eastern shore of the Gulf of Venice. Yet his interests were exclusively antiquarian and architectural, and he was a linguistic cripple. 'He can't or won't speak either German, French or Italian,' wrote his future son-in-law, the archaeologist Arthur Evans, 'and his daughters have to look after him and manage everything.'[20] Another don, William George Clark, who went to Greece in the 1850s, would, like all visitors to Greece at this time, qualify as a 'traveller' according to Hutton's definition. Yet in his written record he hardly mentions the modern Greeks and almost all his attention is devoted to identifying Classical remains and localities and relating what he saw to Classical sources. 'We have then', runs a typical passage, 'to discuss this question: Is

---

[20] Wood, *Letters from Majorca*, 233; Mallock, *Enchanted Island*, 4, 141; E. A. Freeman, *The Subject and Neighbour Lands of Venice*, 26; Evans, *Time and Chance*, 196. See also Coustillas, ed., *Diary of Gissing*, 458.

Pausanius right in identifying this waterfall with the Homeric Styx?'[21] Problems of that sort preoccupied the writers of guidebooks, and even travel books were generally more concerned to expound what the Mediterranean had been than to discover what it was. If the British studied the present, they did so in order to come closer to the past. Only very few studied the past in order to come closer to the present. Victorian writing on the Mediterranean was dominated by the assumption that the modern South was in some crucial sense not authentic. Always looking back, the Victorians related and compared what they saw with what they had read, and they judged the present to be a distortion or a remnant of the real South of Classical or medieval times. Contemporary society was seen as an aberration of the Virgilian idyll; contemporary religion was understood to be a corruption of healthy paganism or of pristine Catholicism; contemporary art was scorned as a travesty of the work of the mighty dead. In the South modernity was the last spasm of decrepit life, and the sun awoke the tired iridescence of exhumed antiquity. The Mediterranean was immensely old, inert, somnolent—'worked out', in the words of D. H. Lawrence[22]—and its true nature was to be found only in the record of antecedent vitality.

Circumstances, no doubt, did something to discourage human intimacy. The cultural inheritance of the South was rich and the visitor's time was limited. As Trollope said, the ordinary English tourist had 'no hope of . . . any sojourn which would make entrance into society possible'; and his advice was that this should not be attempted. 'A few among us', he wrote, 'may so live abroad as to become conversant with the inner life of the people with whom they are dwelling—to know their houses, their sons and their daughters; to see their habits, to talk with them, eat with them and quarrel with them; but to do this is not and should not be the object of the vacation tourist.'[23] Language too was a barrier, because the British were seldom able to speak anything but English. 'How few of the English we meet abroad', demanded George Gaskell in 1875, 'can speak even the one—almost—universal tongue, French? . . . By far the greater number not only know little French, but, speaking what they have picked up with the pure cockney or the drawling Dundreary accent, appear to be

[21] Clark, *Peloponnesus*, 305.
[22] The phrase occurs in *Sea and Sardinia*, Ch. 6.
[23] Trollope, *Travelling Sketches*, 10, 106–7.

talking English when we do not catch what they say.'[24] Yet in the final analysis these circumstances were symptoms of disconnection, not explanations for it. Time and language were lacking because there was no will to acquire them. Priority lay elsewhere. The art and the ruins of the South were deemed more important than the people, and the expectation was that foreigners should speak English. This is made clear by the peevish comment on the Neapolitans in Macmillan's *Guide to the Western Mediterranean*. 'Railway and other officials', we read, 'are not required to speak any language but their own, and their native indolence makes them disinclined to take the trouble of learning any foreign language.'

Association failed, in fact, mainly because the British did not want it. They had no inclination to merge into the background or mingle with the crowd. They were never more insular than when they were abroad; never more self-consciously strangers than in the lands they proclaimed their own. This was true even of artists and intellectuals. The natives were seldom actors, and often unwelcome spectators, in the personal dramas of inspiration and salvation that these people acted out abroad; and those Britons who, like Lawrence and Douglas, were exiles in the land of their birth were no less exiles in the land of their adoption. Their flight was from England as it had become, and their hearts' desire remained England as it might have been. The bulk of the Victorian public in the South were exiles too—but exiles in a single sense. They signified their attachment to home by living in British colonies, travelling in British groups, and cultivating a pose of remoteness and sang-froid—an art in which they did not lack instructors. 'Never pay with your own hands', Eliot Warburton advised travellers to the Levant. 'Insist on the most profound respect; preserve your temper and nonchalance as your best title to influence and security. Never join in a row; let your people fight it out.'[25] Richard Ford had similar counsel for visitors to Spain:

In general a firm, quiet, courteous, and somewhat reserved manner is the most effective. Whenever duties are to be performed, let them see that you are not to be trifled with. The coolness of a determined Englishman's manner, when in earnest, is what few foreigners can withstand. Grimace and gesticulation, sound and fury, bluster, petulance, and impertinence fume and fret in vain

[24] Gaskell, *Algeria*, 95–6.
[25] Warburton, *The Crescent and the Cross*, ii. 343.

against it, as do the spray and foam of the 'French Lake' against the unmoved and immovable rock of Gibraltar.[26]

Murray's *Handbook for Greece* insisted (with italics) on the traveller's nationality being instantly recognisable (*let his dress at all times be obviously that of an Englishman*) and Frances Power Cobbe encouraged intransigence and arrogance by insisting that it was the difficulty of the British that had made life tolerable on the Continent. 'One after another we pour on', she wrote complacently,

staring at every delay, insisting on more and more rapid conveyance, fretting, fuming, making ourselves objects of astonishment to the calm Oriental and of ridicule to our fellow Europeans; but still eventually always conquering, and leaving rough places smooth, and crooked things straight behind us . . . That sign of a thoroughly healthy constitution, the arising of a slight fever after every wound, is peculiarly our own.[27]

The rubric of behaviour prescribed by writers such as these found favour with most British travellers because it appealed to both their racist and their religious sentiments. The Victorians firmly believed that the political and commercial supremacy of their country was owing to their national character, and the fear was current that close involvement with foreign societies would somehow adulterate that character and thereby undermine national wealth and prestige. It was very difficult for a visitor to the Mediterranean not to be reminded of Britain's economic and military might. The English flag flying over the fortifications of Gibraltar, and the appurtenances of trade and empire in Malta, Cyprus, and Egypt, all recalled to the itinerant Victorian the weight of the British ledger and the power of the British sword. 'Most Englishmen at home', wrote Thomas Wemyss Reid in Malta in 1882, 'are so far from warlike sights, that they are apt to forget that their country has after all shown herself great in war as in commerce. But no man can forget that fact as he stands here upon the Barecca of Valetta and looks down upon the great forts and the ironclads which sleep securely beneath their walls.'[28] Mallock's reaction was similar when he saw the English shipping crowding the Suez Canal in 1889: 'A foreigner never knows the greatness of our country till he has visited it,' he reflected; 'we never know its greatness

---

[26] Ford, *Handbook for Spain*, ii. 210.
[27] Cobbe, *Cities of the Past*, 43–4.
[28] Reid, *Land of the Bey*, 248.

till we have left it.'[29] It was the revelation of this greatness that inspired the outburst of patriotic affection expressed by Richard Chenevix Trench in his best-known sonnet, written after a visit to Gibraltar in 1839:

> England, we love thee better than we know—
> And this I learned when after wanderings long
> 'Mid people of another stock and tongue,
> I heard again thy martial music blow,
> And saw thy gallant children to and fro'
> Pace, keeping ward at one of those huge gates,
> Twin giants watching the Herculean Straits.

Moreover, from a vantage point abroad it was easy to detect a nimbus of moral superiority behind this physical prowess. When J. R. Green discovered how readily liberal opinion in the South acknowledged its debt to British influence, he was confirmed in his belief that Britain's virtues outweighed her sins. 'In some ways', he wrote, 'I think being far away makes one fairer to England than when one is at home and worried with all the pettiness and ignorance.'[30] Such evidence of national achievement reinforced a sense of racial superiority and gave rise to the sort of self-congratulation expressed by Mrs Hugh Price Hughes in 1901, when she and her husband embarked at Syracuse:

As the boats came along I could not fail to be struck with the aspect of our English sailors, and my heart swelled with national pride. They came along looking so straight, superior, clean and strong in their dark blue jerseys and caps, with the ship's officer standing erect, calm, immovable in the stern. They threaded their way among the jabbering excited crowds of native boatmen much as a mastiff would walk through a crowd of yelping curs, doing everything deftly, smartly, without a word or a change of expression on their countenances. It was a contrast indeed![31]

Since this contrast was the reason for Britain's supremacy, it was essential to remain aloof. Association with the natives only too easily led to loss of national idiosyncrasy, as the Revd William Arthur had been at pains to emphasize. He rejoiced in the abolition of the petty Italian states in 1859 because he reckoned their courts had been melting pots where his countrymen had had all their Englishness boiled out of them. 'Such schools of manners abroad', he declared,

[29] Mallock, *Enchanted Island*, 393.
[30] Stephen, ed., *Letters of J. R. Green*, 248.
[31] Hughes, *Morning Lands of History*, 48.

'are unfriendly to all English ideas, national and social. Nothing is more unlike a true Englishman or Englishwoman than the sort of creature that has long hung about one of those courts and become enamoured of the society abounding there. Their very language is denationalised.'[32] Segregation therefore became the cardinal article in the expatriates' creed. Henry Rider Haggard saw it in operation in Cyprus and appreciated its vital importance. 'English folk would celebrate book teas and play golf or any other accustomed game upon the brink of Styx', he commented, adding: 'Perhaps that is why they remain a ruling race, for to do this it is necessary to preserve the habits and traditions of the fatherland, refusing persistently to allow them to be overwhelmed by those of any surrounding people.'[33]

Their jealous concern for racial integrity caused British travellers to regard the sexual allure of Southern men as a menace and to ridicule or admonish Englishwomen who showed themselves susceptible to Latin charm. 'That the Italians still condescend to visit English gentlemen and ladies is an honour on which our dear silly country-women pride themselves to one another', scoffed Richard Digby Best, before quoting examples from 'the many instances of their fatuity'.[34] Mabel Sharman Crawford painted a grim picture of the lives of Anglo-Saxon women who had married Latin exiles and returned with them to Italy;[35] and Murray's *Handbook for South Italy*, under the heading 'ITALIAN ADVENTURERS *(A Caution to English Ladies)*', solemnly warned of the risks involved in cultivating intimacies:

Too much care cannot be taken in forming acquaintances with southern Italians, and especially with that class of them which frequents Pensions. One of their chief aims is to marry for money, and keep their families and themselves in idleness. It is a common complaint among them that English wives do not take a beating kindly. The long experience of one who was perfectly qualified to give an opinion on the subject was that, without exception, every Englishwoman married to a Neapolitan was miserable. Englishwomen by marriage with a foreigner forfeit their nationality, and are precluded from seeking redress from British consuls or tribunals.

Their fervent religious loyalties likewise helped to ensure that the British remained strangers in the South. Special churches, special priests, special rituals, and special cemeteries accentuated the maudlin

[32] Arthur, *Italy In Transition*, 260.
[33] Haggard, *Winter Pilgrimage*, 183.
[34] Best, *Nowadays*, i. 351.
[35] Crawford, *Life in Tuscany*, 70.

patriotism of spiritual exiles under siege. 'It was affecting to hear the music and language of our country sounding in that distant place,' wrote Thackeray, stiff upper lip quivering, after attending divine service in the Anglican church at Jerusalem; 'to have the decent and manly ceremonial of our service; the prayers delivered in that noble language. Even that stout anti-prelatist, the American Consul . . . was affected by the good old words and service . . . But it was the music that was the most touching, I thought—the sweet old songs of home.'[36] Frederic Harrison deplored the way in which its votaries dragged the Church of England with them wherever they went, heedless of the susceptibilities and prejudices of the local people. 'Tourists of all other nations', he remonstrated, 'can exist without their national service . . . Is it that we English are the only religious people in Europe? In things spiritual and temporal alike our modern mania abroad is to carry with us our own life, instead of accepting that which we find on the spot.'[37]

Yet ultimately it was religious temperament rather than sectarian loyalty that restricted human contact, because even as Catholics the British were, generally speaking, no closer to the Mediterranean people. In most cases conversion meant substituting one form of religious élitism for another. Ultramontanes reaped where Calvin had sown. The Catholicism of the British—like that of the Germans—was not the popular Catholicism of Italy or the South of France. It was Vatican Catholicism: cosmopolitan, sophisticated, and smart. It flourished amid the Curias, Conclaves, Colleges, and Councils that were peculiar to Rome, and after 1870 it was closely identified with those claims to spiritual absolutism that signified the increasing isolation of the Papacy from modern Italian life. And if English Catholics did happen to forsake the world of fashionable sermons and cardinals' receptions, they did so, it seems, only to bury themselves in ecclesiastical antiquarianism. Frederick Faber, we are told, learnt Italian not in order to communicate with the Italians but 'in order that he might understand the numerous lives of saints published in that language'[38]—and this predilection was common among converts and converts-to-be. Perhaps the most positive thing that can be said about the British Catholics is that they were more ready than their Protestant compatriots to forgive the deviations and perversions of

---

[36] Thackeray, *Cornhill to Grand Cairo*, 208–9.
[37] Harrison, *Memories and Thoughts*, 247–8
[38] Bowden, *Frederick Faber*, 183.

popular religion. It is doubtful that they were more ready to approve them.

But this insularity must have a further explanation, if only because it has outlived the values of the Victorian age. In addition to racist jealousy and religious exclusiveness, and operating at the limits of consciousness, there was an unwillingness to allow the Mediterranean to become mundane and insipid; a desire to delay the dawn of common day and prolong the visitation of enchantment. Visitors to the South, then as now, strove to preserve the sense of novelty, mystery, and potency that suggested a return to childhood and a rebirth of the innocent mind. 'When we travel', said the poet Samuel Rogers, 'all is new and strange. We surrender ourselves, and feel again as children.'[39] But the magic was fragile, because custom quickly staled variety. When Thackeray landed at Smyrna he experienced 'the thrill of that delightful shock which so seldom touches the plain man of the world'; but he realised that this was only because he was spending his first day in the Orient. It was like the first day in a French town, when everything seemed preternaturally French. 'The first day in the East is like that', he wrote. 'After that, there is nothing. The wonder is gone . . . A man only sees the miracle once; though you yearn after it ever so, it won't come again.' And he wistfully advised: 'A person who wishes to understand France or the East should come in a yacht to Calais or Smyrna, land for two hours, and never afterwards go back again.'[40] Writers who would capture the *genius loci* felt the need to work fast, before novelty lost its power and nerves became too slack to vibrate. Theirs was the apocalypse of the brief encounter. D. H. Lawrence, for example, dashed off his accounts of visits to foreign places with reckless haste. According to Rebecca West, Norman Douglas once jokingly complained that Lawrence would go straight from the railway station to his hotel and start pounding his typewriter.[41] But it was Douglas himself who said that things are best perceived by contrasts, and that the Englishman was a good describer of foreign lands because he never submerged his identity.[42] Difference was the traveller's joy and the writer's inspiration; and difference existed only so long as ordinary humanity, the common denominator, was held at bay.

[39] Samuel Rogers, *Italy, A Poem* (1830), 171.
[40] Thackeray, *Cornhill to Grand Cairo*, 81–3.
[41] Mark Holloway, *Norman Douglas* (1976), 297–8.
[42] Douglas, *Siren Land*, 1 38.

This exclusion of the human element from their experience helps to explain why the Victorians' record of their travels to the South is so much more subjective than objective. Denied a life of its own, the Mediterranean submitted to being recreated in the image of British longings and aversions, hopes and fears. Mallock wrote in the 1880s that the purpose of travelling is fulfilled 'when the world shows us our dreams and illusions reflected, instead of our dreams and illusions destroyed'.[43] The Victorians were able to achieve that quest, because their journey was as much a mission as an odyssey. The Mediterranean that they visited was neither real nor ideal, but a world made less than either by prejudice and preconception. It was a landscape that took its colour from their own emotions; an oracle that took its wisdom from their own expectations. Travel did not broaden their minds. Too often their mental horizons contracted as their physical horizons widened, and they returned home settled rather than disturbed in their views about life and art, God and man, good and evil.

Because Victorian and Edwardian travellers never became a truly cosmopolitan class, linguistically versatile and culturally receptive, the revolution in transport failed as a force for greater international harmony and communication. It is sad to have to admit that the level of international goodwill and understanding would not have been reduced, and might even have been enhanced, if the British had stayed at home to cultivate their gardens. But if their visits contributed little to an understanding of the Mediterranean, they have contributed much to an understanding of the Victorians. Although the South did not reveal itself to them, they revealed themselves to the South. The records of their journeys offer images of the Victorians that are by now familiar—that of the disinherited, seeking to reclaim the Wordsworthian hour of splendour in the grass; that of the imprisoned, yearning for deliverance; and that of the guilt-ridden, driven to self-mortification; but they are images minted from a new mine of illustration. Furthermore the records relate these mental characteristics to the physical realities that shaped the existence of the upper reaches of society. They reveal routines adjusted to accommodate frequent contact with remote places and the random visitations of chronic ill-health and fatal disease. Luggage and doctors; timetables and prescriptions; trains and climates; Abroad and invalidism—these

<hr />

[43] Mallock, *Enchanted Island*, 140.

were essential ingredients in the characteristic chemistry of bourgeois and aristocratic life.

Finally it is worth remarking that there is a place for this record in the old debate about where Victorianism ends and post-Victorianism begins. The ruins of the Victorians' paradise no doubt seem like heaven in comparison with the ruins of ours. The railways, boulevards, and hotels that they found so incongruous and disfiguring have become quaint and endearing to generations familiar with the tower blocks of Marbella and Monaco, the car parks and motorways of Italy, the airports of the Greek islands, and the general devastation wrought by concrete and traffic on uncounted miles of Mediterranean coast. Nevertheless their nostalgia was no less potent than ours. Their desire to return to an earlier world was no less ardent than our desire to return to theirs, and they were the first to learn the truth that is part of the modern environmental gospel: that the easiest way to destroy a place is to make it popular. It goes without saying that the Victorians were not the first to experience the Mediterranean Passion. This was a metaphor for a state of mind as old as the tension between nomadic instinct and the constraints and complexities of territorial attachment. Ever since man had given up his primordial, migrating existence he had compensated for the inadequacies of the world in which he lived by elaborating the myth of a distant, antithetical world. But if they were not the first, neither were they the last; and the failure of their odyssey reads like the premonition of a modern neurosis. When they pursued the South as an idea concocted from Classical and Romantic literature and accumulations of travellers' lore, they anticipated the frustration of the modern Ulysses, who, enticed by the fantasies peddled by advertisers and mass entertainers, sets out for places he can never reach. Then again, in the Victorians' quest for the oblivion of the South, for instinctual, unthinking life and the womb-like refuge of the past, it is possible to recognise the *Angst* of the post-Christian consciousness. Their desire to stop the flow of history suggests the despair of men and women confronting the existential Nothingness: the void where there is no imperative save choice and where every choice reveals to the chooser that he is created and abandoned; free to choose because forsaken.

For all these reasons the authors of the guidebooks, letters, and travel memoirs on which this study is based refuse to be anchored in time. They recede and advance, wandering between remoteness and proximity; and the figures we thought strange, too closely identified with a world of their own to be the parents of ours, at times seem disconcertingly familiar. The suspicions arise alternately that the Victorians were not so very Victorian after all, and that we are more Victorian than we supposed. Modern tourists and travel writers have more in common than they realise with those who went before. A throng of pale, overdressed ghosts awaits them to claim kinship in the boulevards and promenades, the galleries and ruins, the piazzas and churches, the museums and the graveyards of the South.

Biographical Notes

AITON, John. 1797–1863. Presbyterian clergyman and religious writer. Minister of Dolphinton, South Lanarkshire.

ALFORD, Henry. 1810–71. Anglican clergyman who became Dean of Canterbury. First editor of the *Contemporary Review*. As theologian, poet, and literary critic was one of the most prolific authors of his time.

ARNOLD, Matthew. 1822–88. Son of Dr Thomas Arnold, Headmaster of Rugby School. Inspector of Schools and Professor of Poetry at Oxford, 1857–67. A poet of the first magnitude and a social and literary critic of enduring influence.

ARTHUR, William. 1819–1901. Irish Protestant polemicist and Loyalist. Missionary in India in the 1840s. President of the Wesleyan Conference, 1866. Died at Cannes, where he had settled in 1888.

ASHBEE, Henry Spencer. 1834–1900. Wealthy merchant, traveller, bibliophile, and, under the pseudonym *Pisanus Fraxi*, bibliographer of pornography.

AUSTIN, Sarah (née Taylor). 1793–1867. Wife of the celebrated jurist, John Austin, and mother of Lucie Duff Gordon. A translator and well-known bluestocking, who helped to introduce modern German literature to the British intelligentsia. In 1836 she accompanied her husband to Malta, where he spent four years on an official commission of inquiry.

BALFOUR, Arthur James. 1848–1930. Philosopher and Conservative politician. Nephew of Lord Salisbury. Held several high offices of state and served as Prime Minister, 1902–5. Known to his friends as 'pretty Fanny' and to Clemenceau as 'cette vieille fille'.

BALL, Eustace Alfred Reynolds. d. 1928. Journalist and traveller. Trained as a barrister, but never practised. Literary Editor, *Court Journal*, 1907–8; Editor, *Travel and Exploration*, 1909–11. Lived latterly in Italy, where he died.

BARNETT, Henrietta Octavia (née Rowland). 1851–1936. Married Samuel Barnett, Anglican divine and social reformer, in 1873, and was closely associated with his work as Rector of St Jude's Whitechapel, Warden of Toynbee Hall, and Canon of Westminster. Created DBE 1924.

BARRINGTON, Mrs Russell (née Emilie Wilson). d. 1933. Artist, connoisseur, and biographer of Watts and Leighton.

BARTLETT, William. 1809–54. Draughtsman. Travelled widely in Europe, the

Near East, and the USA, and published numerous volumes of high-quality engravings of foreign views.

BAXTER, Lucy (née Barnes). 1837–1902. Authority on Italian art and architecture. Wrote under the name Leader Scott and was resident in Florence for many years.

BEAMONT, William John. 1828–68. Fellow of Trinity College, Cambridge, 1852. Arabist and missionary. His early death was attributed to overwork as a parish priest.

BEARDSLEY, Aubrey. 1872–98. One of the most distinctive artists of the 1890s. His black and white illustrations for Wilde's *Salome* and for *The Yellow Book* became a hallmark of the English Decadence. Was converted to Roman Catholicism shortly before he died, at Menton, of tuberculosis.

BELL, Charles Dent. 1818–98. Irish Anglican clergyman. Rector of Cheltenham, 1872–95. Author of several volumes of poems, hymns, and popular biblical exegesis.

BELL, Gertrude Margaret Lowthian. 1868–1926. Explorer and archaeologist. Was the first woman to gain First-class Honours in Modern History at Oxford, but remained a fervent anti-feminist. Became Government Director of Antiquities in Iraq and founded the National Museum at Baghdad.

BELLOC, Hilaire. 1870–1953. Essayist, poet, and historian. Liberal MP, 1906–9. A belligerent Catholic and anti-Semitist.

BENNET, James Henry. 1816–91. Son of a Manchester textile manufacturer. Studied medicine in Paris. Developed tuberculosis and moved to Menton in 1859, where he built up a highly successful practice. The town commemorated his contribution to its newly-found prosperity by naming a street after him and erecting a monument in the Rue Partouneaux.

BENNETT, Enoch Arnold. 1867–1931. Graduated from journalism to highly successful novel-writing. Lived in France 1902–8 and was fascinated by cosmopolitan high-life, but made his reputation as a chronicler of middle-class existence in the English Midlands.

BENT, James Theodore. 1852–97. A gentleman of fortune who travelled widely in the Mediterranean, the Middle East, and Africa, and established a reputation as a learned archaeologist and linguist.

BEST (subsequently Beste), John Richard Digby. 1806–85. Wealthy Catholic landowner with literary pretensions. Despite the failure of his novels to win any popular or critical acclaim he saw himself as a new Walter Scott and was convinced that posterity would recognise his genius.

BLAKESLEY, Joseph. 1808–85. Anglican clergyman and biblical and Classical scholar. Friend and fellow-Apostle of Tennyson at Cambridge. Dean of Lincoln, 1872.

BLUNT, Wilfred Scawen. 1840–1922. Diplomat, poet, philanderer, and lapsed Catholic. Married Byron's granddaughter and inherited Byron's role as champion of oppressed nationalities. Bitterly attacked British rule in Egypt and Ireland. Egypt was his winter home for many years.

BONAR, Andrew Alexander. 1810–92. Clergyman of the Scottish Free Church. Minister of Finnieston, Glasgow.

BORROW, George. 1803–81. Linguist and folklorist who travelled extensively in Spain as agent for the Bible Society.

BOXALL, William. 1800–79. Artist. Achieved fame and wealth as a portrait painter. RA, 1863. Succeeded Eastlake as Director of the National Gallery, 1865. Knighted, 1867.

BOYLE, Mary (née Robins). Wife of the Revd George David Boyle, appointed Dean of Salisbury, 1880.

BREWSTER, Margaret Maria. Wife of Sir David Brewster (1781–1868), the most eminent Scottish scientist of his day.

BROUGHAM, Henry Peter (1st Baron Brougham and Vaux). 1778–1868. Barrister, statesman, and man of letters. Counsel for Queen Caroline in the state trial of 1822. Lord Chancellor, 1830. A prominent figure in campaigns for legal and political reform, and a tireless propagator of 'useful knowledge'. Died in Cannes, where he had made his winter home for many years and whose popularity he did much to establish.

BROWN, Alexander Menzies. Active 1870–1900. Physician and author of several medical treatises.

BROWN, Horatio Robert Forbes. 1854–1926. Archivist and historian. Was commissioned by the Foreign Office to continue the work of his namesake Rawdon Brown and calendar the Venetian state papers relating to British history. Pupil, friend, literary executor, and biographer of John Addington Symonds. Died in Venice. Portrayed as Nelson McTavish in Frederick Rolfe's *The Desire and Pursuit of the Whole*.

BROWNING, Elizabeth Barrett. 1806–61. Poet. Married Robert Browning in 1846 and eloped with him to Italy, where they lived until she died (of pulmonary consumption). Extravagantly praised in her day (Ruskin reckoned her *Aurora Leigh* 'the greatest poem in the English language') her literary reputation slumped dramatically after her death and has never recovered.

BROWNING, Oscar. 1837–1923. Historian, pedagogue, and pederast. Retired from Eton in the wake of a scandal in 1875, and retreated to a fellowship at King's College, Cambridge. Became the most colourful and best-known Cambridge character of his day. One of his many eccentricities was to ride over the Alps to Venice on a tricycle.

BROWNING, Robert. 1812–89. Poet. Initially rated much lower than his wife, in his later years was venerated by the intellectual public. Browning Societies were formed to discuss his work and he was showered with official distinctions.

BRYCE, James. 1838–1922. Liberal politician and constitutional theorist. Regius Professor of Civil Law at Oxford, 1870–93. Held several cabinet posts and was British Ambassador to the United States, 1907–13. Created Viscount, 1914.

BUCKLAND, Anne Walbank. Active 1870–1900. Travel-writer, novelist, and author of popular books on anthropology and nutrition.

BUCKLE, Henry Thomas. 1821–62. Historian and chess virtuoso. His *History of Civilisation in England* introduced scientific method into historiography. Died in Damascus after wintering in Egypt.

BURGESS, Thomas Henry. d. 1865. Irish physician who practised in London.

BURNE-JONES, Edward. 1833–98. The most successful and popular painter in the genre of Victorian medievalism. Friend and disciple of William Morris and D. G. Rossetti. Defended Ruskin in his celebrated legal confrontation with Whistler in 1877. Created Baronet, 1894.

BURTON, Isabel (née Arundell). 1831–96. Explorer and travel-writer. Married Richard Burton, Indian Army officer and explorer, against the wishes of her Catholic parents in 1861, and became his companion and support in his travels and clashes with authority. After his death she expurgated his translation of *The Arabian Nights*, destroyed his private diaries, and published a biography that combined hagiography with romance.

BUTLER, Frances. See KEMBLE.

BUTLER, Samuel. 1825–1902. Essayist, translator, and novelist. His best-known book, the autobiographical novel *The Way of all Flesh*, was published posthumously.

CARLYLE, Thomas. 1795–1881. Scottish historian, social theorist, and sage. Deeply influenced by German metaphysics, he became one of the most strident critics of Victorian positivism and meliorism and interpreted modern history in terms of a catastrophic regression from the medieval principles of authority, faith, and social responsibility.

CHAMBERS, William. 1800–83. Scottish publisher and author. Founded the firm of W. & R. Chambers with his brother Robert. Served as Lord Provost of Edinburgh, 1865–9.

CHESTER, Greville. Active 1860–90. Invalid clergyman who travelled regularly in Egypt and the Levant to recruit his health and collect antiquities. One of the British Museum's chief agents in Egypt.

CHRISTMAS, Henry. 1811–68. Anglican clergyman, theologian, and numismatist. Edited several religious journals, including the *Church of England Quarterly Review*.

CHURCH, Richard William. 1815–90. Historian, biographer, and theologian. A friend of J. H. Newman at Oxford and a High Churchman all his life. Appointed Dean of St Paul's, 1871.

CLARK, James. 1788–1870. Physician in Ordinary to Queen Victoria. A doctor whose fashionable appeal and professional reputation were damaged by frequent indications of incompetence. He attended Keats during his last illness in Rome and was accused of hastening his death; provoked a court scandal in 1839 when he diagnosed Lady Flora Hastings's liver tumour as a pregnancy; and treated the Prince Consort unsuccessfully for typhoid in 1861.

CLARK, William George. 1821–78. Fellow of Trinity College, Cambridge, 1844. Founder and editor of the *Journal of Philology* and editor of *The Cambridge Shakespeare*. Renounced his Clerical Orders after the passing of the Clerical Disabilities Act, 1870. Bequeathed property to Trinity for the endowment of a lectureship in English Literature.

CLOUGH, Arthur Hugh. 1819–61. Poet and civil servant. Pupil of Dr Arnold at Rugby and close friend of Matthew Arnold. One of the most agonised of Victorian writers, his poetry expresses with experimental virtuosity the conflicting claims of negation and affirmation, rebellion and conformity.

COBBE, Frances Power. 1822–1904. Philanthropist, feminist, and social crusader. A leading light in the galaxy of pious Victorian agnosticism.

CRAIG, Edward Henry Gordon. 1872–1966. Artist and stage designer. Son of Ellen Terry and Edward Godwin the architect. An actor until 1897, when he turned to theatre design, making revolutionary use of light and abstract form. Lived in Italy 1907–30 and founded a short-lived school for theatre arts in Florence.

CRAWFORD, Mabel Sharman. Active 1850–90. Daughter and disciple of William Sharman Crawford, an Ulster landlord and politician who campaigned to improve the rights and conditions of the Irish peasantry.

CUNNINGHAM, Alison. 1822–1913. Nurse of Robert Louis Stevenson. Accompanied the Stevensons on their trip abroad in 1863 and kept a diary which gives a unique view of Mediterranean travel as it affected the servants of British families. Stevenson dedicated *A Child's Garden of Verses* to her.

CURZON, George Nathaniel. 1859–1925. Conservative statesman. Viceroy of India, 1898–1905; Foreign Secretary, 1919–24. Created Earl, 1911; Marquis, 1921.

CURZON, Robert (Baron Zouche). 1810–73. Traveller and collector. Visited monasteries in Greece, Egypt, the Holy Land, and Italy collecting and locating early Christian manuscripts. Planned but never completed a history of handwriting.

CUST, Robert Henry Hobart, 1861–1940. Art historian.

DAVIS, Nathan. 1812–82. Traveller, archaeologist, and Nonconformist minister. Lived for many years in an old Moorish palace about ten miles from Tunis.

DAVY, John. 1790–1868. Younger Brother of Sir Humphrey Davy. After serving on the medical staff of the Army in the Mediterranean 1824–35 was appointed Inspector General of Army Hospitals. Elected FRS, 1834.

DE VERE, Aubrey Thomas. 1814–1902. Irish poet, critic, and convert to Catholicism (1851).

DICKENS, Charles. 1812–70. Journalist and novelist. The most popular writer of the Victorian age. Underrated by Victorian intellectuals and mocked by the late Victorian Decadents, his work was rediscovered by academic critics after the First World War and his reputation as one of the major geniuses of English literature is now assured.

DICKINSON, Cato Lowes. 1819–1908. Artist and Christian Socialist. Specialised in portraiture and received many commisions from notabilities and institutions. Taught drawing with Ruskin and D. G. Rossetti at the Working Men's College after his return from Italy in the 1850s.

DICKINSON, Goldsworthy Lowes. 1862–1932. Son of C. L. Dickinson. Classicist, historian, and campaigner for world peace and collective security. Fellow of King's College, Cambridge.

DISRAELI, Benjamin. 1804–81. Novelist and politician. Son of a Jewish man of letters and antiquarian. Leader of the Conservative Party, three times Chancellor of the Exchequer and twice Prime Minister. Created Earl of Beaconsfield, 1876.

DOUGLAS, Lord Alfred. 1870–1945. Poet. 3rd son of the Marquess of Queensberry. His ravishing good looks captivated Oscar Wilde but his temperament was less beautiful and he was involved in many lawsuits. Entered the Roman Church, 1911.

DOUGLAS, Christopher Home. Active 1860–80. Chartered accountant practising in Edinburgh.

DOUGLAS, George Norman. 1868–1952. A writer of Scottish aristocratic origins. Gave up a diplomatic career at the age of twenty-eight and devoted himself to travel and literature. His early travel books were commercial failures but in 1917 he scored a popular success with his novel *South Wind*. A pederast of the rugged, aggressive, anti-decadent type he fled from English justice in 1917 and settled at Posilipo in the Bay of Naples.

EASTLAKE, Elizabeth (née Rigby). 1809–93. Literary critic, art critic, and connoisseur. Wife and helpmate of Sir Charles Eastlake, President of the Royal Academy and Director of the National Gallery. Her most notorious literary exercise was her scathing review of *Jane Eyre*, which she described as written with 'the tone of mind and thought which has overthrown authority abroad and fostered Chartism and rebellion at home'.

EDWARDS, Amelia. 1831–92. Novelist and journalist. A journey to Egypt in the winter of 1873–4 inspired her with the passion for Egyptology that dominated the rest of her life. Champion of Flinders Petrie and indefatigable Secretary of the Egypt Exploration Fund.

EGERTON, Lord Francis, Earl of Ellesmere. 1800–57. Statesman and poet. Younger son of 1st Duke of Sutherland (George Granville Leverson-Gower). Sat in Parliament as a liberal Tory 1822–46 and held several high offices of state.

ELIOT, George (pseudonym of Mary Ann Evans). 1819–80. Translator, novelist, and oracle of the Victorian pious intelligentsia. Lived for twenty-four years with G. H. Lewes, though she was never able to marry him owing to legal impediments in the way of a dissolution of his first marriage.

ELLIOT, Frances (née Dickinson). 1820–98. Novelist, journalist, and art critic. Became the second wife of the Very Revd Gilbert Elliot, Dean of Bristol, in 1863. Lived in Rome for many years, and died in Siena.

EVANS, Arthur. 1851–1941. Traveller, journalist, and archaeologist. Appointed Keeper of the Ashmolean Museum, Oxford, 1884. Began excavation at Knossos, Crete, in 1899, when the island was evacuated by Turkey and acquired by Greece.

FABER, Frederick William. 1814–63. Anglican clergyman who came under Newman's influence at Oxford and followed him into the Roman Church in 1845. Wrote various theological works but was best known for his hymns.

FARR, William. 1807–83. Physician and statistician. Appointed Compiler of Abstracts in the Registrar General's Office, 1838. Principal author of the Census Reports of 1851, 1861, and 1871.

FARRER, Richard Ridley. 1856–83. Fellow of All Souls College, Oxford, 1880.

FELLOWS, Charles. 1799–1860. Archaeologist. Inherited a fortune from his banker father and devoted his time and money to excavation and research, chiefly in Asia Minor. Knighted, 1845.

FINLAY, George. 1799–1875. Philhellene and historian. Joined Byron in the Greek War of Independence and then settled in Greece, on his own estate in Attica. Frustrated in his desire to serve Greece in a political capacity, he turned to writing its history instead.

FLECKER, James Elroy. 1884–1915. Poet and playwright. Employed in the Consular Service until 1911, when ill health forced him to retire. Died in Davos, of consumption, but was buried in Cheltenham.

FLOWER, William Henry. 1831—99. Physician and zoologist. Hunterian Professor of Comparative Anatomy, University of London, 1870—84; Director of Natural History Section, British Museum, 1884—98.

FORD, Richard. 1796—1858. Writer on art and travel. Introduced the work of Velásquez to the British public.

FORSTER, Edward Morgan. 1879—1970. Novelist and critic. Conscious of failing empathy with the world of heterosexual relationships and unable to publish imaginative treatment of homosexual ones, he wrote little fiction after the appearance of *A Passage to India* in 1924.

FREEMAN, Edward Augustus. 1823—92. Historian. Succeeded Stubbs as Professor of Modern History at Oxford in 1884. A bullying controversialist and uncompromising racist. He venerated 'Teutonic' civilisation and despised Turks, Jews, and Negroes.

FROUDE, Richard Hurrell. 1803—36. Son of Archdeacon Froude of Totnes. Fellow of Oriel College, Oxford, 1826. Close friend of J. H. Newman and founder-member of the Oxford Movement. Brother of the historian J. A. Froude.

FRY, Roger. 1866—1934. Artist and art critic. Rebelled against the constraints of a Quaker upbringing and helped to work a revolution in English taste. Associated with the New English Art Club until 1908, when he became a champion of Post-Impressionism and introduced the work of Cézanne, Van Gogh, Seurat, and Matisse to the British public. Later his interest shifted to Oriental and African art.

GALLENGA, Antonio. 1810—95. Historian and journalist. A native of Parma who fled from Italy as a political refugee in 1833 and went first to America, then to England. Took English nationality in 1846. Was employed by *The Times* first as correspondent in Italy, the USA, and Denmark, then as leader-writer.

GASKELL, Elizabeth (née Stevenson). 1810—65. Novelist. The wife of a Manchester Unitarian minister who used her experience among the poor in deeply felt and widely appreciated fiction of social purpose. Closely associated with Dickens's journal *Household Words*.

GASKELL, George G. Active 1850—75. A traveller of whom nothing is recorded save that he published a book on Algeria and a translation of Baron Franz Pillersdorf's *Rückblicke auf die politische Bewegung in Oesterreich in dem Jahren 1848 und 1849*.

GIBSON, John. 1790—1866. Sculptor. Pupil of Canova and Thorwaldsen. Lived and worked in Rome and reintroduced the Greek practice of tinting statues. His patrons included Queen Victoria.

GISSING, George. 1857—1903. Novelist. Son of a Wakefield chemist. His chances of an academic career, after brilliant success as a student at Owen's

College, Manchester, were blighted by conviction on a charge of theft—the first of many misfortunes brought about by poverty and sexual frustration. These dogged Gissing all his life and coloured his fiction with an obsessive pessimism.

GLADSTONE, William Ewart. 1809—98. Statesman and scholar. Leader of the Liberal Party and four times Prime Minister. He brought into politics all the religious idealism and pulpit eloquence that had at one time made him seem destined for the Church.

GORDON, Charles George. 1833—85. Army Officer and Christian mystic who served in the Crimea, China, and the Sudan. His death at the hands of Muslim rebels in the Sudan precipitated a political crisis and almost brought down the government of Mr Gladstone.

GORDON, Lina Duff. See WATERFIELD.

GORDON, Lucie Duff (née Austin). 1821—69. Married Sir Alexander Duff Gordon, a Treasury official and court officer, in 1840. Beautiful, brilliant, and erudite, she was the centre of an adoring circle of famous friends before ill health drove her first to the Cape of Good Hope and then to Egypt, where she died. Tennyson had her in mind when he wrote *The Princess* and Meredith portrayed her as Lady Jocelyn in *Evan Harrington*.

GOWER, Lord Ronald Sutherland. 1845—1916. Sculptor and writer. Younger son of the 2nd Duke of Sutherland. A roving bohemian aristocrat and well-known homosexual. He was on familiar terms with Queen Victoria, yet lived in a tiny house in Earl's Court, travelled by underground, and put up in a room over a florist's shop in Cambridge. His best-known work is the Shakespeare Monument at Stratford-upon-Avon.

GRAHAM, Alexander. 1861—1941. Barrister. Recorder of Bridgnorth, 1905.

GREEN, John Richard. 1837—83. Clergyman, journalist, and historian. His *Short History of the English People* (1874) marked a new departure in historiography by treating social and cultural developments as the chief focus of interest. Plans for further historical writing were cut short by ill health, which kept him from England for most of the remainder of his life.

GROSVENOR, Elizabeth Mary (née Leverson-Gower), 1797—1891. Marchioness of Westminster.

HAGGARD, Henry Rider. 1856—1925. Novelist. Trained for the Bar, but turned to fiction and achieved great popular success with tales of endurance and adventure in exotic settings. Also wrote on farming and English rural life. Spent much time travelling throughout the Empire on official commissions of inquiry. Knighted, 1912.

HARDY, Thomas. 1840—1928. Novelist and poet. Trained as an architect and practised in London and Dorchester, but turned to writing for a living after the success of *Far From the Madding Crowd* (1874) and *The Return of the Native* (1878).

HARE, Augustus John. 1834—1903. Wealthy member of a prominent clerical family with Sussex connections. Led a desultory life of travel, asexual socialising, and literary pottering which he described in six volumes of autobiography.

HARRISON, Frederic. 1831—1923. Essayist, biographer, and historian. Practised at the Bar for fifteen years and served as Professor of Jurisprudence for the Council of Legal Education. Strongly influenced by the Positivist philosophy of Comte, he became one of its chief promoters in England. Founded the *Positivist Review*, 1893.

HENNEN, John. 1779—1828. Army surgeon. Served as Inspector of Military Hospitals and was Medical Superintendent of the Gibraltar Garrison at the time of his death.

HERBERT, Mary Elizabeth (née A'Court). d. 1911. Wife and later widow of the statesman Sidney Herbert (Lord Herbert of Lea), and mother of the 13th and 14th Earls of Pembroke. A penitent and 'spiritual child' of Henry Manning in his Anglican period, she followed him into the Roman Church in 1865.

HEWLETT, Maurice. 1861—1922. Novelist and poet. Drew much of his inspiration from the English countryside and English folklore. According to Laurence Binyon 'his dream was to be read by the common people, rather than by the cultivated and elect'.

HOBHOUSE, Edmund. 1860—1933. Physician who studied in London, Vienna, Berlin, and Paris. Practised in Colorado, USA, before becoming Consulting Physician to the Sussex County Hospital and Children's Hospital.

HOBHOUSE, John Cam (1st Baron Broughton). 1786—1869. Traveller and statesman. Friend of Byron, radical pamphleteer, and Liberal MP. He held several cabinet posts after the Whigs returned to office in 1830.

HORNE, Herbert Percy. 1864—1916. Art historian, architect, designer, and poet. Closely associated with the Century Guild and editor of its magazine the *Hobby Horse*. Retired to Florence in 1900 and bequeathed his art collection (The Museo Horne) to the city.

HOWITT, Mary (née Botham). 1799—1888. Wife of William Howitt. Translator, novelist, and historian. She left the Quaker communion in 1847 and entered the Roman Church in 1882.

HUGHES, Hugh Price. 1847—1902. Welsh Methodist minister. A leading figure in the Wesleyan Methodist 'forward movement' of the 1880s. Elected President of the Wesleyan Methodist Conference, 1898. A moral rearmer and fervent imperialist.

HUNT, William Holman. 1827—1910. Artist. A founder-member, with Millais and Rossetti, of the Pre-Raphaelite Brotherhood. Unlike the others, he remained true to Pre-Raphaelite principles throughout his life.

HUTTON, Edward. 1875—1969. Travel-writer and art historian. Closely associated with the foundation of the British Institute in Florence (1917) and of the Chairs of Italian at Oxford and Cambridge (1918).

JACKSON, Robert Edmund Scoresby. 1835—67. Awarded the degree of MD in 1857 for a thesis on 'Climate, Health and Disease'. Physician and afterwards lecturer at the Royal Infirmary, Edinburgh.

JAMESON, Anna (née Murphy). 1794—1860. Daughter of Dennis Brownell Murphy, a distinguished miniature-painter. Turned her attention to art and literature after the break-up of her marriage to Robert Jameson, a barrister who was subsequently Attorney General of Ontario.

JOHNSON, James. 1777—1845. Physician Extraordinary to William IV. Irish doctor who served in the Navy until 1814. Thereafter practised in London.

KEITH, Alexander. 1791—1880. Theologian and minister of the Scottish Free Church. Declined the Moderatorship of the Scottish Free Church because of ill health.

KELMAN, John. 1864—1929. Scottish Presbyterian theologian and clergyman. Wrote much on religious themes. OBE, 1918.

KEMBLE, Fanny. 1809—93. Actress and writer. Daughter of Charles Kemble, whom she followed on to the stage. Her marriage to the American plantation-owner Pierce Butler was dissolved in 1844 and she lived the remainder of her life in Europe. Sister of the opera singer Adelaide Proctor.

KINGLAKE, Alexander William. 1809—91. Barrister, politician, and historian. Published his eight-volume *History of the Invasion of the Crimea* between 1863 and 1887, and sat as MP for Bridgwater, 1857—68.

KINGSLEY, Charles. 1819—75. Anglican clergyman, novelist, and historian. Closely associated with the Christian Socialist movement. Professor of Modern History at Cambridge, 1860—9.

KNOX, Alexander Andrew. 1818—91. Journalist and lawyer. Travelled to the Mediterranean with Mary Shelley and her son Percy in 1842. Called to the Bar, 1844. Leader-writer for *The Times* until 1860, when he became a London police magistrate.

LANDOR, Walter Savage. 1775—1864. Poet and essayist. Quarrelled with his father (a wealthy physician), his wife, most of his relations, and almost all of his friends; ran through a large fortune; and ended his days in Italy on a pension provided by his brothers.

LANE, Edward William. 1801—76. The son of an engraver. Studied Arabic and lived as a native in Egypt 1825—49. His chief work was an Arabic lexicon, published between 1863 and 1892.

LANG, Robert Hamilton. 1836—1913. Scottish financier who spent almost all his career in Cyprus and Turkey on the staff of the Imperial Ottoman Bank. British Consul in Cyprus, 1871—2. Knighted, 1897.

LAWLEY, Hon. Alethea Jane Weil. d. 1929. Historian. 2nd daughter of the 2nd Baron Wenlock. Married Nobile Cavaliere Taddeo Weil, Librarian of St Mark's, 1890.

LAWRENCE, David Herbert. 1885—1930. Novelist and poet. His career as a scoolmaster was ended by tuberculosis in 1911 and in 1912 he eloped to Germany and Italy with Frieda Weekley, the wife of his former modern languages tutor. In his fiction he played out the sexual apotheosis that eluded him in life.

LAYARD, Austen Henry. 1817—94. Archaeologist, politician, diplomat, and connoisseur of Italian painting. Liberal MP, 1855—69. British Ambassador to Spain, 1869; to Constantinople, 1877. Knighted, 1878.

LEAR, Edward. 1812—88. Artist and author of poetry of surrealistic humour. Travelled extensively in southern Europe and settled in San Remo during the last seventeen years of his life. Epileptic, rheumatic, and homosexual, he waged a constant battle against ill health and depression.

LEE, Edwin. d. 1870. Physician and medical writer. Practised professionally in London and abroad. A controversial figure who made himself unpopular with the London medical establishment. Received the degree of MD from the University of Göttingen and was elected a member of medical associations in Paris, Berlin, and Naples.

LEE, Vernon (pseudonymn of Violet Paget). 1856—1935. Historian, novelist, and writer on aesthetics. Resident in Florence for most of her life. Dressed like a man, adopted a male pseudonym, and wrote with what Henry James called 'intellectualised rowdyism of style'.

LEIGHTON, Frederic. 1830—96. Artist. Became President of the Royal Academy and received the first peerage ever bestowed on a painter. His most characteristic work portrays Classical subjects set in charmed and breathless landscapes immune from decay and death. Depicted as Gaston Phoebus in Disraeli's *Lothair*.

LEVER, Charles James. 1806—72. Irish novelist. Trained as a doctor. A prolific writer in the farcical—picaresque genre. Settled in Italy in 1845 and served as British Consul first at Spezia, then Trieste.

LEWES, George Henry. 1817—78. Man of letters who turned his hand to philosophy, biography, fiction, and theatre criticism. Founded the *Fortnightly Review*, 1865. George Eliot's consort from 1854 until his death.

LEWIS, John. 1805—76. Artist. Abandoned painting animals in order to live as a native in the Middle East, 1838—50. On his return exhibited a series of brilliant canvasses with Oriental subjects.

LINDSAY, Lord (Alexander William Crawford, 25th Earl of Crawford and 8th Earl of Balcarres). 1812—80. Bibliophile, traveller, and art historian. Died in Florence.

LINDSAY, James Alexander. 1856—1931. Irish physician and medical teacher. At the time of his death was Emeritus Professor of the Theory and Practice of Medicine at Queen's University, Belfast.

LYTTON, Lord (Edward George Lytton-Bulwer). 1803—73. Novelist and statesman. Created Baron, 1866.

LYTTON, Lord (Edward Robert Bulwer). 1831—91. Poet and statesman. Son of Baron Lytton. Viceroy of India 1876—80. Created Earl of Lytton, 1880. Published verse under the name 'Owen Meredith'.

MACAULAY, Thomas Babington. 1800—59. Historian, essayist, and statesman. Raised to the peerage in 1857. Ranks with Gibbon as an English historian whose work survives as literature.

MADDEN, Thomas More. 1844—1902. Irish obstetrician and gynaecologist who practised mostly in Dublin. A prolific writer on medical topics.

MAHAFFY, John Pentland. 1839—1919. Historian of Greece and Greek literature. Closely associated with Trinity College, Dublin, all his life, he was finally appointed Provost. An accomplished linguist and brilliant wit and raconteur. Knighted, 1918.

MAINE, Henry Sumner. 1822—88. Jurist. Served in India, held Chairs of Civil Law and Jurisprudence at Oxford and Cambridge, and in 1878 was appointed Master of Trinity Hall, Cambridge. His *Ancient Law* (1861) is a classic of cultural anthropology.

MALLOCK, William Hurrell. 1849—1923. Novelist, poet, and social theorist. A prominent exponent of Conservative ideology and a death-bed convert to Rome.

MANNING, Henry Edward. 1808—92. As an Anglican clergyman was much influenced by the Oxford Movement. Entered the Church of Rome in 1851 and was promoted Cardinal in 1875. A politician rather than an intellectual, he identified with the Ultramontane party in Rome and rallied English Catholics to the causes of social and political reform.

MARCET, William. Active 1870—90. Senior Assistant Physician to the Westminster Hospital and the Brompton Hospital for Consumption and Diseases of the Chest. Spent several winters in practice on the Riviera.

MARZIALS, Theo. 1850—1920. Poet, composer, and librarian at the British Museum. His concert arias and parlour songs were very popular in the late Victorian years.

MAUGHAM, Henry Neville. 1868–1904. Essayist, poet, and playwright.

Cultivated a bohemian lifestyle and lived mostly in Assisi. Committed suicide by drinking nitric acid. Brother of William Somerset Maugham.

MAUGHAM, William Somerset. 1874–1965. Novelist and playwright. Gave up studying medicine after the success of his first novel, *Liza of Lambeth*, in 1897. After the First World War he made a fortune from screen adaptations of his novels and plays.

MEREDITH, George. 1828–1909. Novelist and poet. War Correspondent in Italy for the *Morning Post*, 1866. Reader for the publishers Chapman and Hall for many years. His extremely condensed and fastidious style, which resulted in the notoriously impenetrable 'Meredithean surface', precluded popularity and delayed recognition. Awarded the Order of Merit, 1905.

MILL, John Stuart. 1806–73. Economist and philosopher. One of the chief architects of Victorian liberal ideology and an enduring influence in modern ethics and political science. Married Mrs Harriet Taylor (née Hardy) in 1851. Sat as MP for Westminster, 1865–8. Died at Avignon.

MILNES, Richard Monckton. 1809–85. Poet, Tory politician, and man of the world. The publication of his *Life of John Keats* (1848) marked the beginning of a general recognition of the poet's stature. Disraeli depicted him in *Tancred* as Mr Vavasour, who 'liked to know everybody who was known, and to see everything which ought to be seen ... His life was a gyration of energetic curiosity; an insatiable whirl of social celebrity ... He was everywhere and at everything; he had gone down in a diving bell and up in a balloon...' He collected pornography and acquired a sinister reputation as a corrupter of innocence—especially that of the young Swinburne, with whom he shared an interest in flogging and punishment in boys' schools. Raised to the peerage as Baron Houghton in 1863.

NEWMAN, John Henry. 1801–90. Theologian, priest, and poet. Fellow of Oriel College, Oxford, and leading light of the Oxford Movement. Joined the Church of Rome, 1845; promoted Cardinal, 1879. One of the most influential figures in the Oxford of the 1830s and 1840s and later widely revered as a beacon of spiritual values. His dedication to the principles of dogma and authority and his conversion to Rome have been attributed to his fear of the sceptical tendencies of his own powerful intellect.

NEWTON, Charles Thomas. 1816–94. Archaeologist on the staff of the British Museum. Vice-Consul at Mytilene, 1852–9. Played an important role in excavation in the Levant and was instrumental in the founding of the Society for the Promotion of Hellenic Studies (1879), the British School at Athens (1885), and the Egypt Exploration Society (1882). Knighted, 1887.

NORTH, Marianne. 1830–90. Flower painter. Daughter of Frederick North, MP for Hastings, 1855–65. After her father's death she travelled all over the world in search of botanical specimens. Her sister Catherine married John Addington Symonds.

OLIPHANT, Margaret (née Wilson). 1828–97. Novelist and historian. One of the most prolific of the tribe of popular authors called into being by the expansion of the Victorian reading public.

OTTER, Robert Henry. 1836–1914. Educated at Rugby and Oxford. Practised as a solicitor in Bristol, 1860–72. Thereafter was Justice of the Peace for Surrey.

OUIDA (pseudonym of Louise de la Ramée). 1839–1908. Novelist who climbed from rags to riches and then declined to rags again. Resident in Italy for the second half of her life. Her stories about Italian peasants were inspired by her unrequited love for the Marchese della Stufa, a court officer of the King of Italy. Despite crudities of technique and self-indulgent pathos they have something of the power of Hardy and Zola and remain the best imaginative treatments in English of Italian rural life. *Signa* became the basis of an opera, with music by Frederic Cowen.

PALGRAVE, Francis. 1788–1861. Historian and archivist. Author of Murray's first Italian *Handbook*. Knighted, 1832. His paternal name was Cohen but he assumed his mother-in-law's name of Palgrave on converting to Christianity in 1823.

PALMER, Samuel. 1805–81. Artist. A follower of Blake whose early work consisted of landscapes charged with Christian symbolism. After his visit to Italy (1838) this inspiration faded and his output declined drastically in quality.

PATTERSON, John. Active 1860–70. A British physician employed in the Egyptian Medical Service.

PERRING, John Shae. 1813–69. Civil engineer. In Egypt on professional business, 1836–40. Spent most of 1837 surveying the Pyramids in collaboration with Richard Vyse (q.v.) and published his results in *The Pyramids of Gizeh* (1839).

PETRIE, Flinders. 1853–1942. Archaeologist. His activities in Egypt began in 1880 with a survey of the Pyramids and ended in 1926 when he turned to excavation in Palestine. His technique of stratification and his sequence-dating of Egyptian pottery revolutionised archaeological science. Professor of Egyptology, University of London, 1892–1933. Knighted, 1923.

PHILLIP, John. 1817–67. Artist. A successful portrait and genre painter who was in Spain on medical advice 1851–2. The Mediterranean inspired a complete change in his art and he turned to brilliantly lit scenes of Southern life.

PLAYFAIR, Robert Lambert. 1828–99. Army officer and diplomat. After service in the Middle East and India was appointed British Consul General in Algeria, 1867. Author of Murray's *Handbook for Travellers in Algeria* (1874) and *A Handbook to the Mediterranean Cities, Coasts and Islands* (1881).

POTTER, Beatrice. 1858–1943. Daughter of a wealthy railway and industrial magnate. Became a prominent socialist and social reformer in partnership with Sidney Webb, whom she married in 1892 after her advances to Joseph Chamberlain had been rejected.

PULLAN, Richard Popplewell. 1825–88. Architect and archaeologist. Carried out important excavations in Greece and Asia Minor in the 1850s and 1860s, while continuing to run a successful architectural practice in London.

REID, Thomas Wemyss. 1842–1905. Novelist, biographer, and journalist. Manager of Cassell & Co., 1887–90. Editor of the *Speaker*, 1890–7. Knighted, 1894.

RICHMOND, William Blake. 1842–1921. Painter. Son of the artist John Richmond. Specialised in landscapes of Arcadian idealism, and designed the mosaics for St Paul's Cathedral. Slade Professor at Oxford, 1878–83. RA, 1895. Knighted, 1897.

RIPON, Marquis of. 1827–1909. Liberal statesman, Viceroy of India, 1880–4.

ROBERTS, David. 1796–1864. Scottish artist who began his career as a painter of stage scenery in London. RA, 1841. Travelled extensively and was best known for the published engravings of his landscapes from the Holy Land.

ROBERTS, Richard. 1814–85. Anglican clergyman. Vicar of Milton Abbas, Dorset, 1842–85. Domestic Chaplain to the Earl of Portarlington.

ROLFE, Frederick ('Baron Corvo'). 1860–1913. Artist, photographer, novelist, and historian. A psychopathic curiosity of English literature whose work sometimes exhibits freakish brilliance. It was his custom to try to disguise the homosexual inspiration of his fiction by changing the hero's beloved into a girl, but he always betrayed it by depicting her as a girl with the physical characteristics of a boy.

ROSS, Janet (née Duff Gordon). 1842–1927. Daughter of Alexander and Lucie Duff Gordon. Married Henry Ross, manager of Briggs's Bank in Alexandria, and withdrew with him to Italy after the financial crisis of 1866 had led to the collapse of the bank and the loss of part of their fortune. Meredith depicted her as Rose Jocelyn in *Evan Harrington*.

RUSKIN, John. 1819–1900. Critic of art and society. Son of a wealthy sherry merchant. One of the giants of the Victorian cultural landscape and an entrenched arbiter of Victorian taste. First Slade Professor at Oxford and prolific author and lecturer. Turned to social criticism following the breakdown of his marriage to Effie Gray, when he became convinced that he was living and writing in a society whose economic organisation made the production and appreciation of great art impossible. His clarion call for a new ethic of moral economy in place of the free market awoke a deep response in humanitarians as diverse as William Morris, Tolstoy, and

Gandhi. Manic-depressive illness plagued the latter part of his life, and he passed his final years in almost total silence and seclusion.

SALA, George Augustus. 1828–95. Journalist and novelist. Began his career as an illustrator of books and painter of stage scenery. Subsequently turned to literature, and founded and edited *Temple Bar*. Reported for the *Daily Telegraph* from 1857 until his death. His hobby was pornography.

SENIOR, Nassau William. 1790–1864. Economist and essayist. Twice held the Chair of Political Economy at Oxford. Member of the Poor Law Commission of 1833, and author of its *Report*.

SEVERN, Joseph. 1793–1879. Painter. Accompanied Keats to Italy and remained there until 1841. Returned to Rome in 1860 and served as British Consul 1860–72.

SEYMOUR, Michael Hobart. 1800–74. Irish Protestant clergyman who migrated to England in 1834. He waged a lifelong war of propaganda against the Church of Rome.

SHAFTESBURY, Lord (Antony Ashley Cooper, 7th Earl of Shaftesbury). 1801–85. Prominent philanthropist and Anglican evangelical. Known as 'the People's Earl' for his efforts on behalf of the poor and exploited.

SHELLEY, Mary (née Godwin). 1797–1851. Novelist. Daughter of Mary Wollstonecraft and William Godwin. Went to Italy with the poet Shelley in 1814 and married him two years later. Published *Frankenstein* to great acclaim in 1818, but failed to match its success with other novels.

SMITH, George Adam. 1856–1942. Old Testament scholar and theologian. Served as Presbyterian minister in Aberdeen before being appointed Professor of Old Testament Studies at Free Church College, Glasgow. Principal of Aberdeen University 1909–35. Knighted, 1916.

SMYTH, Ethel. 1858–1944. Composer. Studied in Germany, where her work was better appreciated than in England. Joined the suffragette movement and was jailed in 1911. Created DBE, 1922.

SOLOMON, Simeon. 1840–1905. Jewish painter closely associated with the Pre-Raphaelites, Swinburne, and Pater. Calamity struck in 1873, when he was convicted of a homosexual offence, and he died a chronic alcoholic and a pauper.

SOMERVILLE, Mary (née Fairfax). 1780–1872. Mathematician and populariser of science. Died at Naples, where she lived during the last twelve years of her life.

SPARKS, Edward Isaac. 1844(?)–80. Physician to the Skin Department, Charing Cross Hospital.

SPENCER, Edmund. Active 1840–60. Army Captain, apparently on half-pay after 1815. Wrote travel books and historical romances. Lived in Germany for several years.

SPENCER, Herbert. 1820–1903. Philosopher and sociologist. Originator of the theory of Social Darwinism. The young George Eliot fell in love with him, but he lived and died a bachelor.

SPURGEON, Charles Haddon. 1834–92. Baptist clergyman and revivalist. His church was the Metropolitan Tabernacle, built in 1859. His weekly sermons were published and had an enormous circulation. Edited a monthly magazine called *The Sword and the Trowel: A Record of Combat with Sin and Labour for the Lord.* Bearded, bulky, booming, and biblical-basic: an evangelical bruiser.

STANLEY, Arthur Penrhyn. 1815–81. Anglican clergyman. Historian, biographer, and theologian. Canon of Canterbury, 1851; Canon of Christ Church, Oxford, 1858; Dean of Westminster, 1864. Professor of Ecclesiastical History at Oxford, 1856. Features as 'Arthur' in Thomas Hughes's *Tom Brown's Schooldays.*

STEVENSON, Robert Louis. 1850–94. Scottish novelist and essayist. Called to the Bar in 1875, but never practised. Travelled widely in search of a climatic cure for his tuberculosis, and died in Samoa.

STISTED, Charlotte (1812–90) and Colonel Henry (1786–1859). Resided at Bagni di Lucca for many years and endowed an English chapel and cemetery.

SULLY, James. 1842–1923. Philosopher and psychologist. Emeritus Professor of Philosophy, University College, London.

SYMONDS, John Addington. 1840–93. Historian, poet, biographer, and essayist. His career as a lawyer was cut short by tuberculosis, and most of his life was spent abroad in search of health. Finally settled with his wife and three surviving daughters at Davos, in Switzerland. Collaborated with Havelock Ellis on his study of sexual inversion.

TAYLOR, Herbert Coupland. Active 1880s. Physician and pulmonary invalid.

TAYLOR, Isaac. 1829–1901. Anglican clergyman. Theologian, philologist, and archaeologist. Became Canon of York.

THACKERAY, Anne (Lady Ritchie). 1837–1919. Novelist, biographer, and salon celebrity. Eldest daughter of W. M. Thackeray. Married Sir Richmond Thackeray Willoughby Ritchie, 1877.

THACKERAY, William Makepeace. 1811–63. Novelist and journalist. *Vanity Fair* (1847–8) established him in the first rank of Victorian novelists and only Dickens rivalled him in popularity.

THOMSON, Andrew. 1814–1901. Scottish Presbyterian clergyman. Senior

Minister of the United Presbyterian Church, Broughton Place, Edinburgh, 1842; Moderator, United Presbyterian Church, 1874.

THRING, Edward. 1821–87. Anglican clergyman and schoolmaster. During his thirty-four years as Headmaster of Uppingham he raised it from a small and declining grammar school into one of the foremost public schools of the country. Founded the Headmasters' Conference and held advanced views on the teaching of 'modern' subjects.

TRANT, Thomas Abercromby. Army officer who served in the first Burmese war (1824–6).

TRENCH, Richard Chenevix. 1807–86. Anglican clergyman, poet, and theologian. Professor of Theology, King's College, London, 1847; Dean of Westminster, 1856; Archbishop of Dublin, 1864.

TREVELYAN, George Macaulay. 1876–1962. Historian. Great-nephew of Macaulay and ardent defender of the sort of popular literary historiography that Macaulay represented. Regius Professor of Modern History, Cambridge, 1927; Master of Trinity College, Cambridge, 1940.

TRISTRAM, Henry Baker. 1822–1906. Anglican clergyman and traveller. Rector of Castle Eden, 1846–60; Master of Greatham Hospital, 1860–74; Canon of Durham, 1873–1906.

TROLLOPE, Anthony. 1815–82. Novelist. One of the most widely travelled of Victorian authors. Until 1867 he combined writing with official duties in the Post Office which entailed trips to Ireland, Egypt, the West Indies, and the USA. In the 1870s he also visited Australia, New Zealand, Ceylon, South Africa, and Iceland.

TROLLOPE, Frances (née Milton). 1780–1863. Novelist and travel-writer. Mother of Anthony and Thomas Trollope, and their chief provider in their childhood. Spent the last seventeen years of her life in Florence, where she died.

TROLLOPE, Thomas Adolphus. 1810–93. Journalist and novelist. Lived abroad for most of his life. Settled with his mother in 1846 at Florence, where he met and married Theodosia Garrow. Lived in Rome, 1873–86.

VICARY, M. Active 1840–60. A Protestant clergyman of unidentified affiliation.

VIVIAN, Herbert. 1865–1940. Journalist and traveller. Special Correspondent of the *Morning Post*, 1898–9; and of the *Daily Express*, 1899–1900, 1918. Revived Dr Johnson's *The Rambler* in 1901. An authority on Balkan affairs.

VYSE, Richard William. 1784–1853. Army officer, MP, and amateur Egyptologist. Visited Egypt and Syria, 1835–7. Spent a year and a half exploring and excavating the Pyramids—latterly in association with Perring (q.v.), whose subsequent researches he financed.

WALKER, Frederick. 1840–75. Artist. Son of a jeweller. Began his career as a wood-engraver and illustrator of books. Died of consumption.

WARBURTON, Bartholomew Eliot George. 1810–52. Irish historian. Died a heroic death aboard the steamer *Amazon*, which was destroyed by fire in mid-Atlantic.

WATERFIELD, Lina (née Duff Gordon). 1874–1964. Historian and journalist. Only child of Sir Maurice Duff Gordon and granddaughter of Lucie Duff Gordon. Married the artist Aubrey Waterfield, 1901. Italian Correspondent of the *Observer*, 1921–35.

WATTS, George Frederic. 1817–1904. Artist. Made his living by portraiture but found vocational fulfilment in painting huge allegorical canvases with titles like *Progress*, *Destiny*, *Chaos*, *Hope*, and *Love and Death*. Declined a baronetcy three times but accepted the Order of Merit in 1902.

WELD, Charles Richard. 1813–69. Barrister and scientific writer. Secretary and Librarian to the Royal Society, 1845–61. Published a history of the Royal Society 1848. Helped Sir John Franklin to prepare for his polar expedition of 1850–1. Married Anne Selwood, Tennyson's sister-in-law.

WHITESIDE, James. 1804–76. Irish lawyer. Defended O'Connell in the state trials of 1843, and O'Brien in the state trials of 1848. During his career as a Tory MP (1851–66) was twice Attorney General. Lord Chief Justice of Ireland, 1866.

WILDE, Oscar. 1854–1900. Irish poet, playwright, and novelist. Master of paradox and literary artifice, he domesticated the French Decadence for the British public. The jester and the scapegoat of late-Victorian society. Convicted of homosexual offences in 1895 after unsuccessfully suing the Marquess of Queensberry for criminal libel. Left England after his release from jail in 1897, joined the Roman Church, and died a destitute exile in Paris.

WILDE, William. 1815–76. Irish surgeon and antiquary. Father of Oscar Wilde. Accompanied a wealthy invalid, Mr Robert Meiklam, as private physician during a yacht tour of the Mediterranean, 1837–8. His subsequent professional career in Dublin was turbulent and clouded by scandal. Knighted, 1864.

WILKIE, David. 1785–1841. Scottish artist who succeeded Lawrence as Painter to the King (1830). Abandoned a style influenced by the genre pictures of the Dutch school, for historical subjects treated with bolder technique after seeing the work of Velásquez and Murillo during a tour of Europe 1825–8. Died returning from a journey to the eastern Mediterranean. His burial at sea was the subject of a picture by Turner.

WILKINSON, John Gardner. 1797–1875. Gentleman of fortune who became a well-known explorer and Egyptologist. His magnum opus, *The Manners and*

Customs of the Ancient Egyptians, was published in six volumes (1837–41). Author of the original edition of Murray's *Handbook for Travellers in Egypt* (1847). Knighted, 1839.

WILLIAMS, Charles Theodore. Active 1860–80. Assistant Surgeon to the Hospital for Consumption and Diseases of the Chest, Brompton. A widely recognised authority on tuberculosis.

WILLIAMS, Penry. 1800(?)–85. Welsh artist. Studied at the Royal Academy and exhibited there regularly 1822–69. Settled in Rome in 1827 and specialised in Italian views and scenes of Roman life.

WILSON, Charles William. 1836–1905. Colonel, later Major-General, Royal Engineers. Carried out survey work in Canada, Sinai, and Palestine and served in Egypt, 1882–4. Chairman, Palestine Exploration Fund, 1881; Editor, Murray's *Handbook for Asia Minor and Constantinople*, 1892. Knighted, 1885.

WOOD, Charles William. Active 1870–90. Journalist. Son and biographer of Mrs Henry Wood and co-editor, with his mother, of the *Argosy* (which she founded).

WORDSWORTH, Christopher. 1807–85. Anglican clergyman, theologian and Classical scholar. Nephew of William Wordsworth. Appointed Canon of Westminster, 1844; Bishop of Lincoln, 1868.

WORDSWORTH, William. 1770–1850. Poet. His work embodies the chief Romantic response to the English countryside. Succeeded Southey as Poet Laureate, 1843.

WYSE, Thomas. 1791–1862. Irish Catholic diplomat and politician. Collaborated with O'Connell in the struggle for Catholic emancipation and after this had been achieved (1829) was closely associated with the campaign to establish public education in the UK. Went to Athens on being appointed British Ambassador to Greece in 1849, and remained there until he died.

YEO, Burney. d. 1914. Physician. Closely associated with King's College, London, first as Fellow and Tutor and subsequently as Professor of Clinical Therapeutics, Professor of the Principles and Practice of Medicine, and Emeritus Professor of Medicine.

INDEX

Abbeville 18
Acropolis 176
Acton, Harold 104
Adelaide, Queen 86
Aegean Islands 78, 127
Aeschylus 116
Agamemnon 119
Aitkin, Dr 242
Aiton, Revd John 24, 37, 141, 185, 187, 188, 213, 277
Aix 22
Ajaccio 50
Albania 121, 133
Albano 18
Alcinous 116
alcohol 92
Alexandria 23, 35, 47, 251, 292
Alford, Henry 27, 277
Algeria 29, 49, 63, 64, 84, 87, 119, 137, 142, 153, 164, 234, 250; see also Algiers
Algiers 18, 23, 35, 49, 85, 86, 93, 133, 137, 161, 172, 241, 242, 244, 250
Alicante 4
Allbutt, Dr Clifford 246
Allen, Dr James 249
alternative medicine 88–96
Amalfi 32
American tourists 39, 170
Amitrano 155
Ammon 185, 190
Anatolia 50, 120, 187, 264
Andalusia 97, 98
Anstruther-Thompson, Clementine 66, 79
anthropology, cultural 181, 221
Apollo Belvedere, the 117
'Apostles', the 10, 278
Apulia 119
Arabian Nights 121, 211, 280
Arabs, character of 133, 135, 136, 142–3, 146, 237
Ararat 255
Arcadia 116, 232
Archaeological Journal 83
archaeology, biblical 61, 191–6

archaeology, classical 76, 82–4, 178–9
Areiopagos, the 176
Arezzo 144
Aristotle 116
Arnold, Edwin 60
Arnold, Matthew 64, 73, 115, 129, 131, 149, 154, 179, 180, 181, 183, 228, 235, 277, 281
Arnold, Thomas 75, 189, 277
Arthur, Revd William 139, 141, 213, 215, 216, 219, 220, 225, 270, 277
Art Union Monthly Journal 76
Arundel Society 201
Ashbee, Henry 7, 63, 133, 211, 233, 277
Ashmolean Museum 283
Askalon 190
Aspinall, Mrs 28
Assisi 178, 200
Assyria 61, 62, 192
Aswan 247
Athens 23, 29, 30, 115, 142, 170, 176, 231, 238; British School at 83, 290
atmospheric pollution 151–2
Auden, W. H. 54
Austin, John 277
Austin, Sarah 36, 247, 277
Austria 34, 228, 234
Austrian Lloyd Company 23
automobiles 18, 27
Avignon 22, 26, 290
Avranches 106

Baalbek 170
Babylon 61, 186, 190
Baedeker, Karl 49, 70, 71, 98
Bagehot, Walter 131
Baghdad 278
Balearic Islands 50, 137; see also Majorca
Balfour, Arthur 101, 277
Balkans 50, 115
Ball, Eustace 46, 48, 100, 277
Barcelona 133, 142
Barnes, William 79
Barnett, Henrietta Octavia 70, 277
Barrington, Mrs Russell 120, 156, 277
Bartlett, William 47, 277

Basilica of Constantine (Rome) 176
Baske, Miriam 158–9
Bath 99
Baxter, Lucy 17, 79, 278
Beamont, William 36, 127, 188, 211, 278
Beardsley, Aubrey 4, 95, 278
Beaulieu 87
Beebe, Revd Mr 48
Beerbohm, Max 105
Beirut 30, 35, 36, 119, 122
Bell, Revd Charles 31, 57, 182–3, 193, 278
Bell, Clive 209
Bell, Gertrude 97, 125, 278
Bellini, Giovanni 200, 207
Bellini, Vincenzo 230
Belloc, Hilaire 7, 63–4, 98, 147, 149–50, 153, 234, 278
Bennet, Dr James Henry 19, 26, 63, 86, 94, 95, 116, 120, 124, 241, 252, 260, 278
Bennett, Arnold 41, 74, 77, 78, 101, 278
Bent, James 83, 278
Berenson, Bernhard 79, 98, 209
Bernal, Ralph 76
bersaglieri 119
Bertram, George 49
Bertz, Eduard 208
Best, John Richard Digby 108, 140, 240, 271, 278
Bethany 122
Bethel 189, 195
Bethlehem 122
Beulé, Charles Ernest 62
Bevan, Samuel 72, 233
Bible, the, as a guidebook 55, 57, 122–3, 190
Bible Society, the 279
biblical art 58–9, 191
biblical prophecy 185–96
Bibliolatry 56–7
Bicknell, Elhanan 76
Binyon, Laurence 286
Biskra 164, 247
Blakesley, Joseph 63, 278
Blanc, François and Louis 101
Blanc, Dr Henry 248
Bloomsbury 106
Blunt, Wilfred Scawen 170, 178–9, 240, 279
Bologna 139, 197, 199, 207
Bonar, Revd Andrew 192, 279
Bordighera 44, 45, 46, 86, 87, 95
Borgias, the 236
Borrow, George 134, 225, 279
Botticelli, Sandro 75, 79–80, 200, 207, 208

Boulogne 2, 4, 18, 106
Bourbon dynasty, Neapolitan 138
Bourget, Paul 80
Bowden, Sir George 71
Bowdich, Dr 249
Bowring, Dr John 37
Boxall, William 20, 22, 229, 241, 261, 279
Boyle, Mary 19, 141, 145, 279
Bracebridge, Mr and Mrs 77
Bradford 152
Branchidae 84
Brewster, Lady Margaret 45, 226, 279
brigandage 31–3, 136; *see also* crime
Briggs's Bank 292
Brighton 99, 211
Bright's Disease 95
Brindisi 23, 25
British Museum 4, 83, 280, 289, 290
Broad Church 184, 189, 196
bromine 88
bronchitis 88, 90, 95
Bronson, Katherine de Kay 262
Brooke, Dorothea 155, 157–8, 163
Brougham, Henry 4, 279
Brown, Dr Alexander Menzies 45, 279
Brown, Horatio 80, 124, 143, 160, 168, 264, 279
Brown, Rawdon 279
Browning, Elizabeth Barrett 4, 10, 49, 91, 93, 95, 99, 102, 103, 106, 107, 108, 113, 135, 136, 138, 139–40, 141, 143, 146, 149, 151, 199, 200, 229, 262, 279
Browning, Oscar 21, 27, 72–3, 100, 147, 161, 173, 208, 279
Browning, Robert 4, 102, 103, 107, 108, 126, 153, 172, 200, 201, 217, 233, 236, 262, 279, 280
Brunelleschi 79
Brussels 2, 4
Bryce, James 8, 72, 147, 220–1, 225, 226, 262, 280
Buchanan, Dr 249
Buckland, Anne 109, 173, 178, 233–4, 238–9, 280
Buckle, Henry Thomas 5, 61, 154, 259, 280
Budrum 83
bullfighting 136, 239
Bunyan, John 253
Burano 124
Burgess, Dr Thomas 94, 243, 244, 252–3, 280
Burke, Edmund 179
Burne-Jones, Edward 178, 202, 280

Burton, Lady Isabel 30–1, 280
Burton, Sir Richard 280
Butler, Lady Eleanor 102
Butler, Pierce 287
Butler, Samuel 7, 12, 32, 56, 65, 113, 147, 154, 197, 280
Byron, Lord 5, 9, 48, 102, 168, 173, 232, 233, 234, 279, 283, 286

Cadiz 10, 96
Ca' d'Oro 177
Caesarea 185
Café Florian 87
Caffè Greco 81
Cagliari 29
Cairo 5, 18, 23, 47, 99, 100, 115, 122, 124, 133, 135, 137, 170, 172, 241, 247, 251
Calabria 31, 98, 121, 125, 141, 142, 241
Calah *see* Nimrud
Calais 26, 273
Calatafini 113
Calvary 184
Calvin, John 55, 272
Cambridge 76, 155, 278, 279
Cameron, Julia Margaret 191
Campagna 43, 118, 162, 241, 254
Campbell, Thomasina 50, 142
Campo Santo (Pisa) 208
Canada 249
Cannes 2, 4, 40, 44, 45, 86, 87, 93, 100, 101, 109, 171, 241, 248, 250, 277, 279
Cannes Gazette 45
Canney, Dr Leigh 44
Capri 102, 124, 156
Capua 118
Caracalla, Baths of 73, 178
Carlo Dolci 201
Carlyle, Thomas 9, 40, 130, 179, 234, 280
Carnival 43, 101, 135, 141, 142, 143
Carpaccio, Vittore 207
Carpenter, Edward 159
Carracci, Ludovico, Agostini, and Annibale 197, 198
Carthage 4, 61, 62, 63, 83, 233, 235
Caruso, Enrico 231
Casa Guidi 108
Casa Standish 103
Casaubon, Edward 54, 154–5, 157–8
Castellammare 18
Catania 242
Cavour, Count 139
Cesenatico 98
Chalmers, Thomas 190

Chalon 20, 22
Chambers, Mrs 11
Chambers, William 45, 46, 137, 170, 252, 280
Chambers, Dr William 91, 93, 99
Cheltenham 99, 278
Chester, Greville 5, 280
Childe Harold 48
cholera 35, 36, 37, 38
Christian Art 168, 196–7, 200–10
Christmas, Revd Henry 23, 24, 35, 120, 127, 135, 171, 188, 215, 217, 280–1
Church, Richard 68, 115, 167, 281
churches, Protestant 41, 43, 44–5, 47, 50
Cimabue 200
Clarendon Commission 75
Clark, Sir James 88, 89, 90–1, 93, 94, 241, 243, 248, 250, 254, 281
Clark, Kenneth 206, 210
Clark, William George 124, 127, 140, 214, 266, 281
Classics, the 75–6, 115–21, 220–1
class prejudice 159–60, 162–4
Claude le Lorraine 9
climatology 84
climatotherapy 91–5, 244–50, 253
Clough, Arthur Hugh 4, 10, 154, 167, 180, 233, 281
Cnidus 128
Cobbe, Frances Power 4, 20, 23, 53, 56, 59, 77, 78, 122, 124, 132, 133, 140, 146, 148, 149–50, 152, 172, 216, 233, 238, 262, 269, 281
Coleridge, Samuel Taylor 203
Colonna 120
Colosseum (Rome) 64, 178, 233
Comacchio 98
Comacine Masons 79
Compagnie Générale Transatlantique 24
Comte, Auguste 157, 158, 286
Conder, Capt. Charles 194
conscription, Italian 239
Constantinople 23, 30, 35
Constantinople Sanitary Conference 38
contagionism 38
Contemporary Review 277
Cook, Thomas 2–3, 28, 30–1, 47, 49, 50, 59, 78, 100, 170, 195
Cordova 48, 122
Corfu 30, 36, 119, 124; *see also* Ionian Islands
Cornice 22, 26, 116; *see also* Riviera
Correggio, Antonio 79, 177, 197, 201

Corsairs 31

Corsica 31, 50, 121, 142

Corvo, Baron *see* Rolfe, Frederick

cost of living 106–8

Counter-Reformation 223

Cousin Charlotte 75, 163

Covent Garden theatre 230–1

Cowen, Frederick 291

Craig, Edward Gordon 104, 281

Crawford, Mabel Sharman 8, 34, 68, 113, 140, 143, 271, 281

Crete 50, 78, 83, 121, 283

crime 136–7, 148–9, 239; *see also* brigandage

Criminal Law Amendment Act (1885) 159

crowd behaviour 130, 134–5

Cunningham, Alison 107, 281

Curzon, George Nathaniel 116, 281

Curzon, Robert 7, 172, 212, 217, 224, 281

Cust, Robert Hobart 80, 282

customs inspection 33, 34

Cyprus 5, 47, 50, 84, 97, 123, 137, 153, 233, 266, 269, 271, 288

Cyrene 84

Daily Express 295

Daily Telegraph 293

Dakyns, Graham 155

Dalmatia 97

Damascus 122, 123, 190, 280

Dante, Alighieri 145, 147

Darwin, Charles 56, 180, 181, 182, 238

David, King of Israel 192, 193, 194

Davis, Nathan 61, 83, 235, 282

Davos Platz 246, 250, 254

Davy, Dr John 92, 120, 217, 246, 249, 250, 251, 282

Dawkins, Sabrina 77

Dead Sea 30, 185, 186, 189, 191

Dead Sea Scrolls 195

Dead Sea stone 6

Debir 195

Delos 5

Delphi 68

democracy 131, 144, 146, 160, 164

Dennistoun, James 76

Dernis, 23

Destin, Emmy 231

diabetes 95

Dickens, Charles 6, 7, 22, 70, 81, 102, 105, 106, 108, 113, 124, 132, 135, 140, 143, 151, 198, 201, 215, 232, 233, 241, 259, 262, 282

Dickinson, Cato Lowes 20, 102, 133, 135, 175, 202, 215, 217, 218, 222, 282

Dickinson, Goldsworthy Lowes 155, 282

Dido 62, 235

Didyma 84

digitalis 92

Dijon 85

diligences 20–1

Dinan 106

Dionysus, Theatre of 176

Disraeli, Benjamin 7, 8, 48, 106, 131, 146, 178, 198, 208, 232, 282, 288, 290

doctors, expatriate 87

Dodd family 74

Domenichino 197, 198

Donatello 79

Doney 43

Donizetti, Gaetana 230

Don Pacifico 149

Doria, Princess 262

Douglas, Lord Alfred 159, 161, 282

Douglas, Christopher Home 17, 85, 282

Douglas, Norman 7, 12, 13, 62, 65, 97, 115, 119, 141, 147, 150, 151, 155, 156, 161, 169, 174, 268, 273, 282

doubt, religious 56, 183, 191

dragomen 30

Dresden 99, 106

drugs 92, 95

drunkenness 130, 140–2

Dudgeon, Mrs 45

Dunne, Col. 11

Dyce, William 59

Dying Gladiator, the 117

dyspepsia 90–1, 92, 244

Eager, Revd Cuthbert 65

Eastlake, Sir Charles 4, 81, 82, 113, 200, 279, 283

Eastlake, Elizabeth, Lady 36, 64, 76, 175, 200, 201, 222, 229, 234, 235, 238, 239, 282–3

Eclectic Review 7

Eden, Emily 124

Edinburgh Review 62

Edom 190

education 75–6

Edward, Prince of Wales 60, 101, 189

Edwards, Amelia 5, 283

Egerton, Lord Francis 122, 283

Egypt, ancient 61; *see also* Pyramids

Egypt, modern 3, 5, 9, 25, 29, 35, 46–7, 57, 58, 64, 84, 86, 90, 119, 124, 152, 184–5,

190, 232, 234, 247, 248, 250, 269, 279, 280; *see also* Alexandria; Cairo; Luxor; Nile

Egypt Exploration Fund 283, 290

Elgin, Lord 5, 176

Elgin Marbles, the 117–19, 176

Eliot, George 1, 7, 9, 19, 21, 54, 56, 113, 126, 129, 131, 134, 147, 151, 154–5, 157–8, 163, 180, 183, 207, 208, 231, 283, 288

Elliot, Frances 66, 213, 232, 283

Elliot, Gilbert 283

Ellis, Havelock 294

Emerson, George 163

Engels, Friedrich 131

Ephesus 84, 186, 188, 242

Essays and Reviews 184, 189

Etna 121

Etty, William 81

Eumenides, well of the 176

Eustace, John Chatwode 70–1

evangelicalism 55–7, 67, 183–96, 206–7, 224, 234–8

Evans, Arthur 83, 84, 266, 283

Evolution 179–80

executions, public 135

Exodus, Book of 195

Ezekiel 185, 186, 188, 190, 206

Faber, Frederick 8, 43, 67, 116, 224, 225, 235, 261, 272, 283

Fallmerayer, Jakob 120

Farnese Hercules 117

Farr, Dr William 99, 283

Farrer, Richard 48, 181, 283

Fellows, Charles 83, 84, 120, 264, 283

Fell Railway 26–7

Fergusson, James 60

Ferrara 232

Feuerbach, Ludwig 157

Fiesole 79

Fighting Gladiator, the 118

Finlay, George 70, 120, 228, 234, 283

Fitzgerald, Edward 60

Flaubert, Gustave 62, 168

Flecker, James Elroy 113, 283

Fleming, Contarini 232

Florence 4, 18, 35, 39, 40, 41, 42, 74, 78–9, 81, 87, 102, 103, 106, 113, 135, 139, 143, 173, 175, 177, 182, 197, 198, 201, 205, 207, 208, 229, 237, 241, 242, 262, 281; British Institute in 287

Flower, William 25, 284

folk-song 145

Ford, Richard 31, 159, 239, 268, 284

Forster, Edward Morgan 7, 48, 65, 74–5, 79, 96, 127–8, 156, 159, 160, 161–4, 208, 263, 284

Forster, John 22

Fortnightly Review 246, 288

Forum (Rome) 176

Fra Angelico 200

Fra Bartolommeo 79

Franco-Prussian War 218, 229, 235–6, 260

Frankfurt 106

Fraser's Magazine 183

Frazer, Sir James 181, 182

Frederick, Emperor 86

Freeman, Edward 4, 59, 63, 116, 178, 266, 284

Frith, William 82

Froude, Hurrell 197, 198, 284

Froude, James Anthony 57, 183

Fry, Roger 61, 118, 151, 160, 161, 209, 284

fumigation 36–7

Fusato, Angelo 261

Galilee 30, 127, 172

Gallenga, Antonio 29, 263, 284

Garibaldi, Giuseppe 11, 98, 140

Gaskell, Elizabeth 113, 208, 284

Gaskell, George 63, 137, 142, 267, 284

Gaspard *see* Poussin

Gautier, Theophile 1, 96

Genoa 22, 35, 36, 85, 106, 113, 152, 198

Gethsemane 123

ghetto Inglese 41

Ghiberti, Lorenzo 79, 208

Ghirlandaio, Domenico 200

Gibbon, Edward 199, 232, 289

Gibeah 195

Gibeon 55

Gibraltar 35, 47, 91, 149, 269, 270

Gibson, John 4, 81, 82, 118, 284

Gide, André 124, 153, 161, 164

Gigliucci, Countess 262

Giotto 65, 177, 200, 207, 208

Girgenti 32

Gissing, George 7, 12, 97, 113, 114, 116, 118, 124, 129, 131, 135, 142, 144, 145, 149, 151, 152–3, 156, 158–9, 167, 169, 170, 174, 197, 208, 239, 241, 284

Gladstone, William 10, 65–6, 76, 113, 116, 178, 197, 198, 200, 213, 225, 226–7, 285

Godwin, Edward 281

Golden Age, the 180, 181, 182

Gomorrah 191, 255

gondoliers 143, 160

Gordon, Alexander Duff 285
Gordon Maj.-Gen. Charles 55, 182, 184, 194, 284
Gordon, Janet Duff *see* Ross, Janet
Gordon, Lina Duff 29, 79, 296
Gordon, Lucie Duff 115, 122, 124, 143, 144, 170, 172, 247, 261, 277, 285, 296
'Gordon's Tomb' 194
Gothic architecture 201–5, 207
'Gothic Revival' 202
Gounod, Charles 230, 231
gout 95
Gower, Lord Ronald Sutherland 100, 142, 151, 160, 225, 240–1, 285
Graham, Alexander 7, 63, 133, 211, 232, 284
Grand Tour, the 2, 3, 41, 48
Granville, Lord 33
Grasse 45
Gray, Thomas 232, 233
Great Exhibition, the 130
Greece, ancient 60, 65, 116, 117, 120, 181, 197, 199, 228
Greece, modern 2, 9, 11, 29–30, 32, 33, 35, 48, 68, 119, 127, 137, 152, 155, 176, 231; *see also* Athens; Peloponnese
Greek Church 214, 215, 216, 217, 220
Greek Independence, War of 9, 10, 48, 176, 228, 283
Greeks, character of 137, 142, 234, 235, 237, 238
Green, John Richard 4, 46, 74, 84, 95, 124, 135, 141, 144, 146, 148, 151, 198, 215, 270, 285
Gregory XVI, Pope 214
Grenada 21
Grisi, Giulia 231
Grosvenor, Lady Elizabeth 5, 120, 127, 285
Grove, Sir George 193–4
Grüneisen, Charles 230
Guercino 197, 198, 208
guidebooks 49, 70–2; *see also* Baedeker; Murray
Guido *see* Reni, Guido
Guizot, François 64

Haggard, Henry Rider 28, 30, 47–8, 57, 122, 172, 188, 229, 233, 271, 285
Halicarnassus 84
Hannibal 117
Hardy, Thomas 177, 285
Hare, Augustus 4, 66, 80, 150, 173, 174, 178, 200, 201, 209, 286

Hare, Maria 209
Harris, George 49
Harrison, Frederic 19, 45, 66, 154, 170, 171, 173, 178, 180, 209, 260, 265, 272, 286
Hastings, Lady Flora 281
Hawthorne, Nathaniel 39 n., 82
Haydon, Benjamin 118
Haywood, Abel 76
Hazlitt, William 118
Hazor 195
Hebron 122
hemlock 89, 92
Hennen, Dr John 142, 216, 240, 244, 286
Herbert, Marmion 8
Herbert, Lady Mary 84, 134, 147, 286
Herbert, Sidney 286
Hercegovina 97
Herculaneum 169
Herodotus 70, 116
Herriton, Philip 65, 162
Hervey, James 232
Hesperides, the 116
Hewlett, Maurice 97, 98, 142, 144, 145, 171, 173, 174, 221, 286
High Church 55
Hillard, George 42, 64, 68
Hobhouse, Dr Edmund 47, 86, 286
Hobhouse, John Cam 81, 176, 234, 286
Holland, Lord 81
Holy Fire, miracle of 217–18, 220
Holy Land 3, 8, 17, 29, 30, 35, 50, 58, 59, 122, 182–96, 217–18, 241; *see also* Palestine; Syria
Holy Places, the 184
Holy Sepulchre, the 184, 194, 217–18
Homburg 101
homosexuality 100, 102, 159–64, 221
Honeychurch, Lucy 163
Horne, Herbert 79–80, 286
Homer 116, 152
Hosmer, Harriet 118
hotels 265; in Egypt 47, 247; on the Franco-Italian Riviera 2, 17, 43–4, 46, 171; in Italy 41; *see also* pensions
Housman, A. E. 161
Howells, William Dean 17, 65, 77, 105
Howitt, Mary 4, 286
Howitt, William 4, 286
Hughes, Hugh Price 70, 73, 101, 183, 194, 208, 218, 219, 223, 286
Hughes, Mrs Hugh Price 270
Hughes, Thomas 253, 294
humidity 249

Hunt, William Holman 58–9, 125, 186, 191, 287
Huth, Eddie 5
Hutton, Edward 66, 80, 169, 174, 265, 266, 287
Huxley, Thomas 56, 132
Hyères 40, 44, 45, 85, 86, 87, 150, 241

imperialism: British and French 62–4; Italian 240
Imperial Ottoman Bank 288
India 60, 124, 149, 277
Indian Civil Service 60
Inglis, Sir Robert 132
Inquisition, the 200, 215, 223
International Sanitary Conferences 38
invalids 85–96, 243–54
iodine 88
Ionian Islands 47, 91, 120, 121, 217, 234, 243; *see also* Corfu
Iraq 278
iron 92
Irving, Washington 123, 211
Isaiah 190
Ischia 18
Islam, attitudes to 62–3, 147, 210–11
Israel 190
Italy: art and architecture of *see* Christian Art; Renaissance; climate of *see* climatotherapy; cultural decline of 229–31; landscape of 121–3, 126, 127; unification of *see* Risorgimento
Italian Question, the 10
Italians, character of 133, 134–5, 138–48, 234–5, 237, 238–9
Ithaca 152

Jackson, Holbrook 105
Jackson, Dr Robert Scoresby 63, 86, 88, 92, 94, 245, 248, 251, 252, 253, 287
Jaffa 36, 127
James, Henry 65, 86, 105, 209, 288
Jameson, Anna 113, 130, 200, 201, 202, 262, 287
Jameson, Robert 287
Jennings, George 44
Jeremiah 192, 193, 195
Jeremiah's Grotto 184
Jericho 30, 32, 185, 195
'Jericho Fever' 241
Jerusalem 2, 29, 30, 55, 57, 123, 186, 187, 190, 192, 193, 217–18, 220, 272

Jesuits 200, 215, 216, 223
Jesus Christ 123, 187, 194, 221
Jocelyn, Rose 292
Johnson, Dr James 20, 41, 53, 90, 226, 244, 251, 287
Johnson, Dr Samuel 8, 48, 60, 295
Jones, John 76
Jones, Sir William 211
Joshua 195
Journal of Hellenic Studies 83
Jowett, Benjamin 181
Joyce, James 234
Judea 127, 185, 189

Kahn, Florence 105
Kalamata 30
Karpathos 83
Keats, John 9, 72, 81, 118, 127, 149, 281, 290, 297
Keith, Alexander 188, 190–1, 287
Kelman, John 186, 187, 287
Kemble, Fanny 115, 124, 212, 213, 214, 287
Kinglake, Alexander 211, 217, 218, 287
Kings, Second Book of 195
Kingsley, Charles 8, 9, 54, 130, 154, 222, 253, 287
Kipling, Rudyard 163
Knossos 83, 283
Knox, Alexander 63, 172, 244, 287
Koch, Robert 95
Kokalis, George 261
Koran, the 211

Lachish 195
Ladislaw, Will 54, 157–8
Lancet 38, 246
Landor, Walter Savage 10, 103, 108, 287
landscape, response to 121–3, 125–8
Lane, Edward 210, 287
Lang, Robert 137, 146, 288
la Ramée, Louise de *see* Ouida
laudanum, 92, 93
Lavrion 30
Lawley, Alethea 80, 288
Lawrence, David Herbert 12, 13, 97, 106, 119, 123, 125, 150, 156, 174, 267, 268, 273, 288
Lawrence, Thomas 81
Layard, Austen Henry 61, 76, 80, 100, 139, 175–6, 177, 186, 200, 201, 229, 288
lazarettos 36, 37
Lear, Edward 4, 50, 81, 115, 121, 133, 150, 161, 221, 261, 288

Lebanon 113, 193
Lee, Dr Edwin 86, 89, 93, 102, 249, 288
Lee, Vernon 12, 60, 66, 79, 150, 288
Leghorn 22, 35
Leighton, Frederic 81, 113, 114, 119, 150, 181, 202, 229, 277, 288
Leonardo da Vinci 197
Leoncavallo, Ruggiero 230
Leopold, Prince 87
Lerici 119, 123
Leucaspide 118
Lever, Charles 4, 74, 103, 107, 113, 170, 231, 288
Lewes, George Henry 19, 21, 133, 155, 231, 283, 288
Lewis, John 150, 288
Libya *see* Tripoli
Lindsay, Lord 175, 185, 187, 204–7, 289
Lindsay, Dr James Alexander 90, 94, 247, 250, 251–2, 289
Lisbon 85
Lismore, Lady *see* Butler, Lady Eleanor
Little Dorrit 124
Lippi, Fra Filippo 200, 207
Livy 116
Lombardy 34, 126, 234
London Society for the Promotion of Christianity among the Jews (London Jewish Society) 192
Lowell, James Russell 72, 75
Lucca, 4, 18, 103, 105, 175, 200, 262
luggage 27–8
Luther, Martin 55
Luxor 119
Lycia 83
Lyon 26
Lytton, Bulwer, Lady 113
Lytton, Edward George, Lord 121, 126, 149, 220, 289
Lytton, Edward Robert Bulwer, Lord 102, 289

Macaulay, Thomas Babington, Lord 123, 197, 198, 223, 225, 259, 289, 295
Mackenzie, Compton 7
Macmillan, publisher 32, 50, 63, 100, 101
McTavish, Nelson 279
Madden, Dr Thomas More 21, 22, 48, 85, 86, 88, 90, 136, 289
Madeira 85
Mahaffy, John Pentland 70, 120, 142, 144, 176, 289
Maine, Henry Sumner 4, 289

Majorca 135, 137, 253, 266
Malaga 21, 23, 48–9, 85, 86, 87, 93, 241, 250
malaria 88, 242–3
Mallock, William 50, 96, 97, 123, 129, 150, 153, 233, 266, 269–70, 289
Malta 23, 35, 36, 37, 47, 85, 86, 91, 142, 251, 269, 277
Malthus, Thomas 238
Manchester Town Hall 76
Mann, Thomas 240, 241
Mannerists 197, 201
Manning, Henry 20, 72, 200, 225, 286, 289
Mantegna, Andrea 200
Mantua 232
Marathon massacre 32–3
Marcet, Dr William 87, 88, 289
Marco, Alessandro di 125
Mario, Alberto 11
marriages, Anglo-Italian 262–3
Marsala 36
Marseilles 22, 26, 35, 36, 218
Martineau, Harriet 183, 247
Marzials, Theo 161, 289
Mascagni, Pietro 230
Maugham, Henry Neville 70, 289
Maugham, William Somerset 7, 70, 97, 98, 115, 122, 161, 208, 264, 290
Mazzara 127
Mazzini, Giuseppe 138, 240
Meagles, Mr 37, 74
Medicis, the 236, 237
Medici Venus 117
Meduna, Battista 178
Medway 37
Meiklam, Robert 296
Melba, Nellie 231
Memmi, Simone 200
mendicancy 222
Menton 4, 26, 40, 44, 45, 46, 85, 86, 87, 93, 95, 107, 123, 137, 170, 251, 252, 260, 278
mercury 88
Meredith, George 10, 79, 140, 154, 236, 247, 285, 290, 292
Meredith, Owen *see* Lytton, Edward Robert
Mesopotamia 184, 185–7, 192, 194
Messageries Impériales 24
Messina 98
Mestre 172
Metastasio 145
Metropolitan Tabernacle 46, 294
Meyerbeer, Giacomo 230
miasmatic theory of disease 38, 241

Michaelangelo 197, 198, 199, 201, 205
Milan 98, 106, 138, 141, 200, 201, 242, 243
Mill, Harriet 124, 128, 290
Mill, John Stuart 88, 89, 99, 116, 119, 121, 124, 127, 128, 157, 177, 197, 198, 236–7, 290
Milnes, Richard Monckton 5, 39, 68, 87, 102, 106–7, 211, 290
Minghetti, Donna Laura 143
Moab 190, 191
models, artists' 81, 118, 125
Modena 34, 139
Monaco 26, 87, 252
Monastir 115
Moncrieff, A. R. Hope 87
Montalembert, Comte de 203
Mont Cenis pass 21, 26, 29
Mont Cenis tunnel 27
Monte Carlo 2, 44, 101, 252
Montefiore, Sir Moses 193
Montenegro 97
Montesuelo 11
Montpellier 94
Monypenny, William 208
Morea *see* Peloponnese
Morley, John 56
Morning Chronicle 230
Morning Post 231, 290, 295
Morocco 64
Morris, William 124, 178, 179, 280
Mount Athos 221
Mount Hymettus 120
Mount of Olives 123, 187, 189
Mount Pentelicus 66, 122
Mount Tabor 30
Muller, Max 60, 61, 181
Munich 99, 106
Murano 218
Murillo, Bartolomé 199, 296
Murphy, Dennis 287
Murray, John 49, 70, 71, 80
Murray's Handbooks 70–2, 297; cited 29–30, 32, 33, 36, 68–9, 108, 175, 242, 243, 264, 269
Musset, Alfred de 168, 179
Mycenae 179
Myron 118
Mytilene 83

Nablus 30, 122
Napier, Robert 76
Naples 4, 18, 34, 35, 41, 42, 85, 87, 93, 95, 99, 100, 102, 108, 113, 115, 140, 141, 219, 239, 241, 242
Napoleon I: 21, 48
Napoleon III: 262
National Gallery 82, 279, 283
National Illustrated Library 62
National Vigilance Association 159
Naucides 118
Nazareth 30, 172
Nazzari 43
Neapolitans, character of 140, 238, 268
Nehemiah 193
Nelson, Thomas 192
Newcome, Clive 227, 262
Newman, Francis 56, 185
Newman, John Henry 35, 67, 102, 125, 136, 152, 197, 198, 219, 220, 224, 227, 233, 240, 281, 283, 290
newspapers, English 41, 45
Newton, Charles 83, 84, 137, 290
Nice 2, 17, 20, 40, 43, 45, 85, 86, 87, 93, 94, 101, 250, 252
Nicosia 123, 150
Nightingale, Florence 77, 199
Nile 2, 3, 13, 23, 84, 119, 247
Nimrud 61, 192
Nineveh 61, 62, 186, 190, 192
North, Catherine *see* Symonds, Catherine
North, Frederick 37, 290
North, Marianne 29, 30, 37, 86, 105, 119, 290

Observer 296
Oliphant, Margaret 57, 291
olive trees 8, 123
Omar Khayyám 60
opera 230–1
Orford, Lady 104
orientalism 211
Orvieto 123, 200, 201
Otter, Robert 24, 32, 291
Ouida 4, 7, 103–4, 118, 124, 125, 126, 134, 135, 145–6, 173, 238, 239, 291
Outram, Sir James 247
overland route 47
Oxford Movement 224, 284, 290
ozone 88

Padua 200
Paestum 116, 136, 242
Paget, Violet *see* Lee, Vernon
Palazzo Albani 108

Palazzo Gondi 79
Palermo 32, 38, 138, 242, 250
Palestine 5, 6, 8, 11, 32, 49, 50, 57, 58, 59, 84, 97, 123, 127, 171, 264; *see also* Holy Land
Palestine Exploration Fund 193–5, 297
Palgrave, Sir Francis 71, 175, 200, 291
Pall Mall Gazette 171, 241
Palmer, Samuel 107, 291
Palmerston, Viscount 10, 64
Pan 163
Papacy, the 173–4, 212–15, 236, 272
Papal States 34
Paris 2, 3, 4, 209, 242, 262, 278
parlatorios 36
Parma 36, 139, 201, 232
Parthenon, the 117, 118
Pasqualino, Marchioness 262
passports 33–5
Pasteur, Louis 38, 95
Pater, Walter 202, 209
patriotism 53, 140, 270–4
Patterson, Dr John 90, 251, 291
Patti, Adelena 231
Pausanius 70, 267
Pavia 200
Peard, Col. 11
Peel, Sir Robert 76
Peloponnese 33, 116, 120, 124, 174, 181
penicillin 95
Peninsula and Oriental Steam Navigation Company 23, 24
pensions, English 41; *see also* hotels
Pericles 116, 117
Perring, John 61, 291, 295
Perugia 80, 200
Perugino 200, 203
Petra 190
Petrarch 145
Petrie, Flinders 33 n., 61, 283, 291
Phaethon 163
Phidias 61, 116, 117, 119, 120
Philistia 190
Phillip, John 150, 291
Phillips, L. March 209
Phillips, Sir Thomas 76
phlebotomy 92
Phoebus, Gaston 288
photography 82, 191
Piedmont 34, 228
pirates 31
Pisa 67, 80, 85, 93, 94, 95, 102, 106, 152, 175, 200, 201, 205, 208, 232, 241, 244, 253

Pisani, Countess 262
Pisanus Fraxi 277
plague 35, 38
Plato 116
Playfair, Robert Lambert 63, 291
pleurisy 90
pneumonia 90
Poggio Gherado 79
pollution, atmospheric 151
Pompeii 159, 229
Pontifex, George 65
Porto Torres 29
post, travel by 19–20
Potter, Beatrice 225, 292
Poussin, Gaspard 121
Poussin, Nicholas 121
poverty 237–8
Praxiteles 61, 117, 118
Pre-Raphaelite Brotherhood 191, 287; *see also* Hunt, William Holman
Priene 83
Proctor, Adelaide 287
Promenade des Anglais 101
prostitution 81, 161, 261
protection money 33
Prussia 228
Puccini, Giacomo 230
Pugin, Augustus 203, 205, 207
Pullan, Richard 83, 84, 292
Pyramids, the 61, 170, 172, 247, 295

quarantine 35–8
Quarantine Act (1825) 37, 38
Quarterly Review 175, 201
quinine 88, 92, 243

railways 25–9, 30, 98, 259
Raincock, Miss 105
Ramadge, Dr 89
Ranke, Leopold von 223
Rapallo 106
Raphael 175, 177, 197, 198, 199, 201
Ravenna 98
Rawlinson, Henry 61
Reade, Winwood 259–60
Reformation, the 223
Regulus 117
Reid, Thomas Wemyss 24, 269, 292
Religious Census 132, 183
Renaissance, the 65, 197, 199–207, 236–7
Reni, Guido 197, 198
residents, British 18, 40, 78, 102–6

restoration, of buildings and pictures 176–8

retrenchment, as a motive for expatriation 106–8

rheumatism 95, 244

Rhine 2, 18

Rhodes 84, 137, 232, 240

Rhône 22

Richmond, George 81

Richmond, William 81, 113, 114, 125, 145, 151, 292

Ricketts, Mrs 103

Rio, Alexis 203, 205, 207

Ripon, Lord 178, 292

Risorgimento 9–11, 32, 98, 137–40, 228, 234, 239, 240

Riviera, the 2, 17, 22, 39, 40, 43, 84, 86–7, 99, 101, 108–9, 123, 137, 170, 241, 243, 247, 250, 251; *see also* Beaulieu; Bordighera; Cannes; Cornice; Grasse; Hyères; Menton; Nice; San Remo

Robbia, Luca della 79

Roberts, David 58, 150, 292

Roberts, Richard 142, 239, 212

Robertson, Dr 223

Robinson, Dr Edward 184

Rogers, Samuel 232, 273

Rolfe, Frederick 4, 7, 104–5, 161, 279, 292

Roman Catholic Church 146, 148, 173, 212–27

Romanesque architecture 201, 204, 207

'Roman Fever' 242

Roman Herald 41

Roman Republic 138

Romanticism 9, 179–80, 196, 224

Roman Times 41

Rome, ancient 60, 62, 64, 65, 197, 228, 236

Rome, modern 4, 18, 35, 37, 39, 41–3, 66, 71, 72–3, 81–2, 85, 87, 93, 95, 99, 100, 102, 105, 108, 113, 116, 135, 139, 143, 155, 167, 168, 173–4, 176, 178, 192, 197–8, 229, 232, 233–4, 241–2, 252, 254, 261

Rosa, Salvator 9, 178, 208

Ross, Henry 292

Ross, Janet 79, 104, 118, 122, 247, 292

Rossetti, Dante Gabriel 280, 282, 287

Rossini, Gioacchino 230

Royal Academy 59, 82, 283, 288

Royal College of Physicians 38

Royal Italian Opera 230

Royal Society for the Prevention of Cruelty to Animals 239

Ruins of Sacred and Historic Lands 192

Ruskin, Effie 18, 107, 222, 292

Ruskin, John 2, 13, 14, 54, 56, 59, 65, 80, 98, 107, 108, 113, 118, 123, 126, 145, 147, 150, 151–2, 154, 167, 168–9, 170, 172, 175, 176, 177, 178, 179, 182, 186, 191, 202–10, 212, 218, 222, 223, 225, 226, 233, 235, 236, 254–5, 262, 279, 280, 292

Ruskin, John, senior 76

Russell, Lord John 10

Russia 249

Russia, Empress of 86

Rutherford, Mark 129

Sahara 247

St Augustine 227

St Gotthard: pass 21, 27; tunnel 27

St Moritz 246

St Paul's Cathedral 151, 198, 292

St Peter's (Rome) 70, 72, 73, 115, 197, 201–2, 212, 214, 226–7

Saint-Saens, Camille 214

Sala, George Augustus 3, 11, 21, 26, 41, 42, 65, 212–13, 216, 220, 225, 226, 293

Salamis 233

Salting, George 76

Salvation Army 133

Samaria 122, 127, 185, 186, 187–8, 190

Samos 83

Samuel 195

San Carlo Opera 100

San Damiano 178

San Gimignano 200

sanitation 44, 241

San Lorenzo (Florence) 201

San Marco (Venice) 177, 178, 182, 197, 200, 223

San Remo 4, 17, 44, 45, 46, 86, 87, 93, 95, 126, 241, 251, 252, 288

San Rocco (Venice) 205

Sant' Agnello 217

Santa Croce (Florence) 208

Santa Croce, Princess 262

Saône 22

Saqqara 5

Sardinia 29

Sarto, Andrea del 79

Savonarola 147, 237

Sbeitla 233

Schliemann, Heinrich 179

Schopenhauer, Arthur 158

science, as an aid to religious belief 191

Scott, Geoffrey 209

Scott, Leader *see* Baxter, Lucy
Scott, Walter 211
scrofula 244
Scully, Dr 95
Sechem 122
Selwood, Anne 296
Senior, Nassau 38, 64, 213, 229, 293
Sermoneta, Duchess of 262
Sermoneta, Duke of 64
Seven Churches of Asia 190
Severn, Joseph 81, 293
Seville 48, 201
Seymour, Revd Michael 215, 216, 220, 221, 226, 293
sewers 241
Sforza-Cesarini, Duchess of 262
Shaftesbury, Lord 43, 138, 141, 191–2, 214, 235, 293
Shaw, George Bernard 4, 78, 163
Sheepshanks, John 76
Shelley, Mary 134, 136, 146, 172, 234, 287, 293
Shelley, Percy Bysshe 9, 72, 82, 102, 170, 241, 293
Shiloh 189
Sicilians, character of 134, 140
Sicily 11, 23, 29, 31, 84, 98, 113, 121, 125, 139, 197, 240, 242; *see also* Girgenti; Paestum; Palermo; Syracuse; Taormina
Sidgwick, Henry 132
Sidon 190
Siena 18, 106, 168, 197, 200, 201, 202, 207, 232
sight-seeing 72–3
Sillano 153
Simplon: pass 21, 27, 255; tunnel 27
Sinai 47, 255
Sistine Chapel 199, 201, 212
Smith, George Adam 127, 195, 293
Smith, Lancelot 9
Smyrna 23, 36, 115, 122, 217, 273
Smyth, Ethel 66, 97, 143, 293
Social Darwinism 129, 238
Society for the Promotion of Hellenic Studies 290
Society for the Protection of Ancient Buildings 178, 180
Society for the Protection of the Monuments of Ancient Egypt 5
Society of Dilettanti 82, 83
Society of the Friends of Italy 10
Solomon, Simeon 161, 293

Somerset, Lord Henry 159
Somerville, Mary 4, 139, 293
Sophocles 116
Sorrento 18, 118, 119, 155, 168, 217, 218
souvenirs 6
Spain 21, 48, 122, 142, 171, 223, 228, 235; *see also* Barcelona; Cordova; Grenada; Malaga; Seville
Spaniards, character of 133–4, 136, 142, 146, 235, 264
Sparks, Dr Edward 44, 46, 90, 101, 109, 243, 252, 260, 293
Spencer, Edmund 34, 43, 222, 225, 293
Spencer, Herbert 7, 129, 150, 154, 234, 294
Spengler, Dr Alexander 246
Spezia 103
Sphinx, the 5, 168
Spillman 43
Spinoza 157
Spurgeon, Charles 46, 101, 123, 192, 212, 217, 294
Spurgeon, Thomas 46
Stangate Creek 37
Stanley, Arthur Penrhyn 32, 57, 115, 122, 152, 173, 188–90, 195, 197, 218, 220, 225, 235, 236, 294
Starke, Marianna 71
steamships 22–5, 259
Stendhal 70, 73
Stephen, James Fitzjames 129
Stephen, Leslie 10, 56, 154, 253
Stevenson, Robert Louis 95, 107, 115, 281, 294
Stisted, Charlotte 103, 294
Strachey, Lytton 55
streptomycin 95
Stuttgart 106
Styx 267, 271
Suez Canal 47, 269
Sully, James 8, 27, 68, 261, 294
sulphonamides 95
suntan 123–4
Susa Terminus 29
Sutton, Dr H. G 89
Sweden 249
Swinburne, Algernon 10, 99, 140, 202, 290
Switzerland 2, 18, 25, 160, 222, 246, 248, 250–1, 254–5; *see also* Davos Platz; St Moritz; Zermatt
Symonds, Catherine 32, 254, 290
Symonds, John Addington 4, 6, 13, 14, 32, 55, 60, 80, 97, 98, 113, 114, 116, 123, 126, 145, 147, 151, 155, 159–60, 168, 197, 199–

200, 202, 210, 212, 223, 225, 236, 237, 241, 243, 246, 254, 261, 263–4, 279, 294

Symonds (subsequently Furse), Katherine 161 and n.

Symonds, Margaret 126, 241

Symons, Arthur 167

syphilis 88

Syracuse 36, 116, 164, 235, 242, 270

Syria 58, 59, 97, 125, 184, 185

Syros 23, 36

Taormina 114

Taranto 118

Taunton Commission 75

Taylor, Dr Coupland 94, 95, 245, 294

Taylor, Harriet *see* Mill, Harriet

Taylor, Revd Issac 135, 137, 143, 147, 294

Temple of Solomon 194

Tennyson, Alfred Lord 128, 149, 179–80, 208, 278, 284, 296

Tennyson, Frederick 263

Teos 83

Terry, Ellen 281

Tetrazzini, Luisa 231

Thackeray, Anne 168, 294

Thackeray, William 7, 74, 81, 115, 121, 122, 170, 171, 185, 197, 201, 211, 214, 220, 227, 238, 261, 272, 273, 294

Thasos 83

Theocritus 116

Times, The 29, 139, 284, 287

Thessaly 30

Thomson, Revd Andrew 171, 187–8, 193, 294

Thring, Edward 208, 295

Thucydides 70, 116

Tidey, Dr Stuart 28

Timgad 234

Tintoretto 198, 199, 207

Titian 197, 198, 199, 207

Tocqueville, Alexis de 131

Todd, Miss 78

Torlonia, Prince 261

Torrijos, José 10

tourism 67–78, 169–71, 195, 260, 265; *see also* Cook, Thomas

Toynbee Hall 133, 277

Toynbee Hall Travellers' Club 70

Toynbee Workmen's Travelling Club 2

train bleu 26

transport, revolution in 18–30, 274; *see also* automobiles; railways; steamships

Trant, Abercromby 127, 216, 295

travel books 11–12

Trench, Richard Chenevix 10, 53, 209, 270, 294

Trevelyan, George Macaulay 66, 98, 140, 215, 240, 294

Trieste 4, 23, 288

Trinity College, Cambridge 281

Trinity College, Dublin 289

Tripoli 50, 240

Tristram, Revd Henry 58, 188, 196, 295

Troad, the 83

Trodos Mountains 123

Trollope, Anthony 1, 2, 7, 49–50, 77, 99, 187, 267, 295

Trollope, Frances 126, 198, 212, 295

Trollope, Thomas 103, 136, 144, 148, 262, 295

Trollope family 107

tuberculosis 86, 88–96, 243–55

Tunis 24, 50, 241, 282

Tunisia 50, 63, 64, 116, 133, 233; *see also* Carthage; Tunis

Turin 200, 219, 222

Turkey, 31, 33, 34, 35, 228; *see also* Albania; Anatolia; Balkans; Constantinople; Holy Land; Lebanon; Palestine; Syria

Turks, character of 133

Turner, J. M. W. 81, 150, 207, 296

Tuscan Athanaeum 41

Tuscans, character of 134

Tuscany 34, 126, 134, 139; *see also* Florence; Lucca; Pisa

typhoid 241

Tyre 186, 188, 190, 228, 233

Uffizi, Gallery of the 65, 208

Ultramontanes 272, 289

United Kingdom Alliance 130

Unprotected Females in Sicily, Calabria, and on the Top of Mount Etna 31

Uppingham School 295

Ur 195

Utica 83

vaccination 95

Valetta 36, 85, 241, 269

Vallombrosa 43

vandalism 4–6, 175–9

Vatican, the 70, 73, 175, 201

Vatican Hermes, the 118

Vavasour, Mr 290

Velásquez 284, 296

Venetia 8, 234; *see also* Venice

Venice 2, 4, 17, 35, 41, 77, 80, 87, 113, 138, 155, 160, 161, 167, 169, 172–3, 176, 177, 198, 199, 200, 201, 205, 206, 207, 208, 222, 232, 233, 235, 236, 241, 242, 262
Venice Sanitary Conference 38
Ventimiglia 26
Venus di Milo 118
Verdi, Giuseppe 231
Vere, Aubrey de 120, 170, 203, 210, 215, 220, 225, 226, 282
Verona 113, 200
Veronese, Paolo 197, 198, 207
Vesuvius 121, 159
vetture 19
Viareggio 104
Vicary, Revd M. 198, 214, 216–17, 218, 221, 226, 295
Vicenza 200
Victor Emmanuel, King 139
Victoria, Queen 2, 86, 87, 93, 281
Victorianism 275
Villa Farinola 104
Villa Il Palmerino 79
Villari, Pasquale 262
Villiers, Mrs 203
Virgil 62, 116
visas 33, 34, 35
Vivian, Herbert 116–17, 146, 172, 233, 295
voituriers 18
voiturins 19
Volterra 200
Vyse, Cecil 163
Vyse, Richard 61, 295

Wade, Miss 78
Wagner, Richard 230, 231
wagon-lits 26
Walker, Frederick 133, 142, 152, 296
Walshe, Walter 248
Warburton, Eliot 12, 57, 122, 185, 187, 211, 218, 231, 268, 296
Warren, Capt. Charles 193
Waterfield, Aubrey 296
Waterfield, Lina *see* Gordon, Lina Duff
Watts, George Frederic 20, 81, 82, 119, 125, 150, 202, 277, 296
Webb, Beatrice *see* Potter, Beatrice
Weber, Hermann 249

Weil, Taddeo 288
Weld, Charles 43, 197, 212, 296
Wellington College 56
Wells, H. G. 163
Wesley, John and Charles 55
West, Rebecca 273
Westmacott, Richard 117
Whig philosophy 234
Whistler, James McNeil 280
White, Jessie 11
Whitefield, George 55
Whiteside, James 39, 40, 108, 145, 215, 219, 243, 296
Whitman, Walt 160
Wiesbaden 101, 106
Wilde, Oscar 79, 100, 102, 113, 124, 153, 159, 161, 163, 278, 282, 296
Wilde, William 5, 37, 86, 147, 188, 218, 232, 296
Wilkie, Sir David 4, 58, 150, 191, 296
Wilkinson, Sir John Gardner 23–4, 97, 296
Williams, Dr Charles Theodore 39, 249, 252–3, 297
Williams, Penry 37, 81, 297
Wilson, Col. Sir Charles 187, 297
Winckelmann, Johann 117, 181
Wiseman, Nicholas 224
women tourists 77–8, 271
Wood, Charles 253–4, 266, 297
Wood, Mrs Henry 60, 253, 297
Woolf, Virginia 161 n.
Woolley, Leonard 195
Wordsworth, Revd Christopher 66–7, 148, 214, 219, 228, 233, 297
Wordsworth, William 67, 73, 106, 197, 297
Working Men's College 282
Wyatt, Richard 81
Wyse, Sir Thomas 216, 297

Xanthus 83

yellow fever 38
Yeo, Dr Burney 54, 246, 252, 297
Young, Dr David 39, 73, 242, 251

Zephaniah 186
Zermatt 99
Zorzi, Count 182

MORE OXFORD PAPERBACKS

Details of a selection of other books follow. A complete list of Oxford Paperbacks, including The World's Classics, Twentieth-Century Classics, OPUS, Past Masters, Oxford Authors, Oxford Shakespeare, and Oxford Paperback Reference, is available in the UK from the General Publicity Department, Oxford University Press (JN), Walton Street, Oxford OX2 6DP.

In the USA, complete lists are available from the Paperbacks Marketing Manager, Oxford University Press, 200 Madison Avenue, New York, NY 10016.

Oxford Paperbacks are available from all good bookshops. In case of difficulty, customers in the UK can order direct from Oxford University Press Bookshop, 116 High Street, Oxford, Freepost, OX1 4BR, enclosing full payment. Please add 10 per cent of published price for postage and packing.

FRANCE 1848–1945:

Intellect and Pride

Theodore Zeldin

In what ways are Frenchmen different from other human beings? Zeldin investigates here the ideas they have had about themselves, their attitudes to foreigners, their peculiar habits as travellers, the nature of their nationalism, the significance of being a Breton or an Alsation, a Provençal or an Auvergnat.

To what extent have the French been fashioned by their schools to think, argue and express themselves in ways that are unique? Zeldin examines their teaching methods at all levels, their cultivation of logic, verbalism and competitiveness, their desperate fights against the rebelliousness of their pupils, the chaos of university life.

'The most perspicacious, the most deeply researched, the liveliest and the most enthralling panorama of French passions.' *Paris Match*

'By general agreement, it is one of the outstanding works of history of our generation.' *BBC World Service*

LITTLE DORRIT

Charles Dickens

Edited by Harvey Peter Sucksmith

Highly regarded today as one of the greatest novels in English literature, *Little Dorrit*, first published during 1855–7, the turbulent period of the Crimean War, presents both a scathing indictment of mid-Victorian England and a devastating insight into the human condition. Examining the many social and mental prisons which incarcerate men and women, the novel also considers the nature of true spiritual freedom. Against a background of administrative and financial scandal, Dickens tells the moving story of the old Marshalsea prisoner who inherits a fortune and his devoted daughter's love for a man who believes he has done with love. He draws widely on the events of his own life and times, yet focuses a powerful imaginative vision which is as organic and universal as it is specific, immediate and intense. The author displays his characteristic mastery of irony and pathos, of satire and comedy, and the book contains some of his most mature, ambitious and effective writing.

FRANCE 1848–1945:

Ambition and Love

Theodore Zeldin

Ambition and Love, containing the first two sections of Zeldin's outstanding *France 1848–1945,* offers an entertaining, brilliantly original picture of French society. 'Ambition' deals with the aspirations, pretensions and illusions of different sections of French society. The author overturns many commonly accepted generalizations about France; class conflict, 'the bug held responsible for so many of society's ailments', is placed under the microscope, with surprising results.

'Love' is about the attitudes of parents to their children, of husbands to their wives, of women to their place in society. The tensions beneath the facade of family life, the weakness of the movement for female suffrage, the vigour of prostitution and pornography, and the private world of the child are investigated.

'Masterpieces of the historian's art are rare in any generation. Zeldin's *France* belongs in that category. It is a stunning achievement, a monument of scholarship.' *Times Literary Supplement*

A SENTIMENTAL JOURNEY

with The Journal to Eliza and A Political Romance

Laurence Sterne

This book is far removed from the conventional travel book, and is fiction rather than reportage. Sterne travelled extensively in the 1760s, and drew on his experiences to write the narrative of Mr. Yorick, the Sentimental Traveller. The Journal to Eliza and A Political Romance both demonstrate the rare early satire which marked the beginning of the major phase of Sterne's career.

The World's Classics

FRANCE 1848–1945:

Politics and Anger

Theodore Zeldin

Politics and Anger is about France's illusions and passions. It surveys the emotions, the ideologies, and the social pressures that lay behind the fragmentation of parties. It presents a multitude of portraits, written with both sympathy and irony, of the individuals who led the country's turbulent internal battles. The author shows how the confusions surrounding these have been partly created by the intellectuals, whose interpretations he pulls apart.

'so fluent and lively that it carries the reader effortlessly along. Zeldin's book is truly a work of genius.' *New Republic*

'a masterpiece' *New York Times* and *TLS*

'one of the most important books ever written about French civilisation' *Le Monde*

'probably the most remarkable social history of a modern European nation which has yet been written' *Sunday Telegraph*

PEOPLE AND PLACES

Richard Cobb

This collection of twenty-two articles and reviews from Professor Cobb's multifarious output over the last ten years includes recollections of old University friends—Jack Gallagher, Arthur Marder, and Christopher Hill—as well as less personal essays on authors and historians, such as Pierre Loti and Georges Simenon.

'Richard Cobb has always been a historian of the worm's-eye-view and the grass roots. This collection shows off his virtues admirably . . . A love of his friends and of ordinary people shines through the fun.' Philip Howard in *The Times*

THE EUROPEANS

Henry James

Edited with an Introduction by
Ian Campbell Ross

Eugenia, Baroness Munster, wife of a German princeling who wishes to be rid of her, crosses the ocean with her brother Felix to seek out their American relatives. Their voyage is prompted—so Eugenia says—by natural affection; but the Baroness has also come to seek her fortune. The advent of these visitors is viewed by the Wentworths, in the suburbs of Boston, with wonder and some apprehension. The head of the family advises: 'we must all be careful. This is a great change; we are exposed to peculiar influences.'

Of these, not the least alarming is the fascination exerted by the brilliant Eugenia on her impressionable cousins and their more wordly neighbour, Robert Acton. While Eugenia seems set permanently to unsettle them all, Felix, painter of trifling sketches, would diffuse among his hosts a healing charm. Easing them in and out of various amorous complications, he has, as one might say of the novel itself, 'no fear of not being, in the end, agreeable'.

The World's Classics

DUMAS ON FOOD

Translated by Alan and Jane Davidson

Alexandre Dumas *père* is perhaps best known as the author of *The Three Musketeers*. However, it was for his *Grand Dictionnaire de Cuisine*, published posthumously in 1873, that Dumas himself particularly wished to be remembered.

Alan and Jane Davidson have selected and translated those pieces from the *Dictionnaire* that clearly represent Dumas at his best. The result is a readable and informative dictionary of culinary terms, recipes, and anecdotes which retain all the colour and delight of Dumas's original work.

'Splendid book . . . endlesssly interesting'
Alan Forrest in *Financial Times*

FABLED SHORE

From the Pyrenees to Portugal

Rose Macaulay

With a New Introduction by Raymond Carr

Fabled Shore is the classic account of Rose Macaulay's travels in 1949 along the Catalonian, Valencian, Andalucian, and Algarve shores, from the Pyrenees to Portugal.

Touring alone by car, the author visited major coastal towns, and many minor ones, delighting in the splendours of Spanish History which she found displayed everywhere along the coast. As she says, 'Spain grows Roman walls and basilicas and tenth-century churches like wild figs, leaving them about in the most careless and arrogant profusion, uncharted and unattended, for travellers to stumble on as they will.'

Following previous travellers, from the fourth-century Avienus to the more recent Richard Ford and the inevitable Baedecker, Rose Macaulay draws comparisons with, and makes distinctions between, their observations and her own. In her characteristically elegant style, she points out the ways in which Spain has changed, and, often more interestingly, the ways in which it has not.

FRANCE 1848–1945:

Taste and Corruption

Theodore Zeldin

Taste and Corruption looks, in an entirely new way, at France's *joie de vivre*. It is indispensable for both travellers and students who wish to understand better her painting, her good and bad novels, her cinema, the chic of her fashions, the subtleties of her food and wine, the sensationalism of her press, the sarcasm and sentimentality of her singers, the passion for good living, the unique flavour of French laughter, but also the doubts and disputes that torment the French behind the façade they present.

'The world's foremost authority on Frenchness.' *Time Magazine*

'One of the major historical works of our collective lifetime . . . brilliantly stimulating.' *The Listener*

'The most enjoyable book of its kind in nearly forty years.' *New Statesman*

TEMPLES AND ELEPHANTS

Travels in Siam in 1881–1882

Carl Bock

Carl Bock was an indefatigable traveller. Having written an account of his journeyings in Borneo and Sumatra, in 1881–2 he made another remarkable expedition, this time on the South-East Asian Mainland. The account of his journey—from Bangkok to that area to the north between Burma, Laos and Thailand known today as the Golden Triangle—is the subject of this book.

With vivid detail and telling anecdote the author describes his passage to the north, how he became a target for superstitous villagers, the dangerous moments and shabby treatment he endured at the hands of truculent officials, despite travelling under Royal auspices. He saw much of the life and culture of the countryside, the homes of the peasants and the palaces of Bangkok. In short he restores to life the old Siam as seen through the eyes of a percipient European adventurer in the last quarter of the nineteenth century. The clear, unpretentious style of his writing makes it as exciting to read today as it was when first published a century ago.

AN ENGLISHWOMAN IN INDIA

Harriet Tytler

Edited by Anthony Sattin
With an Introduction by Philip Mason

On 11 May 1857, mutiny broke out in Delhi and Harriet Tytler, eight months pregnant with two children to look after, was forced to flee from the city. Yet when her husband, Captain Robert Tytler, returned to Delhi, she went with him, and for the next three months was the 'only lady' present at the so-called Siege of Delhi, sharing the dangers faced by the soldiers.

This is her story, not just the Siege of Delhi, but also of her childhood and travels in India and England: the record of a courageous, endearing, remarkable woman.

'extraordinarily vivid . . . should appeal to every type of reader'
British Book News

A TALE FROM BALI

Vicki Baum

When Vicki Baum, best known as the writer of *Grand Hotel* and *The Weeping Wood*, visited Bali in 1935 she met Dr Fabius, an old Dutch resident with an unrivalled knowledge of Balinese life. On his death a year later he bequeathed Vicki Baum various papers, including the draft of a novel on which this book is based.

A Tale From Bali highlights a historical event known in the Balinese history as 'Puputan'—'The End'—and embraces the years 1904 to 1906, beginning with the alleged looting of the wreck of the chinese ship from Surabaya off the coast of Sanur (which the Dutch used as a pretext for intervention in the island's affairs) and ending with the battle of Badung, where wave after wave of Balinese, clothed in white, adorned with flowers, and 'set on death' charged the Dutch guns, *Kris* in hand.

First published in English in 1937, *A Tale From Bali* is a free rendering of actual events seen from the Balinese point of view. More important, it is also a remarkably vivid portrayal of the character of the Balinese, their customs and way of life.

THE HOLY LAND

An Archaeological Guide from Earliest times to 1700

Second Edition

Jerome Murphy-O'Connor

Concise, readable, and wittily erudite, this guide is an ideal companion for those who intend to go and see for themselves. It presupposes little knowledge of history or archaeology. The second edition has been completely revised and updated.

ABROAD

British Literary Travelling Between the Wars

Paul Fussell

A literary and cultural study of the period between the two
world wars in which Paul Fussell distinguishes between yesterday's 'travel' and today's 'tourism'. He contends that genuine
travel is a lost art. His book is both an elegy for this art and
a celebration of British writers who, in their travel books,
memorialized that last age of real travel.

'an exemplary piece of criticism. It is immensely readable. It
bristles with ideas . . . It admits a whole area of writing—at
last!—to its proper place in literary history.' Jonathan Raban,
Quarto

'All readers interested in the period between the wars and the
art of travelling will derive great pleasure from *Abroad.*'
Michael Ratcliffe, *The Times*

TRAVELS THROUGH FRANCE AND ITALY

Tobias Smollett

Edited by Frank Felsenstein

In 1763 Tobias Smollett left England for the Mediterranean.
Though claiming to have no quarrel with the French and the
Italians he criticized everything from the food ('I . . . abominate
garlick') to the 'shockingly nasty' beds and the local inhabitants
of Nice where he settled.

Not surprisingly, the *Travels* became notorious and Smollett
was ridiculed by Laurence Sterne as 'the learned Smelfungus'.
Yet his learning shows to good effect, whether he describes
the culture of silk-worms, the French tax system, or the marbles
of Florence, Smollett provides many an insight into eighteenth-
century taste and into his cantankerous perceptive and intelligent personality. This edition includes a letter of Smollett published for the first time.

'any reader of this edition of his *Travels* . . . will be amused,
horrified and aghast—aghast at Smollett (sometimes) as well
as at the French of the eighteenth-century (some of them)'
Country Life

The World's Classics

THE HEAD-HUNTERS OF BORNEO

Carl Bock

Despite its sensational title, Carl Bock's account of his travels in the 1870s in both Borneo and Sumatra covers much more than the well-known head-hunting pursuits of the Dayaks. Commissioned by the Dutch colonial authorities to make a journey into the little-explored districts of West Borneo, Bock proved to be a keen observer not only of the way of life of the peoples of the interior but also their titular Malay overlords and of various aspects of colonial life. Similarly Bock's descriptions of his journeys in Sumatra, portray vividly scenes of contemporary life and society in an era of Dutch expansion along with observations on the flora and fauna. In fact *The Head-Hunters of Borneo* was a pioneer amongst books on Borneo and its inhabitants, and although many have travelled and observed in that island since Bock's account was published, his book still holds pride of place in terms of originality and interest. Written in a clear and unpretentious style, this remarkable volume is further enhanced by a collection of extremely fine colour plates.

FRANCE 1848–1945:

Anxiety and Hypocrisy

Theodore Zeldin

What made French people lonely, self-conscious, worried, bored, hysterical, violent and have more or fewer children? How did they behave as soldiers, colonists and criminals? How can one make sense of their religious and political squabbling? This volume is indispensable to all who are interested not only in France, but in the history of psychology, literature and intellectual life, which it illuminates with a wealth of astonishing insights and amusing detail.

'Brilliant, original, entertaining and inexhaustible' *The Times*

'A very great book . . . A history that is also and above all a great work of sociology and psychology (or psychoanalysis), embracing the whole of life . . . Zeldin's erudition is staggering. His style is deliberately humorous, with a humour that is usually amiable but sometimes ferocious.' *Le Figaro*

'He is a modern Balzac.' *Boston Sunday Globe*